Working People and Hard Times

Working People and Hard Times

Canadian Perspectives

Robert Argue,
Charlene Gannagé,
D.W. Livingstone

Garamond Press
Toronto

Garamond Press
67A Portland St.
Toronto, Ontario
M5V 2M9

Cover design: Heather Guylar
Cover photo: *Toronto Star*
Typeset at ***LaserGraphics*** in Halifax
Printed and bound in Canada

With appreciation to the Ontario Public Service Employees' Union for financial support.

CANADIAN CATALOGUING IN PUBLICATION DATA

Main entry under title:
Working people and hard times

Papers presented at a conference entitled *Workers and their communities* held at the Ontario Institute for Studies in Education in May 1984.
Bibliography: p. 358
ISBN 0-920059-52-X

1. Labor and laboring classes—Canada—Congresses
2. Trade-unions—Canada—Congresses. I. Argue, Robert, 1950- . II. Gannagé, Charlene, 1948- . III. Livingstone, D.W., 1943- .

HD8106.5.W67 1987   331.1'0971   C87-093716-2

Contents

IV. Women's Issues and the Labour Movement

V. Strategy and Tactics for Social Change

Acknowledgements

As conference organizers and editors of this volume, we should like to express our gratitude to the following for aid and assistance. First, for aid tendered to the Fifth Conference: The Social Sciences and Humanities Research Council, the Labour Canada Occasional Grants Program, and the Ontario Public Service Employees' Union for the financial support which made the conference possible; Vivian Ching-Ako, Irene Lepps and the staff of the OISE Conference Office whose organizational skills made the conference work smoothly; Ken Theobald, Chris Schenk, Craig Heron, Winnie Ng, Carolyn Egan, Linda Briskin, Chris Huxley, Meg Luxton, and Don Wells for organizational assistance; and the steering committee of the Fifth Conference who ably and quickly responded to major crises in the process of organization.

Secondly, for aid in the production of this book: the Ontario Public Service Employees' Union for direct financial support; Errol Sharpe for assistance and support in getting the project going; Melodie Mayson-Richmond and Ted Richmond for copy-editing and proofreading; Skye Stollmeyer for help with proofreading; Keith Medcalfe for transcribing interviews and typing parts of the final manuscript, Sharon Nelson for her care and attention to the details of production.

Contributors

RUTH ANNIS is a former social worker in the B.C. Ministry of Human Resources. She was a member of Women Against the Budget and a representative of the Lower Mainland Solidarity Coalition.

BOB ARGUE teaches in the Sociology Department at Ryerson Polytechnical Institute. He is currently conducting research on rodeo cowboys.

HUGH ARMSTRONG teaches Sociology and Humanities at Vanier College. Aside from books and articles written with Pat Armstrong, his published work has been focused on the state and job creation. A member of the Editorial Board of *Studies in Political Economy*, he is the editor of a forthcoming collection of original articles on women and the state.

PAT ARMSTRONG teaches sociology at York University. With Hugh Armstrong, she has authored *The Double Ghetto: Canadian Women and Their Segregated Work*, and *A Working Majority: What Women Must Do for Pay*. She has also written *Labour Pains: Women's Work in Crisis*. In addition to her research on women's work, she has published articles on feminist theory and methods.

JOHN CALVERT has been a senior research officer with the Canadian Union of Public Employees for the past eight years. He has written a number of articles on industrial relations and is a regular contributor to the *CUPE Facts*. He is also the author of *Government Limited* (Canadian Centre for Policy Alternatives, 1984), a study of the Canadian economy. Before joining CUPE, he was a research officer for a British trade union, the Merchant Navy and Airline Officers Association. He has a Ph.D. from the London School of Economics.

DAVID CHUDNOVSKY is President of the Surrey Teachers' Association (STA). In the fall of 1983 he was on the STA Executive Committee and the Strike Committee. He was active in the Lower Mainland Solidarity Coalition and the Surrey Solidarity Coalition.

CAROL CURRIE has been involved with the Retail Wholesale and Department Store Union (RWDSU) for over ten years, after starting as a Dominion Store employee. She's been on full-time staff with the union for six years, and was the Co-ordinating Organizer of the Eaton's-Simpson's Department Store Workers' Organizing Campaign.

CAROLYN EGAN is a member of the International Women's Day Committee, a socialist-feminist organization, and is also active in the Ontario Coalition of Abortion Clinics.

DEIRDRE GALLAGHER is a former member of the Women's Committee of the Ontario Federation of Labour, and is now on the staff of the Public Service Alliance of Canada.

CHARLENE GANNAGÉ teaches sociology at the University of Toronto and is a post-doctoral fellow at York University. She is author of *Double Day, Double Bind: Women Garment Workers* (Women's Press, 1986) and is currently coordinating a union research project on technological change in the garment industry.

STAN GRAY worked for 11 years at Westinghouse in Hamilton where he was a shop steward and chairperson of the union health and safety committee. He is currently director of the Ontario Workers' Health Centre, a labour-sponsored health and safety facility.

CARMENCITA R. HERNANDEZ' political involvement with the Committee to Advance the Movement for Democracy and Independence (CAMDI) - Philippines (formerly known as the Coalition Against the Marcos Dictatorship) was the opening to her work with the Filipino community. A board member of the Kababayan Community Centre, she is also one of the founding members of the Coalition of Visible Minority Women (Ontario). She attended the Non-Governmental Organizations Forum '85 of the United Nations Decade of Women in Nairobi, Kenya, in July 1985. An accountant by profession, she received her Master's of Science degree in Accounting and Quantitative Analysis from the University of Minnesota, U.S.A. She is also a contributing editor of Balita, a Filipino community newspaper with a circulation of 8,000.

ROBERT D. HISCOTT is Assistant Professor of Sociology at Queen's University at Kingston. His previous research work includes a case study of the Beach Appliances Plant Closure in Ottawa, employment outcomes for recent migrants between Atlantic Canada and Ontario, and (in progress) an exploration of the causes and consequences of burn out among health care professionals (with Peter Connop).

FRANCA IACOVETTA is a doctoral candidate in History at York University, who is completing a dissertation on Southern Italian immigrant workers in post-World War Two Toronto. She has published on Canadian women in politics.

TOM LANGFORD for five years worked on the shop floors of two factories which produce appliances and plastic/styrofoam products. He became a sociology graduate student in 1983 at McMaster University.

RONNIE LEAH recently completed her doctorate in sociology, focusing on women's trade-union organizing and the day care issue. A university lecturer since 1976, she currently works as professional officer for the University of Regina Faculty Association Ronnie has been active in both the women's movement and the labour movement for many years. As the mother of two children, she has been involved with day care.

CAMILLE LEGENDRE has been teaching sociology at the Université de Montreal for the past several years. He specialized in the sociology of work and organizations and is currently doing research on the new information technologies and their impact on the work place and organizations. His recent research interests include health and safety at work, discrimination in employment and labour movement history. He has published with Jaques Dofny a study on a mining disaster, *Catastrophe dans une mine d'or.*

D.W. LIVINGSTONE is a professor of sociology at the Ontario Institute for Studies in Education. His recent publications include *Social Crisis and Schooling* (Garamond Press, 1985) and (ed.) *Critical Pedagogy and Cultural Power.* (Bergin and Garvey, 1986). His current research concerns issues of class structure and class consciousness.

STAN MARSHALL is an instructor of Industrial Sociology at the Labour College of Canada in Ottawa and is a candidate for the Ph.D. in Sociology at the University of Alberta.

PETER MEIKSINS was educated at Columbia and York Universities and is currently Assistant Professor of Sociology at the State University of New York—Geneseo. His research focuses on theoretical approaches to the "new middle class" (on which he is now completing a book) and on the sociology of engineering.

STEPHEN MCBRIDE teaches Political Studies at Lakehead University and formerly taught Labour Studies at McMaster University and Politics at Ryerson Polytechnical Institute. While at Ryerson he was an active member of the Canadian Union of Education Workers. His publications include articles on comparative and Canadian politics in *Political Studies, Parliamentary Affairs* and *The Canadian Journal of Political Science.*

JANICE MCCLELLAND is a National Representative for the Communications and Electrical Workers of Canada (CWC) working in the Ontario Region office. In her current assignment she handles grievances for Bell Canada craft employees and operators and is also responsible for women's rights and issues in the Ontario Region for CWC. She is a former telephone operator and was very active in the organizing campaign of the Bell operators into the Union, and was also President of CWC Local 50 (Toronto) during the operators' strike in 1979-80.

PATRICIA MCDERMOTT is a labour lawyer and a sociologist. She has done extensive research on the impact of computerization on the productive process and organizations. She is currently teaching in the Law and Society program, in the Division of Social Science, York University.

DIETER NEUMANN worked for ten years as a wage labourer in the steel fabrication industry. He holds a B.A. in sociology from the University of Guelph which he claims has rendered him unemployable.

WINNIE NG is co-ordinator of the English in the Workplace Program, Centre for Labour Studies. This is a joint project of Humber College and the Labour Council of Metropolitan Toronto. She previously worked at the Immigrant Women's Centre as a counselor and with the International Ladies' Garment Workers' Union as a union organizer.

MARION POLLACK is a postal worker and an activist in the Vancouver local of the Canadian Union of Postal Workers. She was a member of Women Against the Budget and a representative to the Lower Mainland Solidarity Coalition.

BOB RUSSELL teaches in the Sociology Department at the University of Saskatchewan, Saskatoon. He is the co-editor of *Family, Economy and State: The Social Reproduction Process Under Capitalism* (Garamond Press, 1986) and has published articles on political economy, labour and the state in *Studies In Political Economy, The Canadian Review of Sociology and Anthropology*, and *The Insurgent Sociologist*. He is currently authoring a book which examines the Canadian industrial relations system and its implications for state theory.

GERI SHEEDY has worked for Dominion Stores and has been involved for sixteen years with the Retail Wholesale and Department Store Union (RWDSU), where she currently sits on the Executive Board of local 414. She was active as a volunteer in the Eaton's-Simpson's Organizing Campaign.

James Stafford is an associate professor in the Department of Sociology, Lakehead University, Thunder Bay, Ontario. He has conducted studies of pensions and retirement in Thunder Bay and Northwestern Ontario, to complement his historical work on the development of private pensions in Canada.

Erma Stultz is the President of Tolpuddle Farm Labour Information Centre and Vice-president of the Rural Learning Association. Previously, she was a staff representative of the Canadian Farmworker's Union in Ontario. In 1985, she visited India and Bangladesh to study the methods of organizing landless labourers, and to learn of a holistic approach to organizing which attempts to deal with the problems of the rural poor.

Julian Tanner is an assistant professor of sociology at the Scarborough campus of the University of Toronto. He is currently engaged in a collaborative research study of youth unemployment in Canada.

Sean Usher is Director of Resarch, Education and Campaigns with the Ontario Public Service Employees' Union.

Jim Ward is a former Executive Director of Dixon Hall Community Centre in east-end Toronto. He is currently working with the Metro Toronto Parks and Recreation Department.

Peter Warrian is a Labour Economist and Consultant working in Toronto. From 1974 to 1983 he was on the staff of the United Steelworkers of America, serving as Canadian Legislative Director and later as Research Director. From 1983 to 1985 he was Executive Assistant to the President of the Ontario Public Service Employees' Union. He has served on the Economic Policy Committee, Pension Committee and Energy Committee of the Canadian Labour Congress. In addition to private consulting, he is a part-time Vice-Chair of the Workers' Compensation Appeals Tribunal.

Barry Weisleder is a substitute teacher for the City of Toronto Board of Education, an activist in the Ontario Public Service Employees' Union and was the organizer and first President of OPSEU Local 595. He first became politically active in the Toronto high school student rights movement: he was President of the Ontario New Democratic Youth in the early 1970s, and graduated from the University of Toronto with a B.A. and B.Ed. in 1975. Founder and chairperson of the Toronto Anti-Intervention Coalition, a broad anti-war coalition focusing on Central America, he is also a leader of the Alliance for Socialist Action.

Introduction

The articles in this volume are a selection from papers presented at the *Fifth Conference on Workers and Their Communities*, held at the Ontario Institute for Studies in Education (OISE) May 11-13, 1984.

History and Nature of the "Blue-Collar Conference"

Since the first meeting at York University in 1975, the *Conference on Workers and Their Communities* (formerly the *Conference on Blue-Collar Workers and Their Communities*), has attempted to provide the broadest possible forum for academic and government researchers, trade unionists, rank and file workers and community activists to discuss important social and political aspects of work and community issues in terms of class, gender and ethnic relations. It is one of the few conferences in Canada to bring together such diverse groups. Furthermore, it is one of the few such meetings to attempt a sharing of findings and experiences between researchers and union and community activists.

Since its inception, the conference has grown both in size and scope. The first conference was organized primarily to provide an opportunity for Central Canadian labour researchers to share findings and to debate theoretical formulations on work and the working class, in a more informal setting than is normally found at academic conferences. Thirty papers were presented to approximately 100 participants over a period of two days. The Fifth Conference had approximately 130 people presenting or discussing papers to at least 450 registered participants. While the original focus was Central Canadian, the conference now regularly includes analyses of regional and international issues, and draws participants from all regions of Canada and at least a few from abroad. While the conference is now organized on a much grander scale, the original intent of the "Blue-Collar Conference" has remained intact: sessions are still informal, and participants reflect a wide range of interests and backgrounds.

Special Features of the 1984 Conference

A major concern of participants in all five conferences has been the effect of the deepening economic crisis of capitalism upon working-class organization and community. This concern was reflected in the Fifth Conference Theme: *Coping With Hard Times in the Workplace, the Family, and the Schools.* The current economic crisis is not "merely" located in localized conditions of work and employment, but pervades all aspects of working-class life and is international in scope; this was fully reflected in the topics discussed at the conference. The scope of discussion is indicated in just a small sampling of session topics, which included: *The Impact of Microtechnology, Strategies and Tactics for Social Change, The Current Crisis and Working People in the Third World, Women's Wage and Non-Wage Work, White Collar Work, Trade Unions and Social Issues, Occupational Health and Safety,* and *Organizing Women.* Two plenary sessions: *Women's Issues and the Labour Movement* and *Women's Struggles and the Labour Movement—Strategies for the Future,* gave added prominence to the issues of the relationship of gender and class. Trade unionists were involved in the plenary session, *Unions in the 1980's* and in numerous other sessions.

The business meeting of the Fourth Conference gave us a mandate to make a concerted effort to highlight women's issues, including the two plenary sessions. Women were integrated into all other sessions and made up more than 40 percent of the conference participants. Since very few had responded to the initial call for papers, women in trade unions and community groups were individually contacted and motivated to participate. To avoid tokenism, care was taken to increase the participation of immigrant women and women of colour. Carolyn Egan and Winnie Ng helped extend our network into the immigrant women's community. Free childcare was provided and a women's caucus was scheduled early during the conference. The conference fee was kept at a reasonable amount: twenty dollars for faculty, ten dollars for students and employed workers; the unemployed were asked to make a two dollar donation.

Since some women had not previously spoken at a conference such as ours, an orientation meeting was arranged for the women who were speaking at the plenaries. At that meeting, we discussed the unique features and traditions of the conference as well as participants' speeches. The meeting was taped and sent to a conference participant in British Columbia who, for obvious reasons, was not able to attend the orientation. Last minute additions to the conference schedule were confirmed by telephone. The chairs of the plenary sessions took the additional precaution of telephoning the participants to confirm times and places and to offer a word of encouragement.

Recognizing the importance of establishing links with the labour movement, we worked very closely with Chris Schenk from the Ontario Public Service Employees' Union (OPSEU) who smoothed the way by contacting key people and soliciting their participation. In recognition of their busy schedule, we made sure that trade-unionists and working people were scheduled at convenient times as far as possible. We followed up on initial contact with a letter specifically designed for trade-union and community participants, and we sent thank-you notes to all trade unionists and community activists following the conference. Programs were distributed at meetings of the Metro Labour Council, placed in bookstores and displayed in community centres. Non-sectarian socialist organizations generously volunteered to include our programs in their mailings. Ads were placed in local socialist and feminist newspapers.

At all stages of building this conference, care was taken to facilitate the participation of trade unionists and community activists. While we may have made some mistakes along the way, we felt that special attention had to be devoted to extending our conference beyond the traditional academic networks and reach out to the broader community. It is this which is our unique tradition: a conference not simply about but with Workers and Their Communities.

Production Of This Volume

When the Fifth Conference was over, three of the main organizers—Bob Argue, Charlene Gannagé, and D.W. Livingstone—decided that it would be valuable to prepare a selection of conference papers for publication. Given the number and range of papers presented, the editors of this volume were faced with a difficult task: to select a group of papers which would reflect the nature of the conference and which would be of use and interest to both researchers and activists. We decided therefore to give this volume a somewhat narrower focus than was presented at the conference: issues of contemporary importance in Canada. Thus, with some regret, we have excluded discussions of the international working-class. We contacted conference participants by letter and gave them an opportunity to submit written manuscripts. At the conference we followed the tradition that academics had to submit written papers whereas trade unionists and communtiy activists did not need to put their remarks into a formal paper. Charlene Gannagé followed up these letters with phone calls to women trade unionists and community activists. In several cases circumstances did not permit speakers to write down their presentations. Charlene therefore interviewed Deirdre Gallagher in her home and Carol Currie and Geri Sheedy at the women's conference of the Canadian Labour Conference in Ottawa. The transcripts of these interviews are presented here.

As should be apparent from the discussion of the conference, the articles in this collection are necessarily very diverse in their style, ranging from academic studies to direct accounts of organizing experiences by militants active in their workplaces and communities. While this has made it impossible to produce the kind of uniformity in style that normally is found in similar collections, it is this very diversity of experiences and approaches among the contributors which makes this collection both unique and invaluable.

Taken as a whole, this collection provides an integrated view of the concrete effects of the current Canadian economic crisis based on the views and experiences of a highly representative cross-section of people active in different milieus. In order to allow the reader to focus on more particular questions, we have grouped the various contributions together by theme into the following sections: I.*"Current Struggles Over Working Conditions"*, which addresses the pressing issues of occupational health and safety and the effects of technological change. II. *"The State, Economic Crisis and Working People"*, which discusses state policies of restraining the social wage and legislative restrictions on the labour movement as responses to the crisis of capital. III. *"Class Formation and Class Consciousness"*, where the relationship between recent changes in class structure and class consciousness is examined. IV. *"Women's Issues and the Labour Movement"* discusses the special impact of the crisis upon women and the response of women's groups and women in the labour movement to those specific issues. Finally, part V., *"Strategy and Tactics for Social Change"*, raises the question of appropriate responses by the labour movement to the new problems raised by the recent and often disturbing features of the economic crisis.

In the production process we have made every effort to make these articles accessible to the widest possible audience. The articles have been edited for simplicity in language and style, while remaining faithful to the diversity of original styles of the contributors.

A list of all abbreviations used in the articles, footnotes and bibliography is supplied at the end of this volume for the reader's reference. The majority of the bibliographic references have been integrated and organized alphabetically, at the end of the book, while a number of more specialized references have been left with the footnotes accompanying particular articles.

We are hopeful that this collection will provide a valuable source of study and reference for an audience as diverse as the contributors to this volume: for workers, for women involved in workplace community struggles; for university students of labour studies and the sociology and politics of work and class.

SECTION I

Current Struggles Over Working Conditions

Introduction

During the economic slump that has persisted since the early 1970s, relations in paid workplaces in Canada have become increasingly marked by uncertainty and dispute over the social contract between employers and workers. Declining profitability under the terms of established collective bargaining agreements and social welfare provisions, coupled with industrial production technologies movable to regions with cheaper labour, have led to numerous plant closures and demands for employee wage concessions by corporate decision makers. Corporate efforts to increase productivity through combining new, typically computer-based, technologies with workforce reorganization of the labour process, characterized by speed-ups, lay-offs, and programs to secure the motivation of remaining employees (e.g. Quality of Working Life), have been even more widespread.

Canadian working people's responses to such new corporate initiatives have been quite varied. Trade-union leaders have frequently been forced to attempt to defend agreement clauses whose terms have become largely irrelevant to reorganized enterprises, while much of the effective opposition has come from rank-and-file activists among the workers who have been directly on the receiving end of these changes. The papers in this section attempt to outline the global economic context and established legal provisions that condition Canadian working people's current struggles over working conditions, and to illustrate these struggles through several case studies.

Peter Warrian analyzes the crisis of the labour movement in light of the international movements of capital. He argues that capital is reorganizing on a global scale, shifting investment to Newly Industrializing Countries (NICs) without increasing effective demand in those countries. As a result, working people in the advanced capitalist nations are progressively weakened in terms of established trade-union rights and their standards of living. The international mobility of capital thus poses a critical challenge to the labour movement, a challenge which is especially acute in Canada because of the structural weaknesses and resource dependency of our economy.

In the face of capital's global mobility, the response of the capitalist state in Canada as elsewhere has been an assault on the social wage in order to secure investment. Working-class standards of living are being attacked at the level of both the individual pay packet and the social wage in order to secure investment. Warrian observes that this two-front assault on standards of living has been effectively cloaked in a monetarist ideology with strong populist appeal, while organized labour and social democratic political parties are left defending an unpalatable status quo.

Thus the traditional labour strategy of collective bargaining and support for the New Democratic Party is no longer appropriate in Canada. To date the labour left response has been confused, even stumbling. Warrian suggests that what is needed is a broadening of ideological focus from purely quantitative economic demands to qualitative demands for economic and social right. Such a broadening would make possible the necessary alliances between the working class and non-working class popular movements for social change.

The remaining papers in the section focus more closely on particular working conditions in Canada. Robert Hiscott documents the closure of an electrical appliances plant. He reviews the critical events in this process including the political conditions surrounding the initial decision, a wildcat strike, and the resultant severance benefit negotiations, as well as the subsequent experiences of displaced workers. He notes the contractually restricted role of labour unions in closure decisions, and examines options for greater labour involvement, especially conversion to employee ownership as an alternative to closure.

Camille Legendre examines the views of goldminers toward occupational hazards in the wake of the 1980 Val d'Or mine disaster. In this situation, miners were inclined to perceive some employer negligence and some failure by inspectors to enforce government safety regulations. But their predominant response to hazards was to attempt to deny the high level of danger in their work, to be fatalistic about "uncontrollable" factors such as accidents, and to express considerable pride in their individual responsibility for their own work and personal safety. Legendre points to the correspondence of such individualistic coping strategies with the paternalistic way of life that still prevails in this mining community—and perhaps quite widely in single-resource towns across the country.

In contrast, Stan Gray describes a number of successful efforts by rank-and-file workers in Hamilton manufacturing industries to improve health and safety conditions in their plants. He argues that workers can rely on neither employers nor government authorities to implement even minimum established safety standards in the absence of persistent worker struggles with diverse tactics. Gray's accounts should be very suggestive for health and safety activists dealing with the currently widespread problems of continuing use of faulty equipment and toxic substances.

Patricia McDermott assesses the legal processes that have been associated with the implementation of technological change since the early 1970's. She evaluates the extensiveness and effectiveness of the main legal tools available to working people to contend with management's technological change initiatives: government legislation, collective bargaining, and grievance arbitration. McDermott surveys the very limited protection afforded to workers by each of these legal processes in relation to the major technological restructuring of the economy now occurring, and suggests that political rather than legal solutions are needed.

Finally, Janice McClelland offers a case history of the employment effects of technological change since 1957 on Bell Canada telephone operators in Ontario and Quebec. She documents the halving of the operator staff, work speed-ups and consolidation of centralization in conjunction with major technological changes in the telephone system. McClelland's account both illustrates the positive if limited role that contract language can play in worker's struggles with management, and also confirms McDermott's more general analysis, in terms of the vulnerability of the operators to management's technological change initiatives and the importance of engaging in wider political actions.

Trade Unions and the New International Division of Labour

Peter Warrian

Introduction

The steelworkers, autoworkers, textile and electrical workers of Canada, the United States, Britain and West Germany know that the global system of production and trade has dramatically shifted in the last decade. Beginning in the mid 1960s, there was a slowdown in the industrial economies of the Organization for Economic Cooperation and Development (OECD) countries. The classic smokestack industries suffered a slowdown of growth and profitability, and subsequently a crisis of capital accumulation. During the 1970s there was a dramatic shift of new investment to install new industrial capacity in the steel, auto, shipbuilding, mining, electronics and textile industries of the NIC's (Newly Industrialized Countries). Without a social revolution in the NIC's, however, there is no way their own markets can digest this new industrial capacity. Therefore this new industrial capacity comes to be seen by workers and unions in North America and Western Europe, with validity, as a threat to their trade-union rights and living standards. This paper discusses the implications of the new international division of labour for the trade-union movement and its political allies.

The Crisis of Accumulation and the Threat of Capital Mobility

In the 1970s the long wave of post World War Two prosperity and rising incomes came to a halt. Rather than simply an interruption, however, we now perceive the beast for what it is, a crisis in the global capitalist economy (Wolfe, 1983). The root of the crisis is an erosion of private capital accumulation. The system is going through a global restructuring to try to re-establish a basis of sustained profitability and accumulation comparable to that of the post-war period.

There are few more devastating threats to trade unionism and working-class living standards than those posed by the international mobility of capital. They can be expressed in such terms as international competitiveness or a climate of investment or as the direct threat of a capital flight, but their effect is the same. They undermine trade-union bargaining strength, terrorize and demoralize communities, and destablize progressive political regimes.

Understanding the movements of capital is the key to understanding the restructuring currently underway in the international economy. This has a decisive and direct impact on trade unions. Capital flight has always been a tactic at management's disposal in order to discipline workers. However, in the last two decades systematic disinvestment has become, from management's perspective, a necessary strategy; and from a technological perspective, a feasible one. Management would claim that trade unions have forced this on them (Bluestone and Harrison, 1982).

From the mid-1940s, unions, particularly in North America, had won concessions from management in regard to seniority, work rules, health and safety, etc. These union gains have constricted management's previously unfettered rights and power. Large industrial collective agreements now run to hundreds of pages, and much of their content is directed at increasing job security and limiting the discretionary power of management. The crucial exception, in most cases, has been retention by management of the right to determine the aggregate size of the work force and to make decisions on capital investment. The ultimate weapon for management to undercut organized labour's standard armor of grievance procedures, job actions and strikes, has been capital mobility.

To this situation have now been added the new technologies, which tilt the balance of bargaining power in favour of capital, and have severely undermined the power of trade unions in North America.

The study by Barry Bluestone and Ben Harrison, *The Deindustrialization of America* (1982) is the best analysis yet of the process of disinvestment and its social effects. The process of disinvestment has meant a diversion away from productive investment in basic industries such as steel, auto, electrical, textiles, etc., into unproductive speculation, mergers and acquisitions, and foreign investments. Bluestone and Harrison estimate that 32-38 million jobs were lost during the 1970s as the direct result of private disinvestment in American business. As an example, U.S. steel has, since 1976, reduced its capital expenditure in steel making by one-fifth. Profits were instead redirected into the aquisition of chemical firms, shopping malls and other activities; by 1979, 46¢ of every new dollar of U.S. Steel's capital investment was going into the corporation's non-steel ventures.

Moreover in 1979, while each dollar of depreciated non-steel plant and equipment was being replaced by $2.90 of new capital investment, the replacement rate for steel operations was only $1.40. In the United States during the 1970's, two out of every three new Fortune 500 manufacturing plants were not "new" at all, but rather acquired from other owners.

In many cases, it is the exact same corporations laying off workers in North America who are investing in the Third World. These include the new wave, high tech operators such as Texas Instruments and Atari. During the 1980s General Electric expanded its worldwide payroll by 5,000, but it did so by adding 30,000 foreign jobs and reducing its U.S. employment by 25,000. RCA cut its U.S. workforce by 19,000.

The attraction of overseas investment is in part the low wages paid. Young women are the bulk of the workforce in the microchip assembly plants of Southeast Asia, where they labour for $1.00–$1.50 per day. Their inhuman working conditions result in an estimated working life of four years. Even further, the NICs represent an environment where the corporations have a greater general social control over production.

The New International Division of Labour is a reflection of the crisis of accumulation, that is, a shift in the global distribution of production and trade. It is not in itself the cause of the crisis, though it is often the most perceivable evil for trade unions seeking to defend wages and jobs. It is also the subject of many of the most aggressive trade-union economic policies, in the form of "Buy America" programs, national content laws, tariff and non-tariff barriers to trade, etc. Such policies are a necessary form of self-defense for trade unions seeking to determine some of the terms of restructuring. The fundamental problem is not that of national autonomy, but rather the functioning of the global capitalist system. Its solution lies in international trade union and social solidarity.

Global Fordism?

Fordism[1] is the mode of mass production and mass consumption that has dominated the relations of capital and labour during the last fifty years, particularly since the Second World War. Its political expression is the class compromise of Keynesianism and the Welfare State. This model served the mutual short-term interests of organized workers (by raising real income) and corporations (by facilitating social peace and promoting steadily-increasing profits and capital accumulation). However, this mode of production/consumption has been declared null and void by the bankers, industrialists and politicians of the OECD countries in the late 1980s. The one remaining market prospect for expansion of Fordism has been the Third World (Lipietz, 1982). This has not happened, and there is little prospect of its happening in the future. The industrialization strategy being followed in the NICs is not the import-substitution policy of introductory economic text books. It is rather one of export substitution, that is, the installation of large new industrial capacity with the explicit purpose of exporting to other, mostly North American and Western European, markets.

The relocation of production has been made possible by advances in industrial, transportation and communications technologies. The transnational corporations have thereby been able to establish parallel production and multiple sourcing on a global scale, undermining local trade-union and political responses. Concessions by North American workers have not been matched by income transfers and self-sustaining growth in the NICs.

The unequal distribution of income in the Third World continues and indeed worsens globally. Some 34 countries are now in the World Bank's low income category, defined as having a per capita Gross National Product (GNP) of less than $410 in 1981. Their combined population was then 2.2 billion: almost half the world's people living on only a fifth of its land.

Consider the fate of the Brazilian Economic Model. In June of 1983, the number of people employed in Sao Paulo was 1.6 million, the same as in June of 1973. However, during those ten years the population had increased by 50% to 12 million. Sao Paulo accounts for over half of Brazil's industrial production, but it recently lost 500,000 jobs in only two years (*Manchester Guardian*, August 7, 1983)

The credit crunch in the Third World is being forced by the conservative policies of the International Monetary Fund (IMF) and the World Bank in order to constrict incomes even further, and boost exports even at "dumping" level prices to earn foreign exchange and to pay off foreign banks.

Recently, new lending to the Third World has been almost completely cut off, other than the re-financing of existing loans. Including the IMF-linked loans to Brazil and Mexico, net new lending to countries outside the OECD grew by only $500 million in the first quarter of 1983.

This compares with a growth of $9 billion in the preceding quarter, and about $25 billion or more during average quarters in 1978 and 1979. The amount of new loans received by smaller or less industrialized countries (LDCs) declined to $300 million from $3.5 billion. The Bank for International Settlements warns that "more belt tightening by debtor nations may be needed" (*Globe and Mail*, July 19, 1983)

The "rescue efforts" to save Mexico, Brazil, etc. from debt are in fact missions of rescue for the over-extended Western private banks, who took over the major share of international lending from public agencies in the 1970s. The banks supplied the major means of capital relocation to the Third World, while promoting monetarism and credit restrictions at home. That credit restriction has now come back to haunt them; the global recession induced by the success of monetarism has caught both the banks and their corporate clients with over-extended Third World debts that have little or no likelihood of being paid. Indeed, the paradox is that without a resumption of growth in demand in the OCED countries, there is little hope for an economic recovery in the NICs.

Third World countries currently have debts of about $800 billion, while accounting for 30 percent of world trade. Even within a new international division of labour, it will take a real growth rate of 2 percent per year within the OECD countries for the rest of this decade just to enable the NICs to meet their debt payments. As a group, the Third World countries used 13.5 percent of their exports to service their debt in 1979. By 1983 this burden had soared to 20 percent while several of the biggest Latin American borrowers faced debt-service ratios of more than 100 percent.

These "structural adjustments" are not expressed simply by the abstract movement of statistical aggregates. As an example, in the summer of 1983 there were widespread demonstrations and strikes in Brazil, shutting down oil, chemical and auto industries. The strikers were demanding wage readjustments, a rent and price freeze, and the cancellation of two governmental austerity packages. The Brazilian government has been under continual pressure from the International Monetary Fund to cut wages and reduce social spending, as a condition for extension on the Brazilian loans. (*Manchester Guardian*, July 17, 1983).

The struggles for trade-union rights and redistribution of income in the Third World are a necessary concern for the trade-union movement in the industrialized countries. However, there is little prospect in sight of the kind of revival of Fordism in the Third World that would lead to a revitalization of global production and growth.

In summary, the global capitalist economy is in a dilemma in both the industrialized countries and the Third World. The slow growth scenarios for the remainder of this decade are anchored in this underlying reality.

Domestic Impact: Distribution of Income

Whether the shifting division of labour is seen analytically as a reflection or as a cause of the crisis, its impact has been dramatic on workers and unions.

Real wages have fallen behind inflation in the OECD countries for much of the last decade. Labour's share of the national income has been shrinking. The attacks on public sector spending have reduced the "social wage" of human services and income support programs. Much of the blame for this situation is placed by conventional commentators on the long-term decline in productivity.

Numerous reports and studies have pointed to the decline in productivity being much more marked in Canada than in other industrialized countries. When this decline was combined with falling prices during the recent recession, the result was to put pressure on the rates of return on capital, even though real wages had been falling for the previous several years. The rate of return from investment in manufacturing has undergone a trend decline. The fear is that unless this fall in profits is rectified, there could be a diversion of investment dollars into financial assets rather than industrial plant and equipment, or even a flight of capital out of the country.

Recent Canadian federal budgets, both Liberal and Conservative, have made various proposals to accelerate a recovery in profit margins and provide incentives for investment. However, the OECD in Paris has made it clear that a substantial erosion of profits took place during the course of the recession. A 1983 report points out that, on a pre-tax basis, corporate profits as a share of the national income shrank to 8 percent in the second half of 1983, down from 14 percent in the second half of 1982. During the same period the shares of labour and investment income rose 3 percent and 2 percent respectively. Companies' rate of internal funding of capital outlays was almost halved, to 36 percent from 65 percent over the same period. The OECD concluded that for the economy to reach its full potential "an adequate return to investment in real capital is essential" (*Globe and Mail*, July 21, 1983), a conclusion which appears to have become an article of faith for conventional politicians in Canada.

The OECD also points to the structural weakness and resource dependency in the Canadian economy as further dangers. If there is a sustained recovery in the international economy, increased prices for raw materials could be transferred into rising wages and prices spiralling again throughout the entire economy, as happened in the early 1970s. The OECD coyly noted as well that "normal economic tools might not be sufficient in this kind of event".

Domestic Impact: Segmented Labour Market

The restructuring of the division of labour is also taking place domestically. The phenomenon of segmented labour markets has spread, partitioning workers between employed and unemployed, and full- versus part-time. The segmentation can easily be correlated with age, sex and ethnic divisions. (Gordon, Edwards, and Reich, 1982)

The current phase of the transformation of the labour process began in the 1920s, following the triumph of Taylorism over craft forms of organization. There was a large expansion of the managerial workforce to intensify pressure for increased production through the "drive" system. Industrial workers in North America responded by forming the Congress of Industrial Organizations (CIO) in the 1930s. The labour-capital accord in the postwar period resulted in union recognition, grievance procedures, and seniority rules for allocation of work. In return, the management right to determine the organization of work was consolidated, so long as wage increases were granted in return for increases in productivity.

The wave of industrial unionism came to be concentrated in the large firms. Value added per production worker increased, as did the earnings of unionized workers. The ratio of production workers to total employees in these core firms declined, but the incidence of layoffs fell in comparison to the number experienced by workers in smaller peripheral firms.

In summary, the segmentation in the work force created a division between a primary labour market, composed of highly-unionized, relatively-tenured, well-paid, white and male workers; and a secondary labour market of non-unionized, low-paid, part-time, casual and unstable employment reserved for a work force made up largely of women, youth and ethnic minorities. (Gordon, Edward and Reich, 1982:190-200)

However, in the 1980s, the core firms were no longer able to share their prosperity with organized labour as they had during the postwar booms. They have declared the accord off, and pushed for wage concessions and the dismantling of workers' contractual rights. Falling real wages, layoffs, and a loss of rights for primary labour market workers is resulting in a re-shuffling of the boundaries of privilege within the working class, such that all workers may become "secondary".

Domestic Impact: New Technologies

To this portrait we must add the impact of the new microchip, robotic and microbiological technologies. One of their major impacts is to skew the income distribution patterns away from the 'Bell Curve' pattern and towards a 'Two Hump' model, with the middle-income jobs—the heart of the unionized work-force—being eliminated. Steelworker and auto-worker jobs disappear; the replacement jobs, when they appear—usually re-employ people at lower skill levels and poorer wages and benefits, without union protection, in smaller industrial firms or in the service sector. The result is what Robert Reich (1983) has called 'the disappearing middle', the combined effect of North American corporate decline and technological change.

More fundamentally, work itself is disappearing. Most of the job creation currently going on is part-time, low-wage, and low-benefit, and unstable employment. The proponents of small business continually proclaim that small business is creating 7 out of every 10 new jobs. The fact of the matter is that the Massachussets Institute of Technology studies that were the foundation of those claims analyzed *establishments*—many of which were subsidiaries of large firms—and not small, independent businesses. Further, in addition to providing poor wages, benefits and conditions for their workers, 4 out of 5 new businesses also fail in the first 5 years of operation.

The conventional wisdom is that the OECD economies must first re-establish profitability, so as to facilitate re-structuring and resumption of growth. The goal of full employment is seen as 'unrealistic' and unattainable. Canada's unemployment, at the official rate, has hovered around 10% for most of this decade, and this level may well become a permanent feature of the economy until demographic changes intervene in the middle 1990's.

Conventional Political Responses

The conservative political response, currently in the ascendency, is that the welfare state, worker's wages and trade-union rights must be suppressed. The gains of the last fifty years, in other words, must be reversed in order that capital accumulation may be reinvigorated and economic growth resumed. The liberal political response, epoused by the likes of Lester

Thurow, is that wages and trade union rights must be restrained and the national income redirected to investment in high-tech industries to re-establish the economy and reintroduce growth.

The direction of federal Liberal and Conservative policies has been to address, in pro-business terms, the weakness in the manufacturing sector and the need for a resurgence in the rate of return on industrial capital investment by emphasizing the new technologies. According to Informetrica, investment in machinery and equipment will have to rise from 7 to 7.5 percent of the GNP in the 1960s and 1970s, to 8.5 percent in the 1980s and 11.4 percent in the 1990s. Total investment is expected to rise from its customary 24 percent of the GNP to 28 percent, a significant shift given that the portion of national income remaining must be distributed to a growing number of households. (*Globe and Mail*, July 29, 1983).

In British Columbia, the Socred government has reacted differently by making a pre-emptive strike against public sector unions, social services and human rights. It is no secret that B.C. has been the key area of the country for resource-based working class militancy.

Both these political responses are clearly unacceptable to labour. However, we are left with a dilemma. With the apparent exhaustion of the internal limits of Fordism in the OECD in the last decade, the struggle over the distribution of the national income between trade unions and corporations has resulted in major bouts of inflation. At the same time, inflation as a social-political issue has been confronted in a way adverse to labour's interest.

The 'liberal' consensus, be it from the Liberal or Conservative parties, or even some sections of the New Democratic Party (NDP), is that wage controls or an incomes policies are necessary. An incomes policy is most often superficially justified as an anti-inflationary measure. However, nowhere in the Western world has an incomes policy been introduced which goes beyond wage controls to equitably control prices and profits. As a result, incomes policies have in reality been mechanisms of income redistribution. They are not, and arguably cannot be, effective anti-inflationary measures in capitalist ecomomies.[2]

Anyone making a substantive argument for an incomes policy would have to do so on the basis of its real re-distributive effects. Some, like Thurow, will rationalize this against the background of the restructuring in the world economy.

This usually leaves trade unionists to reply on the basis of the social costs and distribution of the benefits in such a forced march of re-adjustment. We must candidly admit that so far in the current socio-economic battle, rightwing populism and monetarism have succeeded over the labour/left response. I shall argue further that, within the existing political economy, this situation will continue.

The Labour/Left Political Response

The labour/left response to the crisis, be it in Canada, Britain or Europe, has been to formulate an ideologically aggressive Alternate Economic Strategy (AES). The components of the AES have emphasized reflation, protectionism, public sector interventionism and a renewal of growth. In effect we have been trying to say that we should get things back to where they used to be.

A few years ago, most of us on the left euphemistically hoped and believed we saw a tidal shift, wherein Europe had turned its back on Reaganism and monetarism, and would initiate a new course of a social democratic-socialist political economy based on an AES and a Britain/France/West Germany/Greece progressive block. Within a year, however, this pipe dream was replaced by the reality of the Reagan-Thatcher-Kohl axis, and a resurgent right appealing to a populist base.

The recent economic policy statements of such labour bodies as the International Confederation of Free Trade Unions (ICFTU), International Metalworkers' Federation (IMF), the British Trades Union Congress (TUC) and the Canadian Labour Congress (CLC) express a consensus around a program call for: 1) re-stimulation of the economy, increased budgetary expenditures and a restoration of social services that have been cut back; 2) lowering of interest rates on a domestic and international basis; 3) selective use of exchange and import controls; 4) major new programs of public investments and public works; and 5) greater public accountability and control over the investment process.

Since the mid-70s crisis, there has been a convergence of trade-union economic programs in Europe, particularly in France, Italy, Sweden and Britain (Martin and Ross, 1980). Among the common elements in these programs is the view that each country's industrial structure has made its international economic position more vulnerable to unemployment and susceptible to inflation and the sacrifice of social needs.

To bring about the changes required in those industrial structures, these programs propose that the microeconomic decisions shaping industrial structure be subjected to state and union control. The state cannot be limited to passive economic intervention relying simply on demand management, whether alone or with selective manpower policies. Investment decisions cannot be left to precisely those firms whose decisions, based on private rather than social criteria, created the current economic crisis in the first place. The state therefore has to take over the functions of mobilizing and channelling capital to assure sufficient investment of the right kind—identified by planning instruments at the national, sectoral and enterprise levels—through instruments such as public enterprises, financial intermediaries, incentives and controls.

Similarly, the unions cannot confine themselves to traditional issues of wages and working conditions. Nor can they agree to wage restraint without having the power to assure that the released resources are used for needed investment. Unions must accordingly participate in planning at all levels in a variety of ways, including representation, but primarily through collective bargaining.

Such an extention of state and union power to include investment decisions is conceived (as much by its business opponents as by its union advocates) as introducing a fundamental change in the mixed economy.

Part of the problem lies in the analytical paradigms we have employed, including even those of the 'Left Keynesian' or neo-Marxist economists of the Cambridge School. One weakness in these views, for example, is the ambiguous place of profits and their relationship to growth and jobs.

The Cambridge Economic Policy Group (CEPG) model identifies the struggle by workers to secure a target real wage as the decisive factor in inflation. Further, the struggle by national capitals for shares of the world market determines the growth of output and therefore employment. Indeed, the CEPG's picture of the decline of British capitalism seems to be based on the twin pressures of wage militancy and international competitiveness. Such accounts usually focus on weaknesses in profits—the 'profit squeeze'—leading to insufficient investment, lack of competitiveness, loss of markets and an inability to maintain employment (Glynn, 1982).

As Andrew Glynn has said:

> Even if the CEPG were correct in arguing that until comparatively recently a cut in real wages was not necessary for a return to full employment, seen in a longer term context the model does imply that the excessive cost of employing labour has caused rising unemployment. Since in their view output has been constrained by poor trade performance, which reflects low investment, which in turn reflects low profits, we are led inescapably back to the conclusion that the problem has been precisely excessive real wages. The CEPG seems to be reluctant to draw this conclusion, perhaps feeling understandably though wrongly, that this would be to blame workers for the crisis (Glynn, 1982: 255).

Monetarists also share this view of the key role played by wage levels in determining economic performance. Their goal is to promote the interests of capital by boosting profit levels; their preferred method of doing so is to use the weapon of mass unemployment to weaken the labour movement. One element of their strategy involves cutting back on public spending and redistributing the surplus to private capitalists. Another and more important element is to allow capital to force through the introduction of much higher productivity levels on the shop floor.

Compared with these preceding perspectives—both of which grant a key role to capital's rate of profit in the search for a resumption of economic prosperity—the Alternative Economic Strategy appears as an attempt to transcend the profit system and use the power of the labour movement to force the capitalists to expand, invest and so forth regardless of profitability. Nevertheless, AES proposals include provisions for import controls and planning agreements as a framework within which there can be selective channelling and subsidies to particular firms. These provisions represent a compromise with the logic of profit maximization; they are an attempt to ensure that options that accord with government options remain reasonably profitable for private industry.

The problem with all of this is that it tends to assume: 1) that it is possible to isolate a national economy (or, more bluntly beggar thy neighbour') ; and 2) that there is a stalemate in the domestic class struggle. This dilemma effects the AES program and that of the French government, and closer to home is an unresolved problem in CLC/NDP economic policy.

This is not to say that an economic program of the left is not a vital necessity. It is obviously essential. However, it cannot be just an economic program of quantitative demands. It must essentially be a program of economic rights, including the elimination of want, waste and welfare, as suggested in the "Economic Bill of Rights" proposed in Bowles, Gordon and Weisskopf, *Beyond the Waste Land* (1983). However, these rights themselves are vulnerable to the new international division of labour. Ultimately they cannot be achieved outside of a global social movement.

Labour, Left and Green[3]

The best of the neo-Marxist analyses (Gorz and Bahro) point to the internal shifts of class relations within the global economic reorganization. Andre Gorz's *Farewell to the Working Class* (1982) focuses on the declining place of an industrial proletariat as the agent of historical change. Gorz also draws attention to the key question of the social management of the reduction of total working time in either a transition to post-industrial socialism or a regression into barbarism. His fear is that the industrial unions will simply rally to the defense of the old order, as they are increasingly cut off in a segmented labour market and subject to the dictates of the capitalist accumulation process. In Gorz's (1982:3,6,7,8) words:

> A society based on mass unemployment is coming into being before our eyes. It consists of a growing mass of the permanently unemployed on one hand, an aristocracy of tenured workers on the other and between them a proletariat of temporary workers carrying out the least skilled and most unpleasant types of work....The abolition of work is neither acceptable nor desirable for people who

> identify with their work, define themselves through it and do hope to realize themselves in their work. Thus, the social subject of the abolition of work will not be the stratum of skilled workers who take pride in their trade and in the real or potential power it confers on them. Protecting jobs and skills rather than seeking to control and benefit from the way in which work is abolished will remain the major concern of traditional trade unionism. This is why it is bound to remain on the defensive... The choice is either a socially-controlled emancipatory abolition of work or its oppressive anti-social abolition.

Bahro is another neo-Marxist who analyzes the logic and contradictions of capitalist accumulation; he sees the mode of production and consumption headed towards global nuclear war and trade wars if allowed to continue on its own path. Further, he emphasizes that trade unions and the left will have to qualitatively break with the mode of production and consumption dominant for the past generation if they are to see another generation at all, let alone initiate a transition to a socialist society.

In his *Socialism and Survival,* Bahro (1982: 31) states:

> If there is anything today that really does deserve the label of a single issue movement it is the institutionalized wage struggle which is ultimately subordinated completely to the overall process of capitalist production....
>
> On a world scale industrialization cannot be achieved any longer for the earth will not yield the material consumption of the North American middle class, for the ten to fifteen billion people of the next century, and at the national level industrialization can no longer solve any problems of general interest. Industrialization will only increase the sum of absolute impoverishment....
>
> This does not mean that the many internal social contradictions no longer play a role, but rather that they have a subordinate importance in a wider context and thus obtain a different significance. They must also all be handled in such a way that they do not intensify the international contradictions. The domestic goal must be to live better with a reduced production in terms of material quantity, i.e., with less labour and equalized incomes.

What this means is that the left and the labour movement must first reconsider our assumptions about growth and consumption. We need not and should not perpetually ask for quantitatively more; we must instead insist on qualitatively more and better, so that the economy comes to serve real human needs and not simply the processes of accumulation. We must also develop new approaches to interventionism and control of the accumulation process that bring about democratic and popular control. The right is currently manipulating popular sentiments that seek more individual control of events and are hostile to big institutions. We are not guiltless of the conservative charge that the left and labour represent 'big' and 'bureaucratic'.

A real alternative to right-wing interventionism and wage controls will entail cultural changes that allow us to assert different values, gain control of our lives and build a different kind of society.

This, finally, will require us to reconsider how we practice politics. The young, women, minorities, environmentalists and anti-nuke groups are far from seeing labour and the left as automatic allies. Similarly, we must establish different relations with popular movements in the Third World; an ideologically pure program will not be enough; a strictly economic program will not be enough. Labour and the left will not and cannot succeed without linking up with the popular movements. The problems of the environment, of nuclear arms escalation and of minorities are inherently linked to the dynamics of capitalist accumulation. Only under a banner of labour, left and Green, can the system be changed for the good of all of us.

Notes

1. The name of the original Henry Ford is linked to the introduction of assembly line mass production techniques in the automobile factories of Detroit in the early decades of the 20th century. As these production techniques spread to other industries and countries, the term Fordism came to be associated with the assembly line style of industrial production. (editors)
2. For a fuller discussion of this topic see Warrian and Wolfe (1982).
3. 'Green' as a political term refers both to the Green Party of West Germany, which has representatives elected to the national parliament, and to the followers of this party's general ideology in other Western industrialized countries. While the Greens are associated with left-wing or protest politics, they have profound disagreements with more traditional socialists programs or Marxist perspectives. One of the most important areas of divergency lies in the fact that the Greens reject the idea of industrial 'growth', whether in terms of productive capacity or mass consumption, as a desirable goal for the developed Western countries at this stage of their historical development. (editors)

Union Response to Plant Closure Decisions: The Role of the UAW in the Beach Appliances Plant Closure

Robert D. Hiscott

Introduction[1]

The prevalence of plant closures and employee displacement in contemporary industrial societies has led to an atmosphere of insecurity, particularly in the manufacturing sector of the economy. Workers are increasingly unable to depend on long-term stability in employment—economic circumstances prescribe insecurity, and the legal framework (defined in terms of enacted legislation addressing such problems, and collective agreements between labour and management) is clearly inadequate to alleviate or reduce such problems. This paper examines the case of the Beach Appliances Plant closure (Ottawa, Canada) with specific reference to union-management relations. It is argued that the role of the union representing production workers at Beach Appliances (United Automobile Workers' Union Local 614) was severely restricted due to the legal-contractual nature of relationships between the involved parties. A number of possible remedies to the conflictual, adversarial norm in relationships are explored, with specific reference to the Beach Appliances case.

Reasons Underlying the Beach Plant Closure

Beach Appliances was one of six plant-subsidiary operations of the former Canadian Admiral Corporation engaged in the production of electric ranges for distribution throughout Canada. A total of 255 workers (office and production workers) were employed at this facility, which was very old, yet highly efficient (relative to other Canadian Admiral operations at the time) and profitable (earning a profit of approximately one million dollars in its last year of operation) . On March 19,1980, Canadian Admiral gave notice that the Beach Appliances Plant would be closed at the end of October, 1980, with production of electric ranges being transferred to another plant at Montmagny, Quebec. At the time of announcing the closure, John Raynor, President of Canadian Admiral gave the following rationale: " The Beach Plant is an antiquated factory that is inadequate for our current and anticipated needs." Evidence from newspaper accounts and detailed interview transcripts with 71 percent (181 of 255) of all displaced employees, including senior management at the plant, suggest that the company rationale was indeed superficial, not reflecting the scope and nature of problems affecting Canadian Admiral and Beach, particularly when one compares Beach and Montmagny operations.

Principal reasons for the closure of the plant include financial circumstances, political interference and worker militancy. With respect to financial circumstances, it is accurate to suggest that the United Automobile Workers' (UAW) union representing Beach production workers secured very high wage levels for workers at all skill levels. The average product assembler at Beach (an occupation which could best be classified as semi-skilled) had an income of roughly $ 22,000 in 1980. By comparison, at the Montmagny Plant (the plant to which operations were transferred), workers under different union representation earned an average annual income of around $12,000 to $13,000. The UAW also secured many supplementary benefits for Beach workers, prompting one plant official to conclude that the workers were far better off than others in the rest of the industry; "It (the Beach Plant) was paying automotive wages in an appliance manufacturing sector." Despite these labour costs, the Beach Plant was able to secure a profit of roughly one million dollars a year, compared to a deficit of $500,000 a year at the Montmagny facility.

Hence, while the Beach workers were well-paid by comparison to other appliance manufacturing workers, their factory had a high level of productivity and efficiency leading to substantial profits, even during the early phases of world-wide economic recession in the 1980s. This however, cannot be regarded as an isolated incident of a corporation closing a profitable plant or subsidiary operation. There is ample evidence across industrial sectors in Canada and the United States of viable businesses being treated purely from an economic investment standpoint, and being abandoned if they do not meet specified target rates of return (Bluestone and Harrison, 1980; UAW (Canadian Council),1980; Root, 1979; Stern, Wood and Hammer, 1979).

One must also consider the issue of political interference in the closure decision. Canadian Admiral was controlled by York Lambton, Inc., which in turn was controlled by Sogebry Ltee., a Montreal-based holding company. Further, Canadian Admiral received a Federal D.R.E.E. grant (Department of Regional and Economic Expansion subsidization) for the Montmagny facility (which was in a federally-designated 'depressed region') to the amount of $380,000, in addition to a major investment from the Quebec government in the Montmagny operations. Although Canadian Admiral (or the parent holding companies) never admitted to political interference in the closure and transfer decisions, it would appear that such factors could have had a significant effect in corporate decision-making processes. One former employee commented that the transfer was:

> ...very, very political to the point that even the contractors coming in to move the stuff out (transfer machinery and equipment from Beach to Montmagny) had to be from Quebec. They had Quebec labour coming in and taking the stuff out.

Finally, another factor noted by a number of office and management personnel was the level of militancy of Beach unionized workers. Such militancy was demonstrated by wildcat walk-outs in 1976 and a major month-long strike (union endorsed) in 1978, as well as by escalating contract demands which were deemed unreasonable in comparison to other companies in the appliance manufacturing sector. However, it must be noted that the Montmagny Plant had also had serious labour problems. A major strike at that plant in 1975 resulted in the loss of most contract clientele, a situation from which the plant never fully recovered (this provides a partial explanation of the deficit situation prevalent at the Montmagny Plant for the several years). However, the argument presented by management was that worker militancy at the Beach Plant led to an unstable, insecure environment. This viewpoint led to the ultimate decision that better opportunities existed elsewhere.

The original rationale for closure stated by Canadian Admiral President John Raynor ('antiquated facilities') is partially justified, although, once again, one must make the contrast with the Montmagny facility to which operations were being transferred. Both the Beach and Montmagny Plants were very old; Beach having been constructed in 1922, and the Montmagny Plant dating as far back as 1897 for one section of the facility. However, Beach was a one-floor production operation which was far more efficient than the three-floor manufacturing operations at Montmagny (which could not be built 'out', but only 'up'). Hence, by comparison, the Beach Plant was less 'antiquated' than Montmagny. Employees feel that had the same amount of money been sunk into renovation of Beach as was done at Montmagny, Beach would have been a very efficient operation, quite able to meet increased production quotas.

Worker and Labour Market Profiles

Having described a number of the principal factors underlying the plant closure and operations transfer decisions, it is useful to provide a brief profile of Beach workers and the general Ottawa-Hull labour market context, since both worker and labour market characteristics determine the re-employment prospects of displaced Beach employees. Approximately

80 percent of all plant employees were production workers with the remaining 20 percent being office and management personnel. The average age of Beach employees was just under 40 years with fully one-quarter of the workers over fifty years of age. The average worker had some thirteen years of experience at the Beach Plant at the time of leaving, with many having spent their entire working lives at Beach. One-third of all Beach workers had over twenty years of experience with the company.

The average educational level of the Beach workers was about ten years with a range from four years of public school to sixteen years (indicating completion of a university degree). Fully two-thirds of all Beach employees did not have a high school diploma. Further, one-fifth of all Beach workers had less than nine years of grade school. In terms of occupational classification, it must be noted that most production workers were in semi- or unskilled occupations such as product assemblers and material handlers, or low-skilled trades (often without certification papers) such as welders and spray painters. Previous empirical research has shown that displaced workers with these general characteristics (older workers, under-educated, un- or semi-skilled) are particularly vulnerable in terms of re-employment prospects (Mick, 1975; Root, 1979; Stern, 1971).

This profile of Beach employees is particularly significant given the composition of the Ottawa-Hull labour market, where the vast majority of displaced employees would search for re-employment. Ottawa-Hull has a very small industrial base with a heavy concentration of jobs in the public administration sector (Ottawa being the Nation's capital) by comparison to other parts of Ontario and Canada in general. The proportion of the workforce engaged in the manufacturing occupations in the Ottawa-Hull area at the time of the Beach Plant closure was less than 8 percent (approximately 20,000 persons according to Statistics Canada census material). Of this number, less than 2,000 were working in 'Electrical Products Industries' engaged in the production of major and small home appliances, electrical industrial equipment, wire and cable, and other miscellaneous electrical products. Further, it must be noted that Beach had been the only plant in the Ottawa-Hull area engaged in the manufacture of major household appliances. As summarized by one union representative shortly after the closure:

> There are few industries where they (Beach employees) can fit in .... Most of the other plants are in high technology and the skills are not transferable. There just aren't any jobs out there.

This assessment was further verified by the results of a Manpower Adjustment Committee involving company and union personnel under the auspices of the Ontario Ministry of Labour, designed to find jobs for the displaced workers. The committee drew up a list of prospective employers (through use of trade and business directories) within a 25-mile radius of Ottawa-Hull. A total of 65 prospective employers were discovered in this area. Letters were mailed to each prospective employer informing them of the pending closure and the need to place manufacturing workers. Follow-up letters were mailed one month later to those employers who had not responded.

The committee discovered only five or six prospective employers with job openings; the absolute number of job openings was twenty. Hence, the maximum number of Beach employees who could be placed was twenty, which represented a very small proportion of the plant workforce (less than 10 percent). Further, it was found that many of the job openings were in the field of high technology computing equipment manufacture. These firms were not considered as viable employers, since Beach workers would have had to undergo extensive retraining to earn roughly one-half of Beach wages. No Beach employee was re-employed as a result of this committee's efforts. The results of the initiatives of the Manpower Adjustment Committee were disheartening, yet fully expected, given the profile of the Ottawa-Hull labour market and the displaced Beach production workers.

Consequences of the Plant Closure

Given worker and labour market characteristics, one could fully anticipate a number of serious problems associated with the closure of the Beach Plant and the displacement of all its employees. Interviews were conducted with a major sample (71 percent) of all displaced employees, nine to ten months after the plant closure, to determine the status and adjustment problems of the workers. Interviews with 181 displaced employees revealed that fully 95 workers were unemployed. Of this latter number, seven individuals had retired, leaving 88 involuntarily-unemployed individuals (for an unemployment rate of 48.6 percent of the full sample). Of the remaining 86 individuals who had secured re-employment, 19 (22.1 percent) were re-employed in temporary positions (full or part-time), leaving only 67 individuals (37 percent of the entire sample) who were fortunate enough to secure permanent full-time jobs after the closure of the plant.

Re-employment success was found to be related to age (with younger displaced workers being more successful than older), education (in favour of those workers with higher education), and previous occupational classification (with office personnel and high-skilled tradesmen faring better than general production workers). Table 1 below presents contrasts for re-employed and unemployed groups, and a detailed occupational classification breakdown with the success rate for each group.

Clearly younger, better-educated and skilled workers were in a much more advantageous position in terms of re-employment prospects, relative

Table 1: Summary of Re-employed – Unemployed Group Contrasts

Variables and Categories		Re-employed Workers	Unemployed Workers
Average Age	$\bar{X}$	35.8	43.3
	S.D.	10.0	13.1
Average Education (in years)	$\bar{X}$	11.0	9.4
	S.D.	2.2	2.5
Blishen S.E.S. Scores for prior Beach Occupations	$\bar{X}$	40.9	36.9
	S.D.	11.6	10.0
% Occupational Classification (N= 181)		**47.5**	**52.5**
Production workers (N=143)		**43.4**	**56.6**
Material Handlers (N=5)		20.0	80.0
Warehouse Handlers (N=9)		33.3	66.7
Product Assemblers (N=37)		40.5	59.5
Machine Operators (N=5)		68.0	32.0
Inspectors/Testors (N=16)		43.8	56.2
Low Skill Tradesmen (N=32)		21.9	78.1
High Skill Tradesmen (N=38)		87.5	12.5
Other Production Workers (N=11)		45.5	54.5
Office Personnel (N=38)		**63.2**	**36.8**
Quality Control Managers (N=3)		66.7	33.3
Design/DevelopmentTechs. (N=4)		75.0	25.0
Foremen/Dept. Managers (N=11)		72.7	27.3
Office Staff, Gnl. Clerical (N=8)		37.5	62.5
Office Staff, Accounting (N=7)		71.4	28.5
Senior Plant Management (N=5)		60.0	40.0
Total N		86.0	95.0

to older, less-educated, and un- or semi-skilled workers. A number of problems were reported by displaced Beach workers, including a loss of savings since the closure (reported by 15.9 percent of the re-employed and 36.5 percent of the unemployed workers); a deterioration in health since closure (6.1 percent of the re-employed and 14.1 percent of the unemployed); and a change in spouses' employment status (either taking on new employment or changing from part-time to full-time status—20 percent of the re-employed and 29.9 percent of the unemployed workers). There were also isolated incidents of loss of homes and declarations of bankruptcy since the closure (in a total of seven cases). Also, some of the health problems reported by displaced workers were particularly severe; there were several cases of heart strokes or attacks during or shortly after the closure of the plant. Workers were often unequipped to cope with the stress of job displacement, which could indeed lead directly to their suffering health complications such as nervous tension, ulcers and even heart conditions.

Labour-Management Relations

Having reviewed the major reasons for the plant closure and the consequences in terms of worker unemployment and other social effects, it is useful to describe the role of the United Automobile Workers' union in the context of labour-management relations. Relations between the union and the parent company (Canadian Admiral, headquartered in Toronto) had become increasingly adversarial and conflictual during the years prior to the closure. This was exemplified by wildcat walk-outs in 1976, a major month-long strike in 1978, and no less than 18 cases (involving plant safety, workers' compensation claims, etc.) sent to arbitration between 1979 and 1980. Canadian Admiral had become increasingly distant and disinterested in the day-to-day problems of the Beach Plant. As concluded by one Beach manager:

> We were a *company run on paper* (Beach by Admiral). They weren't there. They didn't know the people, nor did they care to. They didn't wish to get involved. There was a statement at the end of each month and that was it. They were running it strictly on paper.

Management for Canadian Admiral (in Mississauga) precipitated some of the union militancy with its attitude of capricious indifference. The company's attitude could best be summarized as 'let the workers fend for themselves' once the decision to close the plant had been made. By giving a full seven months advanced notice of the closure of the Beach facility (as required by law), the company felt it had met all requirements and obligations to the workers. At the time of the closure announcement, no mention was made of severance-benefits provisions or pension security for older workers. The company's statements indicated that severance benefits were not required by provincial law, since the company provided legally-sufficient notice of the shutdown. Further, the company stated that all other matters, such as workers' pensions, would be settled on October 31, 1980—the date of the closure. No further information was forthcoming.

The union protested, and attempted to force the company to the bargaining table to consider requests for a week of severance pay for each year of employee service, but it was to no avail. The company position remained steadfast: no negotiations for post-closure severance benefits. The union charged with representing Beach production workers was unable to take any actions on their worker's behalf beyond simple verbal protests of company policy. This kind of union impotence in the face of plant closures is the norm, rather than the exception, as noted by Metzgar (1980: 38) in his study of the closure of Johnstown, Pennsylvania steel mills: "Shutdowns and cutbacks are not negotiated. They are announced." The UAW, representing the Beach workers, was obliged to see that the conditions of an existing collective agreement (signed well before the closure announcement) were met; it was legally bound to maintain the status quo in spite of the impending shutdown.

Workers, frustrated by the powerlessness of their union, took matters into their own hands. Five months after the announcement of the closure, plant workers staged an illegal sitdown on August 26, 1980, to protest the shutdown and the lack of action of the company on critical issues. The UAW could in no way endorse or support this move, due to provisions in the existing collective agreement (explicitly procluding the use of such tactics for bargaining or other purposes). However, the action was effective, forcing the company to respond and to negotiate. By September 2, 1980, management and the union had negotiated a severance settlement under the auspices of a labour relations officer from the Ontario Ministry of Labour. This package included scaled compensation from $200 to $250 for each year of service, dependent upon age , seniority and status of the employee. Workers forced the company into action when the union was powerless to do so.

One fully anticipates conflictual, adversarial relations between labour and management, particularly given the circumstances of a pending plant closure. As asserted by Crozier (1964: 193), the bureaucratic system of organization (which best characterizes the mode of organization existing within Beach/Canadian Admiral), is "primarily characterized by the existence of a series of relatively stable vicious circles that stem from centralization and impersonality." What makes the Beach Appliances case rather unique is the way in which the labour actually disrupted the conflictual status quo, and created a new power dynamic, forcing management to consider labours' interests. Crozier (1964: 158) generalizes that a "... whole system of bargaining and power relationships (develop) around those areas where actors' behavior is rather unpredictable." The illegal sitdown by the workers in August, 1980, was clearly unpredictable behavior brought about by shared feelings of desperation; the workers saw an uncompromising management bent on leaving them with nothing and an impotent union which was unduly bound by a legal-collective agreement, and concluded that they alone would have to assert their position to alter the course of events. Sabel's (1982) analysis of European labour conflicts emphasizes the importance of considering the political circumstances serving to unite or isolate groups of workers, provoking or precluding specific actions; the Beach case dramatizes the solidarity of production workers above and beyond faith in their union.

Improving the Responses to Plant Closures

Three decades ago, W.F. Cottrell (1951: 365) in an analysis of technological change in the railway industry, posed a key sociological question: "Who benefits and at whose expense?" This question implicitly recognizes that major change (whether in the form of conversion to diesel train engines affecting entire communities, or plant shutdowns leading to massive employee displacement) benefits some parties at the expense of others . Despite divergent interests among the principal parties concerned, corporate decision-making (which includes shutdowns, relocations and all other long-run strategic decisions) has been defended as a managerial prerogative. In many circumstances, corporations make major decisions purely on the basis of economic criteria and ignore the social costs affecting other corporate participants or stakeholders (especially the workers who have contributed greatly to corporate efficiency and profitability over the years).

As stated above, the strictly legal-contractual framework circumscribing relations and actions between unions and corporate management serves to limit the potential response of unions in defense of their members faced with a plant closure. It is therefore useful to consider possible modifications to the existing legal-contractual framework, modifications which would allow unions to protect the interests of workers who are indeed legitimate stakeholders within the corporation. Changes in the legal-contractual framework could be brought about at a macro level (in the form of state legislation designed to protect the interests of workers in the face of corporate plant closure decisions), or at a micro level (in particular, the modification of individual collective agreements to include various forms of security clauses). Each of these general forms of potential change is considered below.

State legislation designed to deal with cases of plant closure is presently inadequate, given the magnitude of the problems of plant closure and employee displacement. Research into plant closures before the more recent dramatic increases recommended the need for legislation stipulating requirements for advanced notice of an impending closure (Eleen and Bernadine, 1971; Shultz and Weber, 1966; Weber and Taylor, 1963). At the time such recommendations were made (focusing on advance notice to workers in closure situations), plant closures and employee displacement were not yet severe problems affecting a huge segment of the industrial workforce in Canada or the United States. Hence individual plant closures in the 1960s and early 1970s could largely be regarded as fairly isolated incidents, rather than as a part of a more general, pervasive phenomenon. While state legislation calling for advance notice in plant closures may have been an adequate response in earlier periods, it is my analysis that the utility of such legislation, at present, is marginal at best.

The incidence of plant closure and employee displacement has increased dramatically since the mid-1970s, with an accelerating trend during the world-wide economic recession of the early 1980s. To illustrate: in the province of Ontario, Shakeel (1980) reported 227 cases of layoff or plant closure affecting 21,899 workers between April, 1979 and March,1980. These figures represented an increase of over 183 percent in layoffs/closures and 107 percent in the number of affected employees compared with the previous year. Shakeel also reports that 92 percent of all these cases and workers were in manufacturing industries. The UAW Canadian Council (1980) reported no less than 13 plant closures affecting Canadian UAW members in a six-month period in 1980. This kind of evidence of the recent magnitude of the problems of closure and displacement (affecting virtually all manufacturing sectors in all regions) makes it seem quite doubtful that advanced notice legislation will have any significant effect in minimizing the difficulties experienced by displaced workers.

Indeed, there is some evidence that even when advance notice is given (in accordance with the law), workers do not take advantage of such notice. In the Beach Plant case, fully 54.7 percent of workers who looked for a new job did not begin their search until after the closure, despite seven months advance notice of the closure date. This is not an uncommon finding; the shock of a closure announcement is often met with a psychological denial of the pending closure by the workers (Root, 1979). Relating his feelings towards the Beach closure, one production worker noted:

> I didn't take advantage of the advance notice (of the closure) because while you were working, you never realized that you were going to be out of a job. We never really realized it. I think I first realized it when they started taking out the machinery (in the last month of operation).

Hence, it would seem that legislation prescribing advance notice of shutdowns is of limited utility, given the magnitude of such problems and the nature of workers' responses to advance notice. More recently, legislation has been introduced in the United States to deal directly with the costs (economic and social) associated with a corporate decision to close a plant. Freeman (1980: 14) reports that bills to regulate plant shutdowns were

Massachusetts and Rhode Island. Legislation directly attacking the problem can take a variety of forms, ranging from laws requiring companies to indemnify local governments for part of the tax loss incurred due to a plant closure (such as the Riegle-Ford Bill referred to by Freeman, 1980: 18), to laws prescribing a moratorium and forcing companies to justify their closure decisions before a public tribunal. This latter course is favoured by the UAW's Canadian Council (1980: 16) and by Eleen and Bernardine (1971: 88). Hence there are a number of possible responses in the form of state legislation that are designed to better protect workers' interests and to help minimize the social costs associated with closure decisions.

Despite the fact that there is a potential for legislative intervention challenging the corporate-managerial prerogative to close plants without consideration of all the costs (for all the parties involved), we should also see that unions can play a more direct role in protecting their members' interests by negotiating security clauses as part of general collective agreements. Available evidence suggests that collective agreements negotiated between unions and companies in Canada and the United States generally lack clauses concerning the possibility of a plant closure. Mick (1975: 207), for example, in a study of 1,823 U.S. contracts applying to collective bargaining units with at least 1000 employees, found that only 3.7 percent of the contracts contained clauses on advance notice of a plant move, and only 3.3 percent of all contracts included clauses for union notification of or participation in management decisions to move plants. More recently McKersie (1980: 16), in a study of U.S. collective agreements, found that only a minority had provisions for such matters as advance notice of a closure (11 percent) or severance pay (38 percent)

The Economic Council of Canada (1976: 277) analyzed collective agreements for units of over 200 employees in Canada and reported that less than 10 percent of all employees were covered by clauses respecting notice of layoff in the case of technological change.

The evidence therefore suggests that unions in the past have not bargained for provisions designed to deal with the potential circumstances of a plant closure. While this is slowly changing (as exemplified by the 1982 Chrysler-UAW collective agreement designed to assure the security of auto workers through 'no layoff' provisions), it would seem that a concerted effort is necessary on the part of union officials to make the long-term employment security of union members a standard part of collective agreements. Far too often a Union's hands are tied because a collective agreement says nothing about plant closure circumstances, leaving the company to act in its own interests with little threat of worker-union retaliation. The existence of security clauses in collective agreements can at least guarantee worker severance benefits in the event of a closure, and can potentially place the union in a negotiating position, able to challenge the least guarantee worker severance benefits in the event of a closure, and can potentially place the union in a negotiating position, able to challenge the company's closure decisions and rationale.

Another possible alternative to plant closure is the recent phenomenon of employee ownership schemes, which has been shown to be successful in Sweden, the United States and elsewhere. In a 1975 U.S. national poll of industrial workers, Stern, Wood and Hammer (1979: 24) found that 66 percent of the respondents expressed a preference for working in an employee-owned organization (relative to other forms of ownership) and that "opinions supportive of the employee ownership concept were widespread." Despite the level of labour support for such schemes, employee ownership plans are attainable only in certain circumstances. Stern and Hammer (1978: 1105), in a study of six cases of ownership transition, identify seven factors directly associated with the success of such schemes: 1) entrepreneurial and managerial leadership, 2) parent corporation response, 3) institutional support, 4) environmental pressures, 5) product market, 6) free professional help, and 7) labour unions.

The success of such schemes is often a function of the level of organization (the presence of dynamic leaders, trusted and supported by the workers to see the plan through) and of the ability to solicit external support (such as convincing government agencies that such a scheme is viable and warrants support—capital investment or other forms—from governmental programs). Trade unions could contribute greatly to the success of such schemes by providing the essential organization and leadership to oversee ownership conversion. In the Beach Plant case, however, it is doubtful that conversion to employee ownership would have been possible, even with strong union leadership and support. The response of Canadian Admiral, the parent corporation, would have been very negative (Admiral would have seen Beach as potentially strong competition in a tight electrical appliance market).

Despite the appeal and success of employee ownership and other forms of workplace democracy, Nightingale (1982) has noted that there has been considerable opposition to any shift in power relationships in Canadian work organizations. Nightingale (1982: 141) regards this opposition as stemming in large measure from Canadian trade unions, which perceive workplace democracy schemes as direct threats to their traditional role and indeed to their survival. He suggests that while workplace democracy is based upon collaborative relationships between parties, trade unionism (particularly in Canada) has been based on an adversarial relationship between labour and management. Nightingale (1982: 145) emphasizes that the negotiation process implicit in trade union-management relationships results in either domination or compromise, rather than integration. Instead of a spirit of 'working together towards common objectives', trade unionism has often resulted in the polarization of interests between parties, leading in turn to ill-feelings and instability. Nightingale (1982: 153) concludes that "The win-lose mentality and the 'low trust dynamic' generated by the adversarial relationship will inevitably colour all aspects of the relationship between labour and management."

Employee ownership plans and other forms of workplace democracy constitute viable alternatives to many situations of plant closure and employee displacement. Yet unions (in Canada in particular) have been largely reluctant to organize or to otherwise participate in such schemes. This type of non-adaptive response by unions (supporting a conflictual status quo to the distinct detriment of their members) deserves serious scrutiny. The role that unions play in situations of plant closure must be expanded considerably, in order to protect the interests of the workers they represent.

Notes

1. Funding for the Beach Appliances Plant Closure case study was received from the research branch of the Ontario Ministry of Labour and Queen's University at Kingston. The United Automobile Workers furnished a complete list of Beach union (local 614) members with addresses and phone numbers which was essential for conducting such research. The parent corporation (Canadian Admiral) was unwilling to cooperate in the research.

When Your Time Has Come... Gold Miners' Views on Occupational Hazards

Camille Legendre

On May 20, 1980, the roof of the Ferderber Mine (also called the Belmoral Mine) in Val d'Or caved in and the ramp, drifts, raises and stopes were rapidly invaded by a gushing mass of muddy water carrying sand, rocks and tree trunks. Eight of the twenty-four miners working underground at the time were trapped. Days and weeks were spent digging through the mine to try to rescue those who were believed to be still alive for a while, trapped in the still unfinished ventilation shaft, and to finally bring the bodies of the miners to the surface.

The accident had a profound effect on the miners and, to a smaller degree, on the population in the Val d'Or area. The magnitude of the tragedy, its suddenness, its surrounding circumstances and the problems which plagued the rescue operations created a crisis which was well publicized across Quebec by the media. Under pressure from the labour movement and concerned public opinion, the government appointed a commission of enquiry, presided over by the same judge who had headed a previous enquiry into the asbestos mining industry (which was very instrumental in the adoption of Quebec's occupational health and safety regulation of 1979). The Commission's mandate was to investigate the circumstances and the causes of the mining accident and to advise the government about the measures which should be taken in the future to avoid such an occurrence.[1]

After conducting its public hearings in the fall of 1980, and commissioning an independent study on the management of the Belmoral Company by a consultant firm, the Commission also decided to have research carried out on some of the social issues that neither the hearings nor the management study had properly covered. Because of their quasi-judiciary nature and the dominant role of the lawyers representing the various parties involved, the hearings had revealed little about the organization of work and the working conditions in the mine, and still less about workers' attitudes and opinions about the accident and their working environment, especially concerning safety conditions.

The Study

The original research done for the Commission comprised two parts: a study of the perceptions and attitudes of Belmoral miners together with a matching sample of miners working in the other gold mines in the Val d'Or area and, secondly, a study of the organization of work and safety conditions in 10 of the most important underground mining operations in Quebec. This paper is based on the first part of the research.[2]

The research mandate from the Commission provided us with a unique opportunity to study workers' perceptions and attitudes under unusual conditions and circumstances. For various reasons, we decided to proceed with semi-directed interviews as our major source of information and with various documents provided by the commission as our secondary source.

The mine, one of three properties in that area owned by Belmoral Mines, had come into operation in July, 1979. As of May, 1980, the company employed 52 miners at its Ferderber site out of a total of 187 employees in production and services (excluding supervisory and administrative personnel).

Of the 42 miners who were traced back and reached, 32 were interviewed. The others declined for various reasons. A non-representative sample of 35 miners from five other mines in the same area produced 25 more interviews, equally distributed by location. All these mines were gold mines but one, which primarily produced zinc and silver. Two of the mines were about the same size as Belmoral (around 80 miners underground); the other three had a larger work force (between 250 and 300 underground workers) and were older than Belmoral (two of them had been in operation since the 1930s). One mine was owned by the government of Quebec mining corporation (SOQUEM), while the others belonged to absentee owners from outside Quebec. Two mines, including Belmoral, were not unionized. At three other mines workers were represented by the United Steel Workers, and at the last mine they were organized in an independent union.[3]

The interview schedule was tailored to cover the topics of primary interest to the Commission as well as some other items which we thought to be useful. The list of topics included the following:

1. Complete job history: a) first job and b) other subsequent jobs previous to the present one ; c) job at Belmoral as of May, 1980: detailed description of how the miner got hired and of the various tasks performed while at Belmoral; nature of work and organization of work, system of remuneration, wages and bonus, other working conditions, and organizational structure of the company; d) subsequent jobs (if any) after the mining disaster; e) comparison

between the organization of work and working conditions at Belmoral and those existing at other mines.

2. Problems of safety at work: a) frequency of accidents; b) miners and safety; c) company and safety; d) government and safety.

3. Other issues: a) the May 20 tragedy; b) unions and health and safety at work; c) black listing; d) miners' general attitudes toward their work and their life in the mining industry.

This paper reviews Belmoral miners' perceptions and attitudes concerning various aspects of the safety of working in the mines, including their own responsibility towards safety at work and that of the employers and the government. These perceptions and attitudes are discussed, and some implications are drawn out about the problems of safety at work and concerning research in this field.

Miners' Perceptions and Attitudes

The Level of Danger

One of our first concerns was to assess the degree of danger perceived by the miners. Almost all Belmoral miners agreed that work in the mines was dangerous. However, the majority promptly gave reasons to minimize this fact, by comparing it with work in other industries or with other activities in life. Thus, work in the mines was not believed to be more dangerous than in other jobs that they knew very well, such as work in the logging or construction industries. However, they believed that work in the factories, which very few of them had experienced before, was less dangerous. Furthermore, they believed that work in the mines involved no more risks than other life activities such as driving on the highways. Many believed that there were more fatalities on the roads than in the stopes.

But on this score, their exact knowledge was poor. When asked to give figures regarding the number of accidents in the mines, the majority of the miners could not answer. Among those who answered, opinions varied widely in completely opposite directions: for some there were very few fatal accidents, while for others there were a lot. In fact, the latter group was closer to the truth than the former. Between 1961 and 1976, 141 miners died in Quebec following work injuries suffered in underground operations.

Fear

Did this relative awareness of danger translate into a feeling of fear, especially after the tragedy of May 1980?

In general, miners admitted that they had experienced fear in the past on some occasions (such as following an accident or in a situation involving high risks), or else a constant latent feeling of insecurity when working in a dangerous mine—such as Belmoral. This awareness of danger was related to cave-ins, but also to air blasts, to the use of explosives and to work in isolation and darkness. They believed that other miners (especially the newly-hired and those who had had an accident in the past) experienced the same feeling, but that self-pride prevented them from showing or acknowledging it.

Belmoral was a mine in which a third of the workers were afraid of working (and that is before the tragedy). The ore vein was especially bad. For instance, one miner said that the ground never gave him a sense of security. Another one said that in the 10 years that he had worked in the mines, Belmoral was the only place that he was constantly afraid. It was work in the stopes that the miners feared the most. A miner who had replaced another miner one day reported that he was so upset that he did not want to go back into that stope the following day. Another sometimes left the job pretending that he was sick, in order to hide the fact that he was afraid after the roof of his stope had caved in several times.

According to a third of the miners, the feeling of fear increased after the tragedy and was widely spread among their work mates. Several miners did not return to work for the company after the accident. But for others, feelings got back to normal after a while, as they were convinced that the company would take more precautions from now on.

Fatalism

People like traditional fisherman, involved in activities in which there are a large number of unknown and uncontrollable factors that represent a constant threat to their well-being, often become fatalistic and believe that events unfold in an unpredictable way (fate) which must be accepted as such since it is beyond one's control. We found many instances of this attitude among the miners. The explanation of mining accidents is a fertile ground to show and express fatalism. Emotions generated by accidents exacerbate the contradiction between the awareness of danger in the mines and the remote possibility of escaping completely from it. The frustration is increased when it is impossible to find someone responsible upon whom to cast one's anguish and bitterness. Since mining accidents are usually perceived as a result of uncontrollable natural forces and hazards (falling "looses", for instance), when miners are themselves victims of accidents (or see them happening to people close to them), they tend to look for explanations in non-material and super-natural realities, such as one's own destiny.

As one of the miners put it: "Everyone of us has a time to die, and a fate to meet. You cannot escape from it. I believe in that since I almost lost my life, and nobody will be able to convince me of the contrary."

Most of the miners previously involved in an accident showed fatalistic attitudes during the interviews. "When your hour has come", as one said, "there is nothing you can do. Wherever you are, you die. You cannot escape from it." For another miner, this belief was clearly a way out of the contradiction between the consciousness of danger and the impossibility to avoid it. "If it is your day to die, you will die. You may die while you are working, or in a car accident, or anywhere else and in a thousand ways. It does not matter. Destiny will come and get you wherever you are." This was of course a way to minimize the danger involved in the work since, if it is a matter of fate, "it is not more dangerous in the mines than anywhere else."

Nonetheless, common-sense explanations, as we all know, have a tendency to be used at cross purposes. The same explanation can be used to explain why, in one case, the miner survived and why, in another case, he died. Thus, in telling the story about a miner who got involved in an accident with dynamite but who survived, a miner concluded that "there was a God for this man."

We found expressions of this fatalistic attitude in miners' perceptions of the May tragedy, although it was mixed with their generally critical opinion toward the company. One miner expressed it well when he said that "It (the tragedy) was bad luck. It could have happened during the weekend, but we are not the one who runs that." The majority, however, found matter-of-fact explanations which they drew from their own daily experience in the mine, where it is fairly easy for an experienced miner to notice errors and acts of negligence on the part of the company.[4] But despite their realism and the fact that the accident could be explained by the material causes (as the hearings of the Commission showed), there was still something unaccounted for by these material explanations for the majority of the miners. Why was one not there when it happened, or why did it not happen while another was there? So, as one said: "It could have been me. It's only because it was not yet my turn. I am not the only one who thought like that."

Miners' Responsibility Regarding Their Safety

Faced with this widespread fatalistic attitude, should we conclude that the miners did not see any point in paying attention to their own safety and taking measures to ensure it? Not quite so. According to one miner: "It doesn't mean that you have to run after your own death. You must still take precautions." Or more bluntly, in another one's words: "When you have a chance to find ways to live longer, well you take it." For still another one: "You must try to cheat fate by doing your very best for your own safety." In fact, contrary to our expectations, miners who expressed the most fatalistic attitudes were those who were the most preoccupied by safety measures.

How then did the miners perceive their responsibility regarding safety? It should not surprise many of us to learn that half of the miners believed that the responsibility rested first and foremost with the workers themselves. "It was up to the miner himself to ensure his own safety", said several of them. Moreover, many believed that, in most cases, accidents were the result of an error or an act of negligence by the victim himself, either because of his lack of experience or due to his decision to take a chance. To support their view, many miners gave the example of a fellow worker who was crushed to death by a loose rock a year earlier. Although he was an experienced miner, he had not followed the proper safety procedure before starting to drill (he had not scaled his stope thoroughly and placed rock bolts where needed).

Several factors may account for this prevalent view among the miners, which comes very close to a "blaming the victim" attitude. The organization of work in the mines created conditions which necessitated to some extent that workers take charge of their own safety.[5] On the one hand, miners were responsible for their respective working area. They worked either alone (an exceptional thing at Belmoral) or with one or two other fellow miners, and had to accomplish almost all the production tasks. That meant that they had to assume a series of operations to insure the safety of the environment. On the other hand, miners still exercised a good deal of control over their job. Being widely dispersed throughout the mine and paid on piecework and bonuses, they were loosely supervised.

As a result of these working conditions, safety measures were largely left to the workers themselves, and supervisory personnel intervened only through on-the-spot advice and instructions given with more or less insistence. One miner summarized this situation well: "Safety, it is the miner who makes it. Even if he has a chief of safety who tells him to take his precautions, it is the miner who works under the looses."

Many miners perceived their autonomy at work as one advantage of their job which they greatly valued. Others spoke of the pride that that they had about their work and the specific area where they worked, using such expressions as "my stope", "my raise", etc. In such a context, one miner scorned those workers for whom "safety, it is the boss who should do it for them!" Others also mentioned cases where miners took advantage of the safety issue to not work. In short, because of the personal pride they took in their autonomy at work, miners exaggerated the importance of their own responsibility for safety.

Recognizing this responsibility, did the miners take appropriate measures to insure their safety? The majority of the miners did generally follow the series of procedures dealing first with loose and falling rocks, and second with the remaining dynamite powder in missed holes. However, miners did not seem to pay much attention to the handling of dynamite and the work involved in the preparation of the blast. Many of them admitted, however, that despite these precautions, their work remained dangerous for several reasons: 1) there could always be loose rocks or missed holes which they had not seen; 2) work routines tended to dull the awareness of danger and workers did not always follow through with the safety measures (for instance in scaling negligently, or drilling in missed holes against the rules, skipping steps, etc.,); and 3) there were tasks or jobs which involved dangerous work that could not be avoided (for instance drilling in a raise).

As a result, several workers said that they were ready to take chances in specific circumstances. Otherwise, as one put it, "At one point, if you think only safety, you do nothing anymore. There's a limit to it." In fact, our interviews showed that only a third of the miners seem to be really concerned by their safety to the point of being meticulous about safety measures.

But were they safety-conscious enough to refuse a dangerous work assignment? And, if so, could they refuse such an assignment without problems, knowing that the new legislation for the first time gave them that right?

Although all the miners believed that they could use such a right, half of them said that there was a price to it. The simple legal statement of the worker's right to refuse dangerous work was not enough to eliminate the various means of pressure at the disposal of the employers. First, one risked being fired (something, however, forbidden by the new law). Then, there was the possibility of being humiliated and losing prestige, by being branded as "weak-kneed" or "a complainer". Miners generally were proud of their job and felt responsible for it; they disliked going to the supervisor to tell him that they did not want to work because the place was too dangerous. They also thought that a pushy supervisor could insist that the worker do the job, or use the refusal as an excuse to assign him to a dirty place or to put him on a bad shift. Finally, there was the possibility of losing part of the bonus through re-assignment to a lesser paying job. This was not always the case, since companies often used the "safety bonus" to maintain the normal level of income for miners who had to change their usual routine to complete a dangerous job.

The protection of the union (if there was one) made it easier to refuse a dangerous job, but it was not fool-proof. Supervisors could always use indirect pressures against the miners. As one miner said: "It is always difficult to refuse. With Bill 17, you have the right to do it, but you get annoyed a lot for it."

Safety and the Employers

If the responsibility for safety rested first and foremost with the miners, what was the role of the companies, and what was their state of concern for safety, according to the miners?

Miners agreed on the whole that the companies showed some concern for safety and were doing something about it. However, most of them observed that their employers acted only when they were forced to do so by governmental regulations, mining inspectors and the unions, or when the level of their contributions to the worker's compensation fund was too high. Many added that the companies were negligent, considered production and profits first, and could do better. The worst offenders were the independent contractors and the small mining outfits, especially at the beginning of their operations. Large and well-established companies had, according to the miners, a much better record.

The companies' role was defined along two dimensions. The first was related to miner's responsibility for their own safety. Belmoral miners gave much importance to employer's measures directed at informing workers of their duties and encouraging them to fill them efficiently. A third of the miners thought that this was the normal and acceptable role for the companies and that their responsibilities went no further. In fact, for some, the role of the companies was reduced to telling the miners to be careful. This perception was in line with the "individualist orientation" of the miners noted earlier.

Accordingly, Belmoral miners suggested that appropriate measures should deal with safety training and instruction, safety tips by supervisors, and disciplinary measures against negligent miners. However, several workers mentioned that, in the past, disciplinary measures had been used arbitrarily against undesirable miners; their enforcement followed the state of labour relations in the mines. At Belmoral, however, since the organizational climate was good and working conditions satisfying (except for the poor ground conditions of the ore vein), there were no such problems.

The second dimension of the companies' role had to do with taking care of roadways, emergency exits, ventilation, equipment maintenance, etc., as long as these were under the direct responsibility of the company. But since these responsibilities were more costly, companies had a tendency to neglect them (as the Commission of enquiry found out in investigating the May tragedy.[6]

Government Role

For several decades, the provincial government has been involved in policing work in the mining industry through its regulations and its inspecting service. How did the miners assess the role of the government regarding work safety? Were they satisfied with present regulations and the way these were enforced? Were there specific changes to be made to improve the situation?

Miners' opinions on these matters were very clear and in line with their other views. First, the majority considered that existing regulations were adequate and gave them good protection. There had been improvements in the recent years, and new regulations were promised by the government to prevent cave-ins like the one that had just happened. However, a majority expressed the view that these regulations were not only sufficient, but also exaggerated and, in some cases, could even become a safety hazard (for instance, the obligation to wear safety glasses, which tend to get dirty because of condensation and dust). These regulations were an obstacle for the normal accomplishment of the miner's tasks and did not take into account the great variety of situations with which they are confronted. As one miner said: "If we were to follow them to the letter, we wouldn't be able to work anymore. We would be better to stay home."

It is no wonder then to hear from most of the miners that existing regulations were not followed by employers and employees alike, and that many miners had hardly any notion of them at all.

Belmoral miners repeated the oft-heard complaint that governmental regulations were not properly enforced. The majority believed that the inspectors were insufficient, to the point of notifying the companies of their upcoming visit. As a result, employers could straighten things out before the inspection and steer the inspector away from the worst areas. Moreover, inspectors were in small numbers and, as a result, their visits were few and far-between. Miners believed that they were too lenient and sometimes lacked consciousness. Finally, some miners questioned their competency, since most of the inspectors had never worked in the mines and did not know the practical aspects of the job. As a result, they could not identify the real safety hazards and dangerous procedures.

Improvements to the present situation proposed by the miners centered on four aspects: 1) to increase the power and efficiency of the mine inspectors (increase their number, have miners' representatives accompany them during their visits, etc.); 2) to oblige companies to assume their full responsibilities (organize training sessions for miners, generalize team work in the mines, etc.); 3) to increase the severity of certain existing rules (raise the norms regarding air and noise pollution, improve emergency exits, supply better medical treatment,etc.); and 4) to abolish the piecework and bonus system of remuneration, without reducing the miner's income.

Other Miners' Views

So far, the views expressed have been from the Belmoral miners, those most directly affected by the tragedy. However the views expressed by the second group of miners, those from other gold mines, were very similar, with only some minor differences. In general, these latter miners had a tendency to consider work in the mines as less dangerous than did the Belmoral miners, and to be less affected by the fear of an accident even after the tragedy at Belmoral. This event made them more safety conscious for a while, but it did not change their basic attitudes. They were also less fatalistic and defeatist than Belmoral miners.

These other miners also expressed an individualist orientation concerning responsibility for their own safety, but they were less inclined to blame the victim of an accident, especially those who belonged to a union. More sensitized to noise and dust problems by their unions, they were also less fearful of the consequences of using their right to refuse dangerous work.

Contrary to our expectations, these miners were more satisfied with the efforts made by their company regarding safety at work than were the Belmoral miners. That difference could be explained by the impression left by the tragedy and nourished by the enquiry and reports in the media—that Belmoral had been negligent. But if they were less critical of their employers, these other miners were critical of the government. They put more blame on the process of governmental inspection, and more emphasis on better regulation and stiffer penalties than did the Belmoral miners — an indication of union influence.

Discussion[7]

The miners at Belmoral were between 25 and 52 years old and had accumulated between five and 30 years of experience in the mines—in Quebec, elsewhere in Canada, or even in the U.S.A. With only a primary school education, they had held jobs in farming, logging and sawmills, and had worked for an average of five mines and often for a mining contractor. Very few of them had ever experienced work in a factory; none of them had ever worked in a Montreal factory. They were part of a close family network in which people shared similar occupational experiences in life.

Their trade is a hard one which, like other similar occupations in farming and logging, requires experience and personal skills. It also gives the miner a relative autonomy at work, an autonomy that is accentuated by the bonus system of remuneration.

The social origin of the miner, the types of jobs available in the area and the specific organization of work in the mines contribute to the development of an individualistic orientation in their attitude toward work and its various aspects (safety, work relations, unionization, etc.).[8]

If we compare the miners we can identify two types: those who have internalized the value of individual responsibility (more numerous at Belmoral than at any other mines), and those who put more emphasis on the organizational causes of accidents and rely more on their collective defense against risk (which translates into a recourse to the action and protection of unions).

Those in the first group often see themselves as free entrepreneurs, aware of their antagonistic interests with the company, but convinced that they can reach an agreement without the help of a union. Having worked before for mining contractors and having learned the hard way, they are often known to be going after high bonuses ("bonusmen"). They cherish their personal autonomy, and count on their own capacities to go through the difficult periods which miners experience. Work in the mines is their life and they derive a great deal of pride and personal satisfaction from the relative autonomy that they still enjoy at work. But if they were to quit this life, they would see themselves as becoming small independent merchants or entrepreneurs.

The second type of miner is almost the opposite of the first. For these miners, work in the mine is not their life, and they would like to get out of it. They are preoccupied with their safety at work, and unfavourable to the piecework system. They see themselves as having opposite and irreconcilable interests with the company. Facing economic interests which are too powerful to be confronted by an isolated individual, they consider unions as their only recourse to assure their immediate security or to provide a way out for their professional mobility in the future.

The first type of miner seems to be the basic one. How does this fit in with the miners' social and working environment?

The Social and Working Environment

The community in which these miners live is in an isolated region which was opened to colonization at the turn of the century, with the first mine being established in 1926 at Noranda. This is frontier country. It is a dependent economy, dominated by natural resource-based industries that are subject to a lot of fluctuations. As a result, the economic and social environment has been largely unstable and unpredictable, and its evolution, of course, beyond the miners and other members of their communities. Layoffs, mine closings, unemployment and other calamities have been a staple of life in the mining areas, especially in gold mining. In this type of environment, one has to be prepared to face reality largely on his own.

Along with a few large-scale enterprises (such as Noranda mines),[9] one finds a lot of small-scale enterprises in this economic environment. A mine like Belmoral is a very small world within another small world.[10] The social distance is not great between the manager of the mine and his men who cross each other's paths at the food store, the credit union, the church, the tavern, or the cinema. The men who had been recruited for the new mine had previously worked for contractors, so they had gone to the right school; they would not cause problems. Besides, the company pays good wages, fringe benefits compare well and problems can be solved by a good talk man-to-man. The manager knows; he was a miner himself. There is no need to complicate things and jeopardize the system by bringing in the union and a complicated grievance procedure.

This paternalistic system fits in well with the individualistic orientation of the miners hired at Belmoral, and further reinforces this orientation. One consequence of this system is that workers like the management of the mine and trust its competency... until there is an accident. But by then it is too late to check on this competency. It is also on the basis of this complex of conditions and attitudes that fatalism develops and expresses itself whenever things seem to evolve beyond one's control.

The mine is a microcosm with its social norms, its professional life habits, its human relations, its dangers, its failures and its successes. We could say that there are two mines. The first one belongs to its legal owners, far-away speculators for whom the mine is only one piece of the action. With the profits these owners make, it is a "gold mine" in both the literal and the popular sense of the term....

Then there is the other mine, the one which belongs a little bit more to those who work there everyday, from the manager to the stope miner. It is home to their good relationships, their tensions, their conflicts and also their complicity in the losses and profits. It is also the mine of sickness, accidents and death.

Compared to a large factory, the mine is a small, closed world where everybody knows each other, but also a physical environment which also allows isolation, with miners working alone or two or three together. The supervisor comes twice per shift, and the rest of the time the miner is alone in the place of his work, like the tradesman in front of his workbench. The relative autonomy of his work is highly valued.

The hierarchy of the organization is based on seniority and experience. At the top are the first-hired miners and the most experienced ones, recruited by the manager who had known them before in other mines. They get the jobs paying the highest bonuses. Then come the other miners, most often hired on the recommendation of the first ones, and so on down the list.

The Impact of the Tragedy

Before the accident, miners had a very positive opinion about the company and their job. It was a new mine, and well-equipped; the pay was one of the best of the region; and management was comprehensive. So it was all worth it, even if the underground was not the best around.

Did this opinion change after the accident? Yes and no. The mine was reopened less than a year after, and many miners returned to work, while others decided that they had had enough. For these latter miners, it was a dangerous mine, and dangerously exploited. For the others, the tragedy was bad luck, an accident. After all, it was only a mine like the other ones, even if the underground was not very safe; one might as well earn his living there as anywhere else. Besides, the job market was bad, the price of gold was holding for a while at least, and the pay was good. Not much of a choice, but there were risks in all the mines.

The miners believed that the company knew that an accident was coming and they also believed that it could have been avoided.[11] But it was impossible to predict, they thought, that it would turn into a tragedy. The miners were divided, however, about the immediate cause of the accident. Some attributed it to "nature" (the nature of the ground); some thought that it would have been possible to keep these natural factors under control; and others used both explanations at the same time.

Conclusion

Our studies indicate that the complex of perceptions, attitudes and behaviors that we have identified under the names of individualism and fatalism cannot be properly understood without reference to the miners' social characteristics, such as their occupational history and their social background. But these individual characteristics themselves are related to a particular socio-economic and cultural context, that is to the capitalist economic exploitation of primary resources (mines, forests, fisheries, hydro-electricity), and to a peripheral and dependent regional society. We have a better knowledge of this society, thanks to the numerous works done in the last 20 years or so in the field of regional studies, but we know much less about the working environment of those who live there, and how they view it.[12]

Our study shows that workers' views about occupational health and safety (and about the relationship between health and safety conditions and the characteristics of the working environment) cannot be explained satisfactorily without taking into account individual social characteristics and the particular socio-economic and cultural environment. Within this specific environment, factors such as the type of work organization and the existence of unions constitute important elements to consider.

This paper did not allow us to examine the impact of a significant event like a mining disaster on workers' views and on their employing organizations. Pursuit of this area of study, however, could be fruitful in understanding the process of change in perceptions and attitudes in the field of occupational health and safety.

Notes

1. For further information, see Commission d'enquête sur la tragédie de la mine Belmoral et les conditions de sécurité dans les mines souterraines, *Volume 1, Rapport final sur les circonstances, les conditions préalables et les cause de la tragédie du 20 mai 1980,* Ministére des Communications, Government du Québec, Québec, mars 1981; *Volume 2, Le Sauvetage minier,* Ministére des Communictions, Government du Quebec, Quebec, novembre, 1981; *Volume 3, La sécurité dans les mines souterraines,* Ministére des Communications, Gouvernement du Quebec, Quebec, janvier 1982. For the report of the enquiry on the asbestos industry, see Comité d'etude sur la salubrité dans l'industrie de l'amiante, *Rapport final,* Gouvernement du Québec, Québec, octobre 1976. Three volumes and one Appendix.
2. Legendre and Dofny (1982). See the Introduction and the four annexes for further details on the nature of the study and its design.
3. For more information, see Legendre and Dofny (1982). Introduction and Chapter 2.
4. By the time we interviewed the miners, the enquiry had already revealed a good number of questionable actions by the company.
5. For further details on the organization of the mine and the work process, see Legendre and Dofny (1982), Chapter 3, sections 1, 2, and 3.
6. See especially Volume 1 of the report, as detailed in footnote #1.
7. This chapter is based on Legendre and Dofny (1982), chapter 7.
8. Regarding safety at work, the predominant individualistic orientation which has been observed is no doubt related to the specific organization of work in the mines, which allows for a good deal of autonomy, and to the bonus system. There is no doubt that the miners were conditioned by the companies in general to adopt such an orientation. A phrase repeated over and over again by the miners—"It is up to the miner to create his own safety"—sounded like a conditioning slogan widely used by the authorities. Moreover, once a safety measure had become an official regulation (for instance, the obligation to wear safety glasses, or the interdiction of keeping explosives near the working area during the drilling operations), and the workers were obliged to abide by it, companies had a tendency to wash their hands of it and to rely on the miners' own work routines.
9. It is important to underline here that we are dealing with small-scale operations which are of a very speculative nature. Conditions are different in larger companies, and miners were usually aware of the differences, especially if they had worked for bigger mines before. For the study of a large mining operation, see for instance Wallace Clement, (1981).
10. See Legendre and Dofny (1982), chapter 3 for details.
11. See Legendre and Dofny (1982), chapter 1 for details.
12. Marchak (1983) is a good example of a recent study devoted to these kinds of concerns.

Worker Enforcement of Health and Safety

Stan Gray

You get what you fight for. That pretty well sums up Ontario labour's experience in trying to get unsafe working conditions cleaned up.

A new health and safety act was passed in 1979. It contained many positive reforms but the government authorities charged with enforcing the law have refused to do their job. They have responded too directly to the pressures of the employers. So workers have been left to their own resources. Where the rank-and-file have been able to organize and mobilize these resources in various ways, they have eliminated unsafe and unhealthy conditions. Where they have not been able to, the laws and regulations have remained meaningless pieces of paper.

Employers have resisted work-place clean-ups because these cost money. They also treat health and safety demands as a challenge to their unfettered control over the workplace, an erosion of their management authority.

The new law provides no resolution here because it created joint management-worker safety commissions but gave them no power. The authority over the plant and its production processes remained wholely in the management's hands: management alone determines what chemicals are used and how they are applied, designs the jobs and assembly operations, organizes inspection, maintenance and repair, etc.

The joint committees, even if both sides on them were to agree, cannot make management fix an unsafe condition. The act gives that remedial authority to the government: directly to the inspectors of the Ministry of Labour, and indirectly to the courts.

The employers in Ontario are well organized and have successfully used their considerable economic and political influence to cripple the Minister's enforcement of health and safety. The very top levels, from Cabinet down, have set a policy of weak enforcement.

The inspectors have wide-ranging powers to compel management to clean up but they have refused to use these. They hear, see and speak no evil when they enter the plants, on inspection tours or in response to worker complaints or refusals. When they do acknowledge violations of the regulations, they downplay them or write recommendations that are not enforceable. When they are pushed to write orders, very often these are ignored by the companies and the ministry leaves it at that... or re-writes the orders but never makes management comply.

The court system has not been used as an enforcement mechanism either. There have been very few charges laid over health and safety violations. Even deaths and critical injuries don't necessarily stimulate prosecutions. The few prosecutions to date have not been seriously done and when convictions have been attained, the fines are ridiculously small. They have come to represent a minor cost of doing business, less expensive than clean-up measures would have been. All this simply breeds more contempt by the employers for the safety laws of the province. It tells them their facilities can continue to cause disease and crippling injuries to their employees without serious consequence to their business operations.

And so workers have been left on their own: they have been able to use but not rely upon the official channels the law set up on health and safety. These channels have been obstructed and resisted. This resistance has been rooted in those with vested interests in unsafe and unhealthy conditions.

On toxic substances like asbestos and on unsafe physical conditions with cranes or scaffolding, both the employers and the government officials have made workers scrap and fight to get the minimum of the legal regulations enforced. Since 1979, the bosses have fought every inch of the way, have re-interpreted every clause in the act, have resisted on every front, have twisted every word in the law, and every arm in the government bureaucracy to frustrate compliance with the health and safety standards.

But where workers and unions have been persistent, have not been turned off by the first obstacles, they have been able to get something done. When workers have organized and mobilized their collective strength and confronted the employer with that power, they have managed to force through what they needed for safer conditions of work.

That strength comes first and foremost from the rank-and-file in the shops or offices, and it can be exerted there directly. It also comes through the collective organization of the union in the many arenas open to it. It also comes from the use of public pressure: the media and the political forum (the efforts of the New Democratic members of the legislature who have spoken up against unsafe conditions and government cover-ups).

Workers and labour in general have had to be inventive—constantly seeking out and using new fronts of struggle, finding other avenues and arenas, developing new forms of battle. When they stop you one way, try others. Use ingenuity. Be persistent. There are many ways to skin a cat.

Lessons from the Shop Floor

Some examples I am familiar with from the Hamilton area show this process.

One of the early lessons at the Westinghouse transformer plant in Hamilton where I worked occurred in 1978 in a fight over a band saw in poor condition. The blade often broke, flew off and cut the user. We complained to the boss and to the committee, but to no avail. The department manager claimed it was okay and wouldn't have it fixed.

The Ministry of Labour inspector came in and carefully looked it over. He pronounced it safe, having all the required guards and devices, no evident problems... despite what the workers told him about its performance.

Well, we weren't too much in awe of the law or the expertise of its officials. After all, we were being cut by the saw that he could see no problems with.

The next morning, a guy went to use the saw. Immediately, all of us stopped work, got out of the tanks, climbed down from the scaffolds, quit our machines, even left the cranes, to go to the manager. Under the Safety Act, workers had a duty to report any safety hazard of which they were aware. So we stopped work to tell the manager of an unsafe band saw. We weren't refusing to work, we just wanted to tell him of the danger.

The manager was arrogant about it and told us the government inspector had already checked out the saw, it was safe and we were all to go back to work. Which we did.

Twenty minutes later, another guy went to use the saw and we all left our machines, climbed down from our scaffolds, exited from the tanks to report that unsafe band saw to the manager. As the plant safety representative, I had my book in hand and once again outlined the hazards. The manager huffed and puffed, told us all it was okay and it had been approved by the inspector and we were to immediately return to our work stations. Which we did.

Half an hour later, another guy came to use the saw and we all left our machines. This went on all morning. At one point that manager did some calculations and figured out that he was losing more money in lost production time by leaving the saw there in unsafe condition. So, before noon, he ordered the machine red-tagged, even got the maintenance department to cut the floor bolts off and remove it from the shop. It had become such a red flag, a provocative symbol to the whole shop. And he bought us a new band saw.

All of this, despite the inspector's okays, and within a few hours. That manager, faced with some unorthodox collective action on the shop floor, found it more economical to listen to his own workers than to the authority of law and government.

Things often get more complicated, of course. In 1979, two months after the new act was passed, an explosion in our plant blinded a young worker, Terry Ryan.

We had pretty strong indications that unsafe procedures with flammables, encouraged by management, caused the accident. But the ministry inspectors who came to investigate could find no company negligence. They weren't interested in finding any. They did a snappy investigation, ignored leads that we presented to them, bulldozed their way through to exonerate the company, and let them off the hook.

We weren't happy with this and weren't going to let things drop. The new law had a clause in it that allowed the union safety rep to do his own investigation of a fatal or critical accident. So, as the rep, I conducted my own, completely independent of the company and ministry. I took many months to do it, interviewed witnesses, checked documents, followed leads, probed many possibilities. I eventually found sufficient evidence of company responsibility for unsafe practices that had led to the explosion.

In July, 1980, I issued a long report saying so and itemizing the facts. This forced the ministry to lay charges, seven months after they had whitewashed the company. But things didn't stop there. They laid the charges mainly to clear themselves, but arranged for the case to be scuttled.[1] They put incorrect information in the charges, including the wrong date of the accident, such that it would have been thrown out of court. We forced them to reverse that and revise the charges. We pushed, over a period of months, for a serious prosecution. But the ministry was interested in losing the case and did a very poor prosecution.

When the time came for me and the other shop witnesses to take the stand, the ministry made a dirty deal with the company: 'plea-bargained' and let them get off the hook. They stopped the trial, lowered the charges for a guilty plea and a small fine of $5,000. The truth never came out in court and the company never had to take real responsibility for the accident and pay a real serious penalty.

So, our investigation and efforts got somewhere, namely in forcing the laying of charges and some acknowledgement of guilt. But that was all eventually short-circuited by company-government collusion to bury the case.

Others learned from our experience and developed different tactics. Across the street from Westinghouse is National Steel Car, a very unsafe workplace. The Steelworkers Union safety chairman there was Mike Skinner, a friend of mine who watched the events in the Ryan case with us. He had some concerns about dangerous practices with flammables in his paint area, namely cutting operations which could ignite the solvent vapours. The very day the ministry inspectors were in the plant to check out that and other safety complaints, a fire broke out due to cutting torch ignition. The inspectors, however couldn't see a problem, despite the fact that a worker ended up in the hospital with serious burns. They wouldn't issue orders or lay a charge.

Learning from our frustrations in the Ryan case, Mike didn't push the ministry to prosecute National Steel Car—he did it himself. The act allows any individual or union to prosecute, so Mike laid charges and prosecuted with the help of the union's lawyer. And they did a better job than any ministry prosecutor ever did, obtaining a conviction and a $20,000 fine, one of the largest levied in Ontario—a deterrent to National Steel Car and to other employers.

All of which shows a basic lesson: don't rely on the authorities to do the job for you, they'll mess it up in one way or another. Use the officials, but don't trust or depend on them. They're working for your adversaries. Find other ways; rely upon and trust yourselves, your own abilities and strengths. Don't wait for them to do it, do it yourself. Seek other methods. You'll get a lot further that way.

Don't be held back by the dead weight of official inaction and inertia. Seek ways around it. Be flexible and adaptable.

Persistence is the key. When you use your resources and build up shop floor strength, there's not much you can't do over time.

We had horribly unhealthy conditions in our welding shop in 1982. Guys were getting nauseated; they had headaches, breathing ailments, nosebleeds, burning eyes and more. The company could see no problem, wouldn't install better ventilation. The guys waged a long campaign with work refusals, petitions and other actions.

The ministry's so-called experts came in again and again, and reassured us the place was safe. They based this on various tests and air quality surveys. We didn't believe any of this and charged cover-up. We did our own research and showed that they had taken tests for the wrong substances—carbon monoxide, for example, that isn't even produced by the industrial processes in that plant.

When other tests were taken later, they showed high levels of toxic nitrogen oxides and welding fume. The ministry disavowed some of these results and wouldn't force any ventilation improvements. We challenged those. We found our experts, pushed for better tests.

The paint vapours there were also harmful and the ministry's test reports proclaimed the paint to be safe by using the wrong standards and calculations. We exposed those also. We waged a guerilla war in the shop and also went public with the evidence that incriminated the ministry. The New Democratic Party raised these issues in the legislature.

We fought it out in the shop, in the committee, and in the public arena, and eventually won out. After a year, the company had to install a whole new ventilation system in the building. It cost them a lot of money, but it made things healthier for our workers.

In the process, the company threatened us with discipline and court action, the ministry threatened to dissolve our committee, the guys were subjected to a lot of intimidation and blackmail in the shop... but we kept it up, never surrendered, kept coming back at them with new weapons and new strategies. And today we have a cleaner and safer fabrication shop.

The officials won't do the job unless you force them to. We have had a lot of problems in Hamilton industry with unsafe overhead cranes. A worker was killed at National Steel Car in 1979 after being hit by another crane on the crane runways. After an inquest, the union was able to force the company to install 'stop blocks'. A crane coming along the rails would be stopped by these before it hit a man on the runway in the same bay.

This was an elementary safety precaution. But despite that, and despite the National Steel Car experience, the riggers at Stelco had to engage the company in a lengthy battle to get the same rule enforced there. In the spring of 1981 they refused to work without those blocks. The ministry inspector was called in and upheld their refusal, but that was reversed once the company spoke to the ministry. The riggers were suspended by Stelco, the ministry would do nothing and then all the riggers got involved with other refusals. Eventually, the union won it on appeal and the head office ministry director issued a policy directive that stop-blocks or a lock-out of the power was compulsory in all work on overhead crane rails.

That may have been the law and the director's edict, but that didn't mean that we were entitled to that at Westinghouse down the street. We had been fighting management for years to get such a policy enforced. We had many accidents or near misses on those rails on high. In one case, the guys had to jump off the rails to save themselves from an oncoming crane.

After the Stelco decision, we pressed the company, but to no avail. It took us about a year before we could force the ministry to recognize their own laws and order Westinghouse to abide by the stop-blocks or lock-out regulations. (In full knowledge that Westinghouse was not complying with this rule, the ministry area manager once told us it was not needed because it would cost Westinghouse too much money... he evidently being the self-appointed guardian of the company's financial interests which overrode the safety laws he was charged with enforcing.)

It had taken us years of runarounds and evasions and apologies and the authorities turning a blind eye to accidents and hazards before the government would act. We had years of griping and fighting by our committee men, stewards and rank-and-file. But we won and the workers are better protected as a result.

You have to develop a confidence in your own expertise, and a proper contempt for the pronouncements of the authorities. This is evident in all the wars we have had concerning cranes, a situation we take extra seriously because they carry loads of many tons. In one year, for example, we had three overhead crane cables snap. Two jib cranes fell off the wall. There were other malfunctions.

One overhead crane often went down when you pushed the 'up' button. We said that was unsafe. The company's managers and experts okayed it... as did the Ministry of Labour's engineers and inspectors.

This went on for years, and all those officials and engineers complained about those crazy factory hosers who didn't understand how the equipment was designed to operate. "Go back to work and do what you're told. Stop wasting our valuable time," was their attitude.

We finally mustered up enough evidence and shop floor fightback to force the ministry officials to rule the crane unsafe. The very next day the crane was repaired and it went up, not down, when you pressed the "up" button.

For years we had been given lectures on how that couldn't be done. But our insolent workers had stuck to their guns. The expensive experts were forced to reverse themselves.

A good example of what you may have to go through, and how persistence and militancy pay off, is the fight we had at Westinghouse in 1982-83 to get the lead regulation enforced. It shows how much you have to mobilize the workers and then scrap and fight to get the very minimum of the law enforced, against the resistance of both the company and the government.

The 'designated substance' regulations were the government's answer to the lack of enforcement in toxic emmissions. When these came out, labour was often told, you'll have detailed controls on harmful substances. The first regulation to come out was for lead and that became a sort of test case for the rest of them like asbestos and mercury, which were later issued.

The lead regulation was passed in August of 1981 and was to be complied with by November, 1981. By March, 1982, Westinghouse of course had done nothing. We complained to the ministry about the paint fumes in our shipping department. They came in and duly issued an order for the company to do a lead assessment, in March of 1982.

The ministry returned in May to do air sampling for paint fumes. They tested for everything—solvents, particulate—but not for lead. Lead was the main hazard and the first designated substance, and they had recently tested for lead with the same paint in the fabrication shop and the paint barrel labels clearly specified lead content... but by this time they forgot, or so they said. Based on these test results, they pronounced the shipping floor hazard-free.

But the company took their own tests in April, and did sample for lead. We got those results at the end of June and they showed the lead contamination was over three times the safe level the regulation allowed. We squawked and insisted on control: ventilation improvements or substitution with lead-free paints.

The company didn't agree. Their hygienists saw no problem; the workers were adequately protected. And who were we untrained workers to contradict their credentialled experts? Anyhow, they said, the government had also been in and found no hazard (because they never tested for lead, we replied).

Lead exposure can cause damage to kidneys, blood, and reproductive and central nervous systems. We had no intention of letting the company drag the issue on forever. We raised some hell, and eventually the company said they would take more tests to prove to us our fears were unfounded.

We had been fooled, they now said, by the fact that the earlier tests were done over a few hours. When we would see the results of tests done over the length of a whole shift, eight hours, and averaged out, there would be low lead levels and nothing to worry about.

So Westinghouse tested in August, 1982, for the full eight hours. And those tests showed a level of lead contamination six times the safe limit!

We were pretty mad by then and escalated our campaign. The ministry came in. Rather than cracking down on the company to do proper controls, as we insisted was the law, they said—well, no, they wouldn't enforce such a clean-up but would rather do their own air sampling. We objected, because the evidence was already there of unsafe levels, done twice. We didn't want an endless game of testing and re-testing. They had always lectured and berated us when we challenged the company expert's findings. Would they only re-do the Westinghouse specialists' work when the results showed an unhealthy condition?

As we suspected, the ministry did some curious testing. They came in one day when the company was using the lowest leaded paint of all, did a brief test and misrepresented the lead percentage in their report, and produced a result just below the legal limits.

We weren't going to put up with that kind of cover-up and so went public with the high lead readings. We put our case to the NDP and the media carried the story prominently. The NDP raised the issue in the provincial legislature, repeatedly demanding that the minister enforce his own law on the toxic pollution at Westinghouse. All this heated up over the months with more charges and revelations.

In the midst of all this, the company replied with stepped-up repression in the plant. I was suspended for a day for getting information on the leaded paint cans. And when the ministry came in to investigate this reprisal, its area manager threatened me with "big trouble" if I was giving information on the lead levels to the NDP in the legislature.

The company and the ministry jointly came up with a new answer in October: we'd all been under an illusion, focusing on the wrong problem. Sure, the levels in the earlier tests were high but they were not typical of the paints regularly used on the shipping floor. "Colour" was now the real point. They had tested for grey, gold, and one variety of green, but, in fact, the most typical paint was actually "Hydro-green". When that variety was tested, we were told, we'd see there was really no hazard to the workers from leaded paints at Westinghouse.

So we went through the same exercises again, of re-testing the airborne levels. And when these results were in (November, 1982), they showed levels not three or six times the standard, but *20 times higher!*

When those results were available, but not yet publicly released, the ministry claimed that Westinghouse had been exonerated: the lead regulation was not being violated, the company had a clean bill of health and in fact had gone beyond legal requirements in protecting their workers. All this according to a high-powered investigation by none other than Ontario's Assistant Deputy Minister of Labour.

Well, that was nothing but a pile of crap, and we were able to show that these officials had made these misleading statements *after* they had the results showing the levels 20 times the safe standard. They were hiding the results, trying to grab a headline and make themselves look good, all the while doing nothing to help the workers in the shop subject to lead contamination... more concerned, it seems, with protecting themselves than with defending the workers they were paid to protect.

Even now, however, we couldn't get the company or government to force compliance by proper ventilation or substitution of non-leaded paints. Back in September, the ministry had begun using a simple device: issue and re-issue orders, but never enforce them.

In September they had issued an order on lead control to Westinghouse, to be complied with by October 6. October 6 came and went and nothing happened. They then issued another order, to be complied with "forthwith".

October went by, November came and went, December came and went, but "forthwith" never arrived.

The company was just ignoring these pieces of paper, taking their cue from a lack of seriousness by the Ministry. We had this big stage-managed meeting in the plant in December. The minister informed the legislature he was sending in his top guns to the plant to resolve all the issues. So we had the Director of Health and Safety of the Ontario government with a team of big shots from various divisions of the bureaucracy, along with the company officials, union officials, safety committee, etc.

Our committee reps pushed the ministry to force Westinghouse to implement a proper lead control program. That was the law and the company had already been ordered to comply and we'd been suffering excess lead exposures.

The director waffled, urging cooperation and better communication all around. We said that communication wasn't the problem, lead contamination was. The company fully understood us, we had both communicated very well to each other. The real problem lay not in labour-management relations but in the high lead levels in the shop; the ministry should address itself to that, as was its statutory obligation. The ministry should crack down, for the company had developed a contempt for the law when they saw the government back off from enforcement, content to put out reams of paperwork and do little else.

The director couldn't agree. He urged us to negotiate our problem with the company. We said there was nothing to negotiate. We weren't going to compromise on the legal safe standards. He ought to be there with us, ought to see it as his problem too, ought to enforce his own law.

The director asked if the union and company could talk and agree on a date whereby the company would come up with a proposal indicating future compliance with the lead regulation.

We refused to enter such a process. It was not appropriate to the problem. We told the director his ministry had repeatedly found Westinghouse in violation of the lead regulation, had issued a number of orders, none of which the company had complied with. Stop urging us to cooperate with the lawbreaker polluting our shop, we said—get after them to clean up and respect your orders.

What would you think, we asked, if a policeman stopped a highway speeder doing 100 miles per hour, and then asked him if he could propose a date whereby he would produce a plan for future compliance with the speed limit? The driver would laugh at the law on speed limits, just like Westinghouse laughs at Ontario's safety laws and its so-called safety police.

These shananigans went on and on. We escalated the public campaign and eventually so embarrassed and incriminated the ministry that the minister personally intervened, cracking down and personally issuing orders for compliance, in January, 1984. Two weeks after those orders, Westinghouse announced it was getting rid of all its leaded paints, and by the end of February, had the shipping department lead-free

Instant compliance. Those substitute lead-free paints had existed all along, but Westinghouse didn't feel compelled to use them. It was more costly. Also they felt obligated to resist as a test-case for all employers with the new designated substance regulations. Not until we forced the ministry to get serious about enforcement did anything happen. Once that political will was there, the compliance was immediate.

That political will was produced by the concerted efforts of the workers on the shop floor, and the safety reps and stewards, along with the public campaign and support from the NDP and the labour movement.

As I indicated, there was a lot of intimidation and reprisals coming from the government and company during this extended battle. In the midst of it, I laid charges at the Ontario Labour Relations Board, in self protection, against both the company and the ministry. This also opened up another front of the battle, as it turned out. We were able to put the ministry on trial.

The public hearings at the board went on for almost a year. They highlighted, case by case, detail by detail, how the ministry refused since 1979 to enforce the safety act and repeatedly covered for the company. All this had a good public educational value and also served to demonstrate the collusion at the heart of the problem.

We managed to show that the misconduct and whitewashes were not the isolated actions of negligent government inspectors. Rather, they were authored and manipulated by the higher-ups of the ministry. The ministry's own witnesses showed, for example, that the top officials had ordered the unscientific methods that distorted the welding fume hazards in 1982. Similarly, it came from the mouth of a ministry witness that a key document on the lead assessment, produced in the midst of the struggle in December, 1983, though signed by a Hamilton inspector, had been written by the deputy minister himself.

All of this was done, we charged, to conceal the real responsibility of top government officials in collaboration with Westinghouse to scuttle their own safety laws.

We saw and documented the collusion in process. Memos were produced that showed Westinghouse and the ministry having a number of secret discussions in the last part of 1982. These were unknown to us at the time and it was at those sessions that they jointly developed lead control programs below the legal standards. They then presented these to us as company suggestions... to be approved by government officials when we later appealed to them. All of which belied the public stance of the government as impartial referee asking the company and the union to work things out among themselves.

In fact, the company and government were always jointly working things out and would then confront the plant committee as an adversary, though maintaining a public front of independence from each other.

There were other victories won, apart from replacing the lead. One was comprehensive lead assessment programs with committee participation, later to become a model for all Ontario workplaces in the ministry's published guidelines.

We won a victory on the lead in Westinghouse. But the overall balance of forces did not improve in the province in the succeeding months. In the spring of 1984, for example, a major skirmish developed over the lead regulation at Mack Trucks in Oakville. This seemed like a repeat performance of ours at Westinghouse, with even the same cast of characters involved. The lead levels were shown to be over 21 times the legal standard; the ministry wouldn't compel the compliance; the issue was raised in the legislature. But this time, rather than enforce a crackdown, the minister replied that there wasn't enough evidence of lead-poisoned workers to merit engineering controls. You'd have to produce a 'body count' of dead and diseased workers, he seemed to say, before the government would seriously consider enforcing compliance with the safety regulations.[2]

The workers were stymied at Mack Truck, whereas we had won a big victory on the same issue at Westinghouse. There were other victories and other defeats in the same year at other workplaces. All of which shows how uneven things are in their development. There are steps forward and steps backward. In the final analysis, how much progress you make depends on the degree of organization and persistence of the workers and their collective efforts, and also on the intensity of the political pressure. Your efforts are always related to the constellation of class forces in the shop and at other levels at any point in time, and this is forever shifting.

To the extent the safety laws will mean anything, it is workers who will make it mean something. We cannot rely upon our adversaries for protection, whether employers or government.[3] We have to rely upon ourselves and we will get what we fight for.

Notes

1. For a more detailed account of these events see Gray (1982).
2. A more complete description of the struggle at Mack can be found in Gray (1984).
3. For further reference see Eli Martel (New Democratic Party), "Not yet healthy, not yet safe". This is a dramatic summary of the large number of cases of health and safety non-enforcement uncovered during the ten-city Task Force investigation headed by Eli Martel, MPP, in 1982.

Canadian Labour Law and Technological Change: An Overview

Patricia McDermott

The current wave of computerized technology, rapidly being introduced into every type of workplace throughout the industrialized world, tends to decrease the need for experience and knowledge that workers possess. Once computerized equipment is in place, there is also a tendency to require fewer employees to do the same amount of work.[1] These closely related problems of deskilling and displacement, which have been examined in extensive literature on the labour process,[2] are two of the most critical issues facing workers today.

Well over half of the Canadian labour force work is in unionized settings and are therefore covered by collective agreements.[3] This paper will assess the extent to which legal processes enable organized workers to respond effectively to the possible negative impacts of technological change. People working without collective agreements have no meaningful way to achieve protection from the harmful results of the extensive technological restructuring of work currently taking place. Since unions have access to potentially powerful mechanisms that are part of our industrial relations system, they must play a key role in gaining effective protection for their members and, indirectly, for non-organized workers.

The major legal tools which Canadian unions have available to meet the challenge presented by management's move to introduce new technology are: legislation, collective bargaining, and grievance arbitration. As we examine the relationship between technology and Canadian labour law we should not forget that we are talking about the relationship between labour and management. It is not the technology itself that is changing work processes and introducing new practices such as electronic monitoring. It is people in management who make decisions about what technology to buy, how it will be designed, what it will do, and how and when it will be introduced. Thus the decisions over technology are, in essence, about the power between labour and management.

Since it is assumed that many readers are not familiar with the complex web of Canadian labour law, the basic structure of our legislative scheme will be outlined. Once this is done, the next section will look at which

Canadian jurisdictions have technological change protection in their labour acts and what this legislation does. The following section will describe the extent and type of technological-change coverage unions have negotiated through collective bargaining. Because contract language is only as good as its ability to withstand the rigorous process of grievance and arbitration, the final section will examine some telling examples of what can happen to seemingly tight contract language during this process.

A word of warning to the industrial relations novice; this is a considerable amount of material to cover in one paper. Despite an attempt to present a clear discussion of legal processes, it may get a bit confusing. My only suggestion is to read slowly.

An Overview

Each province has a labour act (also called a labour code) which sets out the rules that govern the general behavior between unions and management. Beside the ten provincial labour acts, there is also a federal labour act. Basically, if you are a private sector employee who spends most of the time working in one province, and the work you do is *not* considered a 'federal undertaking', you will likely come under the jurisdiction of your provincial labour act.

A 'federal undertaking' is work that, according to the division of federal-provincial powers specified in the *B.N.A. Act*,[4] is under the jurisdiction of the federal government. For example, banking, air or ground interprovincial travel, national communications, including all types of media, telephone and postal work, would all be considered federal undertakings. Organized workers in these jobs would therefore belong to unions covered by the *Canada Labour Code*.

It should be pointed out that most public sector employees—those people who work for the government, whether federal or provincial—are usually covered by their own specific piece of legislation that essentially replaces the general labour act. There are over thirty such acts covering public sector workers.[5] Thus it is important to remember that this discussion about legislative protection deals only with people who are covered either by the federal or one of the general provincial labour acts and of course, only those covered by acts that contain technological change provisions. This includes all organized private sector workers as well as some 'quasi-public' sector workers who, although they may belong to a largely public sector union, are still covered by the general labour legislation.[6] So-called 'quasi-public' employees typically work in institutions and agencies that may be funded by the government, but these employees do not work directly for the government.

Organized public sector workers, who represent only about a quarter[7] of all unionized workers in Canada, are often under legislation that severely restricts what is called their 'scope of bargaining'. This simply means they can't negotiate in certain areas; one such area they typically do not have the right to bargain about is technological change. This fact essentially lumps organized public sector workers together with non-unionized workers, to the extent that both groups are unable to negotiate protection from the impact of technological change in their workplaces.[8] Therefore in the section where we discuss what unions have achieved in bargaining over technological change, we are again primarily talking about private sector and quasi-public employees, along with a small minority of public sector workers who have the right to negotiate in this area.

Organized workers who come under the jurisdiction of general labour legislation comprise about three-quarters of all unionized workers in Canada.[9] So when we focus on these workers and their collective bargaining agents (their unions), we are analyzing a healthy majority of the organized Canadian labour force.

Labour acts are administered by labour boards. These are administrative tribunals affiliated with the provincial Ministry of Labour or the federal Department of Labour. Labour boards oversee such processes as union certification, decertification and representation votes. They also provide adjudicative panels to hear cases involving any type of dispute that arises under the labour act. Such disputes are termed 'unfair labour practices' and they range from interfering with the formation of unions, to the failure of the 'duty to bargain in good faith'.

Technological Change Legislation

There are only four jurisdictions in Canada that have technological change language in their labour acts: the federal, British Columbia, Manitoba and Saskatchewan. The other seven provincial labour acts are, as they say, 'silent' on the issue. So if organized workers in these provinces want protection from technological change they must bargain it into their collective agreements.

Rather than going through the technological change provisions of these four labour codes individually, the provisions will instead be compared with each other as we describe the basic features of the language. Perhaps the most significant point that can be made about this technological change protection is that, despite the fact that all four acts have had these provisions for well over a decade, there have been very few cases decided by the respective labour boards under them.

There have been fewer than ten significant written decisions concerning technological change, from all four boards combined, since the early 1970s when the language was introduced. For example, the Canada Labour

Board has issued only two written decisions under the technological change clauses since 1973. As we shall see, the main reason the legislation has attracted so few applications from unions is the decidedly restrictive structure of the provisions.

The first problem with legislation is the definitions of technological change used in the four acts. In the *Canada Labour Code* technological change occurs (a) where the employer introduces new equipment or materials; *and* (b) where there is a change in the manner in which the work is carried out; *and* (c) when that particular change is *directly* related to the introduction of the new equipment or material.[10] This is clearly a very restrictive definition. By defining technological change in this way, all three requirements (a, b, and c) must be present before it can be recognized as such by the Canada Board.

British Columbia has adopted a broader definition in which technological change occurs when an employer introduces simply (a) a change in his work; *or* (b) a change in his equipment or material; *or* (c) a change in the manner an employer carries on his work, related to that equipment or material.[11] Not only does the B.C. definition encompass more employer activities—such as contracting out that is related to new equipment[12]—but gone too is the *Canada Code's* requirement that the change be directly related to the equipment or material introduced. The B.C. Act allows for a change to affect the employees indirectly and still be considered a technological change. For instance, a 1977 B.C. Labour Relations Board case held that an employee who was "bumped" from his position by someone whose job had become redundant, was indirectly displaced by technological change and hence entitled to benefits under his collective agreement.[13]

The Manitoba code has the same definition as the Canada code, but has broadened its impact by adding a clause requiring notice when the change will "alter significantly the basis upon which the collective agreement was negotiated". Saskatchewan's code has substantially the same definition as the Canada code, but it has added a clause that similarly helps broaden the definition of technological change in that it includes the removal by an employer of any *part* of his work, undertaking or business. This section has been interpreted to insist that only a partial closing fall under this definition. In 1978 the Saskatchewan Board held that a total plant closure was not a technological change. This interpretation poses a problem if a company decides to shut down an outdated facility and re-open an automated one. Even if "successor rights clauses", which are included in virtually all Canadian labour legislation, would likely ensure that the union still represents the employees in the new operation, there are typically many important issues that must be decided. Questions of major concern would be in the areas of new job descriptions and especially seniority rights if fewer workers are needed. If the union does not have input into these discussions, it will find it difficult to fully protect its members.

Thus we can see the first major hurdle that a union must overcome in attempting to use technological change legislation in those jurisdictions in which it is available, is in bringing a specific workplace problem within the definition under which the bargaining agent must operate. This is obviously an easier task for unions under the *B.C. Labour Relations Act* than it is for those under the *Canadian Labour Code.*

The second major problem with trying to get protection from technological change legislation is in overcoming what are called "opting-out" clauses. Three of the four labour acts that contain provisions (the federal, Manitoba and Saskatchewan acts) have sections which state that where a collective agreement has language that is, as the Canada code puts it, "intended to assist employees to adjust to the effects of any technological change", the agreement may specify that the sections of the labour act do not apply. In 1977, five years after the technological change sections were first introduced to the federal code, the Canada Labour Board Chairperson, Marc Lapointe, speculated that what he termed these "escape clauses" were one of the reasons for so few applications arising under the technological change provisions.[14] It is likely that this is also true for the Manitoba and Saskatchewan Acts. Clearly without such opting-out language, legislated technological change protection would not be on the table during negotiations and therefore could not be bargained away for other items or for technological change language that has typically done little to protect members.[15]

Perhaps it is the restrictive nature of the protection that encourages unions to cop out. Clearly workers could achieve better protection if legislation required that both parties sit down and negotiate a fair settlement over the proposed change. Furthermore, if a settlement can not be reached, it should be mandatory that the matter be submitted to binding arbitration.

All four labour codes also have a requirement that the technological change must affect a 'significant number' of employees to whom the collective agreement applies, before the legislation will come into operation. Saskatchewan's jurisdiction has defined 'significant number' in a regulation setting out precisely how many employees will be considered significant. Where there are 2 to 9 employees, for example, 2 will be considered significant; where there are 10 to 19 employees, 3 will be considered significant; and where there are over 30 employees, 20 percent of the total will be considered significant. With this regulation, the Saskatchewan Code essentially excludes a situation where only one employee is affected by a change. More importantly, the 20 percent rule will tolerate situations which many people would indeed consider significant before the legislation comes into effect. For example, a plant with 1,000 employees could lose up to 199 workers in one instance of technological change, and the change would likely not be found to be 'significant'.

Although the B.C. legislation does not set out a formula to determine a significant number, a 1977 decision, *City of Port Moody,*[16] found that technological change affecting two employees was "significant" because "a portion of the bargaining unit was wiped out". In a more recent B.C. case, *Modern Die and Stamping,*[17] it was further held that the technological change provisions could apply when only one employee was affected. To date the Canada Labour Board has not ruled on what "significant number" means, but the federal code allows the question to be referred to the Governor in Council. The Manitoba Labour Board has also not ruled on what it would find to be a "significant number." Nor has a formula similar to that of Saskatchewan been set out in either the Manitoba or the federal code.

The fourth major weakness of the technological change protection is the length of the notice period that employers are required to give to the bargaining agents about a proposed change. The federal, Manitoba and Saskatchewan requirements vary from 90 to 120 days. Notice typically means informing the union of the nature of the change, the date when the change is to take place, the number and type of employees likely to be affected and the impact that the change is likely to have on the "terms and conditions or security of employment of the employees affected".[18]

Although after the notice is received the legislation does allow bargaining to commence regarding the change, such a short notice period does not enable meaningful union input. The workers are basically presented with a 'fait accompli'; usually the only thing left to discuss is how the lay-offs will occur. If legislation required that management consult the union at the beginning of the planning process, unions would clearly have more of a chance to assist their members to adjust to the change—even if it did mean an eventual lay-off. For people who might have to sell their homes and move to other cities, a three-month notice is not adequate.

When the restrictive definitions, the opting-out provisions, the "significant number" requirements and the relatively short notice periods are added together, the total effect is one of legislation that offers very little real protection. Needless to say, the Canadian labour movement has not mounted a campaign to get technological change language into the seven labour codes which do not have such provisions. The track record in this area has been exceedingly unimpressive. Unions that have decided to protect their members against the possible impacts of new technology being introduced attempt to negotiate this protection in their collective agreements, rather than lobbying for legislative changes to the labour codes.

Collective Bargaining

For the past two decades, technological change clauses in collective agreements have covered four major areas:

a. advanced notice
b. retraining
c. labour-management committees
d. wage and employment guarantees

Labour Canada's survey of provisions in collective agreements covering 500 or more employees is a good source to help assess the extent of each type of coverage organized workers have achieved as a result of bargaining technological change protection. The report surveys 972 agreements in effect as of July 1984, covering 2,060,486 employees.[19]

Unfortunately the data in this survey do not tell us the *total* number of agreements in the sample that have no provisions for technological change or the number of agreements that have one, two, three or four provisions. Nevertheless we can get some idea of the extent of coverage for each type of clause.

Of the 972 agreements in the survey, 609, or 63 percent (covering 57 percent of the total number of employees), do not have a provision giving advance notice of technological change. Of those 37 percent of agreements that have protection, 7 percent have notice of 0 to 2 months; 17 percent have a 3 to 6 month notice; while just over 1 percent of the agreements have more than a 6-month notice.

Advance notice clauses in collective agreements do not usually grant union input into planning for the change itself. Because consultation occurs so late, often the only decisions left to make involve seniority and bumping issues. Some advance notice clauses do not even specify the length of the notice. They state that the employer will notify the union (or the workers affected) "as far in advance as possible", "as far in advance as practical", or "give as much advance notice as is reasonably possible", or simply say that the union "will be notified before implementation". Without a notice period explicitly set out in the agreement, it is management who will decide what is "practical" or "reasonably possible".

Of the 972 agreements in the survey 676, or 70 percent of them (covering 70 percent of the employees) had no provision for training or retraining. Of the 30 percent that did have protection, 13 percent were for training on new equipment, and 10 percent were for training at another job within the firm.

The retraining provisions in the other 7 percent were likely for training programs such as those at community colleges, and they could be for training for a new job, a preparation for lay-off.

As with any form of contract language, there are strong technological change clauses and weak ones. As our examination of the legislation has demonstrated, the strength of a clause depends on its ability to withstand the potential scrutiny of legal proceedings that focus on precisely what the words mean. Any ambiguous word or unclear meaning can be interpreted to the disadvantage of one party who assumed the language provided protection.

For example, a retraining clause may say that in the event that a technological change results in an employee being "rendered redundant" the employee has the right to displace (or "bump") another employee with less seniority. So far so good, seniority is being honoured, but then the clause goes on to say that "where new or greater skills are required", the employer will provide a "maximum of twenty days training". Surely this is not enough time to learn computer skills that may be required.

Even if a clause provides for training of up to six months, such protection may be strewn with phrases like: "provided they [the employees] are retrainable" or "the degree of retraining will be governed by the capacity of the employee to be retrained". And just who is going to decide who is retrainable? What are the criteria? This should all be spelled out. Some of the worst language gives the union very little room to dispute a management decision in this area. For example, two such clauses state:

> a. ...where the Company considers it practicable to do so and where it is of the opinion that the employee has the capacity, experience and academic background to become qualified to perform the new job.
>
> b. ...the Employer is entitled to select the employee(s) eligible for such a training program from among the employees so affected by the change. Where there are no employees having the requisite experience, capacity and academic background to receive such training, the Employer may hire a new employee(s) for the work in question.

As the saying goes, this is language you could drive a truck through. All of these qualifying clauses allow management to do what they want in the area of retraining. Even though these clauses were lifted from a relatively small, random sample of 100 current Ontario agreements, they do suggest that the 30 percent retraining rate found in the Labour Canada survey might overestimate the level of actual protection.

The third major type of technological change clauses provide for labour-management committees. Of the 972 agreements in the survey, 834 or 86 percent (covering 80 percent of the total employees) had no such clause. The 14 percent that had provisions for these committees provided them a mandate to study the problem surrounding implementing technological change. But, like any other labour-management committees, they are only effective if they have the right to put their recommendations into operation.

It would take careful study to assess the success of these committees in giving union members significant protection. Judging from the dozen or so clauses that were in the sample of Ontario agreements mentioned earlier, some of these committees are merely struck to study problems, and have very little power to alter management's proposed introduction of computerized equipment. Furthermore, it may be that most are not standing committees, but are only brought into existence to handle a particular technological change.

When it comes to the critical issues of wage or employment guarantees, 762 or 78 percent of the agreements (covering 77 percent of the employees) in the Labour Canada survey had no provision in this area. What protection is offered by the 22 percent of the contracts that had such language, it is not possible to say; however, the random sample of Ontario agreements demonstrated again that clauses in this area are likely quite varied. Some so-called employment security is simply a clause that reiterates the bumping and seniority rights of employees already established elsewhere in other sections of the agreement. What is significant is that many of the security guarantees appear to dwell on demotion and displacement. For instance, a clause may say that if an employee is demoted as a result of a technological change, his/her wage rate:

> ...shall not be reduced during the subsequent six months and thereafter such wage rate shall not be reduced by more than one job class.

This is very minimal protection indeed.

Very much like the weaknesses with the labour codes we discussed earlier, technological-change language in collective agreements suffers from serious (and similar) problems. For example, many agreements do not define technological change. This may be a problem because the issue of whether or not a change has occurred could be the subject of a lengthy procedure—even before the protection in an agreement is triggered. It appears a good number of agreements simply borrowed a restrictive definition from one of the labour codes.

There are also definition problems with such phrases as "substantial reduction" in operations. Again, who decides what is "substantial"? To be effective, contract language must be tight. It must set out precisely when a technological change occurs, what procedures are to be followed, and so on. Since the world of law is a realm of hair-splitting debate, even the most carefully drafted language can flounder when attacked by experienced counsel.

Grievance Arbitration

When employees have what they think is a right in their collective agreement, and management denies that right, the emerging dispute can usually be settled in a process called grievance arbitration. During this process an arbitrator listens to both sides of a case and decides the issue. The grievance arbitration procedure in Canada is often complex, lengthy and expensive.

To demonstrate what can happen to contract language, let us examine two decisions in which the major issue being decided concerned technological change. In both cases the grievors worked for large libraries and belonged to different locals of the same large union—The Canadian Union of Public Employees (CUPE). The union won one case and lost the other.

The first case, decided in 1983, involved the issue of whether a removal of equipment could be considered a technological change.[20] A library computerization project, that was considered technically obsolete before it was finished being installed, was cancelled. When this occurred a union member's job also disappeared. The main question to be decided by the arbitration was whether this removal of equipment constituted a technological change according to the agreement.

In the decision the arbitrator noted that the contract did not have a definition of technological change, that the phrase "does not have a single definition" and then, as examples, quoted the definition used in the Canada Labour Code and the one used in the B.C. Labour Code. She concluded that there is no definition "which has been universally accepted".

The key point that clearly turned the case in the union's favour was that in the contract previous to the one currently in force, the collective agreement used the words "technological *improvements*". In the next contract these words were coincidentally replaced with the words "technological *change*". Thus the arbitrator found that intent was shown in the language alteration and it suggested that not only improvements should be included, but setbacks or cancellations as well.

This decision demonstrates that if the union still had the former "improvements" wording, they likely would have lost. Similarly, if they had borrowed one of the more restrictive labour code definitions, it is also doubtful they would have won the case. This decision is a good example of the detailed scrutiny contract language may undergo during the grievance arbitration process.

The second case is essentially about whether the introduction of computer software can be considered a technological change.[21] A library at the University of Toronto had introduced a major computer system that displaced six employees. The union argued that such a considerable amount of new software was a technological change. The arbitrator however, found that the extent of the new software was irrelevant:

> ....if the introduction of new software constitutes a technological change, that would be so regardless of the extent or the degree of the new software introduced at any one time. The software is, of course, the program, or programs, fed into a computer and I do not expect that any computer expert would claim that the introduction of a new program into the existing hardware would constitute a technological change in every case.

It is interesting that in this case the union suffered because the agreement did not contain a specific definition of technological change, while in the previous case, it could be argued, not having a precise definition in the agreement was an advantage. In this case the introduction of a new computer program caused a significant change in the work method. Perhaps if a definition that include a "change in method" had been clearly stated in the contract, the union might have won.

As we can see, achieving significant legal protection for organized workers from the negative results of technological change is far from easy. The technological-change legislation in place in four Canadian jurisdictions covers less than 10 percent of all organized workers in Canada, and negotiating good technological-change language appears to be only the first hurdle in a long process.

It is hard not to come to the conclusion that the major structural changes that are taking place in our society as a result of the new wave of computerization cannot adequately be handled by our current industrial relations system. The energy it would take to improve legislation and the complex bargaining and arbitration procedures that would follow would be better spent focusing on the social problems technological change is creating. Furthermore, since only about one-half of the Canadian work force is covered by collective agreements, industrial relations' gains do not always benefit unorganized workers.

Adequate solutions are likely to be political, rather than legal. A legislated shorter work week would not only help solve the problem of displacement of those presently employed, it might also help resolve the dramatic problem of youth unemployment. Furthermore, employers could not only be required to provide retraining for displaced employees for jobs within their firm, but could also be obliged to enable these workers to acquire the skills necessary to qualify for a new job—perhaps in another area. Such solutions require a commitment from all those involved: union management, unorganized workers and the state. The speed with which all types of work are being computerized would suggest that we should begin to find solutions immediately.

Notes

1. When computerized self-serve operations are introduced, customers, not employees, supply an increasing amount of labour that employers used to provide. We see this trend in banking, retail work, gas stations and so on.
2. The first major academic volume on the labour process was Harry Braverman's *Labor and Monopoly Capital*, (1974). This work has generated a considerable body of research and debate on the labour process, much of which concerns the relationship between technology and work.
3. Centre for Industrial Relations (1985: 221). This issue estimates that in 1984, 58 percent of the non-agricultural paid work force in Canada was covered by collective agreements. This represents a drop of 1 percent from 1983.
4. *The British North America Act.*
5. For a complete list see Centre for Industrial Relations (1985).
6. For example, in Ontario "quasi-public" sector workers include: university researchers, part-time high school teachers, ambulance drivers, day care workers, legal clinic workers, etc. A public sector union, Ontario Public Service Employees Union, has about 55,000 members covered by public sector legislation—the *Crown Employees Collective Bargaining Act;* while approximately 30,000 of its members could be considered "quasi-public". For the most part this latter group are under the *Ontario Labour Relations Act*—what we have called the "general" labour legislation.
7. This estimate comes from John Calvert's *Government Limited* (1984). He estimates that from 16 percent to 21 percent of the Canadian labour force are public sector workers (p. 19). Since we know that just under 60 percent of the (non-agriculture) work force are also covered by collective agreements, and 8 percent of all organized workers in Canada are in the public sector. of all organized workers in Canada are in the public sector.
8. Much public sector legislation, such as the *Crown Employees Collective Bargaining Act* (mentioned in note #6) prohibits bargaining over technological change (except for some health and safety provisions which indirectly relate to technological change).
9. See footnote #7.
10. *Canada Labour Code*, section 149(1).

11. *British Columbia Labour Relations Act.*
12. *MacMillan Bloedel, (1977) 2 W.L.A.C. 255.*
13. *Rayonier Canada*, B. C. Labour Relations Board, June 22, 1977, p. 224.
14. Marc Lapointe, "Breathing Life into Law", in F. Bairstow's *The Direction of Labour Policy in Canada*, pp. 146-147.
15. As we shall demonstrate in the next section of this paper, there is little protection and what there is—appears quite weak.
16. *City of Port Moody*, (1977), 1 W.L.A.C. 288.
17. *Modern Die and Stamping*, B.C. Labour Relations Board, January 9, 1979.
18. *Canada Labour Relations Act.*
19. *Provisions in Major Collective Agreements in Canada Covering 500 and More Employees*, Labour Canada, 1984, pp. 144-149.
20. Metropolitan Toronto Library Board and CUPE, Local 1582, unreported, (P. Picher), April 29, 1983.21)The Governing Council of the University of Toronto and CUPE, Local 1230, unreported, (Hinnegan), January 31, 1984.

Technological Change in the Operator Services – Dining Services Group at Bell Canada, 1957-1986

Janice McClelland

In 1957, Bell Canada employed 11,109 full-time telephone operators in Ontario and Quebec. In the same year, there were 10,320 full-time craft employees and 10,106 full-time clerical employees.

By 1981, the operators group had shrunk—drastically—from 10,600 full-time employees to 5,262—a cut of 50 percent. In the same time period the craft group, by contrast, grew from 10,320 to 15,245 full-time employees (an increase of 48 percent) and the clerical group grew from 10,106 to (we estimate) 18,000—an increase of roughly 80 percent).

The slicing in half of the operators unit has not been due, I assure you, to a lack of work. The number of telephone stations has increased during this period as well as the number of long distance calls. For example, between 1974 and 1981, operator-handled calls increased by 15 percent; and this is only a very small portion of the world.

The halving of the operator group is due to the introduction of technological change—in fact a series of technological changes—starting with direct distance dialing (DDD) in 1958, and continuing with the computer-read mark-sense ticket in the early 1960s, the TOPS process of computerization in 1978, and finally MDAR (mechanized directory assistance records) in the 1980s.

In this time period, technological change started in the late 1950s with the introduction of direct distance dialing, whereby operators were no longer required to connect customers in two cities but the customer could instead dial by him or herself. Before the introduction of direct distance dialing, Mother Bell was very interested in the average connection time. In 1939, the Company was proud to record that 93 percent of the calls were handled while the user remained at the telephone and the average connection time for calls within Ontario and Quebec was 78 seconds. In 1955, when the first long distance crossbar facilities were introduced in Toronto, only one operator was required to complete certain out-of-town calls and the connection was made in 32 seconds. In 1958, in Toronto, when DDD became available, *no* operators were required for an inter-city call—the user dialed direct to Montreal and was talking to the distant party in 17 seconds. That year there was a dramatic drop in numbers to 9,542.

The next technological change during this period was the change by the company from hand-written tickets for operator-handled long-distance calls to the use of the "mark-sense ticket" whereby operators recorded billing information on a ticket with a mark-sense pencil. The pencil marks were picked up and read by a computer. This occurred in the early 1960s.

The redundancies that occurred during this time were covered by attrition, by operators moving into clerical jobs (the clerical sector was expanding), and by some operators—especially in the small towns—losing their jobs.

Then in 1978, (1976 approximately in B.C.) the company began doing away with switchboards altogether and introducing VDT screens and computerized methods of receiving and placing long-distance calls - TOPS in Ontario and Quebec.

The first area where Bell Canada introduced the new technology was in Northwestern Ontario. In September 1977, there were five operator-services offices in Northwestern Ontario located in Thunder Bay, Fort Frances, Kenora, Dryden, and Marathon; the total employment was 219 operators. By September of 1980, four offices were closed and gone—Fort Frances, Kenora, Dryden, and Marathon—and the number of operators was slashed in half to 119. Only five of the 84 operators in Fort Frances, Kenora, Dryden, and Marathon were able to move to Thunder Bay and keep their jobs. Seventy-nine operators were terminated due to technological change and were left without jobs, and that's in an area where jobs 'for women' are very few and far between.

At the same time as the axe fell in Northwestern Ontario, Toronto (an important and large centre of operators) also saw the toll cord-boards shut and the offices disbanded. In September 1977, before TOPS was introduced there were 1,048 toll employees in Toronto; one year later, in October, 1978, there were 664 toll employees—a 37 percent reduction. Unlike Northwestern Ontario, where operators actually lost their livelihood, in Toronto the reduction was accomplished mainly through attrition, and by transferring a very minimal number of operators into clerical jobs.

The Communications and Electrical Workers of Canada (CWC) were certified to represent the operator service (OS) and dining services (DS) group in July 1979. (That was a happy event. Previously, the operators were represented by a company association and the president of the company association, Mary Lennox, had cut the ribbon for the opening of the first TOPS office in Toronto!) A bargaining caucus was held in August, 1979, and the caucus decided on proposals to put to the company that embodied a three part philosophy:

1. that the union be given notice in advance of any technological change (the actual proposal stated one year),
2. that employees' jobs and wage rates be protected, and
3. that we make it expensive for the company to close any office through
   — a substantial increase in termination allowance
   — employer pay for re-training, etc.

The company forced a strike during that round of collective bargaining. After three months on the street, a positive settlement was reached with the company. The settlement contained improved contract rights, dramatic wage increases, and significant changes in the technological change article. For example, we ensured that all employees with one year or more of seniority (instead of 10 years) would not be laid off or terminated due to technological change. (The company has to offer them employment.) We also improved the amount of termination allowance so that someone who opted for termination due to technological change with 10 years seniority, for example, received 21 weeks of pay instead of 10 weeks; someone with 15 years seniority received 36 weeks of pay instead of 23 weeks. We also increased the time period to learn a new job from 30 days to 90 days. These changes came into effect in April, 1980.

July 14, 1980, Bell announced the closing of four Quebec operator services in St. Agathe, Sorel, Thetford Mines, and Lac Megantic. Approximately 100 operators were involved and not all could move or travel to another city to keep their jobs. With the assistance of their locals and the Quebec Regional Office, these operators waged a valiant campaign to keep their offices open. In St. Agathe, the CWC local organized a public meeting that was attended by 450 citizens of the area and the local media.

At the same time, the company converted several cord board offices to TOPS in Joliette, St. Jerome, Granby, St. Jean, Valleyfield, St. Hyacinthe, and Riviere du Loup. Altogether with the conversion to TOPS and the closing of four offices, 159 jobs were eliminated. Unfortunately, despite the public campaign, the union was unable to save these jobs.

During this period, operators in other offices in Quebec started to get very uneasy: what was to be the future of their office? Would they stay open? Would their office be shut? Other offices of operators, e.g. Drummondville and Victoriaville began to take action; for example in January 1981, the operators in Drummondville sent a petition to M. Jean de Grandpre with 900 signatures on it. They stated that this petition was just the start and they would not rest until they had a final answer that their office would remain open. Copies of the petitions were sent to the local news media, members of Parliament, etc. In late 1981, they were notified —their offices were remaining open.

By September, 1981, we were again bargaining with the company. George Larter, an operator from Toronto, and Leone Ritchie, a Service Assistant from the small town of Walkerton, joined Nicole Trachy from Montreal and Louise Dubois from Sherbrooke as rank-and-file members on the OS&DS bargaining committee. For the first time ever it was joint bargaining, with both groups—craft and traffic—together, united, sitting at the same table with the company, negotiating issues shared in common. This time there was clearly a lot at stake—the company's TOPS program was forging ahead to cover the better part of both Ontario and Quebec. The future of many small offices was a real question, and also MDAR had begun. The union presented the bargaining proposals in the area of technological change to the company under one package—"Job Security". Our proposals on technological change had several thrusts:

a. that the notice be given to the union at the time the decision is being made,
b. that technological changes be negotiated between employer and union,
c. that the union shall have the right to strike over technological change issues during the life of the contract,
d. that the company provide for maintenance of salary and pension benefits when transfers are due to technological change,
e. that the company provide job security for all those with six months or more seniority,
f. that there be full job security for dining service employees who are affected by technological changes in *other* departments,
g. that where there are insufficient alternate jobs in a smaller community affected by technological change, then the company will use technology to retain the jobs in the small community. Redundancies shall be dealt with in a larger community,
h. termination allowance to employees retiring on pension,
i. a substantial increase in termination allowance,
j. benefit plans to apply for the duration of the termination allowance,
k. improved termination annuity and provision for earlier pensions for senior employees.

The people at the bargaining table worked very hard to convince the company of the necessity for this protection, and to convince them to maintain the jobs in the small communities.

On February 4, 1982, the chairman of company's bargaining committee gave the chairman of the union bargaining committee a letter. The letter stated that 10 small offices across Ontario and Quebec would be kept open and converted to TOPS in 1983. These offices are Sarnia, Walkerton,

Brockville, Barrie, Orillia, Bracebridge, Parry Sound, Chicoutimi, St. Felecien and Alma. These are small offices, for example Parry Sound has approximately 21 employees.

That was the good news, and the bargaining committee and membership were heartened to see that we had moved the company from its earlier philosophy of wholesale closing of all small offices and centralizing jobs.

The bad news was that three offices in small communities would be closing: Tillsonburg and St. Thomas in the second quarter of 1983, and Midland in the fourth quarter of 1983. These closures meant the loss of approximately 50 operator jobs in Ontario. (There were no office closures announced at this time in Quebec.)

These closures meant lost jobs and wages for the three communities and genuine hardship for those involved. The Ontario Regional Office of CWC surveyed the operators in St. Thomas, Tillsonburg, and Midland. Many of the operators in St. Thomas and Midland told us that their job was necessary to the maintenance of the family: some were sole supporters of their family; others reported that their spouse was not employed; some felt that their spouse's job was "secure" but with a question-mark and then added, "on work-sharing" or "plant may close". Others mentioned that their income was necessary to meet mortgage payments, educate children, etc. Most stated that having to travel to another city to keep their job would cause financial and family hardship. For example, some told us the expense of travelling every day would mean less social outings for the children, a cutback in groceries, reduced contributions to the church, etc. For some, it would mean resigning their office in a community organization and, of course, it meant for most that their hours away from home would be greatly extended and, correspondingly, time spent with children and their activities would be reduced and "a disaster" (to use a quote).

The Ontario Region Office of CWC assisted the locals affected to wage a campaign of public embarrassment against Bell, with the focus on the local community. St. Thomas operators were the first off the mark. The company assisted the union when it was suggested to the operators that they should immediately transfer to London, despite the fact that their office was not scheduled to close until one year later. The St. Thomas operators wrote to City Council, their MP and their MPP, and also picketed and leafletted the Bell shareholders meeting in London on April 20, 1982. Paul Keighley, a National Representative CWC, assisted them. Gary Cwitco, a National Representative CWC servicing Local 40, met with Midland operators and the Executive of Local 40; they planned a day of protest in Midland on Saturday, September 18th, 1982. The day included picketing in the afternoon in front of the Bell office; Midland operators were joined by CWC members from Walkerton, Orangeville, Toronto, Barrie, Orillia, and Niagara Falls—with altogether about 60 people.

Then, wearing our signs we marched up the main street of Midland (as shop-keepers and their customers read our signs) to the fall fair. There we took off our signs and went in, and the local people went to meet with their local Member of Parliament. As they approached his booth—decked out in Tory blue—it was being dismantled and they were informed the MP had an appointment in Orillia and had to leave early. (He had known the CWC members were coming to speak with him.)

At the fair, local CWC members got members of the Midland community to sign petitions protesting the closure. Later in the campaign in Midland, on a Saturday, CWC members distributed protest cards door-to-door for Midland residents to fill in. The local radio station informed residents that day to watch for the CWC people and to mail the cards back in to the government.

We knew it would be a very difficult struggle to change Bell's plans and keep these offices open. However, we encouraged our Ontario members to wage this struggle not only to keep these particular offices open, but also as Bell is a public company it is somewhat sensitive to public criticism. We had a long list of offices in Ontario where we had no official word from the Company as to their future. Our idea was: our struggle today may help for tomorrow.

Recapping the 1981-82 negotiations, we saved 10 offices from the chopping block. We again made it more expensive for the company to terminate operators due to technological change, by improving the termination allowance for those with over 25 years seniority, by providing that those who have not yet given their notice to retire when technological change is announced can receive both termination allowance and pension, and by providing that employees who have 15 years seniority who elect termination due to technological change will be entitled to a deferred annuity, regardless of their age (previously someone had to be age 45; other people who were age 40 and had 20 years of service and were terminated due to technological change got nothing down the road). We were able to add the word "reasonable" onto the kind of training that an employee receives when transferred due to technological change.

In 1984-85, the final long-distance offices in Ontario were converted from cord board to VDTs and the technology advanced another step in Directory Assistance to A.O.S.S. (computerized directory assistance on a system). At this point, Bell Canada violated one of the central clauses in the Technological Change article. This clause provides employees who have 12 months or more seniority with job security in the event of technological change, and also provides them with the option of electing termination with termination allowance if they choose *not* to be transferred or reassigned to the new technology. When Bell refused to pay termination allowance to employees who preferred not to be reassigned or transferred, over forty grievances were filed to the last step before arbitration. In the negotiations for a new collective agreement that commenced during this dispute, the union agreed to a revision of this clause limiting its scope (i.e. as of January 1, 1986, it only applies where employees are reassigned or transferred to another city) and subsequent to the contract settlement, the company finally settled up the outstanding grievances. The payout on those grievances alone was over a million and a half dollars—most grievors, due to their high seniority, received in the neighbourhood of $40,000 to $50,000 in termination allowance, in addition to their operator pensions. (Operator pensions are not very high, so this certainly made their retirements healthier and happier.) Most of the operators who took this option were already eligible for pension, so in terms of the overall operator workforce, the termination allowance acted as an incentive and allowed people to leave their job earlier than they had planned, on very positive terms; it also helped ease the surplus of workers that existed at that time due to the introduction of new technology.

Also in the 1984-85 negotiations, CWC negotiated a reduction in the hours of work. The work week for craft and services employees was reduced from 39 hours to 38, and the evening shift for telephone operators was reduced from six and a half hours to six hours. (This of course was accomplished without any loss in pay, and in fact with small percentage increases.) This is the beginning of our struggle to improve job security, and to share the benefits of technological change with the workers via reduced hours of work.

Dealing with technological change in the operators group has increased the challenges for the union and the employees involved and this continues to be the case today. Concerns include the following:

- there are *serious* health and safety concerns regarding the new technology.
- there is the question of de-skilling of the job. The new mechanized jobs tend to be much more boring, operators have less control over work, less contact with customers, work at an inhuman pace, etc. (There is one community where intimidation is prevalent and the average work time on their long distance calls has varied from 13 to 18 seconds.)
- there is the serious issue of monitoring, not only machine monitoring but also being monitored by others.
- there is the question of those who are indirectly affected by technological change i.e. by secondary effects. We have seen the dining service unit decline in numbers very drastically, but not the number of operators to serve food to. The company cuts back on dining service; how do we assist people in these job categories

to make the move to other jobs in the company when the company's position is that they are not qualified to do even the operator's job? We have to look at upgrading their skills, and in many cases we may have to look at, in Ontario, training in English as a second language.

- a very serious question that we have to face is the retraining of those affected by technological change for other kinds of work:
- what type of re-training?
  —for what jobs?
  —who pays?
  —who controls?
  —and the question of normal hours of work?
- the craft and clerical sectors are not expanding as they have in the past—and in fact they are starting to decline in number as technological change also hits them. (The number of craft employees in 1986 is approximately 13,000.) Where will the surplus people be deployed? Where will the jobs be? What kind of jobs will they be? How will we make employment equity programs work when the traditionally male jobs are declining as well?

In June 1986, Bell Canada announced to CWC its plans for the latest round of technological change in Operator Services—Automated Intercept System (the total replacement of Intercept Operators by machines), Voice Response (a computer voice that replaces Operators by giving numbers on Directory Assistance calls), and Customer Charge Calling (allows customers to direct dial credit card calls without Operator Assistance).

The number of full-time operators in Ontario and Quebec is now down to 3,700. The operators who remain are under intense pressure by management regarding the number of seconds they take to process calls, for taking a day off sick, etc. These operators are real, live human beings, but every day their job environment is more and more suited to a machine—not to a human being. Unfortunately the number of operators who are succumbing to stress and who are unable to work for significant periods of time is significantly increasing. These operators suffer anxiety, debilitation, and desolation. I believe they have become crippled by this inhumane machine environment. Their sisters who are still working are suffering other, perhaps less dramatic, but real effects of stress. This is the latest and perhaps most cruel result of the marvel of technology.

In the immediate future, we must struggle together using our creative intelligence and our courage to ensure the right to a job and to a humane job, and to maintain our standard of living and the rights that we have fought so long and hard for in the past. We must convince our co-workers, the companies, and the government of this country that all working people are entitled to these basic, simple rights.

Acknowledgements
Statistics used in this article are from union records and Bell Canada publications. I wish to give special appreciation to Trish Blackstaffe, CWC National Representative, Research, who assisted me in uncovering the statistics. This is the story of technological change facing telephone workers in Ontario and Quebec and of their union. It is by and large a positive story. This is due to the intelligence and courage of these people and their leaders.

SECTION II

The State, Economic Crisis and Working People

Introduction

A fundamental role of the state in capitalist society is the regulation of class relations in the long-term interests of the capitalist class. In order to achieve this end, it must perform two major functions: the achievement of social stability through the partial fulfillment of general social need (i.e., legitimation), and the maintenance of conditions favourable to the continued private accumulation of capital. The chief gains made by workers out of the previous major economic crisis of capitalism were the establishment of the social wage and legally-recognized collective bargaining rights. From these concessions flowed the trade union strategy of the past 40 years: a primary emphasis on redress of economic grievance through collective bargaining, and, secondarily, expansion of the social wage through electoral support of the New Democratic Party (NDP).

The current crisis of capitalism has resulted in a reversal of state strategies *vis á vis* labour, i.e., the state has moved from strategies of mild concession and legislative restriction toward frontal assault. The labour-capital pact and the social wage which resolved the class conflicts arising from the Great Depression are now under attack at all levels. The strategy of collective bargaining and electoral politics, which served labour in the past, is no longer sufficient to protect workers from serious economic and social harm, and certainly insufficient to expand the limited workers' rights and social wage which currently exist.

The papers in this section analyze the relation between workers, the state, and capital. They shed light on either the legitimating role of the state, or the difficult problem of appropriate responses by workers to the current transformation of that role.

Steve McBride's paper discusses the legislative environment of collective bargaining at the level of the federal government. The "social peace" of the post-World War Two period was purchased, in part, through the legal recognition of trade-union collective bargaining rights. As yet there has been no major restructuring of legislation governing capital-labour relations, but we are seeing a steady process of erosion which has begun to undermine the previous mechanisms of legitimation. McBride contends that the current situation requires an alternative strategic vision of labour-capital relations. To date the labour movement has been unable to develop such a vision, which would enable and require labour to move beyond the simple defense of its currently established and severely limited rights.

Bob Russell's paper is an analysis of the relationship of the social wage to the current crisis. Capitalist societies have developed the social wage as a means to deal with problems of legitimacy arising from the economic crises of the 20th Century. Since the social wage has become an essential part of working-class wages, any assault on it represents an attack on the general working-class standard of living. The labour movement has therefore been forced to fight battles on more-or-less unfamiliar terrain: the protection of rights and standards of living which it had assumed to be permanent gains of previous working-class struggles.

While the Russell and McBride papers discuss state action, Stafford, in analyzing the rise of private pensions, sensitizes us to state *inaction* as an alternative tactic in legitimating the subordination of labour. Stafford presents the private pension scheme as both a means of legitimation (for individual corporations) *and* a means of controlling the labour force. It is clear from Stafford's presentation of the evidence that private pensions were not concessions to the labour movement, which consistently pressed for state, rather than private welfare. It was, rather, labour's inability to gain concessions from the state which enabled the rise of private schemes as a means to control the workforce and discourage unionization and strikes. At least part of the current weakness of the social wage can be traced to the rise of private welfare schemes from the 1920s onward.

While the previous papers deal with the federal state environment governing capital-labour relations, and treat in various ways the historical processes underlying the social wage/collective bargaining compromise, the concluding papers of this section by Annis, Chudnovsky and Pollack deal with one particular case example of state response to the current crisis. That is the direct assault on the post-war compromise represented by the British Columbia budget of 1983. These latter papers are complementary and should be read as a unified whole.

Ruth Annis describes the specific harmful effects of the budget on the social wage and collective bargaining. Of particular importance is her assertion that the budget was not only a crude attempt to change the balance between capital and labour, but was also, like Thatcherism and Reaganism, an attempt to create a popular ideology and movement in support of capital.

David Chudnovsky gives us the final denouement of the B.C. Solidarity movement—the walkout by B.C. teachers. Clearly, one effect of "restraint" was a growth in combativity in a traditionally non-militant sector. However, at the crucial juncture, the new social movement, which was close to bypassing the traditional mechanisms of trade-union action, was brought to heel by a weak settlement imposed by the trade-union leadership.

Marion Pollack's paper summarizes the attempts by community groups and organized labour to form coalitions to fight the budget, and, most importantly, details the reasons for the failure of this alliance. It appears that the inability of the trade-union leadership to think beyond the post-war compromise was of particular importance. None of the opposition groups involved was able to find tactics which would have effectively rolled back the budget.

The three papers describing events in B.C. clearly show the need for a broad alliance between trade unions and community groups. More than that, they show the necessity for a movement which is truly an alliance and is prepared to go on the offensive, rather than one dominated by those who wish only to maintain the existing balance of forces between capital and labour.

In sum, all the papers in this section demonstrate that the post-war consensus is now dead, but the trade-union movement as yet has no strategy to address that situation. This question is addressed further in section V of this volume. "Strategies and Tactics for Social Change."

Hard Times and the "Rules of the Game": A Study of the Legislative Environment of Labour-Capital Conflict

Stephen McBride

Introduction

In common with the pattern in other capitalist countries the role played by the Canadian state has steadily expanded during the 20th century. As part of this general tendency the state has become increasingly involved in the regulation of the relationship between labour and capital. The nature of the 'rules of the game' established by the state to govern the interaction of these often antagonistic social actors can be understood in different ways. Here they are viewed as the product of the state's evolving and changing pursuit of an acceptable combination of its contradictory functions of capital accumulation and social legitimation.

This view of the state's function is derived from O'Connor:

> The state must try to maintain or create the condition in which profitable capital accumulation is possible. However, the state must also try to maintain or create the conditions for social harmony.[1]

The balancing of these two functions is always problematic, since there may be important contradictions between policies based on the accumulation function and others based largely on the legitimation function. The intensity of these contradictions has varied over time, with changes in objective economic conditions and the relative strengths of labour and capital, as has the priority accorded by the state to the always potentially and often actually conflicting requirements of capital accumulation and legitimation. Historically the capital accumulation function has predominated, even during the 1944 recasting of the Canadian industrial relations system which gave more priority to legitimation and even considering the further increase in legitimation added by the partial extension of collective bargaining rights to public service workers.

The onset of the economic crisis in the mid-1970s has placed considerable strain on the labour-capital regulatory system established in 1944. To date no major restructuring of the legislative basis of that system has occurred, though a process of incremental erosion may be said to be underway. There have been massive but *ad hoc* emergency back-to-work measures. As a result of these actions the legitimation aspects of the industrial relations system have been undermined. A second strand of state policy, almost exclusively at the federal level, has sought to create a new legitimacy through increasing organized labour's participation in economic policy processes, and through a renewed emphasis on such aspects of employment standards as occupational health and safety. But a detailed examination of these policies that governments view them as also playing an instrumental role in capital accumulation. Recent years, therefore, have seen an even greater imbalance in the compromise between the two functions represented by the 1944 restructuring of the industrial relations system, at the expense of the legitimation function.

Some have argued that these changes add up to a new era in labour policy which has definite characteristics—principally a greater reliance on open forms of coercion to secure the subordination of labour (Panitch and Swartz, 1983). The position taken here is that such arguments, while having considerable force, may be premature. Even regular suspension of the "rules" is not the same as a systematic restructuring. Rather, the industrial relations system seems to be experiencing a rather complex hiatus in which quite different alternatives—ranging from outright coercion to attempts to create new legitimation mechanisms through cooption—are being debated and, to an extent, experimentally put into effect. The end results might be increased fragmentation rather than the emergence of a single new system.

State Regulation of Labour Relations in 1975

During the last century of Canadian labour relations we can identify four aspects of general labour policy, each characteristic of a particular historical period. In chronological order these are:

i) granting the embryonic labour movement immunity from prosecution under conspiracy laws;
ii) the development, on the initiative of the federal state, of an authentically Canadian industrial relations system which placed great emphasis on the conciliation and prevention of industrial disputes;
iii) the grafting onto this existing system of elements of the U.S. Wagner Act's encouragement of trade unionism and collective bargaining; and

iv) the emergence of provisions for public sector collective bargaining, and other "special" groups.

(i) Immunity from Conspiracy Laws

The release of unions from the threat of prosecution for criminal conspiracy was achieved with the 1872 Trade Unions Act. Subsequent legislation in 1875-76 legalized peaceful picketing. These initiatives followed closely upon similar moves in Britain but were also a response to considerable Canadian working class agitation around the 1872 Nine Hours Movement. Though clearly an advance for the unions, this type of legislation did nothing to compel recognition of unions by employers and left such questions to be determined by the unequal power relationships of the market (Woods, 1973: 39-42).

(ii) An Authentic Canadian Industrial Relations System

Legislative attempts to provide for voluntary conciliation of worker-employer disputes can be identified in some provinces as early as the 1870s but the construction of a voluntary conciliation system, with some elements of compulsion, really began in the early years of the 20th century with a series of federal enactments.

The essence of the new approach (Woods, 1973: 56-64), most comprehensively developed in the *Industrial Disputes Investigation Act* (I.D.I.A.) (1907), was state intervention, at the request of either party, in an actual or anticipated industrial dispute. Once requested, a compulsory investigation of the dispute occurred, during which suspensions of work were prohibited. The conclusions of a conciliation board were not binding on the parties though there was provision for moral suasion, through the publication of the board's findings as a means of bringing the force of public opinion to bear upon the parties. Although a 1925 judicial decision allocated the bulk of labour relations jurisdiction to the provinces, all provinces except Prince Edward Island passed legislation enabling the I.D.I.A. approach to apply to them. The I.D.I.A. approach, therefore, constituted the Canadian policy toward industrial disputes between 1907 and 1944. The act did little to address the problem which bedevilled Canada's fragile and fragmented labour movement during these years—the refusal by employers to recognize and negotiate with unions. Employers were compelled to participate with unions during the investigation of a dispute but this 'recognition' was merely tacit and temporary. The ban on work stoppages during an investigation also tended to hinder the exercise of labour's maximum sanction, the strike.

In a context in which the coercive apparatus of the Canadian state was regularly employed to enforce legislation, and of common law which went to "great lengths to protect employers' property and freedom to use their property pretty much as they saw fit, while providing little or no protection of workers' freedom to protect their jobs and livelihoods" (Jamieson, 1968: 471-2), the emphasis of the I.D.I.A. on prevention of work stoppages and its failure to compel recognition of unions by employers, clearly reveal that it should be classified as an instrument of capital accumulation.

(iii) Elements of the U.S. Wagner Act

Not until the full-employment conditions of World War Two was organized labour able to extract from the state a modicum of support in establishing an ongoing bargaining relationship with employers.[2] The response came in 1944 through a federal order-in-council (P.C. 1003).[3] Often referred to as Canada's *Wagner Act*, the order-in-council did implement certain aspects of the Wagner approach to labour-capital relationships, notably, acceptance of trade unionism and collective bargaining as a right, provided there was evidence of a certain level of worker support, and the establishment of an enforcement machinery.

The legal framework for labour relations which emerged from P.C. 1003 was characterized by a highly formal system of bargaining with elaborate certification procedures, legally enforceable contracts, no-strike provisions for the duration of contracts, and liability for trade unions and their members if illegal strikes occurred. Clearly this package was not an unqualified victory for labour. But the legislation guaranteed the right to organize and to bargain collectively, forced employers to recognize unions once certain conditions were met, defined unfair labour practices and provided remedies under the law for violations. Labour had lacked sufficient power to force recognition and bargaining out of employers, and pressure on the state to provide assistance in establishing a bargaining relationship had finally proved successful. But the price for this assistance was extensive state regulation and the continuation of the compulsory conciliation and 'work-stoppage delay', features of the earlier legislation. The cumulative effect of the restrictions was to severely curtail labour's right to strike.[4]

Overall, however, the legitimacy of organized labour was enhanced by the compulsory recognition provisions of the new labour relations system established by P.C. 1003.

Labour relations policy returned to a largely provincial area of jurisdiction in the post-war period. Despite this a *Canadian* collective bargaining system continued to exist because most provinces adopted legislation patterned after P.C. 1003. One province, Saskatchewan, under a Co-operative Commonwealth Federation (CCF) government, deviated from the pattern in the direction of less restriction but, in general, any deviations were in the direction of greater restrictiveness and exhibited a greater concern for capital accumulation. Examples of the latter trend included restrictions on picketing, secondary boycotts and sympathy strikes (British Columbia, Newfoundland, Alberta); prohibition of strikes in essential services (Alberta); government supervision of strike votes (British Columbia, Manitoba); regulation of the internal affairs of trade unions (Ontario, Newfoundland, British Columbia); limits on the ability of unions to provide funds for political parties (British Columbia, Prince Edward Island, Newfoundland); and decertification of allegedly communist-led unions (Quebec). In general, however, the basic pattern of P.C. 1003 (I.D.I.A. plus Wagner) was established.

(iv) Provisions for Public Sector Bargaining

The major adjustment to this situation was the emergence of special provisions for public service collective bargaining in the 1960s and early 1970s. Saskatchewan's 1944 *Trade Union Act* had treated public servants in the same way as private sector workers. With that one exception no other public servants enjoyed bargaining rights until 1964. A decade later public service employees in all jurisdictions enjoyed some form of bargaining rights.[5] The principal variations centered around the extent to which the right to strike was granted to public servants, the scope of collective bargaining, and differential treatment of public agency (but not public service) workers.

(v) Other State Initiatives

The state's efforts to legitimize both the overall economic system and the place of labour within it were not confined to simply regulating the process of labour-capital interaction. A broad range of policies regarding minimum wages, permissible hours of work, vacations with pay and statutory holidays, anti-discrimination provisions, health and safety protection, and other measures can be viewed as attempts to fulfill the legitimation function.

In contrast to regulation of labour-capital bargaining and confrontation, in which the federal level of government has played the leading role, the initiative for employment standards seems to have rested at the provincial level. The most industrialized province, Ontario, led the way with the first Factory Act (1884), the Employer's Liability Act (1886), the Workmen's Compensation scheme (1914), and the establishment of a division of industrial hygiene (1920). British Columbia was first into the minimum wage area (1918). This initiative was swiftly adopted by most other provinces, though its implementation was sometimes postponed, or confined only to women workers or urban workers (as in the case of the Prairie provinces).

For the most part, the legislation promised more than it delivered. The inspectorates appointed to administer the Factory Acts were inadequately staffed (Baggaley, 1981: 19-20) and the wording of the legislation was often vague, with the onus of proof being placed on the worker.[6] The priority given to occupational health and safety tended to be a function of labour shortages. Whenever labour became a scarce and valuable factor of production, as in wartime, federal government contracts contained clauses which required "the employer to maintain a safe and healthful workplace" (Manga, Brayles and Reschenthaler, 1981: 119). As labour became more plentiful, this concern slackened.

For all its weaknesses, however, employment standards legislation and policy can be understood as a form of social legitimation. Concerns for sweatshop female and child labour and overcrowded and unsafe factories tended to merge with concerns over other threats to "the fabric of society" such as intemperance and deserted wives and children. Employment standards legislation, like efforts to stamp out such social ills, "was an attempt to protect the social order" (Baggaley, 1981: 23). The rather inadequate enforcement mechanisms attached to such policies serve to highlight their cosmetic rather than effective nature.

The Economic Crisis and Canadian Labour Policy

In response to the crisis, the federal and provincial governments have resorted to determining the *outcome* of labour-capital (and labour-state) conflicts with wage controls policies on two occasions, and by the frequent use of *ad hoc* emergency back-to-work legislation. Both policy instruments are classified in the capital accumulation category. Wage controls are designed to achieve a general weakening of labour's bargaining position. If successful, wage controls will freeze or, more likely, reduce the share of wages in the national income (Nuti, 1972: 433-38; Miliband, 1969: 81). Back-to-work legislation which typically includes an imposed settlement, or sets guidelines within which a settlement must be reached, accomplishes the same goals on a smaller scale.

The use of these policies has created a legitimacy crisis in governments' relations with organized labour. This has been explicitly recognized by a former federal minister of labour, at least insofar as emergency legislation is concerned:

> Governments in Canada have been intervening, perhaps too often, to terminate labour disputes and impose settlements by *ad hoc* legislation... Governments have, of course, felt obliged to intervene in these cases, but what has perhaps been overlooked in this incremental process is the long-term effect on the labour relations system and the role it is meant to play. The frequency and predictability of government interventions in both strikes and wage settle-

> ments may have created a contradiction. On the one hand, the political process has sanctioned a wage determination system that is based on free collective bargaining which guarantees the right to strike. On the other hand, *ad hoc* measures have been taken that may have paralyzed the system and removed various rights essential to its smooth functioning. That system is our principal method of determining wage differentials and working conditions... The threat of economic sanction makes it work. Without that threat, the whole system would have to be redesigned (Oullet, 1983: 4-5).

Mr. Ouellet's remarks are an indication that the contradictions between the accumulation and legitimation functions of Canadian labour policy had, under the impact of economic crisis, become more acute.

The federal government has attempted to repair the damage. It has sought to improve its policies concerning the working environment and has also promoted the creation of consultative institutions designed to increase labour's participation and voice in ongoing economic policy decisions. There have been few provincial attempts to emulate these federal initiatives except, perhaps, in the area of occupational health and safety.

The legislative framework within which labour-management interaction takes place has remained largely intact. No government has attempted to 'redesign the whole system.' There have, nevertheless, been a number of incremental changes which are worthy of attention.

The current economic crisis, then, has led to state activity in four aspects of labour policy. Each of these will be briefly outlined below.

Wage Controls

Though they were billed as an Anti-inflation Program, virtually all the actors connected with the decision viewed the federal government's measures, on October 14, 1975, as a wage control program. The program covered[7] federal government and Crown corporation employees, public sector employees in participating provinces,[8] workers in larger firms in the private sector, and professionals. Allowable wage increases varied according to a complex formula under which the incomes of most Canadian workers were controlled and their collective bargaining rights correspondingly curtailed.

A second round of wage controls from 1982 onwards was targeted specifically at public sector workers. In June, 1982, the federal government announced a two-year wage control policy in which federal public sector employees would be limited to 6 percent in the first year and 5 percent in the second. Two provinces had already taken initiatives in this area (Alberta and B.C.). Within a year, the other eight provinces and the two territories had also adopted some form of wage restraint for public sector workers. It soon became clear that public sector wage controls, at least in some jurisdictions, would extend beyond the two year period originally envisaged.

While considerable variation existed in the categories of public sector employees covered by restraint, and in the wage limits to which they were subject, these policies—following on from the 1975-78 wage controls—have severely undermined the already circumscribed collective bargaining rights that were granted to public sector workers in the 1960s and early 1970s. With the exception of the 1975-78 period, however, and in spite of occasional calls for voluntary restraint, governments seemed content to allow rising unemployment to discipline wage demands in the private sector.

Emergency Labour Legislation

The incidence of emergency labour legislation has increased considerably since the onset of the economic crisis. Public sector workers are most affected, especially teachers, hospital workers and transit and hydro workers. An examination of 34 pieces of such legislation since 1975 yielded the following data.[9]

The negative impact of this type of legislation in terms of the legitimation function of the state has already been noted.

The Search for New Methods of Legitimation

Motivated by a perception of crisis in Canadian industrial relations, and by the search for a role for itself, the federal Department of Labour had begun,

Table 1: Emergency Labour Legislation, 1975-83

	Public Sector	Private Sector	Total
Federal	2	4	6
Provincial	26	2	28
Quebec	(11)	(0)	(11)
Ontario	(7)	(0)	(7)
British Columbia	(3)	(1)	(4)
Other	(5)	(1)	(6)
Total	**28**	**6**	**34**

in the period prior to wage controls, to canvas the creation of new mechanisms to promote a "healthier" labour-capital relationship. An early manifestation of this activity was the creation, in early 1975, of the Canada Labour Relations Council (CLRC), a tripartite advisory body. Amongst the Council's terms of reference was the consideration of

> ...ways and means to promote industrial peace by exploring methods and developing procedures by which labour and management may better reconcile their differences through constructive collective bargaining, thereby reducing conflict in their own and the public interest.[10]

The death knell of the CLRC was sounded by the imposition of wage controls in October 1975. This led Canada's largest labour federation, the Canadian Labour Congress (CLC), a participant in the Council, to spearhead a vigorous campaign against the controls policy. The government was accused of planning to establish some form of corporate state in which previously autonomous interest groups would be submerged and converted into agencies of social control. In a concrete expression of its opposition to such developments, the CLC in March, 1976, withdrew its representatives from bodies such as the Canada Labour Relations Council, on the grounds that such participation constituted encouragement of trends towards corporatism. The episode typifies the contradiction between the capital accumulation aspects of labour policy (represented by wage controls) and the legitimation aspects (represented by the search for new cooperative forums in which labour and business, together with the state, could interact).

But in an abrupt about-turn, the CLC, from May 1976—without dropping its opposition to wage controls - began to advocate the creation of corporatist political structures.[11] Though unsuccessful in terms of its ambitions, the new policy did lead to a search for new methods of cooperation with business and government. Despite the delegitimizing aspects of government policy, this new spirit of collaboration—frequently played down by the CLC leadership because of radical criticism within labour's ranks—led to labour participation in a number of bipartite (with business) and tripartite (with business and government) agencies.[12] The establishment of these structures has been described as a series of state initiatives "to restore international competitiveness by *reducing labour costs*, while attempting to maintain labour peace through the establishment of a variety of 'consultative mechanisms'" (Mahon, 1983). In a sense the federally orchestrated drive towards the creation of tripartite collaborative structures represents an attempt to *merge* the capital accumulation and legitimation functions of labour policy.

And while labour's internal opposition to the CLC leadership's corporatist strategy forced its reversal at the 1978 CLC convention, the practice of piecemeal participation in consultative, rather than decision-making, structures has proved a more elusive target for opponents.

The 1983 Speech from the Throne attached tremendous importance to the forging of a "national partnership for prosperity" in which labour would be admitted to full partnership with "an equal voice in the resolution of issues like technological change and productivity improvement." The offers of new consultative opportunities for labour were a far cry indeed from the traditional government attitude to the ambitions of organized labour for a say in government policy.[13] But they were nevertheless qualified in almost every line by the imperatives of the capital accumulation function—increased international competitiveness and greater productivity.[14] Some sections of organized labour see in these overtures an opportunity to escape from the impotence which has been their organization's lot. Others remain profoundly distrustful of government initiatives in this area, a perception reinforced by the wage controls and emergency legislation discussed earlier.

More traditional methods of legitimation have continued and, in some areas, received a new impetus. As well as adjustments to the range and level of employment standards in well-established fields, there has been a considerably increased emphasis on occupational health and safety.

Increased pressure for an expanded definition of occupational health and safety and improved enforcement mechanisms produced legislative results during the 1970s. A number of provinces have rationalized and strengthened both legislation and enforcement mechanisms. As well, efforts have been made to involve labour and management in the policing of workplace conditions.

To some extent this legislative response has operated independently of the crisis-associated tensions which have been central to other aspects of labour policy. At least in the federal case, however, increased emphasis on occupational health and safety, together with other legitimation items, was associated with labour is hostility to the 1975 wage controls program. The Department of Labour was given "almost carte blanche to initiate programs which would appease organized labour" (Swimmer, 1981: 159-161). In response, the department developed a 14-point program which included the establishment of an Institute for Occupational Health and Safety, substantial revisions to the Canada Labour Code in the employment standards area, a task force to study paid educational leave, grants to unions to conduct labour education, provisions for greater worker participation in health and safety issues, and a Quality of Working Life program study to assist the development of ways to increase industrial democracy and humanize the workplace.

The unfavourable economic climate seems to have inhibited workers from seeking the implementation of some of their new rights,[15] such as the right to refuse dangerous work; and many of the measures may have been largely symbolic. One observer has concluded that "there is a higher government priority for programs which pay symbolic lip service to occupational health and safety than for those aimed at enforcing health and safety legislation" (Simmer, 1981: 180).

Nonetheless these measures, together with the search for tripartite cooperative boards, agencies and consultative committees, represent a major attempt to salvage legitimacy after the damage wreaked by other, stop-gap, responses to the economic crisis. Even in this sphere, however, one can note the merging of the accumulation and legitimation functions mentioned previously. More precisely, we can see the use of legitimacy measures to promote the accumulation function. One example is the administrative reform of 1979, in which the Cabinet developed an expenditure "envelope" system. The Department of Labour was included in the economic, rather than social affairs envelope, on the grounds that "a harmonious work environment is essential to the economic well being of Canada" (Swimmer, 1981: 162). Or, as the 1983 Speech from the Throne put it, "This government believes that the maintenance and improvement of workers' rights are fully consistent with, and indeed essential to, increased productivity... A fundamental aspect of productivity is a secure, safe environment for workers." Thus in the recent period labour policies based on the legitimation function have evolved away from support of the political and economic system in the broader sense to become more narrowly instrumental.

Regulation of Labour Relations

In the years since 1975 the rather untidy, varied and partial extension of collective bargaining rights to public sector workers has continued to undergo a process of definition.

The extensive subjection of public sector employees to wage controls and *ad hoc* emergency legislation has mushroomed, but there has been no wholesale drive to directly eliminate (still less of course to expand) the legal protection for their bargaining rights. However in one province, British Columbia, there has been a determined government effort to dramatically roll back the gains public sector workers had already achieved.

The Social Credit administration in British Columbia clearly sees itself as being in the vanguard of a new wave of neo-conservatism in Canada. If its example is copied in other state jurisdictions, then labour policy will be on the way back to its pre-1960s sphere of operation. To date, however, the British Columbia example remains an atypical one.

The main features of the private sector legislative framework also remain intact, although there have been a number of incremental changes to the system. A few have expanded labour's rights. These include the check-off of union dues on demand (Quebec 1975, Alberta 1977, Ontario 1980), and the prohibition of the use of professional strike breakers (Quebec 1977, Ontario 1983). Other changes, often explicitly designed to counterbalance changes perceived to be pro-labour, increase employers' rights. Examples include granting employers greater latitude in opposing unionization drives (Manitoba 1976, Saskatchewan 1983), increasing the majorities necessary for certification or strike votes (Manitoba 1976, Alberta 1981, Saskatchewan 1981), and clarifying the status of unions as entities capable of being sued (Newfoundland 1977, Saskatchewan 1983).

More serious changes to the status quo have occurred in Nova Scotia (1979) and Alberta (1983). In Nova Scotia the so-called Michelin Bill altered the requirements for union certification, in the interests of the anti-union Michelin Tire Company. In 1983 Alberta passed legislation to allow unionized construction companies to set up non-union subsidiaries with relative ease, hence circumventing the effects of unionization. Both these measures strike hard blows at the "encouragement of collective bargaining" aspects of labour policy. They clearly represent a shift from concern for legitimacy to an emphasis on capital accumulation. For the moment, however, they remain fairly isolated as major deviations from the post-war pattern.[16]

For both the private and public sectors, then, the legislative framework of the labour-management relationship has yet to see drastic structural change as a result of the economic crisis, although suspension of the established rules has become quite common.

Conclusions

The economic crisis which began in the 1970s has produced a lot of initiatives in Canadian labour policy. Much of this activity—wage controls and back-to-work legislation in particular—has tended to suspend the operation of the labour relations system constructed in the post-war years. Coercive in form, the substance of these state interventions has been to emphasize the state's capital accumulation function to such an extent that a legitimation crisis may be said to have developed.

Amongst the effects of this situation, the following are noteworthy. First, the labour movement has been forced into a series of mainly defensive struggles to maintain a legislative status quo which, from a labour point of view, was really far from satisfactory. The defense of free collective bargaining is really no such thing since the 1944 labour relations system is hedged with regulations and restrictions, many of which work to the disadvantage of labour. Second, in combination with other factors, this defense of the status quo has been successful to the extent that the legislative "rules of the game" have not yet been dismantled and replaced with a more openly restrictive or coercive labour relations system. The 'rules' have been suspended fairly regularly, but periodic suspension does not amount to demolition.

Some levels of the state (for example, the provincial governments of British Columbia and, possibly, Alberta) do seem to have decided upon a coercive restructuring of the labour relations system. But the vigorous response of the British Columbia labour movement may well deter potential imitators. In any case, other levels of the state (the federal Liberal government being a notable representative), hoping to take advantage of the class collaborationist elements in Canada's labour movement, believed that measures designed to fulfill the legitimation function could also be made instrumental to the needs of capital accumulation. These measures, combined with *ad hoc* coercive interventions and reliance on high levels of unemployment to discipline organized labour, may well constitute an acceptable alternative to a major restructuring of the system and the social and political costs that it might involve.

Labour's lack of an alternative vision of the legislative environment in which the labour-capital conflict should occur has been cruelly exposed by the economic crisis. Though the issue is beyond the scope of this paper, it must be admitted that Canada's labour movement has not developed a view of how the labour relations legislative system should look, let alone mobilized its forces to fight for such a view. Until such a program is developed, however, labour is likely to find itself in a weak and essentially reactive position. It will be perpetually dealing with an agenda prepared by forces hostile to the labour movement, and one in which "victory" is represented by a continuation of the unsatisfactory and highly restrictive system developed after 1944.

Notes

1. O'Connor, 1973. This view of the state's functions has been applied to Canadian labour policy. See Craven, 1980:160.
2. For an account of this development, see MacDowell, 1978.
3. Because of the war, and under the rubric of the War Measures Act, labour relations had once again become (temporarily) an area of predominantly federal jurisdiction.
4. Woods, 1973: 64-70, 86-93. Strikes over jurisdiction disputes, recognition issues, the application and interpretation of collective agreements, and during conciliation procedures were now illegal.

5. For a useful comparison of the details of these provisions see Phillips, 1977: 19-20.
6. As was the case, for example, with Ontario's Employers' Liability Act. See Manga, Broyles and Reschenthaler, 1981: 119.
7. For a detailed summary see Maslove and Swimmer, 1980: 33-8.
8. Only Saskatchewan and Quebec opted out of the program. In each case these provinces set up their own provincial boards to regulate wages.
9. Based on legislation reported in Labour Canada, *Legislative Review* (Numbers 1 to 16.)
10. For an account of the brief existence of the CLRC, see McVittie, 1984. As he notes (p. 14), the existence of the CLRC was always imperilled by its linkage, in the federal government's thinking, to the possibility of a voluntary incomes policy.
11. On the development of this corporatist initiative and its failure to come to fruition, see McBride, 1983; and Giles, 1982: 37.
12. For an overview of one such consultative process see Brown and Eastman with Robinson, 1981.
13. Kwavnick, 1972 (Chapter 9) documents the inability of the CLC to influence government policy outside of a narrow range of *directly* labour-related policy areas on which the government chose to regard the CLC's representation as legitimate.
14. For a less critical interpretation of government policy, see Adams, 1982.
15. *Globe and Mail*, 28 November 1983.
16. British Columbia has recently set up an advisory committee to help draft changes to the B.C. Labour Code (*Globe and Mail*, 16 February 1984). Given the labour relations 'philosophy' of the B.C. government, this could imply a drastic dismantling of the existing system.

Social Wages in a Period of Economic Crisis

Bob Russell

Of what real interest are social wage issues to working-class people? This question is of more than academic concern as social wage entitlements come under increasing review in an era of official restraint.

The social wage concept, as used here, is a term which refers to the variety of direct income transfers and public goods which are made available by state authorities to income earners and household members.[1] In advanced capitalist democracies such as Canada, receipt of social wages has been increasingly construed as a right of citizenship and thus a right to the basic provision of such public goods as education and health services as well as an entitlement to at least minimal levels of overall income. The latter, is in turn regulated by such transfer programs as the social insurances for unemployment and retirement income as well as through measures such as family allowances and the Canada Assistance program.

The development of the social wage has behind it a long history which varies in specifics from country to country (Flora and Heidenheimer, 1981; Guest, 1980; Rimlinger, 1973; Therborn, 1984). Suffice it to say here that the appearance of social wages, or of the so-called welfare state, has been one of the means by which capitalist societies have weathered the periodic storms for the 20th century which have threatened their further reproduction as historical systems. Thus, the extension of social wages is intimately related to the social reproduction of capitalism in at least three senses: such entitlements enter directly as an integral element into the reproduction of the labour power of the working class (Gough, 1980; Russell, 1984a); they also enter into a system of hegemony by bestowing legitimacy in the eyes of the citizenry on the polity which issues them (O'Connor, 1973); and finally social wages have been used to maintain aggregate levels of consumer demand in economies that are characterized by the existence of monopoly capitalism and which are prone to cyclical stagnation (Gonick, 1975; Steindl, 1976).[2]

To return to the question with which we opened this paper, it can be stated that the social wage has become an essential constituent of working-class income. Thus, according to calculations which were made for the Canadian labour force, social wages approximated 30 percent of personal wage and salary income by the mid 1970s (Russell, 1984b). For the 'average' wage earning household, a sizeable proportion of gross income assumes the form of or is derived from social wage payments. Of course, the actual amounts for any given household will vary over time. Some elements of the social wage and especially the public goods aspect are consumed on a periodic basis throughout a lifetime. These aspects are often related to directly equipping or maintaining a national labour force in such conditions as to permit it to earn a living through the sale of labour power. Other elements of the social wage are best thought of as a substitute wage system which comes into operation when income derived from the sale of labour power is either insufficient or altogether absent for household reproduction as during bouts of unemployment or in old age (Dickinson, 1985). Any contraction of the social wage, or of the elements that are factored into it, represents an assault upon the living standards of the vast majority of wage earners.

In an era in which *direct* onslaughts against the wage bill is still, (mercifully), the exception, the social wage becomes a vulnerable target.[3] In fact, one of the more striking aspects of the current capitalist crisis is the centrality of the state and social wage issues in political debates. Ideologically, this is reflected in the common perception that state policy may no longer be part of the solution, (as it was during the 1930s for example), but instead is part of the problem which besets the advanced capitalist economies in the 1980s. As the results of the recent Canadian federal election demonstrate, this mode of reasoning has gained a considerable currency in Canada. At the same time, and as the recent history of British Columbia's Operation Solidarity goes to show, struggles over the social wage represent a new and unchartered terrain for the labour movement in Canada (Magnusson *et al.*, 1984). Ultimately, a successful defense of, or at least an improvement in, the social wage system is dependent upon an accurate appreciation of its place and importance within the capitalist political-economy.

The remainder of this paper examines specific aspects of the social wage crisis that are immediately relevant to working people in Canada. In it, I attempt to provide a diagnostic account of the crisis that has provoked calls for restrictive social policies and the 'implementation of hardship'. The central thesis of the paper concerns the contradiction that exists between the state's role as an agent of social reproduction and its place in anchoring a system of class rights. As the state has assumed greater levels of responsibility for the former, in addition to traditional engagements, this antagonism has blossomed forth into the current crisis which has the social wage system as its principal object. Thus, the current situation arises from the subordination of labour and reproduction to accumulation rather than from over generous welfare provisions or from other factors which lay blame on the victims. The dynamics of this process are described in greater length below with an analysis of the unemployment insurance and Canada Pension plans, two of the largest components of the social wage system. This analysis is undertaken in the belief that a thorough understanding of the current malaise is only one step in combatting its reactionary effects.

The Operation of the Social Insurances and the Unemployment Insurance Debate

Concern with unemployment insurance and its 'abuse' has become as periodic in Canada as the inevitability of the cyclical downturn. In fact, one cannot help but suspect a relation. Useful discussions on the origins of unemployment insurance in Canada have recently been provided (Cuneo, 1979, 1980; Finkel, 1979). However, the on-going operation of the program has not been subject to the same scrutiny.

Unemployment insurance, along with the Canada Pension Plan, which is discussed below represent the two most important social insurance schemes in Canada. Each system is premised upon a contractual obligation between the individual wage earner and the state, such that over the lifetime of the wage earner so much in foregone income is deposited as special ear-marked tax contributions into separate social wage account funds. In other words, a certain proportion of total wage income is socialized by the state and tucked away in the specialized social insurance accounts from which designated payments can be made to recipients. Such social wage trust funds may be operated in accordance with two funding principals. 'Accumulation' techniques, as the name suggests, implies the accumulation of large reserves through special social security taxes. Benefits in this case are paid out of accumulated reserves. 'Pay-as-you-go' plans, on the other hand, do not countenance a build-up of funds. Contributions are periodically reset to meet current obligations. Presumably, the former principal of funding has a 'safety-cushion' effect in that reserves are built into it to meet unexpected contingencies.

A number of social wage expenses, characterized by uncertain future liabilities such as unemployment or long-term but distant expenditures (e.g., pensions) are particularly amendable to 'accumulation' techniques, whereby large deposits are built up from special earmarked revenues in anticipation of future claims. Since the total capacity of such funds are not usually drawn upon at any single moment, the balance of such accounts are available to the state on a continuing basis. While such savings could be deployed in a variety of ways, in practice their use has been almost entirely devoted to the refunding of state debt. The increasing dependence of governments on loans contracted from these funds over a short space of time is one of the more remarkable aspects of contemporary public finance.

There are two aspects to this development. In the past, prior to the advent of the social wage, state finances were formally dependent upon tax revenues and loans from personal savings (both domestic and foreign). Whenever tax receipts fell short of expenditures, the state would have to enter the open market and bid competitively for loan capital, using future tax obligations as collateral for public borrowing. The direct taxation of wage income and the centralization of these revenues in special social wage accounts for future expenditures opens up an alternate possibility: that of borrowing on tax revenues which have *already been received and allocated*. No longer reliant on the vagaries of private lenders, state administrators were able to go directly to social wage accounts and borrow from them; moreover in most cases funds were borrowed at substantially below-market rates of interest.

The extension of state financing as described above therefore includes not only borrowing on private savings secured with future tax receipts, but also calls on tax revenues already collected and set aside for designated purposes. This has important implications for the future of the welfare state. When state authorities borrow on the private loan market, certificates that stand for the taxing power of the state are issued to creditors in exchange for loan capital. From the perspective of the creditors, investment in state issues is identical to the advancement of money capital for any other undertaking; it is carried out as a source of gain, rather than as a means of saving or hoarding. Because of this, state certificates are tradeable. As a form of *money capital*, it is therefore only necessary that the state, at any given time, possess sufficient revenues with respect to its debt as are required to ensure interest payments at rates which are acceptable to its creditors. Although sinking funds were originally established for this purpose, the most significant and revolutionary aspect of capitalist state finances is the creation of a permanently-funded state debt. As implied by the term, the noteworthy feature here is that state debt is permanently refunded, regardless of the fact that the principal debt is never discharged.

The contemporary practice of borrowing on state social wage accounts differs from this procedure in vital aspects. Social wage trust funds such as the unemployment insurance or Canada Pension plans do not exist as a source of profit for owners of money capital or for fund contributors, but rather as a means of reproduction through which wage income may be spread out over the life span of the wage-earner and the wage dependent household. It is thus absolutely necessary that such funds be fully replenished, in order to serve the purposes for which they were established. Now, the interesting question in respect to social wage funds and state transfer expenditures in the current conjuncture revolves around the problem of whether such reserves can be recomposed to meet future social wage payments, given the borrowing that has taken place against them.

Table 1: Unemployment Insurance Fund Account (in millions of Canadian dollars)

	Current Surplus/Deficit*	Balance of Account
1942	425.7	114.0
1943	325.4	190.4
1944	138.4	268.1
1945	248.5	317.9
1946	55.6	372.8
1947	82.9	455.8
1948	80.5	536.4
1949	53.4	589.9
1950	84.6	674.5
1951	108.2	782.8
1952	74.4	857.3
1953	30.2	887.5
1954	-41.2	846.2
1955	13.1	859.4
1956	18.9	878.4
1957	-134.2	744.2
1958	-244.3	499.8
1959	133.9	365.8
1960	-181.2	184.6
1961	-118.0	66.5
1962	-56.9	9.6
1963	-8.8	0.87
1964	39.6	404.4
1965	100.9	141.4
1966	116.7	258.2
1967	44.4	302.6
1968	79.6	382.3
1969	75.8	479.7
1970	-134.5	323.6
1971	-286.6	36.8
1972	-59.0	-22.0
1973	-38.0	-60.0
1974	-40.0	-100.1
1975	-67.0	-167.0

* Current surplus/deficit includes payments of benefits, and purchase of securities collections and interest income and income from sale of assets

Source: Calculated by author from Government of Canada, *Public Accounts of Canada* (Supply and Services, Ottawa 1945-1975).

It is possible to observe all of the above dynamics at work in the operation of the unemployment insurance plan. In 1971 the Canadian Unemployment insurance Act was revamped for the first time since its introduction thirty years earlier. Although accompanied by a great deal of fanfare, including the publication of a 'white paper' prior to debate on the bill, very little in the way of rationale was provided for the new act by either state spokespersons or other analysts. A glimpse at the Unemployment Insurance Account fund (Table 1) furnishes much of the missing information. Launched in the boom years of World War Two, this fund accumulated considerable cash reserves until the 1957 recession. From these funds substantive loans were made to the state as part of its deficit financing strategy; (this accounts for the difference between the yearly surplus or deficit and the overall balance of account). Approaching insolvency in the early 1960s this condition was finally realized in 1972 just as Canada was entering the world economic downturn.

The essence of the new insurance proposals that were brought forward in response to the fiscal crisis of the Unemployment Insurance Commission (UIC) fund consisted of a unique blend of punitive and atoning measures. For the first time claimants of unemployment insurance benefits were required to attend mandatory interviews at Commission offices for maintenance of eligibility. This extension in surveillance was combined with the raising of wage income ceilings on which weekly premiums were paid, as well as with the extension of coverage to an additional 1.6 million workers (virtually covering the entire wage labour force) which permitted a significant increase in benefit levels to 66.6 percent of normal wage earnings, as well as an extension of the contribution base.

Perhaps the most interesting feature of the new plan, however, were the financing arrangements. Previously, the state had contributed 20 percent to a 40-40-20 tripartite scheme which included employers and workers. Under the new provisions, labour and capital would each contribute 50 percent of total contributions until the unemployment rate reached 4 percent. At this level of unemployment, which is usually defined as optimal in contemporary capitalist economies, a system of extended benefits would be triggered, financed totally out of state contributions (i.e. general revenues). The counterpart of this massive increase in state participation through general revenue expenditures was the termination of a separate unemployment insurance account fund. Henceforth, the unemployment insurance account was simply merged with the general accounts of the state. This 'reorganization' was, of course, a tacit admission of the bankruptcy of the old scheme, although at the time this appears to have gone unnoticed. Indeed, in the hundreds of pages of debate on the new Unemployment Insurance Act, only one mention concerning the restructuring of the fund is to be found (Dominion of Canada, *Debates*, 1971). Previously as the unemployment wage fund went further into debt, loans that had been made to the federal government on its accumulated surpluses were called in, and the fund quickly moved form the status of creditor to the state to the position of taking out loans on its own accord. This no doubt contributed to the mushrooming federal budget deficit that appeared in the early 1970s as well as to the disbanding of the fund and its merger with general state revenues.

Two important points emerge from this review of unemployment insurance expenditures. First, no method of financing such schemes is inviolable to the exigencies of capitalist accumulation. Although the 'accumulation' method of social wage funding whereby large surplus reserves are accumulated prior to the making of significant disbursements, does provide a cushion for social insurance assets, sizeable reserves can dwindle over a short period of time as witnessed by the UIC fund. This tendency is all the more marked when generalized stag-flationary pressures are brought to bear on the real value of social wage reserves. When this occurs, programs such as unemployment insurance undergo a *de facto* conversion from 'accumulation' principals of funding. Increasing pressure on general state reserves follow directly from this and are exacerbated by the large scale non-public borrowing which has been permitted on such funds. If such programs are rescued from the precipice, and there seems to be little alternative, the operation does carry important costs. Thus, what little autonomy such programs enjoyed to reflect working-class concerns are whittled away, as the Department of Finance assumes tacit responsibility for their financial operation.

In fact it did not take long for the cost involved in the rescue of the unemployment insurance fund to become apparent. In both 1976 and 1977 major new modifications were introduced into a program that had only just been overhauled. These changes were intended to bolster a flaccid work ethic by reinforcing stable work environments. Apparently from the government's perspective, the sting of unemployment was not having its customary effect of reinforcing work place discipline. On the other hand, with the new UIC financing arrangements, a growing burden of expenditure was being placed directly on the state. Consequently, it was necessary to tighten up the unemployment insurance regulations (Dominion of Canada, Debates, 1976: 8567).

Henceforth, the waiting period for collection of benefits was doubled for those who voluntarily left jobs, as well as for those who turned down 'appropriate' employment or were dismissed from employment for misconduct. Under this provision legitimate recipients of unemployment insurance could wait for up to 2 months before receiving their first payments. In addition, the benefit rate for claimants with dependents was cut back from 75 percent of normal wage earnings to the standard 66.6 percent. Finally, state contributions were decreased by a significant change in the funding formula. Rather than directly funding the costs of unemployment insurance when the rate of unemployment exceeded 4 percent, future government contributions would kick in only once unemployment rates exceeded the previous 8 year average. As unemployment has spiralled, the base average has been forced up and this in turn has placed more and more of the fiscal responsibility for the program on wage earners. Thus, by one estimate the 1976 revisions totalled to an average of $89.00 in additional premium payments for a more impoverished program (Dominion of Canada, Debates, 1976: 8577).

That was 1976. The following year was to bring new erosion, in the form of an increase in the number of weeks of work required for qualification. Secondly, a new benefit structure was announced, which for the first time factored local labour market conditions into the calculation of insured earnings. Thus, whereas the previous year major emphasis had been placed on reducing state expenditures into UIC, in 1977 attention was directed towards the further reduction of claims on the program. This again was combined with a nod in the direction of work ethic ideology through encouraging UIC recipients to participate in job retraining, job sharing and volunteer work programs.

The crisis in the unemployment insurance fund and the restrictive measures that have been adopted to deal with it represent a contradiction between the socialization of reproduction through the extension of substitute wages on the one hand, and the continued dominance of private accumulation on the other. This was manifested along the following lines: a crisis in the fund that was occasioned by high rates of unemployment and supplemented by non-public borrowing on the fund; and government cutbacks in funding as part of an overall turn towards the labour market and its utilization as a means of coercion in the restoration of industrial profitability. In this case, the contingencies arising from the operation of the Canadian state's plan can be taken as providing an omen for future developments. The dissipation of the UIC fund points to a major weakness or to the fragility of social security systems in a wage economy. As can be seen from an analysis of worker' pension plans, the mode of organizing public accounts and in particular the conversion of social wage deposits into loan capital for the financing of state debt exacerbates the impact of the crisis on the welfare state and converts it into a fiscal crisis of the state.

Genesis of a Fiscal Crisis: The Canada Pension Plan

Placing the issues in perspective, it should be noted that the sums involved in the unemployment insurance system pale by comparison with those of the largest social wage transfers, the public pensions. Thus, if the above argument is correct in its essentials we should observe the same dynamic working itself out in the case of the social wage component that has been set aside for the provision of retirement income.

By the latter 1970s, the wages which had been accumulated in the Canada and Quebec Pension Plans were financing over 30 percent of total government debt. Statistics Canada, 1976, 1978). In other words, deferred wages to the extent of almost $22 billion had been loaned to the federal and provincial governments by 1983, as a means of financing the mushrooming state debt. This has been made possible by a number of factors including the profile of the Canadian labour force at the time contributory pensions were introduced in 1968. As a result, over the past 17 years contributions to the pension plans have been much larger than claims on the fund. These surpluses have become one of the principal sources for financing state debt along with the accrued interest on such loans, which as a matter of course were also regularly reloaned back to the state.

This arrangement will only be altered when expenditures from the plan exceed contributions, a prospect that is likely to be realized for the first time as early as this year (National Council of Welfare, 1982). When this occurs pension plan premiums plus accrued interest on previous loans will suffice to keep the plan solvent for about another 10 years or until about the middle of the next decade. Shortly thereafter full interest paybacks in addition to normal contributions will no longer suffice to keep the fund afloat. At this point governments will have to start repaying the principal of the loans they have contracted, thereby adding a strain of several billion dollars more per year to their budgets. How likely is it that Canadian governments will be able to undertake such a commitment? On this point it is instructive to refer directly to the debate within state circles. Citing the debt repayment problem to the Canada Pension Plan, the Royal Commission on the Status of Pensions found that:

> A continuation of the present borrowing structure with the monies in a fully funded Canada Pension Plan would not be in the best interest of the people... (sic). It (Royal Commission on the Status of Pensions) considers that only when monies are borrowed in the money market, at market rates, with payment guaranteed by the tax base and with scheduled repayments can there be any meaningful restraint on government borrowing. It is significant that no one suggested to the Commission that the provinces be obliged to pay back the capital sums already borrowed from the Canada Pension Plan fund. In fact it may be that some provinces would be hard pressed to do so. (Royal Commission on the Status of Pensions in Ontario, Vol. 5, p. 97.)

In conclusion, it is highly unlikely that this element of the social wage will be 'rescued' with the same degree of alacrity as was unemployment insurance—in effect—by an appeal to general revenues. Pension plans and retirement income differ significantly from unemployment allowances in that the period of claim on the fund is normally much longer than is the case with unemployment insurance, (i.e. a matter of years rather than weeks or months). Thus, turning towards general state budgets as a source of refunding retirement pensions is increasingly problematic simply by virtue of the magnitude of the sums involved. In other words it is far from certain that even if the 'political will' was present, the fiscal resources of the state could measure up to the lengthy commitment involved in balancing the pension fund. Rather the more likely outcome is that given the forthcoming defaults on the loans made from the Canada Pension Plan, the payroll taxes which support the plan will have to be increased sooner and to a greater extent than would otherwise have been necessary, while the structure of benefits, including possibly the age of retirement, will also have to undergo re-evaluation.

Concluding Remarks

Somewhat ironically, social security measures which were effected in the wake of the last grave crisis of capitalism have turned out to be major targets in the present conjuncture. While the advent of social insurance was a reform measure, the social wage system now constitutes an important component of their standard of living. The defense of the social wage thus represents a significant dimension of the political agenda for the 1980s.

Today it is fashionable to attribute the crisis in the social wage system to past excessive 'generosity' on the part of political decision-makers which in turn was fueled by the rising expectations of a demanding public. The explanation tendered in this paper is at odds with this ideology. Rather, it commences from the ever-present contradiction between the reproduction of labour-power and the accumulation of surplus value. Through the extension of social wages, extra-market support in the form of state pensions, unemployment insurance, family allowances and subsidized consumption is administered to designated sections of the working population. Such support, however, must ultimately confront the dominant logic of capitalist market society which the state is pledged to guarantee. This conflict between market and extra-market forces, between the accumulation of surplus value and the reproduction of labour power, is basic to public sector economics. It is one of the principal features of the current crisis, which is centred on the social wage.

Concretely, we have seen these forces at work in the preceeding analysis. Thus, while the state is charged with the creation and administration of social wage funds, it is also obliged to consign funds which directly subsidize the accumulation of capital (infra-structural investments, social capital, etc.) In the process, social wage funds are converted into money capital while their subsumption into state debt is experienced as a crisis of the pensions system. Analogously, the state is expected to look after the problems of unemployment, while at the same time be responsible for the maintenance of 'social discipline' in the labour force. The result—a contraction in unemployment insurance monies just as the call upon such funds continues to expand. In brief, the crisis in the social wage system is one of the novel aspects of the current economic crisis and this results from the contradictory roles that the state has assumed in occupying both reproductive and accumulation functions.

Fortunately, state involvement in these dual circuits is not carried out in a political vacuum. While pressure for a revision of social security taxes, combined with calls for more restrictive applications of eligibility rules can be expected to accompany the failure of the social insurance accounts, an increasing awareness on the part of labour of the stakes involved in the social wage question is also becoming apparent. Recently, for example, the Canadian Union of Public Employees has gone on record as advocating that surplus funds from the Canada Pension Plan be used to repatriate the Canadian economy from foreign control with such monies forming part of a publicly oriented industrial strategy in lieu of their consumption in financing the investment requirements of corporate capital (CUPE, 1977). There are the indications that the funding and utilization of social wage resources will become a much more important public issue in the future. When this occurs, the traditional range of trade-union concerns will have been significantly extended in a movement towards a new social trade unionism.

Notes

1. For purposes of clarification the *social wage* may be defined as sources of income that go to individuals via the state. As such they may be contrasted with the wages that individuals receives from employers in return for expenditures of labour-power, that is, for the performance of work. Income derived from the state treasury may either take the form of direct transfers of revenue (e.g. state pensions, unemployment insurance monies, etc.), or it may represent payment in kind, such as access to services which are operated by the state (e.g. hospital care, education facilities). The latter are referred to as *public goods* because they must be consumed collectively—one individual cannot monopolize consumption of the services provided by an entire hospital, for instance. Due to their special qualities it is often difficult for individual capitalists to *profitably* produce such goods or services, thereby obliging the state to fill the void which is left for these necessary items.

2. The concept of hegemony, as used here, was developed by the Italian Marxist, Antonio Gramsci. It is best described as the consent which the oppressed classes render to the social system which is responsible for their oppression. Monopoly capitalism is also a concept that was produced by the classical Marxist tradition. It references a specific *stage* of capitalist development that is characterized by such features as giant corporations which exercise dominant control over their markets and the competitive struggle of national capitals for control over world markets. More recent analyses of monopoly capitalism have focused on the rise of multi-national corporations and their consequences for political-economic development and underdevelopment.
3. Here I am referring to actual wage cuts as have occurred recently in the incidence of concessionary bargaining. This is not meant to imply that real wage reductions have not also been effected through the mechanism of inflation, or by means of creating 'open-shop' conditions in areas of the economy that were previously "closed-shop".

The Rise of Pensions in Canada

James Stafford

Although private pensions have existed throughout history, their occurrence as standardized plans for designated classes of employees is a recent phenomenon dating back little more than 100 years. They are not to be confused with public pensions which have been more common and which have a longer history.

In Canada and the United States, the incidence of private plans is marked by two periods. The first was in 1874-1914, when they were first established, and the second in the post-World War Two era, when they proliferated. The context of growth in the two periods is distinctively different. During the early rise of pensions, a reluctant labour force had private pensions thrust upon it while attempting to gain public pension legislation from the state. Capital unilaterally introduced pensions as one aspect of corporate welfare designed to encourage obedience and loyalty among the workers.

The second period of escalation of private pension plans took place in the context of Second World War legislation. After the Canadian government placed a tax on all profits in support of the war efforts, corporations looked for loop holes in the tax laws and found that contributions to pension plans were tax deductible. Allocating money to pension funds not only pleased labour, which at this time accepted private pension plans, but it also allowed the company to retain control of the money which would otherwise have been lost to taxes. Companies were able to retain control of the money for investment or transfer it back into the operating budget at a later date if they wished.

The goal of this paper is to explain the rise of private pensions in the initial period of growth. Popular explanations credit corporate altruism or union pressure with causing such a development. Labour certainly benefits from pensions and has pressed for greater security, but careful scrutiny of the circumstances and events surrounding the rise of this aspect of corporate welfare reveals a more self-serving motivation on the part of capital than is allowed by the above explanations.

The Political Economic Context of the Rise of Private Pensions

From the 1870s to the 1890s Canada experienced a long period of economic difficulty with serious depressions and periods of uneven recovery. The external demand for staples tapered off while investments in canals proved ill-timed, as they were swiftly rendered obsolete by the railway. The railways absorbed enormous amounts of capital and were slow to produce returns on their investment.

The struggle for accumulation of capital led to depressed wages and working conditions. The continuous influx of immigrants at the turn of the century helped to keep wages down, even when market conditions began to provide increased accumulation in the first decades of the 20th century. In Toronto, for example, net value of production increased 409 percent from 1900 to 1915 while gross value, which includes wages, increased only 260 percent (Piva, 1979:5).

Evidence of mounting tension between capital and labour led to a Royal Commission on the Relations of Labor and Capital in 1887-1889. The Commission found cases of poverty, brutality and injustice suffered by labour. The Report treats us to spectacles of eleven and twelve year-olds maimed by machinery while putting in 12-hour days that began at 6:00 a.m. (Kealey, 1973: 194-9). In the cigar-making industry in Montreal children aged 10-14 were beaten across the head by fist for making mistakes, fined for dropping food on the floor while eating, put in a blackhole for wasting time and thrown in jail for skipping work (Kealey, 1973: 215ff, 256-7).

Shantymen were fed victuals that sometimes made them sick. They were forced to purchase clothing and supplies from the company store at prices that were inflated by 25 percent to 40 percent (Kealey, 1973: 205). In some cases men who quit work had deductions from their wages equal to the cost of transporting a replacement to the job site.

The industrialization of the boot and shoe trade caused men to be replaced by machines. Unskilled, low-wage labour operating the machines forced older, skilled workers out of work. The machines reduced both wages and the labour force while depriving workers of a sense of craft and achievement (Kealey, 1973: 244-6).

The shortage of industrial capital coupled with a desperate drive for accumulation led to the deterioration of working conditions, lengthening of the work day, reduction of wages, employment of women and children and the utilization of machines to replace men. Incidents documenting these trends are included in the Royal Commission Report on the Relations of Labor and Capital, but general statistics on such trends are not readily available. Unemployment statistics do not exist although Piva has used arrests for vagrancy as an indication of levels of unemployment. Arrests for vagrancy in Toronto rose from 1.8 per 1,000 population in 1901-1906 to 2.0 per 1,000 population in the depression years of 1907-1908 (Piva, 1979: 67).

Wages for those who did have jobs were not adequate to support a family, forcing mothers and children into the work place at wages that were even lower than those paid to men. Piva calculates that in 1901, the average weekly expenditure of a family of five for food, shelter, fuel and light in Toronto was $9.68. This compares unfavourably with the average weekly earnings of $7.57 in manufacturing industries in Ontario (Piva, 1979: 45, 52). Piva quotes a *Mail and Empire* interview of a single mother in 1897.

> ...the clothes at which she had been working were lying with a heap of rubbish on the dirty floor. She could hardly speak with a consumptive cough, which was fast taking her life away. She had worked at the garment trade for many years, but had been unable to save enough to permit of her children getting a proper schooling. A little girl, sixteen years of age, who was thin and sickly in appearance, stood by her side and related how she had worked for eight years past for a large wholesale house, most of the time at $2 a week. She now intended to help her mother at the machine. She had a little sister, nine years of age, who also served at the machine. Another sister got $3 a week in a large shop for making button holes in coats....[1]

In order to facilitate accumulation, capitalists were increasing the scale of their operations as well as reducing wages and scrimping on expenses in the work place. As early as the 1890s, the Grand Trunk shops in Montreal employed 3,000 men (Pentland, 1950: 469). By the turn of the century many other firms had work forces of similar size. In 1900 Dominion Iron and Steel Company employed 2,500 men at Sydney; the Montreal Cotton Company employed 3,000 at Valleyfield; while the Canadian Pacific Railway (CPR) employed 35,000 across Canada.[2]

The expansion in the size of firms required new techniques of control of the labour force to guarantee sustained productivity. During the early part of the 20th century, scientific management procedures as well as scientific managers were introduced from the United States to deal with large numbers of employees (Craven, 1980: 93ff). The methods of technological regimentation and scientific efficiency brought into focus the vulnerable position of labour *vis a vis* capital.

Labour responded to its plight with resentment, agitation and militance. Unions were formed in spite of formidable opposition from capital and state. Workers struck with the knowledge that they might lose their jobs, suffer physical beatings from strike breakers, police or the militia, and possibly be incarcerated. Apparently, physical abuse and economic reprisal were not a deterrent to workers who were already pushed beyond the threshold of sustenance and self-respect.

The level of strike activity increased throughout the last half of the 19th and the first two decades of the 20th centuries. The 1850s saw a sudden rise of strike activity. Craft workers in two months in 1853 struck more than they had in the previous 50 years (Palmer, 1983: 63). A continued rise in such incidents is reflected in Kealey's statistics which show that the number of strikes in Toronto increased from 36 in the 1870s to 99 in the 1880s (Kealey, 1980: 319). Across Canada, the number of labour-capital conflicts in the 1880s exceeded 430, more than double the number of the 1870s (Palmer, 1983: 125).

As Canada entered the 20th century, strife between labour and capital accelerated. More strikes were staged in Halifax in 1901-1914 (54) than in 1851-1900 (42) (McKay, 1983: 10). Labour unrest reached a final high in 1919 when 320 strikes occurred across Canada, more than in any previous year (Palmer, 1983: 173).

Ultimately, labour discontent was contained by a number of factors, not the least of which were concessions of better wages and working conditions to labour. The growth and eventual legitimacy of unions forced capital to allocate large proportions of accumulated wealth to the working man. These concessions were usually made by capital with an eye towards further improving productivity.

One procedure that was used to an increasing extent was welfare provided to the worker by his employer in the form of disability payments, profit-sharing plans and pension plans. These were granted without any pressure from labour. Indeed, the early unions and working men's associations provided their members with those services that they could afford. The records of early unions show that labour looked to the state for welfare assistance. The private pension plans that were introduced were often not embraced with enthusiasm by employees. In 1906 the British Columbia Electric Railway Company Limited submitted a pension scheme to its employees for approval. The proposal was rejected, although the terms of the scheme were similar to those of other pension plans of the time.[3]

An intriguing question arises, one which addresses the *raison d'etre* of early private pensions, as to why companies would provide such benefits at their own expense. Concessions to labour usually come after extensive pressure from unions and sacrifices by workers. Yet nowhere in the literature is there evidence that labour pressed employers for provision of old age security. Logan reports that first reference to old age pensions in the proceedings of the Canadian Trades and Labour Congress is found in 1905 (Logan, 1948: 503). In that year the resolution was adopted "that in our opinion the time is opportune to introduce legislation making provision for the maintenance of deserving poor, old, or disabled citizens who are unable to maintain themselves" (Logan, 1948: 503). More specific resolutions submitted by the Amalgamated Society of Carpenters and Joiners in 1906 and 1907 that would have required the government to contribute one-half the amount paid out by unions for old age security and unemployment benefits did not gain the approval of the Congress (Logan, 1948: 503).

United States unions also believed that the state should be responsible for the well-being of the aged and infirm. The first mention of old age security in American Federation of Labour (AFL) Convention proceedings occurs in 1902, when it was resolved that the United States Congress "enact an old age pension law that will do for the aged who have given so much of their lives to the industrial struggle what the soldier's pension is designed to do for the old soldier."[4] At the meetings held in Toronto in 1909, the AFL added its support to Canadian labour's request for state supported pensions by recommending "the adoption by the Canadian parliament of an old age pension bill similar to the one now in operation in the mother country Great Britain."[5]

Thus labour in North America at the turn of the century turned to the state for old age security. Precedents were already established in other countries. Germany had introduced the first universal pension for all wage earners and low-paid salary workers in 1889 (Bryden, 1974: 45). Two years later Denmark established the first means-tested universal plan that was later adopted by New Zealand in 1898, Australia and Great Britain in 1908, Newfoundland in 1911 and Sweden in 1913. The Newfoundland plan was the first of its kind in North America. It provided an annual pension of $50 for those who had attained the age of 75 after residing in the colony for the previous 20 years and who could demonstrate the need for such a pension.[6]

Government pensions in Canada and the United States were slow to come because of the dictates of their respective charters. The United States Constitution and the B.N.A. Act placed welfare jurisdiction in the hands of the individual states and provinces. The task of coordinating all of the respective states and provinces or of repeating pressure on each unit in return to enact legislation was difficult enough that other alternatives were attempted. The problem led to an amusing submission to the United States Congress by the AFL in 1909. It recommended that Congress enact a bill which would put all persons into the military who reach the age of 65 and meet other qualifications of residence, citizenship and lack of means. They would become members of the Old Age Home Guard of the United States Army with maximum wages of $125.[7]

The plan was not adopted although it was again recommended in 1922. Instead individual state pensions were later introduced, the first in Arizona in 1915. It was promptly declared unconstitutional on a technicality the following year. The second state pension was passed by the Pennsylvania legislature in 1923 but met the fate of the Arizona bill in 1925.[8] Other state pensions introduced in the 1920s were inadequate in provisions and limited in coverage. Families were made responsible for their indigent parents while paupers with no families were placed in almshouses (Olson, 1982: 39). Finally the economic conditions that prevailed in the depression led to the federal Social Security Act of 1935 which established a universal, compulsory plan covering the entire work force, financed by a payroll tax and providing benefits according to the amount contributed.

The Canadian government dealt with the problem by passing the Government Annuities Act of 1908 authorizing the sale of Government Annuities to residents of Canada. Young adults were encouraged by means of advertisements to purchase deferred annuities payable in monthly installments after retirement. Needless to say the voluntary nature of the plan precluded its use by the bulk of the working class, who were in greatest need of the derived benefits. Instead the annuities were purchased largely by the middle class who could afford to take advantage of their favourable interest rates and anachronistic mortality assumptions (Clark, 1960:5).

The bulk of the earlier pensions established in the civil service and public institutions slightly preceded those in private industry. The 1912 Inquiry of the Select Committee into Old Age Pensions found that a number of banks, police and fire departments, teachers' federations, and judges had pension plans.[9] Few provincial and municipal governments and private companies had them. Among the earliest plans to be established in Canada were those of the Bank of Montreal and the Bank of British North America, established in 1885 and 1886, respectively. Prior these dates the pension for the federal civil service was enacted by Canadian parliament in 1870.

The title of the federal civil service pension act is insightful. An Act for better ensuring the efficiency of the Civil Service of Canada, by providing for Superannuation of persons employed therein, in certain cases.[10] The preamble is more explicit, with the statement that:

> Whereas, for better ensuring the efficiency and economy in the Civil Service of Canada, it is expedient to provide for the retirement therefrom, on equitable terms, of persons, who, from age or infirmity cannot properly perform the duties assigned to them.[11]

Public pensions, at least in this case, were designed to ensure efficiency and to provide a means of forcing employees out of their offices once age had eroded their ability to function.

The Rise of Private Pensions

Private pensions arose within the context that has just been described. Capital faced increasing militancy from labour and feared further growth in unionization. At the same time the shortage of industrial capital forced employers to pay minimum wages and to adopt economies of scale that further weakened their control of activities in the workplace. Although employers were under no pressure to provide pensions, the target of union demands for such security being the state, they saw pension plans as an alternative that would help them maintain control and increase worker loyalty with minimal immediate expense.

The first private pension plan in North America was that of the Grand Trunk Railway, centred in Montreal but owned and managed in London, England. The man who introduced the plan was President Richard Potter, father of Beatrice Webb. His father was "Radical Dick" Potter, who co-founded the Manchester Guardian and his mother was an eccentric who, among other adventures, attempted to personally lead the Jews back to Israel.

Potter's life style was much more conservative. He conducted himself in the accepted manner of the landed gentry until the economic crash of 1847-1848 when he lost most of his inherited wealth and was forced to go to work. His father-in-law, a Liverpool merchant, made him director of the Great Western Railway.

Potter eschewed the socialist views his daughter later embraced but believed that a work force could be made more productive with a carrot than a stick (Stevens, 1960: 319). He introduced a compulsory pension scheme in 1874 that covered all office staff with salaries over $400,000 per year who started work with the Company before age 37. Employees contributed 2 1/2 percent of their salaries, the aggregate of which was matched by the Company. Retirement was compulsory at age 55 unless the employee was deemed to be providing efficient service (Riebenack, 1905: 182).

The Grand Trunk plan was implemented for reasons similar to those that instigated the plan in the Canadian civil service—to impart loyalty and to provide a legitimate method to rid the offices of old, inefficient workers. The second private plan in North America was introduced by the American Express Company in 1875, while the third belonged to the Baltimore and Ohio Railroad Company and was introduced in 1880. Pension plans were introduced by the CPR in 1902 and the Intercolonial Railways in 1904, and a more comprehensive plan replaced that of the Grand Trunk line in 1908.

They became a standard part of the employment contract in the railway industry by the second decade of the 20th century. Almost 75 percent of railway employees in Canada and 40 percent in the United States were covered by pension plans in 1908 (Latimer, 1932: 29). The fact that the railway industry was the first to introduce pensions in the private sphere is evidence that corporate welfare was introduced for purposes other than the well-being of employees. Railways were the first industry to have to deal with a large, skilled labour force distributed over a wide geographical area. They required a bureaucratic organization and employees with specialized skills which management lacked. At the same time the railways were in constant conflict with a public that felt it was charged unfair freight rates and inadequate compensation for the death of livestock and the destruction of property. The high accident rate of railroads left the industry with continual court battles for injuries and property losses. It also left a large number of employees crippled or debilitated to the extent that they could not carry out their duties adequately. The industry was faced with the dilemma of retaining older, less efficient workers, or letting them go and exacerbating already frayed public relations.

On top of all of these problems, the railroads were in constant economic crisis. Although the construction of railroads was a lucrative endeavour, their operation was precarious. When a depression struck North America in the 1870s, thousands of employees were laid off or had their wages cut back, which led to strikes, riots and clashes with federal troops. Indeed when railway officials appealed to municipal authorities for police protection, their requests were granted reluctantly (Morton, 1977: 22). In the context of scarce capital, a critical public and a resentful labour force, the railroad industry was desperate for procedures that would help to improve public and labour relations without incurring large expenses.

Examination of the terms of the early plans provides further evidence that they were established primarily to control the work force and to discourage unionization and strikes. Most of the industrial plans were non-contributory which meant that the company provided all of the funds for the plan and therefore had complete jurisdiction over its terms. The CPR prefaced its first set of pension regulations with an honest statement of the purpose of the plan:

> The company hopes, by thus voluntarily establishing a system under which a continued income will be assured to those who after years of continuous service are by age or infirmity no longer fitted to perform their duties, and with which they might be left entirely without means of support, to build up amongst them a feeling of permanency in their employment, an enlarged interest in the Company's welfare and a desire to remain in and to devote their best efforts and attention to the Company's service.[12]

The decision as to when employees were no longer "fitted to perform their duties" was made entirely by CPR officials. The Pension Committee consisted of the President, Vice-President and the Chief Solicitor of the Company, and was delegated the power to set rules and regulations although all Committee proceedings were subject to the approval of the Board. The Committee was empowered to make rules and regulations for determining eligibility for receipt of pensions and the amount of such allowances. Furthermore, it could make exceptions to certain rules it passed if such exceptions were in the interest of the Company.[13]

Details of one other plan, that of the Grand Trunk Railway Company drawn up in 1908, shall be examined for further evidence of its primary function as a mechanism of control. Once again rules and regulations were established by a Pension Committee consisting of Company Officials, in this case, three Vice-Presidents, the General Solicitor and the General Transportation Manager. The Committee made rules and regulations which were confirmed by the Board.

Although the official retirement age was established as 65 years, article eight of the rules gave the Committee the power to retain an employee for an additional five years, with that employee's consent, and to retire an employee early for reason of physical or mental disability which left him unsuited for employment, as evaluated by the Chief Medical Officer. Article 14 specified that pension privileges of an employee who sued the Company for damages on account of personal injuries sustained by him in the course of his service be withdrawn, while Article 19 gave the Committee power to "withhold permanently or temporarily the payment of any person or allowance in case of any misconduct on the part of the recipient of the same of any action on his part inimical to the interest of the Company."[14] The Company put Article 19 into operation in 1910 when its trainmen went on strike. The strikers were cut from pension benefits for service prior to the date of the strike.[15]

The Intercolonial Railway had a similar article in its pension regulation but chose to interpret it as having retroactive jurisdiction. Although the Intercolonial Railway did not introduce the pension plan until 1904, it voided service credits for those maintenance-of-way men who worked for the Company before 1899, the date of the strike. The Company chose to interpret the regulation as if the trainmen had had the foresight in 1899 to know that five years later the Company would include such an article in their pension regulations.[16]

Returning briefly to the CPR pension plan regulation, we find a similar incident arising from the 1919 strikes. At that time Canadian Pacific trainmen struck or stayed off the job because of fear or respect for their more militant co-workers. The CPR chose to interpret its regulation that "Persons voluntarily leaving the employment of the company when their services are required thereby become ineligible for pension allowance as being applicable to all employees who did not report for work during the strike."[17]

The Role of the State

The question of state activity must be considered in a study of labour and capital relations. Briefly stated, the rise of private pensions as a means of control of labour was supported by inaction on the part of the Canadian government. With the introduction of public pensions in European and Commonwealth countries, some pressure was mounted by trade unions and Members of Parliament to follow suit. Had the state acted promptly, the rise of private pensions would have been much slower. However, the government resisted such pressures and ignored problems related to the welfare of its elderly.

The year 1906 represents the first attempt to bring the matter of public pensions before the House of Commons. In 1908 a select committee was formed ostensibly to investigate a scheme to provide state aid to the elderly, but it met only three times and was simply a political ploy to cool out the voices of concern. In the same year the voluntary annuities plan was put into effect, in spite of acknowledgement that it would serve the middle class who could afford the payments rather than the labouring class who most needed support.[18]

Under continued pressure the government set up a special committee to investigate the old age pension system in 1911, but it was disbanded in 1913 because the government could not be "burdened at the present time by any scheme no matter how desirable it may be."[19] The reason given was that the government was too busy providing for the economic development of the country to direct any funds towards the welfare of labour. The government policy was stated eloquently in the 1911 conference of the Trades and Labour Congress that government responded willingly to the demands of capital for subsidies and grants but that "a sickening silence in parliament follows every request for old age pensions."[20]

At the same time that the state did little to encourage public pensions, it did less to regulate and control private pension plans. No general legislation was passed dealing with such plans. Instead, companies requested individual statutes which provided them with the legal power to design the terms of the pension plan in the way that suited them.

A typical example is the statute legislated in 1887 incorporating the Guarantee and Pension Fund Society of the Dominion Bank. The preamble indicates that the purpose of the plan is to improve the efficiency of the bank:

> Whereas the persons hereinafter named, employees of the Dominion Bank, have, by petition, set forth that it is desirable that the employees of the said Bank should be empowered, with the sanction of the said Bank, to make efficient arrangements for giving security to the said Bank for the good conduct of its employees...[21]

The act goes on to name those who are empowered to pass by-laws pertaining to the Fund:

> [These named persons]...may make such laws, not contrary to law, as may be deemed advisable for the formation and maintenance of the said fund, and for the application to such purposes of the said fund, and for its investment and administration generally, and for defining and regulating in anywise as to them may seem meet, all manner of rights of the corporation and of the individual members thereof, and of the Bank in the promises and of such officers and employees and their widows and children, and the mode of enforcement thereof, and for imposing and enforcing any description of conditonal penalty or forfeiture in the promises which to them may seem meet, and for the government and ordering of all business and affairs of the corporation.[22]

The statute in effect makes the decisions of the officers laws unto themselves. No employee is able to lodge a complaint except at the discretion of the officers of the fund.

The government continued this hands-off policy until the 1960s when pension funds were being used as a tax dodge. This loop hole had been opened in 1917 when corporations and individuals were first required to pay an income tax. At that time any contributions to a pension fund by a corporation were declared tax deductible according to the newly enacted Income War Tax Act. The Act was amended in 1919 to allow individuals a similar tax deduction.

The role of government with respect to private pension plans was one which supported the efforts of capital. It blatantly directed all available monies towards capital development while turning a blind eye to the exploitation of men, women and children in the labour force. When pressed to act, it set up royal commissions but did little to convert recommendations into law. A case in point is the 1889 Royal Commission on the Relations of Labor and Capital. In spite of findings of widespread poverty and abuse, the only action of the government was to institute a national Labour Day Holiday to take place annually on the first Monday of September.

Summary

The argument presented herein is that private pensions were instigated by capital as part of the program of corporate welfare that burgeoned at the turn of the century to control and appease labour without undue expense. Capital has used a variety of methods to achieve greater production. At the turn of the century wages were lowered, hours of work lengthened, and women and children were hired or machines utilized to replace men. In addition, other practices such as accelerating the pace of production, rationalizing work procedures and introducing assembly lines were adopted to augment productivity.

Needless to say, none of these procedures met with the approval of labour. A crisis of control resulted as labour struggled for unionization rights, higher wages, shorter hours and improved working conditions. Capital countered with the installation of machines, which dictated what work had to be done by the employee; the arrangement of a bureaucratic structure, which placed the control of workers in the hands of other workers; and the advent of corporate welfare programs, which motivated the worker to endorse the goals of the firm (Edwards, 1979: 177-83). One form of corporate welfare was the company pension plan which promised the worker economic salvation upon retirement, conditional upon long, loyal service without complaint.

The struggle for accumulation of industrial capital in Canada was particularly difficult because of the country's dependence on the export of staples, the policies of the government which favoured mercantile capitalism, and the advantages inherited by competitors in the United States. Shortages of industrial capital led to increased exploitation of workers which in turn exacerbated the crisis of control of the labour force in Canada.

Private pension plans represented one aspect of the effort of capital to deal with the widening rift between itself and labour at the end of the 19th century. They were brought forward by capital in spite of the prevailing tendency in the industrial world for old age security to be made the responsibility of the state. The paradox of capital shouldering this burden while continuing to deprive workers of reasonable wages and working conditions can only be interpreted in the context of the inevitable struggle between classes in a capitalist system.

Further evidence of pensions as a tool to control labour is revealed in the terms drawn up in the early pension plans. Details of the plans reveal that power to set these terms was given to company officials while labour had no official influence. These officers interpreted the terms of the pension plan and were given the right to arbitrarily withhold pension payments if they wished. Pension plan terms decreed that an individual was to be denied benefits if he struck or otherwise acted in any way deemed contrary to the best interests of the company. The conclusion to be drawn from this evidence is that pension plans, now commonly seen as a concession to labour, were introduced as part of a strategy by capital to maintain its domination over the labour force.

Notes

1. *Daily Mail and Empire*, October 9, 1987, quoted in Piva (1979: 95). Piva notes that William Lyon Mackenzie King was the author of the newspaper article in question.
2. *The Labour Gazette*, Volume I, King's Printer, Ottawa, October 1900, pp. 101, 223; and Riebeneck, 1905: 149.
3. *The Labour Gazette*, Volume 8, 1908, pp. 551-2.
4. American Federation of Labor (AFL), *Report of Proceedings*, 22nd Annual Convention, 1902 (Washington, D.C.: The Law Reporter Company, 1902), p. 112.
5. AFL, *Report of Proceedings*, 29th Annual Convention, 1909 (Washington, D.C.: The Law Reporter Company, 1909), p. 331.
6. *Newfoundland Legislative Acts, 1911* (St. John's: King's Printer, 1911), p. 98.
7. AFL, 1909, p. 98.
8. AFL, Report of Proceedings, 48th Annual Convention, 1928 (Washington, D.C.: The Law Reporter Publishing Company, 1928), p. 96.
9. *Inquiry of Select Committee into the Old-Age Pensions System for Canada (Ottawa:* Government Printing Bureau, 1912), pp. 23-47.
10. *Statutes of Canada, 1870* (Ottawa: Queen's Printer, 1870), Cap. IV, p. 27.
11. *Statutes of Canada, 1870*, Cap. IV, p. 27.
12. *The Labour Gazette*, Volume 25, (1925), p. 29.
13. *The Labour Gazette*, Volume 25, p. 29.
14. *The Labour Gazette*, Volume 8, p. 996.
15. *House of Commons Debates*, June 25, 1925, p. 4930.
16. *House of Commons Debates*, June 25, 1925, p. 4929.
17. H. S. Johnstone, "Pension Rights of Certain Employees of the CPR and Associated Express and Steamship Companies" (Report to Minister of Labour, Ottawa, 1945).
18. Canada, Parliament, Senate, *Old Age Annuities: Reprints of Speeches Delivered During the Tenth Parliament, Third Session* (Ottawa: Government Printing Bureau, 1907), pp. 14-18, 38.
19. *House of Commons Debates*, 1914, p. 1341.
20. *Conventions Proceedings*, Trades and Labour Congress, 1911, p. 56, quoted in Bryden (1974: 48).
21. *Statutes of Canada*, Volume 2, Chapter 55 (Ottawa: Queen's Printer, 1887), p. 7.
22. *Statutes of Canada*, Volume 2, Chapter 55, p. 8

The Impact of the B.C. Government's "Restraint Program" on Provincial Employees, Social Services and Women

Ruth Annis

Nineteen eighty-four came early in B. C. It started on July 7, 1983 when the Social Credit government launched an unprecedented attack on workers, democratic rights, human rights, union rights, women, children, the disabled, minorities, and the poor in B. C.

In the name of restraint, the government increased the provincial budget by 12.3 percent. Meanwhile they dismantled social services and education, and laid off 25 percent of the public service.

The purpose of this offensive on workers is to restructure the political balance of power back in the absolute favour of the capitalist class squeezed by the international crisis of capitalism.

The Socred attack has been a one-two punch. First, smack the public sector hard, then use the state apparatus to assault the organized private sector labour.

Their target in the public sector has been the 40,000-strong B. C. Government Employees Union (BCGEU). The government introduced Bills 2 and 3, giving themselves the right to fire any public sector worker without cause, ignoring seniority and dismissing on the basis of political belief, age, sex, race, sexual orientation, union activity, personal dislike, resistance to sexual harassment, or any other reason that suited them.

Bill 2 eliminated large parts of the BCGEU collective agreement seen to be too costly for the employer. It eliminated the right to negotiate work schedules, overtime, and protection against contracting out.

Without waiting for their own legislation to be enacted, the government overnight closed down whole departments and fired thousands and thousands of workers. They gave notice that 10,000 would be fired before the end of the year. As well they moved to privatize government projects and services wherever possible.

Their intention was clear—to bust the BCGEU.

In July the Socreds tried to create the impression that they were mainly hitting the public sector. They were counting on the historic division between public and private sector workers. They were expecting workers themselves to buy the line that the public sector was fat, privileged and unchecked in the handout of services to free-loaders. They were banking on the rise of right-wing ideology.

The Socreds have promoted the myth that money transferred from unnecessary public services to the private sector would create private sector jobs. This is not true. It's another example of 'doublespeak', like the so-called 'restraint' budget. Out of one side of its mouth, Social Credit has heralded "more jobs", and out the other side, "high technology schemes".

But high technology spells not more jobs but fewer. For the Western countries, unemployment increased from 16 million in 1975 to 34 million in 1983. Technological change will inevitably escalate unemployment, even if there is some economic recovery for capitalist profits.

The real attractiveness of B. C. for 'high tech' capital would be a cheaper, more docile labour force and a 'friendly' political climate for free enterprise. This the Socreds are committed to deliver. This is where their second punch—against private sector unions and worker—fits in.

Bill 26, the Employment Standards Amendment Act, was introduced in July. There will no longer be a Board to resolve disputes between non-unionized workers and employers. There is no longer the possibility of suing individual directors of private companies for wages if the company goes bankrupt.

There are no longer minimum standards of employment that apply to everyone. It is possible that union workers could have less protection than non-unionized workers, if in negotiations they were forced to accept terms below the minimum standard.

Most important, when contracts expire any person can apply to have the contract or any part of it declared void and the terms set by the Employment Standards Branch.

But Bill 26 was just the tip of the iceberg. In July proposed amendments to the Labour Code were leaked, and on May 8, 1984, the Social Credit government introduced sweeping changes to the Labour Code.

Political strikes are now illegal. In other words all of the protest job action taken by the Solidarity movement in the past nine months, if repeated, would now be illegal work stoppages.

The Cabinet now has the power to declare any construction site an "Economic Development Project", making strikes illegal. Unionized workers are forced to accept non-union labour on union work sites. Secondary picketing is severely restricted. Union organizing is more difficult: there is no longer automatic certification when 55 percent of employees join the union. But there *are* automatic decertification procedures. The Cabinet has extensive powers to declare jobs as "essential services" and ban all strikes. This union busting and right to work legislation is at the heart of the Socred program.

And what about social services?

In terms of service cutbacks, there has never been such a vicious attack on children, women, the elderly, the disabled and the poor in B. C.

The Ministry of Human Resources is cutting back services which work directly with abused children, many of whom have been sexually assaulted. Treatment centres for these children have been privatized. As well, 25 percent of government employees who provide social services have been laid off.

Some 230 Family Support Workers worked with thousands of families each year. They are gone. They worked with families in crisis to prevent children coming into care. Many of these families are headed by single-parent women, who will go under without support.

Homemakers—who step in temporarily when small children are left unattended or at risk of being abused by parents in crisis—are gone. Post-partum counselling is gone—leaving mothers who are depressed in isolation. The Child Abuse Teams and specialized expertise are gone, leaving overworked front line social workers to cope with impossible caseloads.

Women are particularly hurt by social service cutbacks. When crisis and family support services are eliminated, the burden falls back on to women. Although the economic and social load women have been carrying can no longer be tolerated, women's services and advocacy have been eliminated: Planned Parenthood, Vancouver Status of Women, the Women's Health Collective.

In B. C. there are 30,000 single parents on welfare. The vast majority of these are women. In 1983, the number of single parents on welfare went up 25 percent. While women and children sink further and further into poverty, the Social Credit slammed us with still more welfare cuts in February, 1984, in their second restraint budget.

And what does the Socred master plan have in store for education?

Some 3,000 teachers were laid off in 1984. Classroom size is increasing. Cutbacks particularly affect immigrant children and children who need special education. Higher education has been cut back, while subsidies to private schools have been increased. 'Back to basics' curriculum and radical streaming between academic and vocational training, combined with a regimented exam system, have degraded the concept of universal education.

But this program of Socred 'restraint' is not limited to economic assaults, service cutbacks and attacks on unionized workers. It is also a political ideology that uses the economic crisis to find greater support from the public for its whole program. It eats away at human rights and democratic rights. This program is not unique to the Social Credit party, but rather finds its inspiration from B. C.'s Fraser Institute, the local Milton Friedman club.

The new Human Rights Bill eliminates the Human Rights Commission and the Human Rights Branch, and replaces them with a government-appointed council that has no enforcement powers. It puts the burden of proof of discrimination on the complainant; it requires proof that there was intention to discriminate; and the complainant pays the cost of complaining.

Other legislation is equally savage. The Residential Tenancy Act has eliminated rent controls and opens the way for massive evictions and rent hikes. Landlords may now evict without cause. This is an invitation to discriminate against racial minorities, lesbians and gays, and welfare recipients. But in all of this there was one thing the Social Credit Government miscalculated badly in the endeavour—the degree of people's anger and their willingness to fight back. Within days after the introduction of the July 1983 legislation, the Lower Mainland Budget Coalition had formed, uniting hundreds of individuals and organizations. This initiative came from the Communist Party, feminists, and leftists active in community groups and unions. Within three weeks, there was a demonstration of 30,000 people in Vancouver.

The Coalition grew overnight. It united tenant groups, feminists, leftists, churches, welfare recipients, seniors' groups, the disabled, students, gays, lesbians, and minority groups. It united conservative groups like the Consumers Association with others like the Sikh Solidarity Association. It drew out many people who had never been politically active before (who now worked with communists and lesbians.) The Coalition met weekly, with 200-300 people attending. Everyone had the right to speak.

The spontaneous demonstration of 30,000 surprised everyone. It particularly surprised the leadership of the B.C. Federation of Labour (BCFL). They were still reeling from the announced legislation and the lack of Socred willingness to be 'reasonable'. They tried to negotiate a solution to this new crisis in the back rooms, but the Socreds weren't interested.

The Socred determination to make no concessions forced the BCFL to consider that it might actually need to unite with community groups. These groups potentially had broader community support on the issues of human rights, social services, and education cutbacks. This support would be needed to build popular support for union demands. The BCFL recognized two things at this point: First, that the movement needed to be broadened around the province, and second, that the BCFL would only be involved if it could gain control of this emerging movement.

In order to achieve these two purposes, the BCFL initiated a province-wide network of coalitions under its control and organized into two separate bodies. The Solidarity Coalitions united community groups, and Operation Solidarity united the trade-union movement.

Operation Solidarity initially included all unions: the B.C. Federation of Labour, the Confederation of Canadian Unions (CCU) affiliates, and non-affiliates alike.

The dual structure of the solidarity movement—divided into the union coalition and the community coalition—was questioned time and again by Coalition activists who pushed the BCFL leadership to clarify its position on joint demands and a joint strategy. But the BCFL repeatedly evaded a clear commitment to a united movement under a united leadership.

The coming months were marked by steadily-growing popular support for solidarity. The coalitions expanded into every major community in B. C. The demonstrations grew larger in response to Bennett's contemptuous disregard for the oppostion movement developing in the streets.

In Victoria, 25,000 turned out in August; and 45,000 were out in Vancouver for August 10.

As the move to the streets increased, the B. C. Federation of Labour nervously tried to spark alternative tactics by launching a petition campaign in August and stalling on further popular mobilization.

By October the Lower Mainland Coalition—which had never completely folded under the leadership of the BCFL—forced the BCFL to go with another demonstration.

The BCFL leadership speculated that only 8,000 would come out, but over 70,000 people marched against the Social Credit convention at the Hotel Vancouver - the largest anti-government protest ever held in B. C. history.

From August through November problems emerged: the lack of a clear political program and strategy, and the political differences within the movement. But these problems were overshadowed by the rapid pace of events.

The political perspective of the BCFL leadership was clearly a problem from the outset. Their slogans were "Restraint is no excuse for repression" and "Restraint is no excuse for revenge". While the B. C. Federation of Labour vacillated, the Solidarity Coalition became firmer and clearer on its demands. The coalition demanded the withdrawal of all the offensive legislation and the full restoration of social services. It demanded that there be no secret or closed negotiations between members of the movement and the government. It called for using all tactics necessary, up to and including a general strike. The BCFL reassured wary coalition members that they would not settle on union issues only, that they would not sell out the coalition, and that they would not compromise on human rights and democratic rights.

But the B. C. Federation of Labour never expected the Social Credit government to be so unwilling to compromise. They wanted to cut a deal with the government—assuming that a little flexing of union muscle would bring the government to the bargaining table.

The story of the B. C. Government Employees Union's (BCGEU) response to the Socreds' all-out attack was an object lesson in this kind of "give a bit and get a bit" tactic.

The central offensive of the Socreds challenged the BCGEU's right to exist. The first response of the BCGEU was to threaten the government with an immediate, full-scale strike of its 40,000 members if a single member was fired without cause. The government went ahead anyway, and fired thousands.

The BCGEU leadership started spinning its wheels, trying to placate an expectant membership by saying it needed to use the grievance procedure first. It tried to keep up a new face of militancy through weekly demonstrations and harassment tactics.

By August, the membership was becoming demoralized with the lack of strike action, even though the BCGEU leadership was talking a more-and-more militant line. The leaders said they would do anything, including going to jail in an illegal strike, but that the membership had to be patient and not put forward the BCFL resolutions calling for a general strike just yet. Parts of the labour movement weren't ready for the general strike, the leaders said.

The strike vote of the BCGEU was over 90 percent in favour. At union meetings the membership called on the union to not limit our fight simply to the negotiation of a new contract and a withdrawal of Bills 2 and 3. The membership also called for fighting the layoffs, not just protecting seniority rights.

While the Coalition called for preparing a general strike, the BCFL leadership reluctantly began to organize an escalating strike strategy.

The smashing of the BCGEU or the smashing of the fundamental principle of seniority would have forced even the reluctant union leadership to an all-out confrontation. The political atmosphere in B. C. at this point was very volatile. It's possible that the government could have been pulled down, but the opposition leadership feared there would be no clear victory for their forces.

On November 1, 1983 the BCGEU strike began in full force. It was a massive shutdown, with a bar minimum of essential services left in place. A week later the B. C. Teachers Federation (BCTF) joined the walkout, in the second wave of the escalating strike strategy.

Notes

Editor's Note: Both the factual description and the political analysis of the events described here by Ruth Annis continue in the following article by David Chudnovsky.

The Impact of the B.C. Government Restraint Program on Teachers

David Chudnovsky

I want to take a look at British Columbia teachers and their involvement in Solidarity and the strike movement. Since I am a teacher, that's the perspective from which I experienced these events. More important, Ruth Annis has summarized events up to the climatic last week of the strike in November 1983, the point at which the education sector came out on strike.[1] So in the course of this paper I will try to take the chronology on from that point, while at the same time making some general comments and trying to draw some lessons and conclusions.

The B. C. Teachers Federation (BCTF) is an organization of about 30,000 members, representing all of the teachers in the public schools of British Columbia, both elementary and secondary, as well as principals and vice-principals and some supervisory personnel. It has been seen by its members, as well as by the government and public at large, as a traditional professional-type organization. However, over the last number of years, the elected Executive of the BCTF has had what can be described as a 'trade-unionist' perspective. The organization itself has a tradition of remarkable democratic structures and procedures.

This trade-unionist executive has attempted over the last five years or so to lead the membership in a more militant and activist direction - with some success. But one measure of the limited nature of this success is that in 1982 the membership voted, about 60 to 40 percent *against* asking the government to change our bargaining structures to allow for the right to strike. That is, they voted to stay with compulsory arbitration. The significance of this referendum vote will shortly become clear.

After the introduction of the budget and its accompanying legislation in July of 1981, the BCTF was an early and active member of Operation Solidarity and the Solidarity Coalitions. An important reason for this enthusiasm on the part of teachers was that massive cutbacks in the public education system had not begun with the July budget. Education cutbacks had been a kind of 'test case' for the Socreds and had been proceeding for two years previously. Along with the cutbacks had gone a furious ideological attack on teachers and public education, carried out by the previous ministers of education. Teachers correctly understood that after the events of July 1983, they would no longer be involved in a lonely and isolated struggle against the Socreds.

In the fall of 1983, B. C. teachers were asked to vote on a strike in conjunction with Operation Solidarity's campaign against the budget and accompanying legislation. Significantly, 59 percent of the membership voted to strike. Thousands of our members, faced with the reality of the Socred attack, had changed their minds about striking. But, equally significantly, another 41 percent were still opposed to strike action. Militants like me were thrilled with the results of the vote, and terrified at its implications. Had we won a decisive battle in the history of our organization, only to see the BCTF ripped apart by a partial strike with thousands of members crossing picket lines?

I will digress from the chronology for a moment to take a look at the demands of Solidarity and the perceptions of teachers (and many thousands of others) as to what the strike was to be about. The Solidarity Coalition reaffirmed many times throughout the summer and fall that its goals were the complete withdrawal of the July budget and its accompanying legislation, and the restoration of social services. To a lesser extent, especially in the early days of the fightback movement, the leaders of Operation Solidarity also took this position. Certainly the President of the BCTF, an active participant in the Operation Solidarity leadership, stressed publicly and in internal communications over and over (to his great credit) that teachers were being asked to strike to defend public education and levels of service and jobs, to oppose the deterioration of human rights and tenants' rights, and to support the rights of families and children as well as to assert the legitimate right of teachers to seniority provisions in their contracts.

With this incessant repetition by the BCTF leadership of the goals of the movement, with the continued intransigence of the government, with the strength and high spirits of the British Columbia Government Employees Union (BCGEU) workers in the first week of the strike, and with the recognition of the democratic traditions of the BCTF among members, we began to see a shift in the position of the membership. On the morning of November 8, more than 90 percent of BCTF members were on strike. Thousands from Colleges, Universities, Canadian Union of Public Employees (CUPE) support staff and others in the education sector came out as well.

They were on strike, as their leaders had convinced them, for the removal of the budget and legislation. In fact it should be remembered that after the initial walkout by government workers, no group that joined the strike and no group that was slated to join the strike was in a formal position to walk out. The strike was being transformed from an economic struggle into a political struggle.

The day before the teachers' strike was to begin, several School Boards sought and were granted injunctions. The Vancouver School Board, largest in the province, had picketing of the schools by the teachers made illegal. What happened in response to this injunction can perhaps say more about the atmosphere in B. C. in November than any number of speeches. Members of Women Against the Budget, the Lower Mainland Solidarity Coalition and the BCGEU spent all night phoning their members and contacts. The next morning, every school in Vancouver had a picket line around it, and several dozen picket lines were maintained by the volunteer pickets who had been organized throughout the night. The rest were put up by maintenance, janitorial, and clerical workers who had not been called upon to do so. Our picket lines in Surrey were a wonderful collection of teachers, CUPE workers, parents, Solidarity Coalition supporters, building trade workers, visiting BCGEU pickets, and others. Clearly, something unusual was going on.

The great strength of the teachers' walkout was shocking—shocking to three different groups.

1. The government was shocked. It was clear that the government had stalled on negotiations with the BCGEU, expecting that the strike movement would fizzle on the morning that the teachers were supposed to join.

2. Teachers themselves were shocked—they had received letters from the Ministry of Education threatening that their teaching certificates could be removed. Many had been intimidated by their local Boards. Yet they had the courage of their convictions, and they found that even in the rain teachers' pickets don't melt.

3. But the group that probably was most shocked by the gathering strike movement were the leadership of the B. C. Federation of Labour and Operation Solidarity. After all, almost 90,000 people were on strike, and thousands more were poised to join them.

Clearly an agreement had become necessary. Negotiations began immediately, at the request of the labour leaders, between the government and the highest levels of Operation Solidarity. An additional incentive for a quick settlement was the public promise made by Operation Solidarity leaders that with the second wave of the strike, and with each additional group that joined, Solidarity would "up the ante". When it was only the government workers who were on strike, Bills 2 and 3 were the issues. With the education sector out on strike, the issues of human rights, tenants' rights, education funding and other so-called 'social issues' were now to follow. It was these very demands which most threatened the structure of collective bargaining, the leadership of Operation Solidarity (OPSOL), the government, and the New Democratic Party (NDP).

Ironically, however it was precisely these demands which had galvanized the public sector, particularly the teachers, and which, because of the grassroots work of the Solidarity Coalitions around the province, were beginning to have a wider impact. It can fairly be said that the situation in the province during the week of the teachers' strike was unstable and in flux. By this I don't mean that there was an imminent revolutionary situation, but rather that it was genuinely unclear which side was going to win the hearts and minds of the people, and that the momentum was certainly with our forces.

But the leadership of Operation Solidarity, no matter what they say now, had never abandoned the business-unionist perspective that seniority rights were the only legitimate issue over which to bargain. Therefore the negotiations which proceeded under the threat of escalation (and further "upping the ante") in the coming weeks were aimed at developing exemptions to Bill 3, which would have wiped out seniority rights. These negotiations took place among the Premier's principal advisor, the President of the Employers Council of B. C., the Vice-President of B. C. Federation of Labour, and representatives of the Government Employees.

And so the stage was set for high drama on the Sunday night, less than a week after the teachers had gone on strike. Word that a settlement was imminent was everywhere. Members of the Lower Mainland Solidarity Coalition (representing for the most part the non-trade unionist elements of the movement) tried desperately to find out what was happening in the negotiations, and to slow down the process so that the agreement reflected their needs and the needs of the wider constituency. But they were frozen out of discussions. An agreement in principle had been achieved, and all that was left to do was for the Vice-President of the B. C. Federation of Labour to fly to Premier Bennett's home town in a private jet to "iron out the details".

The deal was even worse than we might have imagined. Bill 3, which would have abolished seniority rights in the Public Sector, stays on the books but unions can bargain exemptions for their members. On tenants' rights and Human Rights there was to be consultation, but no commitment whatsoever, from the government. Legislation on these issues has since been introduced and passed in the legislature; it differs only marginally from what was proposed in July 1983. On education funding, a commitment was made to put the money saved during the strike back into the system, but so far not a penny of that money has been seen by the School Boards.

A measure of the drama we experienced that Sunday night, and of the opportunity that was missed, is that despite the fact that the President of the BCTF had appeared on T.V. and told our members to report for work the next morning (by then he was taking the same position as the other Operation Solidarity leaders), I still received call after call throughout the night from our local members and school strike contacts. These people wanted the news confirmed by their local leadership, and were ready to stay out if they were asked, although not one of them had ever been on strike before. We found out later that similar reactions were common across the whole province. (It must be said, however, that there were also locals in which strength was beginning to ebb, and there were dozens of injunctions coming to court on the coming Monday and Tuesday).

I want to look at some of the issues of democracy as they affected our members and others, in order to try to explain some of what happened and to attempt to derive some lessons. The *key* problem of democracy was that tens of thousands of workers were on strike for a set of demands which the leadership of Operation Solidarity were never committed to winning. For the business-union leaders, the mass mobilization was merely a particularly good hand in a game of high-stakes poker played by all the old rules. They never intended to fight for the Coalitions' demands; but we were naive enough to believe that they would be forced to do so by the momentum of events. This was a critical error.

From the beginning, the strategy of an escalating strike with escalating demands left too many escape routes for both the government and the B. C. Federation of Labour leadership, while simultaneously leaving thousands of trade unionists vulnerable to injunctions. Many rank and filers in my union (you see at the beginning I called it an organization and now I call it a Union), and many of our members who had never been involved in strikes before, had enough common sense to know that everyone should have been called out at the same time—or that, at the very least, the escalation would need to be daily rather than bi-weekly.

We didn't fight hard enough for a structural involvement of the Coalitions in the negotiations. While Operation Solidarity was supposed to be simply a component part of the Coalitions, this was really a fiction. It was the Operation Solidarity leadership, not even the union membership, who made all the key strike decisions. This leadership could not have accepted a democratic movement—it was simply not in their nature to do so. They had never before operated democratically—why should they start in the middle of a crisis? Furthermore, to have accepted democratic procedures would have been to encourage the formation and birth of a new labour and people's movement in B. C.—one which would have left these leaders out in the cold.

The negotiations took place in secret, even though the Coalition voted several times that there should be no secret deals. We should have taken our own demand for open negotiations much more seriously, and insisted on it, as did the Solidarity movement in Poland.

Finally, a word about the aftermath. Another important anti-democratic trend is that the leaders of the strike have painted the November agreement as at least a partial, and important, victory. This includes the president of the BCTF who played, at least up to the time of the strike, the most positive role of any of the union leaders. And while especially in the case of teachers there were some gains (we had never had seniority rights before), it does nothing but spread cynicism, demoralization and despair to invent silver linings for very black clouds.

Notes

1. See the preceding article by Ruth Annis in this volume (editors).

The Politics of "Restraint" and the Response of the Trade-Union Bureaucracy in B.C.

Marion Pollack

On July 7, 1983 British Columbia heard about the 'new reality' for the first time. On that infamous date, the Social Credit Government of B. C. introduced a draconian legislative package. Virtually no group of British Columbians would escape unscathed. Under the guise of restraint, the Social Credit Program eliminated rent controls and rental protection in B.C., abolished the Human Rights Commission, privatized a number of social service agencies, extended provincial government control over local school boards' finances, and dissolved the alcohol and drug commission. The legislative package also included a frontal attack on labour by removing the right of government employees to negotiate job security, work hours, transfers etc. It gave public sector employers the right to lay-off and fire people without just case, and extended wage controls. For the first time in British Columbia the 'ability to pay' was enshrined as the primary determination of wages and salaries. In addition the Employment Standards Branch was abolished, wiping out protection for non-union workers.

The primary reason behind the 'restraint program' was that the government wanted to reallocate its resources away from wages and services towards mega-projects. It is no coincidence that two years after the restraint program was introduced, the B.C. Government has introduced legislation to create special economic zones. B.C. cabinet ministers have been quoted as saying that they want to transform this province into the "intellectual Philippines of the North".

The response to this restraint program was virtually instantaneous. Opposition groups sprang up immediately throughout the province. The two that received the most media attention were the Solidarity Coalitions and Operation Solidarity. The former were coalitions of community groups and some unions; the latter was exclusively a union formation. Despite the fact that most press coverage went to these two groups, it was clear that the opposition to the Socred package was widespread. Anti-budget groups sprang up everywhere. In Vancouver, for example, some of the organizations that emerged included the Disabled Peoples Coalition

Against the Budget, Cultural Workers Against the Budget, Gays and Lesbians Against the Budget, and Women Against the Budget.

Operation Solidarity was formed on July 15, 1983. Initiated by the B.C. Federation of Labour (BCFL), it included representatives of most unions in British Columbia. In many ways this represented a historic moment, as it was the first time that both affiliates and non-affiliates to the B.C. Federation of Labour had met together for a common purpose.

The basis of unity for Operation Solidarity was the following ten point progam (BCFL, 1983):

> "1. That all unions in B.C., through bilateral agreements respect, for the next four years, each other's sanctity of established bargaining rights.
> 2. That, under the leadership of the B.C. Federation of Labour Executive Council, we establish a Trade Union Solidarity Committee, which will be comprised of the Executive Council of the B.C. Federation of Labour and fair representation from non-affiliated unions, for the purpose of mounting an effective fight-back campaign against the vicious attack on government on social, economic, human and trade union rights.
> 3. That the B.C. trade union movement, under the leadership of the B.C. Federation of Labour, enter into a broad-based coalition with other groups such as the churches, the unemployed, peace groups, tenants' organizations, minority groups, small business groups, women's groups and any other groups who have a sense of moral and social responsibility to the overall community, for the purpose of:
>
> > a. Opposing the brutal attack of government against the social, economic and democratic fibre of this province;
> > b. To help individuals and groups directly affected by this government onslaught; and
> > c. To start broad public discussion in this province in an effort to develop public policies for a social and economic recovery alter native designed to meet the real needs of people in the 1980's.
>
> 4. That we ask non-affiliates to pay an amount equal to Federation monthly per capita into a defence fund for the purpose of partially funding Operation Solidarity.
> 5. That we set up regional Trade Union Solidarity Committees who, under the direction of the Provincial Committee, will do the work of building the coalition. These regional committees will work though the framework of local Labour Councils and will be involved in the overall mobilization.

6. All trade unions in the province will hold special local union meetings to discuss with the membership the implications of the budget and the accompanying legislation on workers and the general public. Local unions shall engage in letter writing campaigns, post-card campaigns and lobbying. They shall also appoint delegates to the local Labour Council Solidarity Committees and also mobilize their membership for mass rallies.
7. The B.C. Federation of Labour, through the Communication Advisory Committee will start a massive membership and public education program in the form of radio spots, newspaper advertisements, billboards, pamphlets and briefing notes, beginning on Monday, July 18th, 1983. This program will run for a minimum of two months.
8. Operation Solidarity will hold its first in a series of mass public rallies on Wednesday, July 27th, 1983 starting at 3:00 p.m. at the steps of the Provincial Legislature in Victoria. All other groups which will form the broad-based coalition will be asked to participate. The Committee will set into motion organizational talent to assist regional coalitions to plan and execute regional mass rallies.
9. The Provincial Trade Union Solidarity Committee will work out all the major policy decisions on the fight-back campaign as far as B.C. Labour is concerned. Its chief spokesperson will be the President of the B.C. Federation Labour. Each trade union group shall agree to allow the chief spokesperson of the Provincial Trade Union Solidarity Committee to make all public representations on behalf of the Committee and its constituents.
10. Operation Solidarity will renew its mandate every twelve months through a delegated conference."

A number of unions in the Confederation of Canadian Unions (CCU) felt the point on no raiding was gratuitous. As a result, they were forced to leave Operation Solidarity.

The leadership of Operation Solidarity was largely dominated by the officers of the B.C. Federation of Labour. For example, the "Trade Union solidarity steering committee", which served coordinating committee functions, consisted of 16 members of the BCFL executive, staff members from both the Canadian Labour Congress (CLC) and the B.C. Federation of Labour, and seven other trade unionists.

The Solidarity Coalitions were the community arm of the fight-back. There were Coalitions in most towns and cities in British Columbia. These coalitions were very diverse, encompassing church groups, anti-poverty organizations, college and university groups, lesbian and gay organizations, women's groups, daycare and school groups, civil liberties groups, ethnic groups, tenants organizations, human rights groups and seniors' organizations.

Operation Solidarity (OPSOL) had no structure. The 1983 report to the B.C. Federation of Labour Convention stated that

> the crisis nature of much of the past several months has led to many hurried meetings, and many of the decisions have been made by the steering committee. In fact, Operation Solidarity had been run with a very informal structure. It has no formal constitution or bylaws, and runs on goodwill and unity of purpose.

Although Operation Solidarity was supposed to be in partnership with the Solidarity Coalitions, in reality there was a master-and-servant relationship. Operation Solidarity had total control of the money. Any action by the Solidarity Coalitions that involved any spending of money had to be approved by Operation Solidarity. A case in point was the October 15 demonstration in Vancouver, which was billed as a demonstration giving Bennett "one last chance". The proposal for the demonstration originated with the Lower Mainland Solidarity Coalition, who wanted to hold it in front of the hotel where the Socreds were hiding their annual convention. It required a series of negotiations with the leadership of Operation Solidarity not only to get the demonstration endorsed but to determine the route. There were many discussions with OPSOL leaders about whether the demonstration could go around one side, two sides, or three sides of the hotel.

In early July a group called together by the Vancouver and District Labour Council unemployment committee met together to form the Lower Mainland Budget Coalition. The makeup of this coalition included trade unions, community groups, church groups, and women's organizations.

This group did not have the official sanction of the B.C. Federation of Labour. It organized the first public antibudget rally on July 23, initially without the support of the B.C. Federation of Labour.

The weekly meetings of the Lower Mainland Budget Coalition attracted over 300 people. It was an alive, and militant, body.

However, things changed drastically as of August 5, 1983. The regular meeting of the Lower Mainland Budget Coalition was attended by the leadership of both the Vancouver and District and the New Westminster Labour Councils, who announced they were setting up a Lower Mainland Solidarity Coalition. This would parallel exactly the Lower Mainland Budget Coalition. It was a takeover. The Solidarity Coalition had the official endorsation of the bucks, so it got the control.

The Provincial Solidarity Coalition was the baby of Operation Solidarity. The 1983 report to the B.C. Federation of Labour Convention stated:

> ...of equal significance and importance was the decision of Operation Solidarity to take the lead in the creation and development of the Solidarity Coalition. The labour movement often has united with various community groups on an ad hoc basis; however, their decision to form a structured coalition and to accept decision making by that coalition, represented an important innovation with profound ongoing implications.

The report goes on to state that the coalition was funded by Operation Solidarity.

The acceptance of the decisions made by the Provincial Solidarity coalition did not go as far as allowing the delegates to elect their own steering committee. The choice came rather from a decision made by Operation Solidarity.

The rest of the steering committee were people either appointed or elected from various sectors. In reality the Provincial Solidarity Coalition was a body with little positive power. It could not make major decisions, as those were under the auspices of Operation Solidarity. It could not make major decisions concerning the direction of the Solidarity Coalitions, as it had no base.

In retrospect one of the primary roles of the Provincial Solidarity Coalition seemed to be that of exerting negative power over the local Solidarity Coalitions. For example, it authorized Art Kube to make statements denouncing "Luncheon at Gracie's," an action by Women against the Budget, prior to it occurring. It also strongly advised the Lower Mainland Solidarity Coalition to sit tight when they saw a sell-out coming down.

The steering committee of the Provincial Solidarity Coalition was by no means homogeneous. There were always significant discussions and debates.

The Provincial Solidarity Coalition initiated a petition campaign. It also developed a week-by-week program: one week was health care week; the next week, education, and so on. However, in many cases these weeks were started without discussion with the affected groups. As the weeks dragged on, it became clearer and clearer that the Provincial Solidarity Coalition did not have the base to carry out these activities.

All this was a prelude to the night of November 13, 1983. On that evening Jack Munro, with the full knowledge and support of the Operation Solidarity steering committee, boarded a jet to Kelowna. When he returned later that night, a deal had been worked out between the Social Credit government and Operation Solidarity. It was a sellout.

Reasons for the Sellout

In the next section of this article I will briefly analyze some of the reasons why I believe this sellout occurred. These include:

- the fact that the trade-union leadership was not willing to take on extra-parliamentary action.
- the fact that the trade-union movement did not have a political program to address the question of restraint.
- the fact that the private sector union leadership did not prepare its membership to participate in a general strike.
- the fact that there was no political alternative. The New Democratic Party (NDP) was not prepared to fight an election, and virtually abstained from the fight.
- the fact that the left was in disarray.

It is clear that the leaders of Operation Solidarity did not want to undertake extra-parliamentary action. This was not because of the individual attributes of any leader, but rather a legacy of the current historical era. After 1945 there was a massive expansion of the labour force, and the growth of large-scale industry. These factors led to considerable unrest among workers. The end product of this unrest was the development of a labour-capital pact, which codified labour-management relations in law. As a result there was increasing stability and growth in the trade-union movement. However, this was accomplished at a fairly heavy price. The trade-off was a loss of dynamism for the labour movement as well as more reliance on legal methods of settling disputes. The leadership of Operation Solidarity are part of this continuum. After July 7, they opted for petitions, attempts at conciliation, clandestine meetings with the premier, and the development of formal structures.

Early on in the struggle the leadership was opposed to mass mobilizations. They were initially hostile to the July 23 anti-budget rally. They publicly condemned an action of Women Against the Budget, before it had even occurred. Instead they opted for small-scale and controllable actions, such as dogging cabinet ministers. The public was not informed beforehand, nor invited to participate.

The leadership of Operation Solidarity emphasized trade-union issues. They argued that these were the main issues that had to be dealt with. At a provincial conference of the Solidarity Coalitions in early fall, Art Kube, spokesperson for both Operation Solidarity and the Provincial Solidarity

Coalition, stated that the aim of the struggle was to get rid of Bills 2 and 3 (the bills that affected collective bargaining). Meanwhile the Solidarity Coalitions had an agenda that included repeal of all the bills, and the expansion of social services. Because these two groups had such different agendas the leadership of Operation Solidarity wanted control. They engineered the maneuver that put the Lower Mainland Budget Coalition directly under the control of the Provincial Solidarity Coalitions.

The participants in the Lower Mainland Solidarity Coalition were explicitly told that they had no right to either have input into or to made demands on the unions. However, when the strike occurred members of this coalition were called upon by the trade-union movement to staff picket lines in front of schools. Some of the first groups to call for a general strike were the Lower Mainland Solidarity Coalition and Women Against The Budget.

Despite the influence of Operation Solidarity, a number of unions mobilized on the basis of opposition to the entire legislative package. For example, the Vancouver Local of the Canadian Union of Postal Workers voted to participate in the general strike on the basis of the attacks against human, social and health care rights.

The leadership of Operation Solidarity was also terrified of extra-parliamentary action, which would have required a drastic change in terms of democracy and structures in the trade-union movement. This is confirmed by a statement made by International Wood Workers of America (IWA) regional President Jack Munro. He said that:

> We were headed for a major disaster. The trade-union movement would have blown itself apart and there was all kinds of shrapnel around that would have affected some other people. It was basically out of control. (*Vancouver Sun*, 22 May 1985).

In part, the leadership rationalized their fear of extra-parliamentary action by consistently underestimating the rank and file. Several days prior to the October 15 demonstration, Art Kube stated that it would draw about 8,000 people. Over 70,000 attended.

The leadership of Operation Solidarity as well as the NDP, and to a lesser extent the coalitions, did not have a program to address the economic crisis. As a result they failed to politically educate their members. While many unions distributed information on the draconian nature of the budget, there was no education on the issue of restraint. The billboards erected by OPSOL read "Restraint is no excuse for revenge", thereby buying the argument that restraint is necessary. This argument was echoed by Jack Munro, who said that he was in favour of restraint. The problem, he said, was how the Socreds were doing it.

The refusal to take on the issue of restraint was completely in line with the reluctance to take up extra-parliamentary action. The fight against restraint would have had to have been a fight that went beyond the ballot box and challenged the fundamental assumptions about the B.C. economy.

As a result, there was no attempt by Operation Solidarity to develop and popularize an alternative economic strategy. To their credit some groups, like the Communist Party of Canada and Women Against The Budget, had slowly begun this process.

In the private sector, there was virtually no mobilization or educational initiative. This is exemplified by the New Westminster Local of the IWA. In late October the local set out a circular letter to the membership commenting on the upcoming municipal elections and the current state of the IWA negotiations. Not a word was mentioned about Solidarity.

This lack of mobilization and education allowed Bennett to drive a wedge in the fightback movement. In a fireside chat shortly before November 1, Premier Bill Bennett address the concerns of private sector workers by rhetorically asking: "Where were the public sectors when you were laid off?" Given the role of Munro in this struggle, the lack of private sector involvement can only be seen as deliberate. This lack of response paved the way for 1984 changes to the B.C. Labour Code.

The labour alliance with the NDP is also responsible for the sellout. The NDP filibustered in the House and sat through all night legislative sessions, but did little else. While many constituency associations and rank-and-file New Democrats were active in the coalitions, both the provincial party and the sitting MLA's abstained from the struggle. When Dave Barrett, the NDP provincial leader, was dragged out of the House for unparliamentary behaviour, he did nothing about it, in spite of calls for him to barnstorm the province. The NDP pushed moderation at all costs.

The NDP was terrified of the prospect of an election, believing that they could not win it, and that the Socreds would be returned with an overwhelming majority. Given their defeat in early May, 1983, due to their refusal to campaign on policy issues, this fear may have been justified. Additionally, the NDP did not want to be tied to the "radicals" in Solidarity, believing that such an alliance would make it impossible for them to appeal to the people in the political centre.

Throughout the entire struggle there was no serious discussion about the need for a call to defeat the government, and, more importantly, no debate on who might form the new government. At the Lower Mainland Solidarity Coalition meeting a motion was passed calling for a new election if the legislation was not repealed. This begged the question of government.

Both the NDP and OPOL felt that the struggle was a four-year one, to be eventually won at the ballot box. The following report adopted at the

November 1983 B.C. Federation of Labour Convention exemplifies this outlook:

> It is only regrettable that the resources devoted to Operation Solidarity could not have been found earlier in the year when a provincial election was being fought. It is only with the removal of the Bennett government that a lasting form of social progress can be achieved. We must not lose sight of that continuing battle that must be fought at the ballot box. While we must continue our fight against all repressive legislation, we must channel our energies in such a way that they will also achieve results at the ballot box. The Operation Solidarity Program must be viewed in that long-term context if we are to achieve the results we desire.

The general strike never occurred. Instead the leadership of Operation and Solidarity developed a program of escalating job action. In November 1, the British Columbia Government Employees Union (BCGEU) went out, and on November 8 the teachers, universities and other educational workers followed suit. Civic unions were slated to go out on the 13th, and so on. This escalating series of job actions allowed OPSOL to maintain control. In addition, it allowed both the union leadership and the Socred Government to pick and choose the issues that they were going to deal on. A full-fledged general strike would have made this impossible.

The left got swept up in this process. We believed that the trade-union movement was the only group capable of carrying out a general strike. As a result we concentrated on pushing the bureaucracy to the left. We were seduced by the doubletalk of the leadership, and blinded by the fantasy of a general strike. We got caught up in the trap of unity, and rarely criticized the leadership. But the left's main weakness was that we failed to develop a left opposition that included broader social perspectives and a class-struggle program. The left was present, but not united. In addition, many groups got too immersed in Coalition activity, and failed to carry out independent actions.

The refusal of both the trade-union leadership and the NDP to develop programs and to engage in extra-parliamentary action resulted in Operation Solidarity approaching the head of the B.C. Employers Council to make a deal. On November 13, the strike was solid and we had a winning hand. But the trade-union leadership is not too good at playing poker.

The union bureaucracy's refusal to address social issues has resulted in new attacks on social services. The newly-privatized social service agencies are finding their funding has been drastically cut; expenditures on health care have plummetted; numerous hospitals beds have been closed.

Education funding has been slashed, resulting in massive layoffs and large class sizes. Welfare rates have been frozen.

Women's services particularly have been attacked. Drop-in centres for parents have been closed, and the Vancouver Status of Women lost all its provincial funding. Vancouver Transition House, a shelter for battered women, has been closed.

The response has been sporadic. A few community groups and unions have carried out small scale activities, but the leadership has not followed suit.

Again a resolution passed at the 1983 BCFL Convention provides further insight into this process. It give a clear indication that social issues were not a priority in the labour movement. It stated that:

> ...all affiliates commit themselves to the taking of whatever action necessary when called upon by the Fed, to protect workers' rights from repressive legislative changes such as indicated in the Labour Code. A commitment must also be made to assist all organizations in obtaining exemptions from the odious dismissal provisions of the Public Sector Restraint Act.

Interestingly enough, when the amendments to the Labour Code came down, there was almost no response from the Federation.

The struggle has been largely demobilized. People feel that they have been silenced by the actions of Solidarity. The tensions between the trade-union movement and community groups have increased. The level of trust has decreased.

We have learned a lot through this process. It is becoming clearer to us that we have to begin a serious discussion on how and in what form we are going to build an alternative movement—one that has the determination to wage a concerted and serious fight.

Acknowledgements

I would like to thank Marcy Cohen and Jackie Larkin for their help in the preparation of this article.

SECTION III

Class Formation and Class Consciousness

Introduction

In the wake of the expansion of private enterprise into tertiary services and rapid growth of public sector employment after World War Two, followed by the widespread initiatives to introduce new technologies and reorganize workplaces in current hard times, the recomposition of class forces in advanced capitalist societies has continued to be a topic of much dispute over the past generation. Many analysts have emphasized the importance of the growth of intermediate strata situated between capitalist owners and industrial workers, and considerable recent research has been devoted to delineating the contours of such imputed 'new middle class' groupings.

In the lead article in this section, Peter Meiksins provides a critical summary review of new middle-class theories. He argues that much of the emphasis on the distinctiveness of intermediate strata has been misplaced, leading analysts to ignore the common objective condition shared by most white collar employees and industrial workers alike: their relationship of exploitation by employers as subordinated wage labourers. Meiksins' argument suggests that the fundamental division of class interests between those with actual ownership of the means of production and the vast majority who are essentially sellers of their labour power provides the most relevant objective basis for the formation of a working-class political movement. He concludes by emphasizing the obstacles that the heterogeneity of wage labourers, in terms of skill levels and places in the labour process—in addition to the mystification of bourgeois ideology, repressive state forces and capitalist divide-and-rule tactics—present to the emergence of class consciousness and concerted political action among the contemporary working-class.

The next two papers examine recent expressions of class consciousness in Canadian settings by people in different objective class locations. Julian Tanner explores the views of Edmonton manual workers about their own class identities and images of class structure. He finds that most manual workers do believe Canada is a class society and, whether they are inclined to use a 'middle class' or 'working class' label, see themselves as part of a broadly defined group of wage and salary earners in the middle of the social structure. But such class awareness is not found to be a central and active part of these manual workers' identities. In particular, subjective class identity is not significantly related to their voting preferences, a condition that Tanner attributes at least partly to the dearth of working-class political parties and radical trade unions in Canada.

D. W. Livingstone looks more specifically at political party preferences and their relationship to different class locations and levels of class consciousness in Ontario in recent years. He finds that, since the late 1970s, corporate capitalists have expressed a high level of consciousness of their own class interest as well as strong majority support for the Progressive Conservative Party. Those in all subordinated class positions have displayed more contradictory forms of class consciousness, as well as growing support through the early 1980s for the Progressive Conservative Party. While employees with a clear sense of working-class interests opposed to capitalist interests have remained more likely than others to prefer the New Democratic Party (NDP), this association does not appear to have strengthened in recent years. In fact, the level of oppositional working-class consciousness may have declined, and some types of class-conscious employees, most notably industrial workers, have expressed growing disaffection for the NDP. Thus, both the Tanner and Livingstone papers provide ample indications of continuing obstacles to the emergence of coherent class consciousness and concerted political action among Canadian working people in hard times.

The final paper by Tom Langford and Dieter Neumann considers the relevance of the university as an educational resource to be used in overcoming such obstacles. Writing from the vantage point of shop-floor activists who have recently entered university, they point to a number of financial, programmatic and political factors that currently inhibit critical social inquiry in Canadian universities. But they also emphasize the importance of a sound and sophisticated theoretical understanding of society for working-class leaders in order to strengthen the intellectual independence of working people. They call upon those university-based intellectuals who have genuine working-class sympathies and a critical grasp of Marxist theory to reach out and encourage the creation of independent workers' study groups which can contribute to the sustained growth of the socialist movement among working people.

White Collar Workers and the Process of Class Formation

Peter Meiksins

As the 20th century has progressed, increasing numbers of the socialist 'orthodoxies' of the 19th century have been called into question. One of the pieces of received wisdom that has taken a particularly severe battering pertains to the concept of class. The traditional socialist view of capitalist social structure was relatively simple. Capitalist society, according to this view, tended to divide into two classes (industrial workers and capitalists) who were locked in mortal combat. Out of this conflict, the industrial working class, which constituted the vast majority, would triumph over the much smaller group of capitalists and create a socialist society devoid of class divisions.

This analysis, however, has become increasingly difficult to sustain in the 20th century. The industrial working class is not longer (if it ever was) the majority in most capitalist countries and a wide variety of white-collar workers has appeared, including clerks, professionals, administrators, technicians and so on. One need not be a proponent of the view that the industrial worker is an endangered species[1] to realize that socialist theory needs to analyze the nature and future role of these strata if socialism is to remain relevant to the countries of the developed West.

This article is an attempt to stimulate discussion of the role of the 'new middle class' in socialist politics. It begins by briefly considering some of the theoretical issues involved in the class analysis of these strata. Before we can develop a meaningful political analysis of these workers, we need to know whether they are by nature the opponents, the potential allies, or even a part of the traditional working class. It is the contention of this article that most neo-Marxist class analyses of the 'new middle class' are unsatisfactory—in their place, it proposes a reformulated version of the Marxist theory of class. This theoretical reformulation leads to a number of important political conclusions, some of which are briefly sketched out in a concluding section.

The Concept of Class

In attempting to develop a viable Marxist class analysis of the 'new middle class', it may be useful to begin by reminding ourselves of the weaknesses of the traditional alternatives. Many academic sociologists, following Max

Weber, see class as defined by certain 'objective' attributes of individuals, such as income, education or prestige. For example, it is argued that if one's income is above a certain point, one is middle class; if it is below it, one is lower class (the precise manner by which this 'point' is determined is, as the non-sociologist will guess, a highly complex, mysterious business). A great deal of academic class analysis has been based on one of the many variations on this general theme. The other motif in academic analysis of class has been a reliance on "subjective" criteria. Thus, many sociologists would argue that what really matters in identifying classes is what 'people' say classes are. There are variations here too—for some, each individual's view of his or her own class membership is critical, while for others it is how people evaluate the class position of *others*. Nevertheless, the common thread is the emphasis on the relative importance of subjective definitions of class.

Each of these approaches points to important and real aspects of contemporary social stratification. However, neither is really adequate as a general theory of class, for they both leave us with the impression that the existence of classes is somehow accidental. For example, consider the influential 'objective' approach which regards the distribution of income as the basis of class. The distribution of income in capitalist societies, as is well known, is not characterized by sharp breaks. Consequently, the appearance of classes—i.e., groups of people with a sense of *shared* difference and even of shared antagonism to other groups of people—is difficult to explain. After all, why should the differences between, say, $15,000 and $17,000 be any more significant than that between $17,000 and $19,000. The sociologist, thus, is forced into one of two unacceptable strategies. Either she must *arbitrarily* decide that a particular point in the income scale is the point around which classes polarize, or else she must argue that, at certain times, for purely contingent reasons, some factor other than income comes into play, giving significance to what are otherwise relatively meaningless differences in income. Either way, the regular, consistent appearance of patterns of class conflict is not adequately explained.

A similar critique may be made of the "subjective" sociological approach to class. For this type of analysis, classes only exist if people say they do; if everyone says that they are "middle class", then there is only one class in that society. This, however, begs the question of how two essentially *similar* social structures may lie beneath radically different perceptions of class. How, for example, is one to explain the very different patterns of class relations characteristic of most Western countries in the 1950s and later in those same countries in the 1960s? Either one is forced to argue that people's perceptions of class bear absolutely no relation to the real, "objective" world (which would make the appearance of class very difficult to explain); or, one is forced to contend that structurally similar societies sometimes are characterized by classes, while at other times they are not, for reasons that are not at all clear. Moreover, if we consider the array of institutions in capitalist societies that help to shape perceptions of class (schools, government, media, etc.), many of which seem to be primarily concerned with convincing people that there are no such things as classes, it seems clear that we should be careful not to accept as accurate uncritically subjective perceptions of class. It may very well be that it is just as arbitrary to accept them as "correct" descriptions of class as it is to impose on reality a class boundary set by the sociologist.

The basic difficulty with all of these approaches is that they attempt to define classes *apart from* class conflict. Since they refuse to regard contemporary society as inherently divided by a fundamental conflict of interests, the appearance of antagonistic groups of people becomes very difficult to explain. Ultimately, they wind up arguing that just a little less mobility, or more unemployment, or some other comparable shift, is enough to "suddenly" produce classes (or at least class conflict) where there were none before. Yet, it seems questionable whether such a relatively minor change as a slowing down of mobility is enough in itself to cause classes to appear. Moreover, there is no consistency here at all—sometimes classes form when unemployment is high, sometimes when it is low; sometimes they form when wages decline, sometimes when they rise. It is in contrast to these approaches that the basic superiority of the Marxist analysis of class may be seen.

For Marx, it was meaningless to define class apart from class conflict—classes are by definition rooted in a fundamental conflict of interest built into the exploitative relationship between capital and labour. It is on the basis of this conflict that classes arise—unlike academic sociologists, Marx has no difficulty accounting for the existence of warring classes. This approach is also able to account for those situations where class conflict is *not* overt and well-organized. Thus, Marx was aware that the intensity of class feeling and conflict can vary as battles are won and lost and as conditions change. But a relatively low level of class feeling does not indicate the absence of class—it signifies rather the temporary success of a variety of forces (such as the state and capitalist ideology) in drawing people's attention away from, or papering over, the basic conflict that is *always* present in capitalist society.

Marxist Analyses of the "New Middle Class"

In its broad outline, then, Marx's class analysis avoids the major difficulty encountered by academic approaches to class. The problem, however, is how it may be applied to contemporary capitalist society, which appears to include far more than just workers and capitalists. As has already been indicated, a number of attempts have been made to 'up-date' Marxist theory to account for the complexities of contemporary social structure. A brief discussion of the general theses that have been advanced will allow us to identify their shortcomings and to underline the need to re-think the Marxist approach to contemporary class structure.

One neo-Marxist approach may be loosely called the 'new class' theory. It includes a wide range of arguments, all of which posit the existence under contemporary capitalism of an intermediate class composed of relatively privileged professional, intellectual, technical and administrative workers.[2] The most influential Marxist version of this thesis has been the Ehrenreichs' critique of the Professional- Managerial Class (PMC). As their criteria for designating this group a new class, the Ehrenreichs point to its a) non-ownership of the means of production and its b) role in the reproduction of capitalist social relations. How adequate is this as a Marxist definition of class? We cannot take the Ehrenreichs to task for failing to identify a basis for conflict between this group and the bourgeoisie, for it is precisely on this conflict that the Ehrenreichs' argument is strongest. It is rather on the relationship between the PMC and the *working* class that the argument is weak. The Ehrenreichs clearly indicate the basis for conflict between the PMC and the bourgeoisie in pointing to the former's employee status. Given that they are employees, members of the PMC, like *all* employees, are exposed to various kinds of conflict with the owners of the means of production.

However, the Ehrenreichs are less successful in establishing that there is a *class* barrier between the PMC and the traditional working class. In essence, they point to the PMC's role in reproducing capitalist social relations as the basis for such a conflict. Yet this confuses a group's function with its class position. It may be that the activities of teachers, or engineers, or administrators in capitalist society are sometimes inimical to the interests of industrial workers. But the same may be said of the seeming short-run conflict between the interests of most workers and those of munitions workers, or public sector workers whose wages are subsidized by the working class as a whole. One must be careful not to assume that a group of workers is in a different class simply because of a distinctive function. Indeed, we must ask why the Ehrenreichs distinguish between labour and capital using the traditional Marxist criterion of relationship to the means of production, yet use another criterion (function) in identifying the PMC.

The only other argument which the Ehrenreichs employ in positing a class distinction between the PMC and the working class is to point to their relative privilege. Yet this is to retreat to the type of class theory employed by academic sociology that we have already seen to be unsatisfactory. In short, while the Ehrenreichs point to some important sociological differences between the PMC and the 'working class' they do not succeed in showing that there is a *class* barrier between them.

A second approach to the class analysis of the 'new middle class' focuses on the question of 'control'. The leading exponent of this school—Erik Olin Wright—argues that because certain types of workers (managers and supervisors, semi-autonomous employees, and small employers) have partial degrees of control over either the means of production, the labour process or investment, they are not fully bourgeois, proletarian or petit bourgeois (Wright, 1978). Instead, Wright argues, they "occupy" what he refers to as "contradictory class locations" which are "objectively torn between class forces". Wright is undoubtedly correct in arguing that degrees of autonomy or supervisory authority may contribute to a particular group of workers' sense of being different. But is he justified in seeing these as constitutive of partial class barriers?

To begin with, we must point out that Wright's analysis is a static class analysis, similar to the sociological approaches discussed above. Instead of focusing on conflictual *relations* among different groups, Wright argues that the possession of certain characteristics (i.e., control) is the basis for class in capitalist society. Consequently we must ask him, where is the line to be drawn? How much control does one have to have (5 percent? 10 percent? 20 percent?) to be excluded from the working class?[3] One suspects that it is as difficult to avoid arbitrarily drawing class barriers within Wright's analysis as it is in most sociological class analyses.

Furthermore, Wright tends to make too little of the fact that the vast majority of these he regards as occupying contradictory class locations share with the 'working class' their status as employees who do *not* control the means of production (obviously, a small number of higher managers are a different matter). Wright seems to feel that this shared characteristic is *overridden* by the fact that certain workers are in partial control of various aspects of their jobs. Yet, is it the case that a moderate amount of control over one's job is of such great importance that it creates a partial conflict of interest (hence a partial class barrier) among different categories of workers, *in spite of* the fact that they are all wage-labourers? And is the difference between top management's control over resources and the types of control characteristic of 'middling' corporate positions simply a question of degree, as Wright's analysis implies? Like the Ehrenreichs', Wright's analysis points to important sociological differences among various types of workers, but it fails to provide an adequate justification for regarding these differences as constitutive of class.

The final neo-Marxist approach we need to consider is that developed by Nicos Poulantzas (1974). This approach emphasizes three important Marxist distinctions—that between productive and unproductive labour, that between mental and manual labour, and that between supervisory and non-supervisory labour—in its analysis of the 'new middle class'. These concepts have been extensively discussed elsewhere (Gough, 1972; Meiksins, 1981), hence we need not define them in detail here. We do need to concern ourselves, however, with the accuracy of Poulantzas' contention that only those workers who are performing productive, manual, non-supervisory labour may be considered part of the working class.[4]

To begin with, there are serious problems involved in equating the distinction between productive and unproductive labour with a class distinction. Marx's analysis of productive labours in capitalist society emphasizes that they are exploited in the sense that they produce surplus value. Unproductive laborers, in contrast, produce no surplus value. Yet, many of them *are* exploited. Salaried unproductive workers, like their productive counterparts, are paid only for their labour-power, not for the actual amount of labour they perform. While this does not produce surplus value, since the labour is not embodied in commodities, it *does* constitute exploitation. Productive and unproductive salaried workers alike are in a similar relation of conflict with their employers—because the latter have a permanent interest in keeping their wages down. Just as commercial or banking capital differ from industrial capital while remaining capital, so do salaried unproductive workers differ from productive workers while remaining workers.[5]

Similar difficulties arise when one attempts to use the mental/labour labour distinction as the basis for class analysis. Braverman has demonstrated that the increasing separation of mental and manual labour is the result of a long historical process. As the capitalist labour process has evolved, the two types of labour have increasingly been assigned to different workers. This analysis raises questions about Poulantzas' allocation of mental and manual labour to different classes. When both types of labour were performed by the same worker, there was no question of his/her belonging simultaneously to two different classes. Moreover, Marx argues that the production of commodities is increasingly performed not by individuals but by large numbers of workers, some mental, some manual, working within what he calls a collective labour process. He was aware that there could be hostility between the two types of labour, especially since the labour process is not arranged cooperatively (as it might be), but as a hierarchy with mental labour in a position of relative authority.[6] Nevertheless, this does not alter the fact that mental labourers are also wage-labourers and are part of the collective labour process which is *collectively exploited* by capital.

Furthermore, Poulantzas' use of the mental/manual distinction seems to suggest, at least implicitly, that it is *ideology* that is the basic determinant of class. Poulantzas would classify clerical workers as mental labour and, on the strength of that alone, 'disqualify' them as members of the working class. Yet, we must ask, are clerical workers privileged? Clearly not. Are they in positions of relative power? Hardly. On what grounds, then, does Poulantzas regard these workers as members of a different class? Inevitably, we are led to conclude that Poulantzas has simply equated the mental/manual distinction with the conventional distinction between blue-collar and white-collar workers. In effect, he has reduced class to an essentially *ideological* distinction, thereby eliminating any objective determinants of class. Class, in this view, becomes what people (or more specifically capitalist ideologues who have been most anxious to stress the white-collar/blue-collar division) say it is.

This critique leads us to Poulantzas' final distinction—that between supervisory and non-supervisory labour. Here too we are confronted with an important sociological distinction, but one which appears on reflection to be premature to classify as a class distinction. The problem with Poulantzas' argument is that most of the people who perform supervisory labour, with the exception of very high managers, are wage-labourers. Indeed, a significant component of their work consists of what Marx called the labour of coordination[7]—i.e., 'managerial' labour that would be necessary even in a non-exploitative mode of production—which is clearly part of what even Poulantzas would consider to be productive labour. But even where they are not performing this type of work, most supervisors are what Marx referred to as "a special kind of wage-labourer", to whom a certain limited amount of authority has been delegated by capital. It would indeed be foolish to ignore the important conflicts that can arise between supervisory and non-supervisory labourers. Yet it is far worse to overlook the importance of their shared status as wage-labourers by postulating the existence of a class barrier between them.

Neo-Marxist Analyses of Class

The common thread running through all of these neo-Marxist approaches to contemporary class structure is their attempt to establish that the 'working class' and the 'new middle class' have different interests. This would be an advance over sociological class analysis, if it were successful, for the identification of a conflict of interests would eliminate the need to draw class barriers arbitrarily. The question for us, then, is whether in fact these analyses succeed in establishing that such different interests exist. Wright points to the different interests generated by 'control'; Poulantzas to those engendered by unproductiveness, supervisory responsibilities and mental labour; and the Ehrenreichs to those produced by the privileges and social functions of the PMC. How adequate are these as analyses of class interests?

There is a sense in which one could say that the two groups discussed do have different interests. For example, one might wish to say that unproductive labourers have an interest in the exploitation of productive labourers, inasmuch as the former's wages are drawn from the surplus value produced by the latter. Or, one could suggest that mental or supervisory workers have an interest in the continued subordination and 'deskilling' of industrial workers, because they provide the conditions for their superior privileged position. Yet, what are we saying by making these statements? We are only saying that, *as long as present social conditions persist*, these two groups have certain different interests, in the short term. It is analogous to saying that in a society where inequality and competition for prestige are the norm, the person with a $5 job has "an interest" in keeping the $3 person down (because it leaves more for him or her and enhances his or her prestige). But there is another sense in which the interests of both are far from incompatible; that is, it is possible to create a society in which *both* people would have plenty (and probably more than $5 jobs!). Moreover, the two share an antagonism to their employer, in whose interest it is to keep both of their wages down. This argument can be applied to virtually all of the 'privileged' new middle class groups. In the long run, the triumph of socialism is in the interest *both* of those groups *and* the traditional working class, for socialism would enable them all to live more comfortable and rewarding lives. It might mean the end of dramatic differences in power, income and prestige—but, in a society where everyone has enough and where everyone has a fulfilling role to play, such differences would cease to have much meaning.

It might be objected, at this point, that much the same could be said of the petite bourgeoisie, which clearly *is* a distinct class. Marx, on several occasions, suggested that ultimately the interests of the petite bourgeoisie lay with the proletariat, with the triumph of the socialist movement.[8] Why then couldn't one argue that the 'new middle class,' also shares an interest with the working class, without actually being part of it? The two situations, however, are rather different. The petite bourgeoisie does *not* have the same relationship to the capitalist class as does the proletariat; their 'shared' interest with the working class is not the result of a shared relationship of exploitation. It is the result, rather, of the fact that they are too weak to press their *own* class project successfully against capital; they are, in a sense, doomed under capitalism. In contrast, the 'new middle class' shared interest with the traditional working class *is* the result of a shared relationship with the capitalist class—i.e., the shared condition of being exploited wage-labourers.

In sum, the 'conflict of interest' between the traditional working class and the 'new middle class' is a short-term one. The same may not be said, however, of the conflict of interest between wage-labour and capital. This cannot be treated as a short-term conflict that ultimately can be transcended. There is *no* sense in which the advent of socialism is in the interest of the capitalist, for it would mean the abolition of exploitation, privilege and status themselves. While one can, under socialism, satisfy the desires of those who are now privileged wage-labourers (perhaps better than under capitalism, in the long run), there is no way under socialism to satisfy the desires of the capitalist. In sum, there is a clear and irreconcilable conflict of interest between wage-labour and capital. Neo-Marxist analyses do not succeed in identifying a similarly irreconcilable conflict between the 'new middle class' and the traditional working class.

What is perhaps most surprising in all of this is the willingness of neo-Marxist theories to *pass over* the traditional Marxist criteria for defining classes (relationship to the means of production). Indeed, they do more than pass over it; they seem to suggest that exploitation is *not* the fundamental relationship on the basis of which class formations develop—that other factors can and do override it. This is not wrong *per se*. If these theorists were able to improve our understanding of class and class conflict, to explain something that traditional Marxist theory cannot, their arguments would be quite justifiable. In reality, however, they do not improve on Marxist theory; in many ways their analyses actually substantially *weaken* the Marxist approach. *None* of them is able to identify a fundamental, irreconcilable conflict of interest between 'the working class' and the 'new middle class'. This means that they all find themselves in the same position as academic stratification theory—forced to resort to arbitrary definitions of class. All of them point to ostensible sociological groupings (which sometimes do not even consider themselves to be a group), and simply *assert* that they are classes without giving an adequate explanation of why such a formation should develop in the first place. In sum, these theorists have eliminated the greatest virtue of Marxist class analysis—its ability to explain why class formations can and do develop.

'Traditional' Marxist theory has no problem answering this last question; it points to the role of exploitative relations of production in constituting classes. As we shall see below, it does not assert that there is an immediate relationship between exploitation and fully conscious class formations, but it does at least allow us to understand why the latter *can* develop. At the same time, Marxist class analysis draws our attention to and helps us to understand a significant aspect of 'new middle class' behaviour that neo-Marxist analyses overlook. That is, although the 'new middle class' differs from the tradition 'working class' in diverse ways, the two 'classes' have a remarkably similar relationship to the capitalist class. Specifically, both classes are constantly in conflict with their employers over the terms and conditions of labour. This is a phenomenon with which neo-Marxist theory seems ill at ease. Traditional Marxist theory, in contrast, has no difficulty explaining it as the result of the fact that the two groups *share* a status as exploited wage-labourers.

An Alternative Approach

The preceding discussion has identified some of the limitations inherent in various neo-Marxist analyses of contemporary class structure, and has pointed to a number of important themes regarding Marxist class analysis that emerge from such a critique. The general conclusion of this discussion is that existing approaches are unsatisfactory, for a variety of reasons, and that an alternative approach is needed. What would such an alternative look like?

The alternative suggested here involves, in a sense, a 'return' to Marxist orthodoxy. Specifically, it involves the reinstatement of the notion that the principal determinant of class is exploitative relations of production—in the case of capitalist society, the relationship between wage-labour and capital. This approach to class analysis is not proposed here simply because it is more orthodox. Rather, it is proposed because it offers a convincing answer to the question that most class theories seem unable to answer—i.e., the question of why there is a persistent tendency for class formations to develop in capitalist society. Marx's original formulation has the virtue of showing that this tendency for society to divide into classes is rooted in the actual conflict built into capitalist production relations, i.e., the very essence of capitalist society itself. Capitalist production relations automatically place individuals in relations of conflict and establish the possibility that individuals will organize into groups on the basis of shared conflict.

But what of all the intermediate groups we have been discussing—how do they fit into the traditional Marxist scheme? The vast majority of them, as has already been suggested, are wage-labourers, obliged to sell their labour-power to capital in exchange for a wage. As a result they, like industrial workers, are in a relation of *conflict* with their employers. True, some of them—say, for example, engineers—may earn much higher wages and have a variety of other privileges. Yet, as anyone familiar with the history of the engineering profession will know, this does not immunize them from conflict with capital. On the contrary, engineers also enter into conflict with their employers over familiar issues such as employment security, work conditions, and even income. And these conflicts have the same *cause* as do those experienced by more subordinate wage-labourers. This is not to suggest that there are no important differences among various types of workers; we need to be very sensitive to the real differences that do exist. What is being suggested here is rather that the vast majority of the so-called 'new middle class' shares with the traditional working class a relationship of conflict with capital that is *precisely the basis for class formation in capitalist society*. Consequently, only the very few who may be truly said to own or control (and not in Wright's partial ways)[9] the means of production, or who are in career paths that will lead them to such a position, may be 'disqualified' as potential members of the working class.

In essence what we are saying is that, as capitalist society has evolved, the category of wage-labour has become more and more internally *differentiated* (again, this differentiation is not the same thing as *class* distinctions). There are a variety of developments behind this differentiation, including the increasing split between mental and manual labour in industry, the vast expansion of capitalist commerce and banking, and the spread of capitalist enterprise beyond industry to what Marx called 'the non-material sphere,' i.e., services. This has meant the expansion of wage-labour, as capitalist relations have spread to areas of the economy they previously had not penetrated; it has also meant the differentiation of wage-labour, since work takes different forms in each of these spheres. Furthermore, within each of these spheres, the labour process has been shaped into a complex hierarchy which is headed by capitalists (in the private sector) or by high officials who generally are closely linked to the capitalist class (in the public sector). In either case, a further differentiation and *stratification* of wage-labour has been the result, because of the rise within these hierarchies of "intermediate" cadres of relatively privileged wage-labourers who often exercise a certain amount of delegated authority. Any expectation that the category of wage-labour would become homogeneous in the foreseeable future has been effectively laid to rest.

A comment on the role played by the process of 'de-skilling' in the constitution of the working class may be appropriate at this point. Many observers have noted that substantial numbers of 'new middle class' occupations have gone through a process of de-skilling, analogous to that undergone earlier by blue-collar workers. Some have gone further, arguing that in being de-skilled, these workers have become proletarian.[10] This, however, is to miss the point entirely. For it is only because these workers were wage-labourers *already* that they could be de-skilled. Only someone who sells his or her labour-power to capital, and therefore does not possess the means of production, would lack control of the labour process such that they could be de-skilled. De-skilling then is a symptom, not a cause, of proletarian status. Nor should we expect that all or most wage-labourers in capitalist society will eventually be de-skilled, making the working class more or less homogenous. All wage-labourers are certainly exposed to this process, but the historical tendency has been for new strata of highly skilled workers to be created as old ones are de-skilled.[11]

To return to the main thread of our argument, we have contended thus far that the basis for class conflict in capitalist society is the inherent conflict between capitalists and the *heterogeneous* group of wage-labourers. This is not, however, all that needs to be said about the nature of class. For to this point we have really only discussed the production relations that give rise to class, and not looked at fully conscious class organizations. The conflicts inherent in capitalist relations of production should not be confused with class organizations, for that would presuppose an 'immediate' relationship between the objective determinants of class and the formation of actual organized classes that clearly does not exist (if it did, there would be no need for theories for class consciousness or working class organization). Rather, these conflicts *set in motion the process of class formation*—it is because of them that individuals enter into conflict with their employers and are encouraged to organize themselves to fight back. For us to speak of class organizations, however, individuals must actually form themselves into conscious classes. And although this does occur, because of the conflicts inherent in capitalist production relations, such forms of organization do not come about automatically. To put this argument into other words, we may say that capitalist society is a class society—one that constantly tends to divide into classes because of the permanent conflicts built into its relations of production. However, the actual development of class organization is, in a real sense, contingent; it depends on the actual reactions of the individual affected by those conflicts.

Similar attempts to define class as an historical process frequently have been criticized for 'dissolving' the objective determinants of class.[12] Such criticisms, however, miss the point. The idea of class as an historical process is an attempt to avoid a double error. First, it attempts to avoid the tendency to reduce class to production relations, an error which completely begs the question of why full-fledged class conflict is not present in capitalist society at all times. At the same time, it also seeks to emphasize that classes *do* have objective determinants. Classes are not simply *ideological* formations whose existence is transient and contingent. Rather, the exploitative character of capitalist production relations generates a constant tendency for class organizations to arise.

A sophisticated approach to the process of class formation is thus clearly of the utmost importance. In particular, we need to emphasize the fact that this process is *not* automatic. Socialists have long been familiar with the various obstacles that can be placed in the path of working class organization—i.e., the mystifications of bourgeois ideology, the repressive force of the state, and the ability of the capitalist class to "play off" one group of workers against another. What also emerges from our analysis is that there is yet another, particularly powerful obstacle—the fact that the category of wage-labour is *not* homogenous. Thus, wage-labourers come in all different forms (ranging from the highly skilled and prestigious to the menial and unskilled, and they occupy different places in the labour process (some may be delegated a degree of authority, while others may be totally subordinate). This means of course that it is extremely difficult to organize wage-labourers into a fully conscious class organization.

In order to get a sense of the difficulties involved, one needs to look for a moment at the manner in which wage-labourers react to the conflicts inherent in their situation. Initially, one would expect workers to react as individuals—"*I* have a conflict with *my* boss" or "*My* boss is exploiting *me*" — for this is the most immediate way in which the conflict is experienced. However, since the worker is likely to find around him or her people in a similar situation, the possibility of forming into a group arises. The most obvious bases for group formation undoubtedly are the workplace or the occupation—it is relatively easy for workers to see that they *share* something with others working in the same part of the organization or in the same type of job elsewhere. Hence, this step in the process of class formation is not terribly difficult (local unions, craft unions), although it may meet powerful resistance from capitalists. However, once one gets beyond this point, organization becomes increasingly difficult. The obvious sociological differences between various kinds of workers, and the ability of employers to exploit these differences, make it very difficult for workers to perceive the relationships of conflict with their employers that they share. Again, the diversity of wage-labour makes the process of class formation one that is extremely complex, but one that is constantly being set in motion by capitalist relations of production.

The process of class formation, then, is just that—a process. The working class does not enter the world fully formed; it needs to be organized. What should we expect the end-product of this process to look like? Since class formation is an *historical* process, its outcome is never given precisely in advance; hence we cannot really answer this question without engaging in speculation. However, a few general points may help us better to understand the process. First, one should not expect all members of a particular occupation to wind up on the same side of the class divide. As has already been suggested, a number of occupations, especially the so-called 'professions', are internally stratified. It is hardly likely that a top corporate attorney and a storefront lawyer would take the same side if capitalist society were to truly polarize into well-organized classes. Second, and more important, we should not expect the outlines of an actual class organization to coincide exactly with the outlines of the "objective" category of wage-labour. The philosophical vision of a class-in-itself becoming conscious of itself and 'coming to life' (this is precisely what the image suggests) is certainly elegant, but it bears little relation to actual historical processes. It is far more likely that the 'fit' between actual class organizations and production relations will be approximate. All wage-labourers will experience the 'pressures' inherent in capitalist production relations, but there are a variety of historical contingencies that may encourage this or that wage-labourer to resist the 'logic' of these pressures. This is not to suggest, however, as some neo-Marxists (e.g., Poulantzas) seem to argue, that ideological factors are *the* factor determining class membership. What makes one part of a class is one's relationship to the means of production. Ideological factors can and do affect an individual's sense of his or her position in class relations; as a result they have a substantial role in the process of class formation. Nevertheless, social groupings constitute class organizations only to the extend that they are rooted in exploitative relations of production.

It should also be remembered that capitalists take advantage of the internal differentiation of wage-labour to consolidate their hegemony. Confronted by the disunity of the working class, capitalists actively seek to drive wedges between its various parts. Thus, through the manner in which they organize the labour process, through the ideologies they create, and through a variety of other methods, attempts are made to *widen* the already existing breach between mental and manual labour. Similarly, efforts are made to persuade workers that the status differences among them are real and meaningful and that the privileges of one are conditional upon the suffering of the other. All of this should serve to remind us that the process of class formation does not occur in a vacuum; it must take place in the context of a constant struggle by the dominant class to prevent its fruition. It should also serve to remind us of the political dangers of capitulating to the ruling class' interpretation of reality.

Before concluding this theoretical discussion, we need to repeat that the diversity of the categories of wage-labour should not be confused with class barriers. For to do so would be to ignore the various types of workers' shared experience of conflict with their employers, and would force us to jettison Marx's convincing analysis of the tendency of capitalist society to divide into classes. We need to remember the point that Gramsci took great pains to make; i.e., that the working class is disorganized in capitalist society.[13] This will allow us to explain why classes arise in capitalist society, why the 'new middle class' is in conflict with its employers, and why it can be de-skilled, *and*, at the same time, allow us to account for the complex and often fractious relationships among various types of workers.

Political Implications

How we define the class nature of the intermediate strata is not a matter of simply theoretical importance. If one views them as members of an intermediate class who also are in conflict with capital, then they may be treated as potential *allies*. But if one agrees with the analysis proposed here, then these 'intermediate' groups become more than allies—they are unambiguously part of the working class movement. A political strategy which is defined by alliances with a 'new middle class', as distinct from one of overcoming *intra-class* differences, is like to be ineffective, for the former approach does not attempt to resolve the differences among the various strata, or attempt to make these strata see the need to change themselves.

An important example of the difference between an alliance strategy and one which focuses on forging class unity can be seen in the politics of contemporary social democracy, for whom an alliance with the so-called 'new middle class' is central. Such parties pursue a strategy of creating a mass *electoral* movement which seeks to attain its goals exclusively by winning a majority of the votes in Parliament. Consequently, in the name of the need for an alliance, chiefly with the 'new middle class' in order to 'win', they become advocates of cautious, innocuous policies whose principal virtue is that they are relatively inoffensive to large numbers of voters and thus might gain adherents from various groups whose interests are perceived as being inevitably different.

But such a strategy, which avoids as much as possible mass mobilization and organization, does little to forge the unity which the working class lacks and desperately needs. Instead, this strategy accepts the divisions as 'givens', and appeals to a diverse group of people primarily on issues where they already presumably agree (papering over the areas of conflict and disagreement). This strategy fails to do anything to break down the real divisions and conflicts within the working class. Thus a general appeal will be made to both 'elite' engineers and 'subordinate' line workers (perhaps on general questions such as inflation). But no attempt is made to bring these two very different groups (not classes) together, and to encourage them to redefine their relationship as one of cooperation rather than of super- and sub-ordination. To repeat, contemporary social democracy makes no attempt to unify the working class. Yet it is only such a united class that can advance a truly socialist perspective. (This should not be taken as a blanket critique of electoral politics as such; it simply indicates the consequences of an exclusive reliance on such tactics.)

A similar critique may be made of the political strategy of Eurocommunism. The big Eurocommunist parties of France and Italy do pay somewhat more attention to mobilization and organization than does contemporary social democracy, but they too are hamstrung by their alliance strategy. Thus their attempt to forge the so-called "anti-monopoly" bloc does very little to overcome the important conflicts among the various components of the bloc. Not to mention the fact that it proposes to bring together groups whose interests in the *long* term, are probably incompatible—e.g., factory workers and small employers.

These strategies of allying the 'new middle class' and the 'working class' are not satisfactory. Yet it would be equally if not more foolish to retreat to a strategy which sees only the traditional working class as part of a unified socialist working class movement.[14] On the contrary, the central problem for contemporary socialism is to devise strategies which can overcome the differences *within* the working class (i.e., unify the intermediate strata and the blue-collar workers, not simply ally them). This is a problem which certainly predates the coming into existence of the new white-collar and professional layers of the working class. But it is no longer just a problem of overcoming the differences between the skilled and the unskilled, the employed and the unemployed. To these unresolved difficulties one must now add the new problems which flow from divisions between mental and manual workers: the ideology of professionalism, the problems posed by supervisory workers, and the complex relations between public and private sector workers. How this diverse class can be moved toward unity, and in that process become a class in the full meaning of the term, is clearly a problem beyond the limits of this essay. But the very fact that several millions of these workers are now in the union movement at least represents and encouraging start.

Canadian socialists must also be careful not to misunderstand the political significance of the 'new middle class'. As has frequently been remarked, Canada has a particularly well-developed 'tertiary sector' (employing at least two-thirds of the labour force in the late 1970s), including a large number of white-collar state workers. Whether this is the result of the peculiarities of Canada's economic development or of more general processes affecting all advanced capitalist countries is a question that cannot be resolved here. Nevertheless, it remains a fact of the Canadian political economy that the traditional manual working class is likely to be a minority force, and may even experience some permanent contraction if present worldwide economic trends continue. As the analysis here suggests, this should not be cause for despair, since the 'new middle class' shares fundamental class interests with the traditional working class. And, in the Canadian context, there are even some encouraging signs, notably the fact that some of the largest unions are *white-collar* unions, particularly in the public sector.

This should not be taken as an indication that the development of a well-organized, socialist working class movement in Canada will be either easy or automatic. The development of class organization in Canada will be just as complex a process as anywhere else, involving contingent human reactions to the experience of exploitation by a heterogeneous (and thus divisible) working class. Moreover, there is reason to be concerned that the Canadian socialist movement may be repeating the political error committed by European social-democrats. Gad Horowitz (1968:261) put his finger on the crucial problem a number of years ago when he remarked that:

> Increased union support and increased middle-class support will become compatible goals for the NDP if and when the *unions* learn how to project a good image among the middle classes in general and the white-collar workers in particular. In the mean-time, the NDP is doing all it can to minimize the harmful effects of its association with labour.

It is certainly correct that the labour movement should endeavor to make unionism more attractive to white-collar workers—it has even had some success in this area. However, a New Democrat Party (NDP) retreat from "its association with labour" would be in direct contradiction to the analysis I have outlined. It would perpetuate the mistaken view that there is a fundamental difference between traditional working class and 'new middle class' interests, leaving the door open to the kind of vague, 'alliance'-oriented appeals to 'the people' that have appeared in recent election campaigns. It would be foolish to assume that it will be easy to unionize all white-collar workers, to attract union members to the socialist movement, or to unify a group of people divided by race, gender, occupation, and degrees of privilege. But in Canada as elsewhere the socialist movement, instead of abandoning class politics, needs to make the forging of class *unity* its number one priority.

It is of course one thing to declare the need for a strategy to develop a unified working class, and another actually to put it into practice. Many questions need to be answered (e.g., how to get workers to stop thinking in terms of status considerations; what types of organization are appropriate) before such a strategy will become a reality. If we are to succeed, however, in developing a viable socialist strategy for late capitalism, the basic theme of this paper will have to be taken seriously. Socialists must drop the antiquated view of the working class to which they have held for so long, and begin to recognize that capitalist social structure and the contemporary working class are far more complex than previously thought. In particular, socialists must stop acquiescing to the interpretations of the social structure that those who dominate society have developed in order to *prevent* the rise of socialism. Instead, socialists should *attack* capital's categories and seek to build the kind of united but diverse class that is essential to the realization of the socialist project.

Acknowledgements and Notes

Thanks are owed to Bob Brenner, Johanna Brenner, Steve Zeluck, Sarah Harrington, Kim Gross and Tara Shaver for their help and advice. I am particularly grateful to Ellen Wood and Joyce Mastboom for providing invaluable intellectual stimulation and encouragement.

1. It has become quite common, in the recent economic crisis, to hear speculation about the demise of industrial labour. Yet, even in Canada, blue-collar workers remain a substantial proportion of the labour force (around 30 percent); and it is unlikely that the much-touted 'robotics' revolution will reduce this proportion dramatically, since the introduction of robots is expensive, confined to large assembly-line industries, and applicable only to certain jobs.

2. For left and right versions of this argument, respectively, see Ehrenreich and Ehrenreich (1978) and Bruce-Biggs (1979). A third variant of the position may be found in Gouldner (1979).
3. Wright has begun an effort to apply his argument empirically. Some preliminary results appear in Wright *et al.* (1982).
4. Interestingly, Poulantzas seems to give precedence to the mental/manual distinction. He excludes from the working class certain categories of unambiguously 'productive' workers—such as technicians—because of the fact that they perform *mental* labour (Poulantzas, 1974: 254). (Thanks to Ellen Wood for drawing this to my attention).
5. It is also important to note, since Poulantzas seems to feel that only workers who produce material commodities can be considered productive, that Marx argued that service work could be productive as well. For an example of his several discussions of service labour, see the analysis of capitalist organization in the "non-material sphere" in Marx, (1975: 411-12).
6. Thus in Volume I of *Capital* Marx points out that the labour process unites the labour of head and hand but that later they "part company" and become "deadly foes" (1973: 508).
7. Marx develops this distinction in Volume I of *Capital* (1973: 330-1). In essence, he is arguing that one part of the supervisor's labour is made necessary by capitalist class relations, while the other portion is made necessary by the collective character of the labour process.
8. See, for example, Marx and Engels, (1964: 21).
9. The problem of defining 'control' of the means of production is a notoriously thorny one. An adequate answer to the question of where exactly to 'draw the line' between capital and labour is still awaited, and it may be that it is incorrect or even impossible to attempt to draw such a line. Perhaps it would be better to concede that there is a relatively small 'grey area', where the distinction between control and non-control becomes fuzzy. Nevertheless, without attempting to resolve this issue here, we may safely say that the vast majority of white-collar workers do not even come close to having meaningful control over the disposition of the means of production.
10. This position is argued in Baudelot *et al.* (1974).
11. This was the case, for example, with turn-of-the-century metalworkers, whose demise was concomitant with a significant growth in the skilled occupation of tool-and-die maker.
12. For example, see the critiques of E. P. Thompson by Anderson (1980) and Johnson (1978). These critiques are in turn critically evaluated by Wood (1982). The discussion of class here owes much to this latter article by Wood.
13. For example, he remarks that "The subaltern classes, by definition, are not unified and cannot unify until they are able to become a 'State'" (Gramsci, 1971: 52).
14. Thus, in rejecting alliance strategies, one has to be careful not to fall the opposite error (a strategy which we may here call "workerism")—that of excluding the "new middle class" from the socialist project. In the name of opposing the pollution of the workers' movement, workerists would restrict the term "working class" to either the industrial working class or to wage-earners who are fully subordinate and/or "de-skilled". The difficulties with this view are evident. First, like the alliance strategy, it merely postpones the task of creating some kind of cooperative relationship between the two groups. Secondly, this self-limiting definition reduces the working class to a minority. Consequently, quite apart from making the task of social revolution more difficult, it would have a negative effect on the prospects for a *democratic* socialist society.

Manual Workers and the Perception of Social Class: An Edmonton Case Study

Julian Tanner

Introduction

The study of subjective social class has a history in the social sciences that can be traced back, at least as far as to the distinction made by Marx between a "class in itself" and a "class for itself". Modern academic sociology is similarly concerned with the relationship between the objective facts of class inequality—differences in material wealth, status, education and so on—and the varying ways in which they are interpreted and responded to.

Manual workers have tended to be at the front and centre of empirical research on subjective social class and this, too, is explainable in terms of Marxist-inspired concerns with the revolutionary potential of the working class. The question of how manual workers perceive the class structure is clearly fundamental to any analysis of how the working class might transform society. This general concern with the ideological orientations and behaviour of the contemporary working class also has a more specific referent: subjective social class has been identified as the crucial mediating variable that explains otherwise anomolous voting behaviour among manual workers. Research has indicated that those politically deviant manual workers who vote for political parties on the right of the political spectrum are more likely to identify themselves as middle-class than workers who vote for parties of the center or left. (Goldthorpe et al., 1969:174; Goyder and Pineo, 1979:432).

In accounting for workers' images of class, causal priority has been accorded to the experiences and relationships of everyday life, particularly those associated with the workplace. As Gavin Mackenzie puts it:

> the work situation provides *the* most important set of conditions shaping the social imagery of industrial man: for it is at work that relationships and experiences of superiority and inferiority, of solidarity and separation, of frustration and achievement are most

persuasive, most visible and therefore most influential (Mackenzie, 1975:173, emphasis in the original).

The empirical referents for this argument tend to be primarily of European or American origin (Bott, 1957; Popitz *et al.*, 1969; Willener, 1957; Blauner, 1960; 1964). In so far as manual workers the world over share similar work settings, it is reasonable to suppose that these research findings apply equally well to Canadian workers. On the other hand, cross-cultural variations in other potential influences upon class imagery means that we cannot automatically assume that research conducted elsewhere necessarily depicts the way Canadian workers view their society.

Unfortunately, there is a dearth of Canadian research dealing with workers and their class attitudes. Whilst there is no shortage of scholars willing and prepared to offer their theories of social class, remarkably little is really known about what class actually means to that group of Canadians who are disproportionately the object of that interest.

What is known about manual workers' perceptions of class in Canada comes from two fairly circumscribed sources. First of all, there has been the research on the class vote (Ogmundson, 1975a; 1975b; 1976; 1980; Myles, 1979; Erikson, 1981; Lambert and Hunter, 1979; Schreiber, 1980). In this research, class functions primarily as a non-problematic, objectively defined independent variable: the focus is upon the linkage between assumed social class membership and political identifications and behaviour. These studies are large-scale surveys; they provide little qualitative information about either the processes whereby images of class are constructed or the meaning that class holds for respondents. Secondly, there have been a handful of studies of class identification employing a forced-choice methodology. Class identification is measured by the class label that respondents choose from pre-determined categories. The deficiencies of this technique have been well documented; the criticisms focus upon unfounded assumptions made about the meaning of class labels for respondents. Nonetheless, it has remained the staple method of investigating subjective social class in Canada (Rinehart and Okraku, 1974; Coburn and Edwards, 1976; Keddie, 1980).

Based upon information provided by manual workers in Edmonton, the present paper constitutes an attempt to more comprehensively explore the perceptions of class and class structure held by those in manual occupations. It tries to transcend the parameters of interest and limitations of method found in previous investigations of class imagery in Canada and, at the same time, place the findings in the context of other recent studies of working-class imagery undertaken in different societies.

The issues in which I was specifically interested concern the part played by social class in the formation of workers' mental constructs of Canadian society, the degree to which class is a source of personal identity, and the bearing that conceptions of class has upon workers' political orientations. Also, the broader concerns of the research—an examination of the relationship between skill and working-class consciousness—stimulated curiosity about whether differences in craft and non-craftmen's work situations produced discernible variations in class imagery.

Research Site and Methods

To explore these issues, a survey of craft and non-craft workers drawn from two different plants in the city of Edmonton was undertaken.

One plant—Airfix—was involved with the repair and overhaul of primarily military aircraft. Most of the men interviewed here were skilled craftsmen—electricians, aircraft mechanics, tool and die makers, and fitters. For purposes of comparison, a smaller number of non-tradesmen—janitors, aircraft cleaners and so on—were also interviewed.

The second plant—Glyberforce—is a manufacturer of home insulation. It employs a large number of men engaged in essentially routinized job tasks, including assembly line work. Most of the men interviewed at Glyberforce were unskilled, though again—for reasons of comparison—a smaller number of maintenance craftsmen were also interviewed.[1]

Thus, in each plant, information was received from samples of skilled and unskilled men. Most of the data was gained through fairly lengthy tape-recorded interviews conducted by the author with 42 craftsmen and 9 non-craftsmen drawn from Airfix and 39 unskilled workers and 9 maintenance men drawn from Glyberforce. Information on one forced-choice question about class was provided by an additional eleven men (6 airfix craftsmen, 2 airfix non-craftsmen, 2 Glyberforce craftsmen and one Glyberforce non-craftsmen), who completed a shortened mailed-out version of the questionnaire in lieu of a personal interview.

Although the sample is small, it is representative of the two plants under investigation; moreover, because the interviews were tape-recorded, I was provided with the kind of detail about respondents' class perceptions that would not be elicited in the course of a brisk interview or through a postal questionnaire.

The analysis of workers' class imagery that follows is mainly based upon the answers given to open-ended questions about perceptions of the number of classes found in Canadian society, respondents' class membership, the size of each class, and the determinants of class.

The apparent straightforwardness of these questions belies the fact that coding—and hence classifying—workers' images of class is no easy matter. The main reason for this is that during the course of the interview respondents did not always adhere to the same terminology when answering seemingly related questions about class. These problems were compounded because the interview schedule contained both 'open' and 'closed' questions about class. Whilst the use of different measures did facilitate the construction of a more accurate picture of workers' views of class, it also encouraged respondents to offer more than one frame of reference in their discussions of class (cf. Cousins and Brown, 1975).

Findings

The topic of class was introduced into the discussion after workers had talked about their jobs and worker-manager relations. It was broached with the aid of the question: "Some people have said that there are social classes in Canada, while other people disagree. What do you think?"

It has been suggested that one part of the dominant Canadian ideology of liberalism is the tenet that Canada is a society devoid of class differences (Hunter, 1981:213; Marchak, 1981:19). In light of this, the finding that 78 percent of the sample felt that Canada is a class society clearly represents at least a minimal rejection of that dominant ideology. Another 14 percent denied that there are social classes, while the remainder (18 percent) were either undecided or failed to answer the question.

The acknowledgement that Canada is a class society leads directly to the question of whether workers' awareness of class is related to particular types or models of the class structure.

To uncover the overall pattern of class imagery, those respondents who viewed Canada as a class society were then asked: "What do you think are the major classes in this country today?" In coding the answers to this question, more attention was paid to the actual number of classes identified than to the nomenclature ("upper", "middle", "lower", and so on) employed by respondents.

Table 1 produces two findings of note. First, 20 percent (15) of the men who agree that there are social classes in Canada were able to provide no further information about their class imagery; the inability of some respon-

Table 1: Perception of Number of Social Classes in Canada

Number	Percentage
4+	12
3	54
2	14
No discernible pattern	20
Total N	**74**

Figure 1: Images of the Social Structure

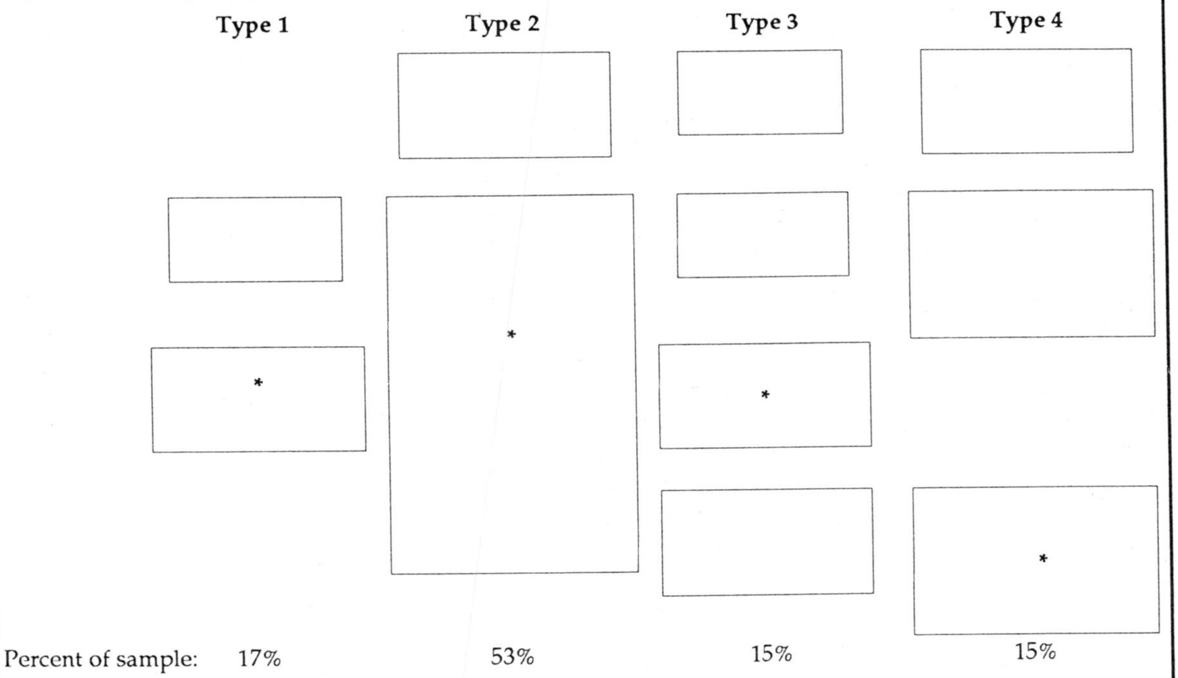

	Type 1	Type 2	Type 3	Type 4
Percent of sample:	17%	53%	15%	15%

* Respondents' own class position (self rated).

dents to identify the major social classes is preliminary warning that although respondents are aware of the phenomenon of class, their emotional and cognitive involvement with the concept is, nonetheless, fairly limited. Secondly, among respondents willing and able to specifically identify social classes in Canada, over half (54 percent)—irrespective of workplace or occupational level—put forward a view of Canada as a three-class society.

A follow-up question then asked respondents which of their identified social classes they felt that they belonged to. The overall pattern of responses can be represented diagramatically as follows:

According to some accounts, (e.g. Lockwood, 1966), a dichotomous power model is the 'prototypical' working-class image of society. However, as Figure 1 indicates, only a small proportion of respondents—(17 percent) in the present study—adhere to a two-tier model of class. Moreover, the actual content of these two-tier models is more varied than that specified by the theoretical construct. Thus, whilst some men do express class divisions in terms that imply power and conflict (for instance, with references to a dichotomy of 'High Society' and 'the poor'), others describe class differences in more neutral terms—by references to 'the rich' and 'the less rich', or 'High Society' and 'the middle-class'. In other words, a two-class view of society does not necessarily imply a 'Them' versus 'Us' conflictual relationship.

There is little equivalent doubt or ambiguity about either the structure or content of the modal image of class held by the sample. A majority (53 percent) claim membership of a large and generously defined 'middle-class' with a small elite group ('High Society', 'the Establishment' and so on) at the top and a small residual group composed of the unemployed, welfare recipients, etc., at the bottom (type 2). This middle class is seen as comprising both manual and non-manual workers. Type 3 is essentially a variant of the Type 2 image. Although more than three classes are visualized, respondents similarly see themselves as occupying an intermediate position in the social structure. Key elements of the Type 2 and 3 images are brought out in the following exchanges. The first respondent is an Airfix aircraft electrician:

> J.R.T.: What do your think are the major social classes in this country today?
>
> You've got the rich, the poor, skilled workers, unskilled workers (pause) I'm trying to think of a word to describe people that don't want to work, like unemployment (laughs)!—'cos I know a lot—unemployment and welfare...

J.R.T.: What social class would you say you were in?

That's hard to say—there are so many.

J.R.T.: Of the ones that you've mentioned, which would you see yourself as belonging to?

Myself as being in? ... I've mentioned myself as a skilled worker. I'm not rich and I'm not poor—I'm just middle-class ... the middle-class varies too much ... where are the limits? Where do you start from, for the middle-class? I'd say I'm average. But I'm a skilled worker.

The second respondent is a forklift truck driver at Glyberforce. Having agreed that there are social classes in Canada, I asked him what he felt were the major social classes:

I dunno, like, I'd say there's the wealthy and what you'd call the normal, and there's the poor.

J.R.T.: What social class would you say you were in?

I'd say normal.

A similar picture is offered by this third respondent, an Airfix craftsman:

J.R.T.: What do you think are the major classes in this country today?

Upper-level or high-income, mid-income, and low-income.

J.R.T. What social class would you say you were in?

I couldn't say that I'm a low income—we don't fit in to the High income either. I would have to say we are probably at the bottom of the mid-income group.

What is also strongly hinted at in these exchanges is that money is viewed as the prime determinant of class membership. This impression was quantified by the responses to a question which revealed that for each of the four occupational groups, 'income' was the most frequently cited determinant of social class position.

Now, references to 'money' or 'income' in surveys about class are notoriously difficult to interpret (Platt, 1971). Some commentators suggest that such references are simply employed by respondents as a convenient shorthand for a wide range of material and symbolic differences between classes (Moorehouse, 1976); others, most notably the authors of the British 'affluent worker' study (Goldthorpe et al., 1969) interpret references to money/income as indicating a primary concern with material living standards and consumptive capacities.

Adjudicating between these different interpretations in the present study was made no easier by the fact that different respondents meant different things when talking about money and class.

Answers to the first question about the existence/non-existence of classes in Canada were an initial portent of this tendency. Respondents who both agreed *and* disagreed that there are classes in Canada did so by reference to money/income. Hence I was getting statements such as the following:

> No, I don't think there is social classes. I think the money is what counts in Canada. If you're a lower-type person with lots of money you've just as much power as the high-falutin' type with no money. It's not like Britain and Europe, where, you know, you meet a lot of people that haven't got a penny to their name, but they flash out their club tie, and stuff like this.

This was the view of an Airfix sheet-metal worker who emigrated to Canada from Britain. Clearly his sense of Canadian classlessness is inspired by comparisons with Britain. But a similar sort of statement was expressed by a Canadian-born aircraft mechanic from the same plant: "I disagree ... they tell us here about blue-collar workers and stuff, but the only thing I see to that is how much money you make".

On the other hand, 'class' and 'income' are inextricably linked for another Airfix craftsman, who argues that "Well, basically, when it comes to classes, I think it's got to be money: money is what divides people into classes".

When discussing the determinants of class, a similar lack of universal meaning was attached to the money references. For some respondents money is merely a simple and convenient approximation of power differences that exist between the classes. This is the essence of such statements as "money is power, eh" (Glyberforce day labourer). Money/income also meant life style differences—the traditional middle-class concern with status and prestige—for other respondents.

However, the most popular meaning attached to money emphasized quantitative rather than qualitative variations between individuals. For the majority of respondents, social class is mainly a matter of consumptive

Table 2: Images of Society by Skill Level and Company

	Skilled			Unskilled		
	Gyber-force	Airfix	Total Skilled	Glyber-force	Airfix	Total Unskilled
A	27%	17%	19%	18%	20%	18%
B	18	13	14	23	10	20
C	55	65	63	59	60	59
None	0	4	7	0	10	2
Total N	**11**	**46**	**57**	**39**	**10**	**49**

capacities: "it's only a matter of how much money you have, that's all" (Airfix, sheet metal worker).

That this is the defining quality of most respondents' views of class is substantiated by the pattern of responses produced by a forced-choice question that was introduced towards the end of the interview.

Respondents were presented with three statements, each reflecting a distinctive overall image of the class structure. They were then asked which of the statements came closest to their own perceptions. The three statements were:

a. There are several classes in Canada; although the upper classes run the country and industry, it is in everybody's interest that they do so.

b. In Canada today, there are basically two main classes—bosses and workers—and these classes have opposing interests.

c. Most people in Canada today belong to the same class—and the only important difference is how much money they earn.

Now, some respondents felt that none of these vignettes very accurately captured the defining characteristics of their conception of the class structure and relationships. Others felt that some—but not all—elements of a given vignette corresponded with their own views: for instance, some respondents did feel that there are basically two main classes in Canada, but did not necessarily think that they had opposing interests.

Table 3: Belief in the Possibility of Social Mobility by Skill Level and Company

	Skilled			Unskilled		
	Glyberforce	Airfix	Total Skilled	Glyberforce	Airfix	Total Unskilled
Yes	78%	61%	64%	56%	75%	58%
No	22	33	31	38	25	36
Don't Know	0	6	4	6	0	6
Total N	**9**	**36**	**45**	**32**	**4**	**36**

Nonetheless, most respondents (61 percent overall) had little trouble in agreeing with statement C ... the vignette that captures the imagery of what has been described as the pecuniary model of society (Lockwood, 1966).

The unskilled Glyberforce workers are a partial and limited exception to this generalization. These are the workers with the most limited job tasks, who were exposed to the worst physical conditions—noise, heat, and dust, etc.—and who were most frequently on the receiving end of the petty tyrannies of front-line supervisors. Hence it comes as no surprise to find that, as a group, the unskilled Glyberforce workers are most likely to favour the traditional proletarian image depicted in statement B. What is perhaps more surprising is that this statement of proletarianism is still only a minority viewpoint—only 23 percent of this group endorse it.

Thus a large, and inclusive, middle class is the centre-piece of most workers' image of the Canadian class structure. Moreover it is evident that, regardless of skill level or workplace, most workers do not regard class boundaries as being particularly immutable or impenetrable. Respondents were asked: "Do you think that many people move from one class to another these days?"

The fact that the majority of respondents perceived Canada as a relatively 'open' society in which it is fairly easy to move from one class to another is further evidence that class divisions are viewed as negotiable and elastic rather than fixed and unchanging. More importantly, this fluid conception of class boundaries suggests that, rather than being a fundamental anchor of world views and personal identity, class has only a superficial bearing upon most workers' social consciousness. That respondents did not accord high intellectual or affective priority to their class schemas is evidenced as follows.

Table 4: Social Class Identification Using Forced-Choice Classification

	Skilled			Unskilled		
	Glyber-force	Airfix	Total Skilled	Glyber-force	Airfix	Total Unskilled
Middle-Class	44%	51%	50%	45%	57%	47%
Working-Class	56	43	46	55	43	53
Don't Know	0	5	4	0	0	0
Total N	**9**	**37**	**46**	**38**	**7**	**45**

First of all, in sharp contrast to the voluminous amount of information volunteered about their jobs, most respondents were far more hesitant, uncertain and generally less forthcoming in expressing their views about class. As Peter Hiller (1973) has remarked, hesitations, pauses, and so on, in interview situations are cues or indicators as to the lack of meaning that a topic holds for the respondent. In the present study this is epitomized by the amount of non-response produced by the open-ended questions.

Additional light is shed on the matter of 'meaning' by looking at the responses given to a forced-choice question on class identification that was asked of respondents after the open-ended discussion of the topic.

The question posed was a varient of the classic one asked by Centers (1949): "Some people seem to think that there are 3 major social classes in Canada: the upper-class, the middle-class, and the working-class. If you had to choose one of those terms, which would you say you were?"

A major effect of introducing a force-choice item—as a number of other researchers have also found (Gross, 1953; Goyder and Pineo, 1979)—is that it reduces the amount of non-response that open-ended questioning generates: inviting workers to respond to pre-defined class categories eliminates much of the doubt and prevarication upon which non-response to the original open-ended question is largely based.

More significantly—as Goyder and Pineo have similarly demonstrated—presenting respondents with a closed question *after* an open-ended one increases the amount of working-class identification. In terms of the present study, this results in nearly half (48 percent) of all respondents identifying themselves as 'working class'. What we also find is a slightly greater tendency on the part of the unskilled workers than the craftsmen to identify with the working class (53 percent compared with 46 percent) and a converse tendency for a greater middle-class identification among the craftsmen than the non-craft workers (50 percent against 47 percent).

The problem now, of course, is whether the reduction of non-response and the increased amount of working-class identification produced by the forced-choice question constitutes a clarification of workers' class imagery or a distortion of it.

Eschewing the temptation to over-interpret what are, after all, only slight differences in class identification between the craft and the non-craftsmen, we want instead to suggest that the significance of these findings lies in terms of what they tell us about the import of social class categories for respondents and in the commentary that they provide about forced-choice formats.

Closed questions have the effect of over-structuring respondents thinking about class: they deny respondents the opportunity to disavow feelings of psychological membership of a class. Such formats thus have the effect of exaggerating the importance and clarity of individuals' conceptions of class. Moreover, the meaning that respondents attach to the class categories that they are required to choose is never unambiguously clear in forced-choice responses (Hiller, 1973). The responses to, and spontaneous comments about, the forced-choice questions indicate that for my informants the terms 'working class' and 'middle class' are not conceptually very distinguishable. In fact, the terms are often inter-changeable ways of describing their meaning of class: membership in a broadly defined group of wage and salary earners in the middle of the social structure. Respondents, by and large, share a view of class that hinges around occupancy of a large central class, membership of which excludes, *a priori*, only the rich, the established professions (doctors and lawyers, and so on) and quite literally, those who do not work—the unemployed and those on welfare. That the terms middle class and working class refer to basically the same phenomenon is illustrated by the following exchanges:

> Now I would have to ask what (is) the middle-class? I'd consider the middle-class as working-class, you know ... myself, the middle-class is the working-class, and I'd class myself as middle-class. (Aircraft electrician, Airfix)

> I'd say the working middle-class (laughs) ... That's what the middle-class is as far as I'm concerned. (Packer, Glyberforce)

> I'm definitely in the working-class. But ... income-wise I'm in the middle-class. (Aircraft mechanic, Airfix)

> Working-class ... because that is what I do a third of my time, I work ... almost all of us are in the working-class. (Hydraulics mechanic, Airfix)

One of the first casualities of this inclusive view of class boundaries is class voting. As suggested earlier, interest in subjective social class has in large part been motivated by the assumption that there is an intimate connection between images of class and political orientations, particularly voting behaviour. On this argument, we would expect those individuals, who in open-choice formats, locate themselves at the bottom of the social structure, to be more inclined than those who place themselves in the middle of that structure to electorally support the New Democratic Party (NDP): the theoretical rationale being, of course, that those who see themselves as occupying a subordinate position in society will be most responsive to the egalitarian pitch of the NDP.

Such is not the case, however. NDP support, in the form of voting in the 1979 Provincial and Federal elections (minimal though it is among the sample as a whole) is no more associated with the bottom-class identifiers than with the middle-class identifiers. The forced-choice question provides a similar picture: those who identify themselves as working class are no more likely to vote for the NDP than those who see themselves as middle-class.

On this evidence, at any rate, the matter of voting seems little effected by respondents' notions of subjective social class. This is because, we would argue, a sense of working-class membership is insufficiently crystalized for it to motivate a distinctive pattern of voting.

Discussion

Although little internal variation in class imagery has been found within this sample, there is another kind of comparison that can be made: between the findings from this study and other recent studies of manual workers conducted in different cultural contexts.

On the one hand, the findings presented here are quite similar to those reported by Gavin Mackenzie in his American examination of the embourgeoisement thesis (1973). He found that over 70 percent of the skilled craftsmen in his sample saw the American class structure as a three-class hierarchy, and placed themselves in the middle class. Moreover, they saw the bases of social class as lying in differences of income, education, and life style, rather than factors pertaining directly to the work and employment situation.

On the other hand, the present findings do differ from the more complex pattern of class imagery reported in recent studies of British manual workers. That research does not support Lockwood's contention that differences in work and community setting produce variations in workers' social consciousness (Lockwood, 1966). Rather, information culled from both particular occupational groups (Goldthorpe et al., 1969; Cousins and Brown, 1975; Allen, 1984) and more random samples (Moorhouse, 1976) indicates that the basic elements of British working-class imagery exist independently of particular industrial milieux. Although most British workers do not view society in the dichotomous term of "Them and Us", the majority do identify themselves as working-class and do see their class of membership as being the largest and, invariably, the most subordinate in society. They also see class divisions as being determined by money, and hold generally pessimistic views about the prospects for social mobility.

Nonetheless, British workers hold less conflictual views of class than do French and Italian workers. Gallie's recent comparative study of British and French manual workers (1983) reveals that class divisions are less keenly felt in Britain than in France. Class is a more important source of personal and group identity for the French than for British workers, who were also less inclined than their French counterparts to place themselves in the bottom class in society. Moreover, French workers are more likely than British workers to explain class differences in terms of experiences deriving from the workplace.

John Low-Beer's (1978) research on the 'new' working class in Italy indicates that Italian technical workers show a pattern of class imagery closer to French than to British models. Thus the proportion of Italian workers who identified themselves as working class and saw themselves as being part of the most subordinate class in society is higher than that found in the British studies.

Whilst concentrating upon these cross-cultural differences, it is also important not to lose sight of the fact that they co-exist with a number of commonalities. Thus in all these studies, including the present one, the majority of workers view the class structure as a hierarchy of three or more classes rather than as a two-class dichotomy; income is consistently regarded as a prime determinant of class; and nowhere is the manual/non-manual occupational divide accorded much significance as a major 'break' in the class structure.

Two broad and inter-related generalizations can be abstracted from these various studies. First, western European workers, particularly those from France and Italy, are more likely than their Anglophone North American counterparts to offer a 'bottom-up' view of the class structure (e.g. Cousins and Brown, 1975); second, patterns of class imagery uncovered in these studies are linked to, and consistent with, other known variations in working-class consciousness found in those societies. That is, on a range of indicators, French and Italian workers are known to be more radical than British workers who, in turn, are more radical than American and Canadian workers.

Common sense strongly suggests that the scope of these cross-cultural variations in working-class imagery are not explained by immediate work-inspired influences, which can reasonably be assumed to be universal in their effect. In fact, the opposite seems to be the case: all the important societal differences in class imagery appear to be attributable to broader cultural and ideological influences, most notably the degree of contact that manual workers have with working-class political parties and radical trade unions. Certainly, the evidence from France and Italy is testament to the proposition that the strength of these influences in a society is directly related to the tendency of workers to offer oppositional interpretations of social inequality (cf. Parkin, 1972; Mann, 1973).

What happens when these ideological influences are absent is apparent from these Canadian findings. If not absolutely denied as an entity, class is nevertheless clearly not a central dynamic in this sample of workers' social consciousness. We can conclude, on the basis of this and other research, that a class outlook on inequality is not a natural or automatic outgrowth of experiences of deprivation and exploitation in industry. The Canadian situation tells us that without the active intervention of working-class political parties and 'Left'-orientated trade unions, a dominant ideology, which explains inequality in individual rather than structural terms, is likely to go uncontested.

Notes

1. A more detailed description of the two plants and the job tasks is provided elsewhere. (Tanner, 1984).

Class Position, Class Consciousness and Political Party Preference in Hard Times

D. W. Livingstone

A general consensus exists among social scientists that class politics are of little relevance in contemporary North America (Myles and Forcese, 1981). Consequently, analyses of actual relations between class position, class consciousness and political party preference in Canada and the U.S. have been limited. Several reasons for this presumed irrelevance will be discussed here. The basic thesis of this paper is as follows: In "hard times", such as in the past decade, relations between social classes are frequently renegotiated, and the political implications of such negotiations should not be simply presumed. More specifically, conditions of protracted economic and fiscal crisis in North America (see O'Connor, 1984; Wolfe, 1983) have been associated with a decline in popular confidence in many established institutions, including governments (see Lipset and Schneider, 1983; Canadian Gallup Poll, 1985), as well as an increase in political conflicts between advocates of enhanced rights for owners of property, and defenders of universal social service entitlements such as unemployment benefits and social assistance payments (see Piven and Cloward, 1983). Some empirical evidence on recent patterns and tendencies in relations between class position, class consciousness and party preference in Canada is offered here to encourage discussion and further study.

The "North American Exception"

In comparison with most other advanced capitalist societies, both Canada and the U.S. have historically shown relatively low organizational capacities to mobilize working people in their own interests, particularly in terms of unionization and the existence of "left" or socialist parties with strong working-class platforms attracting electoral support (Korpi, 1983). Over the past few decades, survey researchers generally have found that the association between measures of objective social class and voting preferences has been very weak in both countries.

Until the mid-1970s, the prevailing view established by Alford's (1963, 1967) comparative analyses of elections in the Anglo-American democracies was that while class-differentiated voting in federal elections in the

U.S. was low, in Canada it was almost non-existent (see Anderson, 1966; Meisel, 1975). Since then, 'revisionist' studies have demonstrated the inaccuracy of Alford's initial classification of the class positions of Canadian parties, especially his description of the Liberals as a party of the left (Ogmundson, 1975a); such studies have also used statistical measures of difference, sensitive to skewed distributions of the overall left or right voting between societies, to indicate that Canada has had a very similar pattern of class voting to the U.S. (Myles, 1979).

More broadly, Canadian revisionists have begun empirical research on possible mediating effects of such factors as the structure and performance of the political party system and individuals' perceptions of the class positions of political parties to better understand the relations between objective social class and voting preferences. With regard to the existing party system, Myles and Forcese (1981:27) have concluded that, within the continental corporate economic context of both Canada and the U.S., "... a dominant center party mobilizes mass support from all social classes and .... the political party system effectively suppresses the electoral expression of working class interests." Ogmundson and Ng (1982) find that measures of social class have been more closely associated with individual Canadians' perceptions of the class position of the political parties they vote for than with voting behaviour designated by imposed criteria such as Alford's classification, and that the difference in class voting between Canada and the United Kingdom (which Alford took as a case of "pure class politics") substantially decreases using these subjective measures. They conclude that differences in popular sentiments regarding class issues in these two countries may be much less than has been widely assumed and that, in accord with Myles and Forcese (1981), explanations of differences in class politics in different countries should pay more attention to organizational factors such as the nature of the electoral options available to the voter.

Thus, mainstream, national survey-based studies of class politics in Canada either argue for the political irrelevance of class divisions and class consciousness, because of a failure to detect their existence, or else assume the existence of class divisions and class consciousness, but continue to argue that they are irrelevant because of the omnipotence of existing political structures. A series of case studies has documented substantial pockets of class voting in Canada (e.g. Wilson, 1968; Wiseman and Taylor, 1982). But the broader significance of such findings typically has been discounted because of the absence of a major working-class party (see Schwartz, 1974).

The main limitations of such arguments are twofold. First, the imputation of extensive consciousness-constraining powers to political parties remains problematic. While considerable consciousness-shaping capacities are typically imputed to electoral parties, actual differences in the class interests represented by their political discourse and programs are downplayed. Surely political parties, along with trade unions, have been crucial organizational and ideological forms historically involved in both shaping and partially resonating the concerns of working people in many advanced capitalist societies (e.g. Gallie, 1983; Lash, 1984). But it is also clear that in particular moments of social crisis, even the left parties have not effectively shaped popular expressions of dissent (e.g. Willener, 1970). More generally, a tendency for the parliamentary left to focus on less threatening "safety net" issues while only sporadically raising class issues has long been observed, even in the advanced capitalist states where class voting has been most strongly detected (e.g. Michels, 1959; Miliband, 1973). With regard to actual variations in political discourse, the U.S. has clearly been, at least since the 1930s, a polar case with "... a party system that reflects relatively loose coalitions that incorporate a variety of often inconsistent policy goals" (Jackman and Jackman, 1983:215). In Canada, the Cooperative Commonwealth Federation (CCF)/New Democratic Party (NDP) has, from the early days of the Regina Manifesto through to the "corporate welfare bums" campaign of the 1970s, quite regularly attacked the interests of big business while attempting to articulate those of a shifting array of working-class, farm and other subordinate groups. Thus, without becoming an explicitly working-class party, the NDP has, as Heron (1983:31) observes, "... become the repository of diffuse radical and reformist traditions of working-class politics". The relative visibility of left parties in English Canada, although still far less than in many European countries, "... offers striking contrast to the situation in the United States" (Christian and Campbell, 1974:116). In addition, the level of unionization in Canada has increased significantly in the past decade,[1] whereas in the U.S. it has declined to roughly half the current Canadian level.

While class voting researchers have typically cited other factors, to be consistent in their use of political organizations as explanatory factors they would at least have to posit a somewhat higher level of working-class consciousness in Canada than in the U.S. The main difficulty in this regard, however, is that *levels of class consciousness simply cannot be inferred in any direct way from the existing political party system*. Whatever class consciousness exists is constructed not only through political organizations, but also through broader public discourse on various political, economic and cultural themes as well as more directly through lives experiences of structured workplace, household and community relations (Livingstone, forthcoming; cf. Chamberlain, 1983). There may be a variety of mediating influences between the emergence of subjective class consciousness and concerted political action. In logical terms, it would be equally reasonable to argue that where substantial variations in subjective class consciousness do exist, the party system may not necessarily reflect such differences. Some class-conscious voters would therefore either discriminate pragmatically among existing parties, or else refrain from participating in electoral politics, along with others with lower levels of class consciousness.

The second major limitation of most North American research on class voting, as with most European research on the topic (e.g. Korpi, 1983), is the use of inadequate conceptualization or measurement of either class position or class consciousness. Typically, objective classes have been treated either as a vague continuum of statuses measured by combinations of occupational categories, educational attainments, and incomes, or as simple manual/non-manual or working/middle class dichotomies using similar measures. Classes should instead be demarcated primarily by relations of ownership and control within production processes (see for example Wright, 1980a). Secondly, when class consciousness has been specifically assessed, it has been only in terms of measures of subjective class identity, with no effort made to differentiate those with higher levels of class consciousness (see Mills, 1956; Hazelrigg, 1973).

Empirical researchers more familiar with a historical materialist perspective have recently begun to redress our ignorance about contemporary class positions (e.g. Wright, 1980b, 1985) but have shown little interest to date in relating class positions to political party preferences. Two major Canadian exceptions are Hunter's (1982) re-analysis of the 1974 *National Election Study* and Ornstein *et al*,'s (1980) report of a 1977 national survey, both of which have attempted to operationalize Marxist class categories based on production relations. Both studies found negligible objective class differences in party preferences in English Canada. While these two studies are steps in the right direction, limitations in their data bases which prevent discrete identification of several class positions, as well as their initial reliance on aggregate linear regression analysis techniques, may make them insensitive to important variations in particular objective class groups. In the latter regard, a third Canadian study based on roughly comparable measures of a Marxist class scheme (and using a multiple discriminant analysis technique) has found more significant associations between objective class position and party preferences in the 1974 federal election. Zipp and Smith (1982) found that professional employees (the "new working class") were significantly more likely to vote NDP or Liberal than Conservative, that traditional working-class people who lived in ridings where the NDP was "viable" were less likely to vote Conservative and more likely to vote NDP, and that non-voters were more similar in class terms to NDP voters than to Liberal or Conservative voters. In any event, further comparable research on more recent patterns is much needed.

No recent large-scale North American studies appear to have gone beyond very limited measures of class identity in examining the relationship of class consciousness to party preferences (e.g. Keddie, 1980; Kornberg et al., 1982; Jackman and Jackman, 1983). Several local studies conducted in the late 1960s did find significant associations between higher levels of working-class consciousness and support for either pro-labour or NDP candidates among urban manual workers (Leggett, 1969, 1979). More current, larger-scale analyses of the association of levels of class consciousness with party preferences, as well as of the interactive relations of class position and class consciousness with party preferences, are of central importance in order to reassess still prevalent assumptions that class politics are irrelevant in North America.

The following sections offer some relevant evidence drawn from a series of opinion surveys conducted in Ontario in March 1978, September 1980, September 1982 and September 1984.[2] I first briefly outline the conceptualizations of class divisions and class consciousness that underlie this empirical analysis and present summary profiles of the distributions of class positions and levels of expressed class consciousness in Ontario at these four points in time. Then I summarize the specific patterns of association found between class position and political party preference, class consciousness and party preference, and finally between class position and party, as mediated by class consciousness.

Several researchers have suggested that whatever class-based voting does exist in English Canada has been strongest in Ontario and British Columbia (see Englemann and Schwartz, 1975; Clarke *el al.*,1979). Numerous Canadian studies have found strong regional patterns of voting behaviour, political attitudes and political loyalties (see Clarke *et al.*, 1979; Mathews and Davis, 1985). One detailed analysis of the 1965 federal election has found that region had no effect on the relationship between objective class measures and voting behaviour, but that region did affect both objective class and vote separately (Erickson, 1981). There may also be important regional differences in the class alignments of voters with regard to federal and provincial politics. Quebec is the most evident case: for example, Hunter (1982) found class effects on voting in the 1973 Quebec provincial election, but not in the 1974 federal election. More recently, B.C. voters have been found to behave much like other voters in English Canada in federal elections, but to be much more highly polarized in left-right terms in provincial politics (Blake, 1985). In view of both the previously-noted limitations of prior North American research on class voting and the documented regional differences in aggregate voting patterns, conclusions from the present study should not be generalized beyond the Ontario case.

Current Class Divisions in Ontario

From a historical materialist perspective, the primary agencies of social change have been assumed to be class groups and alliances. In this conception, classes are not categories, but rather relationships that are lived within historically constructed contexts. In capitalist societies, classes are partially constituted in household and community relations, but their primary determination has come from paid workplace relations. Class positions in production are distinguished in terms of the extent of control exercised over the basic dimensions of the production process: the ownership of the means of production, as well as the technical design of the work process, and the supervision of the worker.[3] As Meiksins has stressed in one of the preceding chapters in this collection, ownership versus wage labour is the most fundamental objective class division.

Very broadly, we can think of the current class structure of the advanced capitalist societies in terms of:

1. Capitalists, who own the major private means of production. Within this class one can distinguish: (a) large corporate employers; (b) small employers, who continue to work alongside their employees; and (c) rentiers, who live off investment income without direct participation in the workplace.

2. Intermediate workers, who have some control over others' labour power and/or discretion over the use of their own labour, but are subordinated to capitalists' ownership claims or production decisions. Four broad types can be identified:
(a) the self-employed, traditionally called the 'petite bourgeoisie', who work for themselves without employing other paid labour (they are now generally dependent on corporate capitalist enterprises);
(b) managers or technocrats—those employees with day-to-day general responsibility for disciplining the rest of the workforce and the conduct of technical design and planning;
(c) supervisors, who are subordinate to managers in capitalist firms and state organizations. They exercise immediate disciplinary control over subordinated workers, but are assigned no control over production design; and
(d) professional employees, who have no role in supervising other workers, but do have responsibility for the detailed problem-solving involved in the design and operation of production systems.

Table 1: Class Structure of the Ontario 18+ Population, 1978-84

General Class Location	Specific Class Position	% of 18+ Population 1978		1980		1982		1984		% of Employed Workforce 1978		1980		1982		1984	
Capitalist	Corporate executives	1		1		1		1		1		2		1		2	
	Small employers	5		5		3		2		9		8		5		7	
	Rentiers	1*		2		3		2		-		-		-		-	
Intermediate workers	Self employed	4		5		4		3		6		9		8		5	
	Managers	4		3		5		4		7		6		9		8	
	Supervisors	9		9		9		9		16	36	18	37	17	39	15	37
	Professional employees	8		7		7		8		13		13		13		14	
Proletariat	Non-industrial wkrs	16		12		14		115		26		22		25		27	
	Industrial workers	11		11		9		11		19	48	21	44	17	45	19	49
	Residual workers	2		1		1		2		3		1		3		3	
Dependent population	Homemakers	18		21		18		22		-		-		-		-	
	Students	3*		7		7		7		-		-		-		-	
	Unemployed	8*	41	3	45	5	43	3	42	-		-		-		-	
	Pensioners	10		13		11		10		-		-		-		-	
	Residual	2		1		2		0									
TOTAL		**100**		**100**		**100**		**100**		**100**		**100**		**100**		**100**	
N		**1032**		**1121**		**1051**		**1046**		**616**		**597**		**557**		**591**	

* Data for rentiers, students and unemployed not directly comparable with later surveys because of less precise question wording.

3. Proletarians, who own only their own labour power and have no real control over other workers. Two types are distinguished:
(a) industrial workers, who are engaged in the manufacture of material goods and related transportation activities; and
(b) non-industrial workers, who are engaged in clerical, sales, and service activities.

4. The dependent population, composed of people outside the employed workforce; many of them are, however, instrumental in its daily and generational reconstitution. The dependent population includes homemakers, students, temporarily unemployed workers, and pensioners, many of whom live in households with members of other classes, as well as lumpen elements. Designation within the dependent population is generally not very informative for class analysis, without specification of either the class positions of others in the household or the trajectory of the dependent people themselves into or out of class positions in the production process.

Any serious account of class structures, practices, and relations must include the lived relations of all class actors within the household and community spheres as well as those within paid workplaces. The empirical analysis presented here, however, uses only fairly arbitrary first approximations, based on individuals' class positions in production relations.

On the basis of our series of sample surveys, estimates can be made of the recent class distribution in Ontario. As Table 1 indicates, the dependent population now includes more than 40 percent of Ontarian adults over 18 years of age, with full-time homemakers being about half of the total. If we also exclude rentiers to focus only on the employed workforce, we find that nearly half of the people actively engaged in production relations are in proletarian class positions, with non-industrial workers outnumbering industrial workers. Over one-third of the people in the employed workforce are in professional, managerial, or supervisory positions; not surprisingly managers are the smallest group. The remaining one-sixth of the employed workforce is made up of proprietors, with self-employed workers and small employers in about equal numbers, as well as corporate employers (including top executives and boards of directors) who represent less than 2 percent of the total employed population.

Taking sampling variations into account, these surveys have not detected any major structural changes in class positions over the six-year period involved. That is, despite substantial restructuring within firms and recomposition within economic sectors, the overall distribution of capitalist, intermediate and proletarian positions appears to have been quite stable.

Class Consciousness in Ontario

Analysts have distinguished at least three basic level of class consciousness:

1. Class identity, which is awareness of classes and identification with one's own class.

2. Oppositional consciousness, which is recognition of one's opposition of interest with another class or classes.

3. Hegemonic consciousness, which is readiness to act to achieve (or maintain) a form of society based on one's own class interests.

In the current study, class identity is assessed in terms of "upper", "upper middle". "lower middle", "working" and "lower" class labels. Oppositional consciousness is considered in terms of support for the right of corporations to unconditionally maximize profits and, conversely, of support for the right of workers to strike. Hegemonic levels of consciousness involve preferences for corporate capitalist or socialist economic structures as well as an acceptance or rejection of the current structure of political power.

In this conception,[4] it is the subjects' individual and collective sense of opposed class interests that is pivotal in the development of class consciousness. However intensely people hold to a subjective class identity, it is unlikely to be of much significance in shaping specific political attitudes or action unless there is also a coherent general recognition of opposed class interests. On the other hand, perceptions of the power structure and preferences for economic futures are unlikely to be of much use for political action if they are grounded in a confused sense of the fundamental class interests operative in present-day capitalist society.

Using these assumptions one can construct a basic class-consciousness schematic:

1. Starting with the midpoint, anyone who expresses inconsistent or noncommitted views on the opposed interests of capital and labour exhibits "contradictory class consciousness", differentiated only by class identity. Upper and upper middle class labels are take to designate "capitalist" identity, working and lower class labels to designate "working class" identity, and lower middle class or other responses to designate "mixed residual" identity.

2. Among those with a coherent sense of opposed class interests, one can distinguish three forms of capitalist consciousness:

Table 2: Levels of Class Consciousness in Ontario, 1978-84

Class Consciousness level	1978		1980		1982		1984	
Hegemonic capitalist	2		3		3		3	
Oppositional capitalist	3	19	2	16	5	27	5	23
Capitalist supporter	14		11		19		15	
Contradictory mixed residual	14		14		15		14	
Contradictory working class	23	64	22	66	21	61	22	69
Contradictory capitalist	27		30		25		33	
Working class supporter	9		10		7		6	
Oppositional working class	7	16	7	18	6	13	3	8
Counter-hegemonic working class	0.3		0.4		0.3		-	
N	**1032**		**1007**		**1051**		**1046**	

(a) "capitalist supporters" express coherent support for capitalist rights and opposition to labour's interests but assign themselves subordinate-class identities;
(b) people with "oppositional capitalist consciousness" exhibit a similar sense of coherent class interests but see themselves as part of the upper classes; and
(c) "hegemonic capitalist consciousness" entails, in addition, a denial of big-business dominance of the political system and a clear preference for a corporatist economic future.

3. Similarly there are three forms of working class consciousness:
(a) "working class supporters" express coherent support for the rights of labour and opposition to capitalist interests, but assign themselves non-working class identities;
(b) people with "oppositional working class consciousness" display a similar sense of coherent class interests but do see themselves as part of the working class; and
(c) "counterhegemonic working class consciousness" requires, in addition, a perception of corporate capital's dominance of the current political system and a clear preference for state or worker control of the economy.

Table 2 summarizes the basic pattern of class consciousness found in our Ontario surveys. While no interview survey is likely to capture the full variety and fluidity of class consciousness, the findings strongly support the prevalence of contradictory class consciousness. Roughly two-thirds of Ontarians expressed such views in each survey. The major change over the six years was an apparent decline in working-class consciousness: in the 1978 and 1980 surveys, the minorities indicating coherent class consciousness were split quite evenly between capitalist and working class consciousness, but in the later surveys, the former was twice as frequent as the latter. Only very small proportions of the population had hegemonic levels of class consciousness, but it is probably worth noting that of the people who did, those with hegemonic capitalist consciousness outnumbered those with counterhegemonic working class consciousness by at least seven to one throughout the survey period.

When we assess the relationship between class position and class consciousness, as summarized in Table 3, contradictory-class consciousness is found to prevail in nearly all class groups. The most coherent class consciousness appears among capitalists. Most notably, the majority of corporate executives consistently express at least oppositional capitalist consciousness, with some indication of increased coherence since 1978. Rentiers have also displayed a marked tendency toward more coherent capitalist consciousness in recent years, while small employers exhibit a more uneven pattern. The majority of people in all subordinate class positions have continued to express contradictory class consciousness. For most of this period working-class consciousness persisted most strongly among industrial workers, with about one-quarter stating such views. But by 1984, even among industrial workers, there appeared to be a larger minority expressing oppositional capitalist consciousness than oppositional working class consciousness.

Political Party Preference in Ontario

The item used in these Ontario surveys to measure party preferences is as follows: 'Which party or social movement is generally closest to your political views?'

- Progressive Conservative
- Liberal
- New Democrat
- Social Credit
- Communist or Radical Socialist
- Libertarian
- Other
- Can't say

Table 3: Class Position by Class Consciousness, Ontario, 1978-84

	Class Consciousness											
	Capitalist				Contradictory				Working Class			
Class Positions	**1978**	**1980**	**1982**	**1984**	**1978**	**1980**	**1982**	**1984**	**1978**	**1980**	**1982**	**1984**
Corporate executives	63	69	80	77	32	28	19	23	5	3	1	0
Small employers	28	25	56	26	66	56	38	60	6	19	6	14
Rentiers	-	26	55	60	-	68	40	33	-	6	5	7
Self employed	19	4	22	22	75	83	61	68	6	13	18	10
Managers	40	24	31	41	51	57	64	54	10	19	6	4
Supervisors	21	15	33	22	64	70	54	68	15	15	12	10
Professional employees	17	17	27	18	57	56	63	71	26	27	10	11
Non-industrial wkrs	23	13	21	19	65	66	67	73	12	21	12	8
Industrial workers	14	11	20	17	59	67	57	74	27	23	24	9
Homemakers	14	13	23	23	72	72	63	71	14	15	14	6
Students	33	18	16	22	51	63	69	71	16	19	15	7
Unemployed	12	15	24	14	71	72	65	76	17	13	11	9
Pensioners	22	20	29	18	62	66	62	73	16	15	9	9
TOTAL SAMPLE %	**19**	**16**	**27**	**23**	**64**	**66**	**61**	**69**	**16**	**18**	**13**	**8**

Table 4: Class Position by Political Party Preference, 1978-84

Political Party Preference (%)

Class Position	Progressive Conservative 1978	1980	1982	1984	Liberal 1978	1980	1982	1984	NDP 1978	1980	1982	1984	Other 1978	1980	1982	1984	Not Stated 1978	1980	1982	1984
Corporate executives	67	71	73	80	23	18	14	12	0	0	0	0	4	4	2	1	6	7	7	3
Small employers	49	41	45	49	26	28	19	26	2	12	10	13	4	5	6	1	19	13	21	11
Rentiers	-	24	48	61	-	51	35	18	-	0	1	11	-	0	3	2	-	25	13	8
Self employed	33	22	40	48	29	36	23	26	3	14	17	7	25	7	0	0	9	22	20	19
Managers	38	27	39	59	38	48	19	15	7	16	8	9	2	0	0	1	15	9	35	15
Supervisors	18	28	42	31	39	33	23	40	16	27	24	18	3	2	2	0	23	10	10	10
Professional employees	22	22	30	47	33	29	18	26	21	28	22	8	3	4	6	8	21	17	25	11
Non-industrial wkrs	29	15	32	45	29	36	25	18	15	23	22	19	2	2	2	1	24	23	19	17
Industrial workers	17	21	27	38	23	38	15	20	30	25	29	25	2	2	3	1	27	14	26	17
Homemakers	29	24	33	51	37	38	19	16	14	12	20	21	1	1	1	0	19	24	28	13
Students	27	22	31	29	50	41	16	34	10	15	24	14	0	1	1	1	12	22	29	22
Unemployed	13	21	22	22	31	46	23	24	17	12	28	28	4	0	3	5	35	20	24	21
Pensioners	26	33	32	45	38	29	27	15	12	14	14	19	1	0	3	4	24	23	24	18
TOTAL	**26**	**25**	**33**	**44**	**33**	**36**	**22**	**22**	**16**	**18**	**19**	**17**	**3**	**2**	**2**	**2**	**23**	**19**	**24**	**15**
Totals excluding undecided	**34**	**30**	**44**	**52**	**42**	**45**	**28**	**26**	**20**	**22**	**25**	**20**	**4**	**3**	**3**	**2**				

This format is intended to elicit a general political party preference and dampen the pragmatic and particular factors which may influence more immediate voting decisions.

The general patterns of party preferences, as summarized in the column marginals of Table 4, were in any case quite close to those of both federal and provincial elections and other opinion polls conducted at the same points during the 1978-84 period. There appeared to be a general if uneven tendency toward increasing Conservative support from 1980 onwards, reaching a slight majority of decided federal and provincial voters by September 1984, and a corresponding decline in Liberal support to about a quarter of decided voters.[5] The relative support for the Conservative and Liberal Parties did fluctuate somewhat within these tendencies in relation to specific federal and provincial elections. But what has been persistently found in all elections and most surveys is that support for the NDP remained *very stable* at about one-fifth of decided voters, and that support for other parties, particularly other socialist parties, remained negligible.

The specific patterns of association between class position and party preference are detailed in the body of Table 4. Corporate executives expressed strong majority support for the Conservative Party throughout this period and no support for the NDP.[6] Other capitalists' views were less consistent, with marked increases in rentiers' support for the Conservatives, and occasional small minority support for the NDP among both rentiers and small employers. The general tendency toward increased Conservative support from 1980 onward was evident among most subordinate workers. Industrial workers expressed the most consistent support for the NDP, but this amounted to less than one-third of their numbers, and was always considerably less than their combined preference for the Conservative and Liberal Parties. In spite of a continuing expression of party indifference or uncertainty by around one-fifth of the electorate, and the existence of discernible support for the NDP among all class positions except corporate executives, majorities in nearly all class positions supported the two mainstream or major parties throughout this period. This majority support for the two mainstream parties was broken only irregularly; in addition to industrial workers this occurred among professional employees, students, and most frequently, the unemployed. But while the unemployed have experienced the greatest personal distress during this economic and fiscal crisis and the NDP has made sustained efforts to speak distinctly to their needs, even the political response of this grouping remained muted, with only a marginal turn detected here toward the political left (cf. Schlozman and Verba, 1979; Economist Intelligence Unit, 1982).

More distinct patterns occur in the relations between class consciousness and party preference. As the columns of Table 5 show, those with working-class consciousness have been much more likely to support the NDP or another socialist party than those with capitalist consciousness, while a reverse pattern occurs with regard to combined Conservative and Liberal Party support. The column differences are quite striking between those with capitalist and working-class consciousness. The pattern of association between levels of class consciousness and party preferences remained quite stable through the 1978-84 period. But several asymmetries in these relations should be noted. First, a decline in the number who combine a strong working-class consciousness and a socialist party prefer-

Table 5: Class Consciousness by Political Party Preference, 1978-84

	Political Party Preference(%)							
	P.C./Liberal				NDP/Other Socialist			
Class Consciousness	1978	1980	1982	1984	1978	1980	1982	1984
Counter-hegemonic working class	20	13	0	-	80	67	58	-
Oppositional working-class	37	38	31	43	43	38	33	40
Working class supporter	53	53	45	62	25	27	37	23
Contradictory working class	50	57	46	62	18	21	23	21
Contradictory mixed residual	59	63	54	60	12	14	24	19
Contradictory capitalist	70	67	70	70	11	12	11	17
Capitalist supporter	65	76	62	77	6	12	10	9
Oppositional capitalist	89	76	72	84	1	2	10	3
Hegemonic capitalist	87	76	72	84	2	4	6	6
TOTAL	59	61	55	66	16	18	19	17

ence is indicated particularly by the absence of any respondents with counter-hegemonic working-class consciousness in the 1984 survey. Secondly, only tiny minorities of those with any level of capitalist class consciousness indicated support for the NDP, whereas the allegiances of those with oppositional working-class consciousness remained quite evenly split between the NDP and the two mainstream parties. Nevertheless, the results do clearly suggest that differences in levels of class consciousness have generally played a substantial role in mediating political party preferences in Ontario during this period.

When the combined associations of class position and class consciousness with party preference are examined, the numbers of cases are smaller and statistical confidence levels lower, but several more specific patterns are suggested. Table 6 summarizes the survey results concerning NDP or other socialist party preferences. Not only all corporate executives but all small employers and rentiers who exhibited capitalist consciousness were opposed to the NDP; among capitalists, only small employers with less coherent levels of class consciousness expressed any sustained support for the NDP. Among intermediate class positions, only self-employed proprietors with capitalist consciousness consistently expressed no support for the NDP. Only among those respondents with working-class consciousness were there pluralities in any class position supporting the NDP. But in no class position was there consistent majority support for the NDP. The unemployed and pensioners with working-class consciousness offered the most consistent plurality support for the NDP through this period. Professional employees expressing forms of working-class consciousness appear to have made an abrupt switch from majority support for the NDP in the early 1980s to the mainstream parties in 1984, exhibiting a political ambiguity similar to that characterizing professionals elsewhere (e.g. Brint, 1985).

Among proletarian workers, the association of working-class consciousness and NDP support sharply diminished during this period for industrial workers. While the majority of industrial workers with working-class consciousness supported the NDP in 1978, by 1984 only a small minority did so; the majority did not state a party preference, which perhaps suggests a growing disenchantment among industrial workers for organized politics. The pattern also suggests that non-industrial workers may have become the most active class conscious proletarian component within the NDP. In sum, this table indicates a quite volatile and recent recomposition of class conscious support for the NDP.

Table 6: Class Position by Socialist Party Preference Controlling for Class Consciousness, 1978-84

	NDP or Other Socialist Party Preference (%)											
	Capitalist Consciousness				Contradictory Consciousness				Working Class Consciousness			
Class Positions	**1978**	**1980**	**1982**	**1984**	**1978**	**1980**	**1982**	**1984**	**1978**	**1980**	**1982**	**1984**
Corporate executives	0	0	0	0	0	0	0	0	0	*	*	*
Small employers	3	0	0	0	1	14	26	7	*	24	*	60
Rentiers	*	0	0	0	*	0	0	23	*	*	*	*
Self employed	0	*	0	0	0	11	20	4	*	27	27	*
Managers	0	0	8	0	11	22	7	11	15	17	*	*
Supervisors	14	7	12	10	17	26	26	16	17	52	44	46
Professional employees	10	0	18	16	18	21	20	6	37	59	55	11
Non-industrial wkrs	9	13	10	14	14	21	24	19	32	35	36	25
Industrial workers	5	18	25	3	23	25	26	32	60	29	38	9
Homemakers	2	8	15	9	17	14	19	24	11	12	32	28
Students	0	7	0	0	11	15	24	21	*	22	49	*
Unemployed	0	0	9	*	16	10	31	29	42	36	51	*
Pensioners	0		7	6	8		16	20	45	43	34	36
TOTAL SAMPLE %	**5**	**9**	**10**	**7**	**15**	**17**	**20**	**19**	**34**	**33**	**36**	**28**
N	202	175	281	233	666	738	637	738	163	194	133	86

* ≤ 5 respondents

Conclusion

Hopefully, this brief summary has been sufficient to demonstrate that class positions, class consciousness and their interaction have had some substantial relationships with recent political party preferences in Ontario. The major trends detected during the 1978 to 1984 period, particularly the general decrease in the expressed level of working-class consciousness and the increase in Conservative Party support, are indicative of a political climate that became increasingly difficult for the practice of socialist politics. The growing disaffection of class conscious industrial workers with established parties, coupled with the continuing stability of general levels of NDP support in opinion polls, suggest that this party itself may have acceded to this climate.[7]

Class-based political struggles obviously continue both in everyday life and at the level of public discourse. The harsh material effects of business restructuring and government cutbacks, as well as the resistance of working people are graphically documented in some of the other chapters in this book. A more recent country-wide opinion poll found that the most significant trend of 1985 was '... a growing and potentially dangerous class disparity' and '... the beginning of class-based thinking' (Newman, 1986:12). Major efforts to encourage wider public discussion of more progressive social futures had previously occurred in Ontario through both the Ontario Federation of Labour's Economic Recovery Alternative campaign, and the Ethical Reflections on the Economic Crisis brief of the Catholic Bishops' Commission on Social Affairs. However, *optimistic presumptions about the progressive effects of such material conditions and public initiatives are no more advisable than the earlier easy presumptions about the irrelevance of class politics in North America.* Certainly, it should be more informative to begin further research into party preferences in North America with attention to their actual association with class positions and class consciousness than with presumptions of the non-existence of class politics. Such a research focus is consistent with a progressive perspective, as the emergence of majority support by class conscious subordinate class groups for some organized political vehicles on the left remains a necessary condition for any effective transformation to a genuine socialist democracy.

Notes

1. It should be noted, however, that since an initial burst of enthusiasm around the formation of the NDP in 1961, the party has been unable to increase the number of affiliated union members. In proportionate terms, NDP affiliation dropped from 19 percent to 12.5 percent of organized Canadian workers between 1964 and 1984. See Crombie (1986).
2. For descriptions of the design and sample composition of these surveys, see Livingstone (1978); Livingstone and Hart (1981); Livingstone, Hart and McLean (1983); and Livingstone, Hart and Davie (1985).
3. A more detailed discussion of these relationships and class structures generally, as well as of the specific measures used, appears in Livingstone (1985; forthcoming).
4. These levels of consciousness are more fully defined and illustrated in Livingstone (1985; forthcoming). To call responses to such general questionnaire items "contradictory" is not to suggest that all working people who so respond necessarily have a confused sense of their individual and class interests in everyday relations with capitalists.
5. For convenient partial summaries of such poll results, see the *Toronto Star*, October 23, 1984, pp. A1,4, and the *Toronto Globe and Mail*, October 28, 1985, p. 1.
6. This finding may be compared with that of Porter (1965) who found that Canadian corporate executives in the early 1960s were about equally divided between the Liberal and Conservative parties with no support for any third parties, and with that of Ornstein (1985:150) who found that in the early 1980s, the majority of corporate executives were aligned with the Conservative party, again with negligible support for the NDP.
7. It should be noted here that post-1984 declines in Conservative party support, both federally and provincially, have not yet resulted in any significant movement in NDP support beyond the 20 percent level in Ontario. See, for example, the *Toronto Globe and Mail*, August 15, 1985, p. 1, and the *Toronto Star*, December 6, 1985, pp. A1,4.

From the Shop Floor to the University Campus – Perspectives for Marxists

Tom Langford and Dieter Neumann

More than a few Marxist activists have decided to return to or newly take up university studies in the past several years. A whole raft of definitive cynical judgements have been made about this trend, directed both towards the involved individuals (middle-class careerism coming to the fore, etc.) and towards the Marxist sector of the socialist movement (more armchair Marxists only illustrates the inability of Marxism to develop a mass base in Canada, etc.). Just so that the authors of this article don't seem to be defensive and uncomfortable in the face of such charges, we will definitively reply: Damn the cynics! At the same time we want to offer some first-hand observations and analysis of the problems confronting Marxist activists in academia, and make a suggestion on the role university Marxists should be playing in building the socialist movement.

Both of the authors entered university in the early 1980s after a number of years of wage labour in large-scale industry which included extensive workplace activism. Our biographies, however, are far from identical. One of us grew up in a professional family, had been to university and had been politicized through involvement with campus-based socialist organizations. The other grew up in a working-class environment, dropped out of school at age 16 and developed a Marxist conviction through self-study during his wage- labouring years. What we have in common is a number of independent years of shop floor activism during which we strongly identified with, learned from and attempted to politically catalyze the groups of anti-company militants we met. Thus, the critical faculties we bring to bear on the problems of Marxist activists in academia owe a large debt to our participation in the social relations of production on industrial shop floors.

Practical Considerations in Pursuing a Marxist Education

The objective of Marxist activists who have recently entered university is to pursue a concentrated period of education which will improve their knowledge of the main currents of Marxist theory, and allow them to make a more theoretically sophisticated contribution to the socialist movement.

Canadian universities are not set up to facilitate this objective; nor is such an objective shared by very many university students or faculty. As a consequence it is largely incumbent on the Marxist activist to design his or her own educational program within the very definite limits imposed by the bourgeois educational system. Two factors are central to the educational experiences of activists: finances and time.

As we write these words, the importance of finances in the university education experience of activists is all too personally evident. One of us secured a scholarship and so he is continuing with graduate studies; the other ran out of money before getting enough credits to enter graduate school, so he is temporarily welding steel for the new skyway bridge in Hamilton. Both of us have had to depend upon financial assistance from our spouses at different times in the past two years, and have student loans to repay. It is obvious that even for individuals with limited family and financial commitments, full-time university study is an option which taxes resources and entails material sacrifices. When material difficulties become severe, the relative peace of mind necessary for concentrated intellectual activity is simply not available.

In any university program, academic requirements exist concerning both what material is covered and how well it is covered. Some of these requirements do not contribute greatly to the goal of socialist education, and are consequently an unwelcome intellectual diversion, but others are flexible enough to be advantageously utilized by the student of Marxism. A certain amount of time must consequently be diverted from what we really want to accomplish intellectually in order to maintain our standing in the university. This is a necessary compromise. The other option would be to attempt a concentrated period of individual study. Such a course of action would rule out the possibility of obtaining employment or scholarship funds as a graduate student; and would cut us off from the intellectual stimulation provided in classes, seminars and informal discussions with students and faculty (this is how the authors met). It would also make the use of university resources such as libraries more difficult. In the short term, a maximum amount of time for study of Marxist theory would certainly be secured by sitting at a table for 14 hours a day of reading, thinking and note taking. In the long term, economic and intellectual factors make formal study at a university the option which secures the most time, month after month, for the study of Marxism.

A further factor which has facilitated the pursuit of our educational objective is closely related to our experiences as wage labourers: we tend to treat formal university requirements as a job to be accomplished in a certain amount of time rather than as an all-consuming obsession. This leaves considerable time for our own intellectual priorities.

Solidarity on Campus

As university students with a well-defined educational objective not shared by the vast majority in the university system, Marxist activists face problems in relating to their fellow students. The elite of university students are being trained as professionals such as lawyers, doctors, veterinarians or, at a somewhat lower notch, university faculty; many others are being groomed to occupy places as managers and supervisors of capitalist labour processes; still others will become skilled technical wage labourers. Even though an increasing number of the university educated are unable to find employment commensurate with a B.A. or higher degree and are thrown into the working class (often after experiencing extended periods of unemployment), they often share the occupational aspirations of their more successful colleagues. What separates us as Marxist activists from most of our fellow students (and faculty) is that we have already turned our backs on capitalist educational and occupational priorities for a number of years, and presumably are willing to do so again. As much as possible within the bourgeois university, we are setting our own agendas.

Put in these terms, it sounds like Marxist activists are the only ones with a critical consciousness and practice in the university: *we* are the enlightened critics; *they* are the products of bourgeois ideology. Such elitist thinking must be guarded against precisely because it is a pitfall for Marxists. Many students and faculty at least partially reject bourgeois values and policies, and some are active in their opposition. Work experiences, in combination with theoretical work, have helped Marxist activists to develop a crisp, gut-level oppositional viewpoint of capitalism. This is an invaluable perspective to have in the university, but it must not blind us to other insurgent trends.

Within the framework of these general perspectives, the question of solidarity has been a problem for the authors. It seems as if we are constantly being challenged to choose between our own intellectual priorities and involvement in the contradictions of the university. The following example provides an illustration of this.

The authors (both male) were enrolled in a graduate social theory course in which the other seven students were female, and the instructor male. It soon became apparent that the dynamics of discussion in the classroom revolved around the three males, and that the women were generally excluded. There were a number of reasons for this situation but the main ones, according to our assessment, were that the course was a prescribed requirement and none of the other students would have voluntarily taken it; and the women had been socialized to be intimidated by theoretical discussion. In the first few classes the authors would often refrain from speaking when the instructor asked for comments in order to give others a chance to speak—long silences would ensue. We investigated informally how the other students perceived what was taking place and found no resentment against our participation or strong desire to participate more. Consequently, we made a pragmatic decision not to take the lead in attempting to qualitatively change the structure of a course which was clearly not optimally serving the educational interests of most participants. Our instrumental decision in this situation is similar to many difficult decisions which Marxists have to make in order to get on with their own priorities in the university.

The question of solidarity also confronts us at the level of socialist politics. Should we commit ourselves to the dozens of hours involved in organizing a study circle to read Volume I of *Capital* (which we did) or involve ourselves in the libertarian left political culture of the university? The question can only be answered in one way if we are to be consistent. Our rationale for entering university indicates the acceptance of a political strategy which stresses the importance of theoretical practice for Marxists at this point in time. We must navigate such a strategic course in an environment where "direct action" on a personal and political level is the dominant strategy of the left. And once again, we must check arrogance and elitism when we observe the naive, often unreflective radicalism of many students, which includes a strong dose of anti-worker sentiment. Quite simply, we must establish our own priorities as Marxists, while making our strategy understandable to others on the left and maintaining cooperative links.

This, of course, doesn't mean a total withdrawal into the university library. In the past year in addition to the study circle on *Capital*, one or both of the authors helped to organize a public speaker series on socialist themes, participated in a teaching assistant union organizing committee, and researched and wrote a leaflet concerning the corporate policy of General Electric which was distributed by a local union to its membership. Our emphasis, however, has always remained on the theoretical objectives which brought us to the university.

Learning Marxism by Negative Example

Turning to the content of our education, the university has proven to be a strangely productive environment for the study of Marxism. Since he is today generally acknowledged as one of the founders of sociology, Karl Marx warrants more than a passing mention in an increasing number of courses. We contend that little in such courses (other than the very few taught by responsible Marxists or Marxist sympathizers) is of any worth in understanding Marx. It seems that instead of the relentless scorn and slander of yesterday, academics today praise and distort Marx and Marxism in a way that largely preserves the negative stereotypes of the past. In what forms have we observed this distortion?

First, there's the balance sheet approach to Marx. "He was correct in these predictions, wrong on these, and most important, his overall theory of social change was wrong. Case closed. Now let's talk about Veblen." This approach is quite popular, and is probably all that most students will remember about Marx. Its logic is based on a tripartite foundation: intellectual laziness, political anti-Marxism, and an epistemology which maintains that the worth of Marx's general theory can be decided by empirical tests of specific statements logically deduced from the theory. We can almost guarantee that anyone promoting this perspective has never taken the trouble to actually read *Capital*; nor does such a person have it on a reading list.

Second, there's the distortion involved in stereotyping current Marxist social science as being nothing more than crude defenses of outdated Marxist theory. During the second week of formal sociology study, one of the authors was subjected to an outburst by a graduate student, lambasting a piece of research conducted by Marxist sociologists in Windsor in which they "inanely" concluded that most of the working class held a Marxist view of society's power structure. No reference was forthcoming—this graduate student was merely relaying a tidbit he had picked up in the course of his "professional socialization" as a student. We learned this when, amazingly enough, other graduate students as well as faculty members were heard spouting the same ill-formed critique. In time we discovered that the reference was actually to a study of class consciousness in London (not Windsor after all). This research (Rinehard and Okraku, 1974) undoubtedly suffers from methodological, conceptual, and interpretive weaknesses; however, the characterization that was being passed on to undergraduates was designed not to educate, but rather to stereotype current Marxist research as a kind of quasi-religious quest to maintain the coherence of a set framework.

A third distortion is closely related to the second: "Marx made an enormous intellectual contribution, but Marxists since then, from Engels to Lenin to Lukacs to Althusser, have had little to say of relevance to social science." This is a convenient excuse for ignoring (or being ignorant of) a century of Marxist theory. The supposed failure of Marxists since Marx is usually attributed to their subservience to Marxist organizations; this political involvement is presented as something that compromised their intellectual creativity and honesty. There is certainly some truth in such an assertion, although it doesn't justify ignoring all Marxist writing. This explanation also overlooks Marx's own lifelong involvement in working class and communist politics. A slight disjunction in this assessment of Marxists, in our experience, concerns Antonio Gramsci. He receives favourable comments in university corridors, although the sad truth of the matter is that few have read him seriously and fewer still include any of his writings in course curricula.

Fourth, there is the attempt to link Marx with various mainstream intellectual traditions, from Weberianism to positivism. This is a philosophical rather than an empirical exercise. Marx is associated with these other traditions on a metaphysical or epistemological level, and any of his unique contributions are viewed as being of secondary importance to what he shares in common with other theorists.

Fifth, Marxism is diminished by reference to the eccentricities and deficiencies of the token Marxists on campus. When even one of these academics is identified as a male chauvinist or an incompetent, Marxism itself is negatively judged by both the campus and broader communities. Furthermore, the complete lack of activism on the part of some of these Marxist academics is justifiably seen by observers as hypocritical. Unfortunately, quite often the Marxists found in tenure-stream jobs seems rather isolated and incapable of engaging in the active, people-oriented political practice expected of them.

How, then, could such an environment be a productive place for the study of Marxism? Only in the sense that the crude distortions, simplistic assessments, and ever-present negative stereotypes provoked us to pursue topics and problems on our own. Next to none of our positive interest or motivation for learning about Marxism was fostered in the classroom. (Of course, this simply reflects our particular educational experiences, rather than ruling out the possibility of Marxism being effectively taught in the university classroom.) The university has been a relatively productive environment for our study of Marxism only because we brought an initial sympathetic understanding with us, along with a substantial background knowledge. This allowed us to utilize the resources of the university for the independent study of Marxist theory.

The Terror of Shop Floor Struggle Tactics

Our experience as Marxist activists in the university has been to attempt to arrange our academic lives so as to facilitate action on personal intellectual priorities. In our own judgement we have been far from armchair revolutionaries. At the same time we have generally refrained from the use of struggle tactics which we learned on industrial shop floors. On one issue, however, an academic contradiction centred on the course participation of one of the authors and he was forced to pursue it with vigour. The introduction of shop floor struggle tactics into the university afforded an opportunity to assess the political reality behind liberal academic education.

When we speak of shop floor struggle tactics, we aren't referring to the grievance procedure outlined in union contracts or the pseudo-grievance procedures contained in the employee guidebooks of most non-union plants. What we have in mind are the tactics used on the shop floor in the day-to-day matters over which workers can attempt to gain some control. The following anecdote illustrates the concept.

Machine operators in a department in which one of the authors worked would get thirty seconds of dead time every three minutes. A quick run to another machine and back would still leave twenty seconds for a brief conversation. Over the course of a half hour a lively and entertaining conversation on the topic of the day could take place. In time the department supervisor introduced a new rule: no wandering from machines. Written warnings were passed out to coerce compliance. The response of the workers was to engage in shouted conversations—certainly less enjoyable, but a response that struggled against the company's imposed discipline. Eventually a further opportunity for struggle presented itself. The supervisor confided in one of the workers that the main reason for the ban on conversations was the fact that he thought the workers had been gossiping about him. (In fact such conversation usually revolved around stories in the morning paper.) Now that shouted conversations were going on, he believed that the machine operators were involved in a continual process of "catcalling" him. Needless to say, from that time on, imitation tomcat "meows" would fill the air whenever the supervisor made an appearance.

One immediate comparison between the shop floor and the university campus can be made: most professors, despite their liberal airs, are if anything more blatant subjectivists than the supervisor in the preceding anecdote. Deference to the professor's authority is generally a necessary, though not sufficient, condition for academic success.

Of course there exists an element of freedom for the student which is unavailable to the factory worker. The student can skirt some troublesome issues, while the factory worker has no room to manoeuvre. In both settings, however, what we've described as shop floor struggle tactics are often dismissed as childishness. In this sense, the expectations of university professors and company officials are exactly parallel; 'mature' people should be able to sit down and work out their differences (according to the framework of power already in place). The following is a brief description of the struggle which allowed us to form these conclusions.

Unhappy with his inability to create a 'group effect' in one of his classes, a sociology professor issued a lengthy written statement near the end of the course which provided his assessment of why this group had failed to develop the dynamics which developed in previous courses. This professor was a self-styled master at 'creating group effects', and over the course of the semester many of the students concluded that this was a fancy way of avoiding serious teaching responsibilities (an attitude which apparently did not lend itself to the professor's intention). The written statement named the students deemed responsible for sabotaging this learning experience, and hinted darkly at the deep-rooted sexual phobias that were the cause of this behaviour.

In response to this document, and to other irregularities in the course, one of the authors launched an appeal through official channels which dragged on for almost a year and eventually went nowhere, largely because the university establishment was of the view that the instructor was merely exercising his academic freedom. The reactionary dimension of the department was revealed when one of the authors embarked on a campaign of informal agitation, photocopying the documents in question and distributing them as widely as possible. What had begun as an attempt by a professor to squelch criticism of his course now backfired. His statement, rife with subjectivist innuendo and numerous obscure doodles, was made public. The response of the department was an attempt to intimidate the student by threatening him with a lawsuit—a threat which only guaranteed that the documents were given an even wider distribution.

On the shop floor the company warns you, transfers you, tries to make life so miserable that you quit and, eventually if it has to, fires you. In the university they try to persuade you in discussion, warn you about academic repercussions, and even threaten you with a lawsuit; if that fails, they ignore you, secure in the knowledge that the intricate academic grievance procedure will eventually tire you out.

Some may object to our sketch of the similarities between the shop floor and the university in comparing the response of authorities to independent, non-deferential struggle tactics. We realize we've failed to draw out some important distinctions. At the same time our experiences show remarkable similarities once the struggle begins; those controlling commodity and intellectual production in bourgeois society are shaken by acts of resistance which show no homage towards their directing authority. In pursuing a socialist education at university, Marxist activists may be able to tactically skirt many situations such as the one which led to the confrontation described above. However, they should never lose sight of the social relations of the institution, or shirk a struggle where the logic of the situation demands political action.

Conclusion: A Suggestion for Marxists in the University

There are undoubtedly more Marxists than ever in the Canadian university system: the tenured professors who studied in the 1960s and early 1970s; the sessional instructors from the past decade; and the current crop of Marxist students which includes activists who have returned to university. Some of these people are doing highly original research which is addressed to frontier questions in Marxist theory and politics and is greatly contributing to our understanding of the social relations characteristic of capitalism in Canada. Others of us are theoretically sophisticated and competent, although we have no claim to high levels of originality and brilliance.

The university system allows an opening for socialist studies which only a few are able to use. This route is cut off for most activists and certainly for militant workers. While we would hardly claim that there are hundreds of workers in every community across Canada who would enroll in socialist educational courses if they were only given the opportunity, we believe that there are many workers whose experiences have raised intellectual problems in their minds, and who have the temperament and ability to pursue those problems at a theoretical level. It is our contention that Marxists in academia must utilize the resources at their disposal, and their relative intellectual freedom, in order to actively build the socialist movement among workers.

What we mean is at once something more and something less than the common practice of socialists today. We are talking about Marxist intellectuals taking the initiative in reaching out to workers - not waiting for an invitation from the local labour council to give a talk. We are not talking about using socialist jargon in an attempt to build the membership of an isolated left group. What we foresee are responsible socialist education courses, advertised in community newspapers, on cable television, and on public bulletin boards, and dealing with a wide range of themes. Such courses should ideally be conducted on a regular basis, and be restricted to theoretical education. As individuals who have left the shop floor to study Marxism in the university system, we see the creation of independent workers' educational groups as being a concrete way in which we can turn our theoretical training into a collective advance. We are not starry-eyed about this—the most optimistic expectation we have is for the involvement of a relatively small number of workers over many years of work. Neither do we have any illusions about imparting a 'correct' socialist perspective to workers; our only goal should be to encourage theoretical sophistication on the part of workers. Such theoretical education is essential for strengthening the intellectual independence, and increasing the confidence, of workers. It is our conviction that Marxists in the university system have at present a unique responsibility to provide independent educational alternatives for workers.

Acknowledgements
For comments which helped originally to develop this paper we thank Barry Fowlie, Vanessa Hyland, Evelyn McCallen and Dave McConnell.

SECTION IV

Women's Issues and the Labour Movement

Introduction

The economic crisis has hit women the hardest and threatens to erode the gains they have made by pushing women back into the home. Because of the gender hierarchy at work, women are found in the low paying sectors of the economy defined as women's work. Oppressed by their position in the household, exploited as cheap labour in the workforce and treated as second class citizens in the labour movement, women have been pivotal in developing effective strategies that link together community, union and workplace. Their increasing militancy in organizing campaigns and in first contract strikes, the forging of alliances between the women's movement and the labour movement, and the importance of raising women's issues alongside economic demands have been the major components of this new strategy. The papers presented here not only provide thoughtful analysis but also explore practical methodologies for democratizing the labour movement, by placing an emphasis on the activities of women in determining their lives.

Unique to this volume, we have highlighted the struggles of the most exploited sectors of the Canadian economy, namely immigrant women and women of colour. The authors implicitly provide a global perspective to women's and workers' struggles. A heightened sensitivity to issues of racism and sexism has been catalysed by the growing pressures from this sector to avoid tokenism, and to truly democratize the labour and women's movements.

Armstrong and Armstrong's paper addresses the effects of the economic crisis on women by examining women's segregation into certain occupations of the Canadian economy threatened by technological change, part-time work and cutbacks in state expenditures. While women's labour force participation has greatly increased since World War Two, official government statistics underestimate women's real unemployment. Through an examination of labour force trends, the authors offer a convincing argument that women's unemployment rates are higher than men's.

Despite hard times epitomized by capital's squeeze on workers' wages, high levels of unemployment, and unfair labour legislation, women at Eaton's were militant in their fight for job security. Carol Currie and Geri Sheedy discuss the historic organizing drive that captured the hearts of the labour and women's movements in 1984.

Women not only defended their rights to bargain collectively but to become full and active participants in the labour movement. Ronnie Leah's paper on "Organizing for Daycare" reveals how the Women's Committee of the Ontario Federation of Labour helped to initiate a women's movement within the labour movement. The campaign for free standing abortion clinics is a further step, according to Carolyn Egan, in winning the union movement to a social movement perspective by going beyond economic issues and focussing on the quality of women's lives.

Increasing pressure on organized labour from the unorganized sector has highlighted the struggles of immigrant women and women of colour. Franca Iacovetta's historical study of Italian immigrant women describes the demands of their domestic and wage labour as they migrate from Southern Italy to Canada. Carmencita Hernandez focuses on the difficulties facing Filipino domestic workers who have lived in fear of reprisals from their home country. Erma Stultz acknowledges the need to organize farm workers who, unprotected by labour legislation, are required to work long hours for less than minimum wages under unsafe working conditions. Winnie Ng offers a vision of hope in her proposal for a Garment Workers Action Centre to house political, educational and service facilities for immigrant garment workers in the heart of downtown Toronto.

Women and the Economic Crisis

Pat Armstrong and Hugh Armstrong

Crises are an integral part of capitalist development, of the drive to accumulate. Such crises are political and social, as well as economic. They involve interruptions in production and in capital accumulation, and result in widespread bankruptcies, unemployment, cutbacks and social unrest. They reflect neither linear development nor uniform tendencies, but rather contradictions and struggle. At one and the same time, some firms are destroyed while others expand and restructure. In some areas, both the firm and the workers suffer; in others, both benefit; in some, little changes; in others, profits grow but employment declines. Competition, accumulation and worker resistance all play a role in these processes. The impact is not the same for all industries, for all classes, or for women and men.

The state actively intervenes to affect the outcome of crises. At one and the same time, it is an instrument of the most powerful economic forces, a mediator of the conflicts amongst them and between them and other forces and a location for these conflicts. Primarily interested in encouraging accumulation, the state also works to limit the worst consequences of that development. State programs and regulations encourage development in some areas and discourage it in others, helping both workers and employers in some cases, having little impact in some instances, assisting owners but having a negative effect on workers in others. The actions and organizations of workers and those without paid work influence the programs introduced or maintained. Here, too, the impact is uneven.

Technological change, both in equipment and in the organization of the labour process, is also an integral part of crises. At one and the same time, technological change is a cause, a reflection and, for many capitalists, a solution to crises. The application of new technologies make some firms uncompetitive, causing jobs and profits to decline; a few areas grow in terms of both profits and jobs, while others expand output but decrease the relative size of their labour force. Technological change is both retarded and accelerated by state intervention and, like state intervention, it is both affected by the strength and strategies of workers and unevenly introduced by industry, occupation, class and sex.

The effects of crises, of technological change and of state intervention are not limited to the formal economy, however. The household and formal economy are interpenetrating, with the conditions of the household set in broad terms by the formal economy but not wholly determined by it. The relationship is dialectical; the connection frequently uneven. Changes in the formal economy are reflected in and influenced by the household. The unevenness of development in the formal economy and in the relationship between the two spheres ensures that the process is not uniform. So does the resistance of household members. Household resources diminish in some areas, grow in others; eliminating some alternatives while expanding other kinds of domestic work, particularly for women.

Such a crisis has been disrupting the western world since the mid-seventies. This paper connects the uneven development during the current crisis, the technological change that is part of it and state intervention in these processes to the sexual division of labour in the formal economy and the household. Given the sexual division of labour in both spheres and the uneven development throughout the entire system, crises in general, and this one in particular, have different consequences for women and men. Initially, labour market segmentation has protected many women from the most obvious effects of the current crisis. But even in the earliest stages, there were many negative consequences for women's jobs, in and out of the labour force. The consequences were less visible and concentrated than those for men but were nonetheless real. Moreover, as the crisis continues, as the state cuts back in some areas and expands in others and as the new technology is put in place, women will lose more—and lose more than men—in and out of the household.

It is possible to make this prediction because the interests of capitalists usually prevail, because they design the technology and the relationships that accompany it and because state programs are primarily intended to encourage accumulation. The outcome is not however entirely determined by these interests. Nor is it without its own contradictions. People acting on the basis of these contradictions can influence the outcome. It is therefore important to analyze the most likely patterns in order to fashion a strategy for the future, one that will work for women as well as for men.

But such an analysis has more than immediate strategic implications. Crises are integral to capitalism and, while each has characteristics that are historically specific, many of the patterns that are emerging in the current crisis are likely to recur in the next. If the purpose is to develop a theory which explains the position of women in Canada, then it is crucial to work towards a theoretical and empirical understanding of women during economic crises. This paper is meant as a contribution to that larger project.

Labour Force Trends

By 1975, there were signs of an impending recession, perhaps of a crisis. In that year, male unemployment went above 6 percent, female unemployment above 8 percent. The rates for both sexes have not fallen lower since then. The overall rates suggest that, as the recession became a crisis, the greatest impact was on male employment. For the first time since the method of collecting unemployment data was changed in 1975,[1] male 1982 unemployment rates were higher than women's and men's share of unemployment increased significantly. Male participation rates also dropped sharply.

Particularly in the early years, most women in the labour force seemed to be protected from the worst consequences of the crisis. Some women appeared to be making gains. Between 1975 and 1982, female participation rates continued their steady climb, women's share of jobs grew by almost 5 percentage points and, with the sole exception of occupations in fabrication, women captured a higher proportion of all jobs. While the increasing concentration of women in managerial jobs seemed to offer the clearest indication of gains for women, there were also signs that some women had moved into other traditional male areas.

These overall figures, however, camouflaged both the meaning of these patterns and the real losses for women that were underway. The labour force remained highly segregated. In addition, an increasing number of jobs were part-time and most of this part-time work went to women. The more detailed the information, the more obvious it becomes that most women were not acquiring men's jobs or jobs in traditional male areas. Rather, some male jobs disappeared at the same time as the demand for workers grew in traditionally female areas, usually in low-paid and often part-time work.

Moreover, there were also indications that, as the crisis continued, many women in the labour force had little protection. Women's unemployment rates were higher than men's in every occupation where there were enough women to make the data reliable. That female participation rates abruptly halted a steady thirty-year climb suggests that many women who would otherwise have sought paid work, and thus been counted as unemployed, had given up in tough economic times. And in those areas where women did compete directly with men, the women usually lost. These patterns of uneven development during the crisis, of early protection for some women's jobs, of less visible deterioration in women's position and of increasing relative loss for women as the crisis deepens, becomes more evident when the occupational categories are examined in turn, as they are below.

Managerial and Professional Occupations

Close to half of all the additional full-time jobs created between 1980 and 1982 appeared in the broad "managerial, etc." category—a group which includes jobs in managerial and related occupations, those in natural sciences, engineering and mathematics, in social sciences and related fields, in religion, in teaching, in medicine and health as well as those in artistic, literary, recreational and related fields. Two-thirds of these full-time jobs went to women. Measured against the growth in the female share of overall employment between 1980 and 1982, women's share of managerial and teaching jobs grew more rapidly, while their share of natural science jobs grew less rapidly. Meanwhile, their share of jobs in medicine and religion remained constant, and their share of social science jobs actually declined slightly. With the exception of natural science, women took the larger share of part-time work.

These variations in patterns suggest that there is no uniform tendency towards greater opportunities for women. Rather, continued segregation has meant that some women in women's jobs have been protected from the crisis while some men in men's jobs have been more vulnerable. Additional jobs have appeared in female-dominated professions and these jobs have gone to women. The increase in female managers may be partially explained by the inclusion of executive secretaries in this category, a group that has been growing as new technology encourages a redefinition of this work and, not incidentally, can result in the exclusion of these women from union jurisdiction. Unlike men, the women who moved into other management jobs were concentrated in the relatively low "occupations related to management." Where women did compete more directly with men, as is the case in social science occupations and in part-time work in the natural sciences, women lost ground.

There are other signs of women's increasing vulnerability in these occupations as the crisis continues. A growing number of women with professional and managerial jobs found only part-time work—itself an indication that they did not capture the best jobs. Moreover, with the exception of those holding jobs in artistic fields, those women with part-time work saw their hours reduced, and reduced much more than those of men. Women's unemployment rates in all these jobs remained consistently higher than those of men; more than three percentage points higher in the natural and social sciences and more than two percentage points higher in teaching and managerial work.

Clerical Occupations

Throughout most of the century, clerical work has been women's work. Full-time clerical jobs have however recently been disappearing[2] especially for men. By 1982, a smaller proportion of women was doing clerical work even though they held a larger share of the jobs. This greater relative loss for men can be largely explained by the uneven impact of the crisis on a still segregated labour force. And the process has resulted in even greater segregation.

This explanation becomes clearer when it is understood that not all those people classified as clerical workers type, file, keep books or act as receptionists. Also included in this group are those involved in material recording, scheduling and distributing occupations. It is these other clerical jobs, concentrated as they are in the manufacturing, transportation and utilities sectors, that have most abruptly disappeared during the crisis and that account for a significant proportion of rising male unemployment in this occupation. By contrast, a high proportion of unemployed women are concentrated in the finance and service industries, where male unemployment is much lower. Only in trade industries are relatively equal proportions of women and men unemployed, and therefore more likely to be competing for scarce jobs.

While on the surface it may appear that men have suffered more, it should be noted that the overwhelming majority of unemployed clerical workers are female. Moreover, women retained their relative position only by acquiring most of the new part-time work, and many of those with part-time jobs saw their hours reduced. In addition, those full-time female jobs that were eliminated probably disappeared as a result of new technology. Such a reduction is likely to be permanent. On the other hand, male jobs disappeared primarily as a result of crisis-induced cutbacks in the private sector. Many of these will reappear if a recovery is sustained.

Sales Occupations

Approximately one in ten women and men in the labour force do what is classified as sales work, jobs ranging from supervisors in insurance companies to those in grocery stores, from service station attendants to delivery people and sales clerks. Less segregated than clerical work, sales work provides less protection for women from male competition. This probably explains why more than 60 percent of those losing full-time work here were women.[3] While full-time jobs disappeared, part-time jobs were created for both women and men. Women did manage to capture a majority of the new part-time work but then they had accounted for the overwhelming majority of part-time sales workers in the past. Their share of part-time jobs declined somewhat, however, indicating that men's relative position improved, that when women and men compete, women lose. Moreover, those women who got or kept part-time jobs had few hours of paid work. More than a quarter usually worked less than 20 hours a week; a fifth usually worked less than 9 hours a week in 1982.

Service Occupations

The service sector has not been as vulnerable to the crisis as other areas. More than one in ten of the additional full-time jobs and over one in five of the part-time ones were created in the service occupations. Women took three-quarters of the new full-time jobs and 60 percent of the new part-time work, in the process increasing their dominance in this occupational group.

What appear as gains for women must be understood in terms of the continuing segregation within this broad occupational group and the uneven development within the sector. Included in the broad service category are those involved in the provision of protection, lodging and accommodation, apparel and furnishing, food and beverages as well as personal and other related services. Men predominate in the protection and "other service occupations", women in the rest. Nearly 13 percent of all employed women prepared food and beverages or did personal service work. Only 3 percent of male employees had jobs in these occupations. In addition, well over a third of all women doing service work held part-time jobs and the majority of new work here was part-time. Moreover, by 1982, more that one in ten of the women with service jobs usually worked 9 hours a week or less; another 15 percent usually worked between 10 and 19 hours. The proportion of men with such short hours was approximately half the size.

Job growth in a still segregated market meant that some women acquired jobs, even if they were often crummy jobs. However, a growing number of women who had done service work found themselves unemployed and the unemployment rates of women remained higher than that of men. Since unemployed male and female service workers were concentrated in different industries, women's unemployment situation probably had more to do with jobs disappearing during the crisis than it did with competition with men.

Primary Occupations

Crisis hit first, and most obviously, jobs in the primary industries. This crisis is no exception. In farming, forestry and mining, full-time jobs have disappeared and have not been compensated for by any increase in part-time work. The high job loss meant little to women but accounted for 12 percent of all full-time jobs lost to men.[4] Since the number of women employed in these occupations is so small, it is difficult to tell whether or not the crisis wiped out the small gains some women had made in acquiring so-called non-traditional work. It seems likely, however, that especially in the highly unionized sectors, seniority rules and women's recent entry would ensure that women would be the first to go. It also seems likely that, if a recovery is sustained, many of the full-time male jobs will reappear, reducing significantly the male unemployment rate but having little effect on that of women.

Processing Occupations

During the crisis, unemployment has risen sharply in manufacturing occupations. Since work here is highly segregated, the sex affected varied significantly from job to job and since men predominate in most manufacturing work, more men than women saw their jobs disappear with falling profits and production.

However, more than half the full-time jobs disappearing in fabricating were lost to women, although they accounted for less than a quarter of the workers in this occupation. In addition, women's highest rates of unemployment are found in these occupations. More than one in four women here are officially counted as unemployed. With the sole exceptions of forestry and logging, women's unemployment rates here are higher than all male unemployment rates. The consistently higher female unemployment rates and women's declining share of part-time work suggest that when women do directly compete with men, the women lost. They certainly indicate that many women have not been protected from the impact of the crisis.

Other Occupations

Work in construction, transport, materials handling and other crafts is also men's work and the relative positions of women and men in these jobs have changed little in recent years. As the crisis deepened, full-time jobs disappeared in these occupations, accounting for over a third of all full-time jobs loss. Since men dominate the field, it is not surprising that most of these jobs were lost to men.

Although full-time jobs disappeared, part-time ones were created. There was some variation from occupation, but in general, men took most of this new part-time work. Consequently, women's share of part-time work declined, reversing the earlier trends. Such patterns suggest that when jobs are scarce, women are unable to compete successfully with men for even the part-time work.

Overall Trends

In general, the occupational data indicate that the labour force remains highly segregated and that this segregation has protected many women from the most obvious consequences of the crisis. However, more of the women who took jobs found only part-time work. And many of those who kept their part-time jobs had their hours and pay reduced. As the crisis continues, men are becoming increasingly successful in acquiring traditionally female part-time work in clerical, sales and service jobs.[5]

Male unemployment has been more visible because it has happened in large centers to large numbers of full-time workers at the same time. It is largely crisis-induced and may therefore be temporary if a recovery takes place. Women's unemployment has been less obvious because unemployed women are more scattered over a range of occupations, because women are more likely to drop out of the labour force and the statistics when unemployed, and because the crisis is more likely to result, at least initially, in underemployment in part-time jobs with reduced hours of work. Nevertheless, women's unemployment rates are higher than those of men in all those occupations where there are enough women to make the statistics reliable. And when women directly compete with men, they usually lose. Even in the early stages, women's jobs have not been unaffected by this crisis. As the technological change and the state restraint and job creation programs take hold, women are likely to bear much more of the burden in the future. The losses they suffer are less likely to be alleviated by a recovery, since a recovery will be based, in part at least, on changes in women's work.

Job Creation Programs

It is difficult to ignore the disappearance of more than 200,000 full-time jobs between 1980 and 1982,[6] especially when most of these jobs have been lost to so-called 'prime age males'. Before the current crisis, this category included males between the ages of 25 and 54. As the crisis deepens, their numbers have been reduced through redefinition. Now, in its most recent labour market study, the Economic Council of Canada counts only males aged 25 to 44 as part of this group.[7] Never considered to be in their prime, at least not in economic terms, women have suffered no such redefinition. Although women's unemployment rates are higher than those of men in most occupations, employment studies and job creation programs have reflected a preoccupation with the employment futures of men in their prime. And such research and projects have become more frequent as more of these men experience unemployment. Women are not ignored in these studies and programs but, lumped together with other 'special problem' groups such as the handicapped, the youth and Native Canadians, they take a distinct second place to that other minority group—the 'prime age males'.

The problem is not simply semantic or academic. These approaches are translated into government job creation programs which are primarily directed towards those males in their prime. In an information bulletin released in February 1983, Employment and Immigration Canada listed eleven job creation programs. Three of the four largest were directed towards increasing employment in industrial sectors dominated by men. With $500 million in federal funding, the largest program (New Employment Expansion and Development, or NEED) is designed to create productive employment for people who have exhausted their unemployment insurance or who are on social assistance. While these criteria seem unbiased in terms of sex, the list of possible projects does not. According to the government advertising, eligible activities include "construction of small craft harbours or fisheries facilities, parks improvement, reforestation, modernization of production plants, improvement or adaption of facilities for the handicapped and tourism development."[8] It is men who work in these areas and therefore they are most likely to benefit from these programs. Moreover, since men are more likely to be considered eligible for and to collect unemployment insurance, there are more male exhaustees to qualify for this program.[9]

The second largest job creation program (Canada Community Development Projects, or CCDP) is intended to "contribute to, maintain or increase" jobs in areas and for groups "suffering continuing high unemployment." The guidelines called for support of affirmative action principles but the projects listed as eligible were the "development of solar energy equipment, construction of wharves and the restoration and development of recreation facilities",[10] once again areas traditionally dominated by men. Government estimates of female participation in these programs range from 32 percent to 27 percent, considerably below the female percentage of the unemployed or of the labour force.[11]

The third program in terms of funding was Summer Canada and here women had a better chance of competing with men for jobs in "the provision of tourism information, the compilation of a home restoration handbook, working with physically handicapped children or the operation of a mobile vision clinic."[12] Indeed, the government estimates that women constituted 60 percent of the participants in 1981-1982.[13] However, this program involves short-term jobs for summer students rather than longer-term employment programs or even relief from unemployment in general.

The fourth largest program is the UI/Job Creation (Unemployment Insurance) scheme which is designed to channel $170 million into Unemployment Insurance funds and $50 million from Consolidated Revenue into job maintenance during 1982-1983. Participants have their normal unemployment benefits supplemented when they voluntarily work on approved projects. Once again, not an obviously discriminatory program, but with projects primarily in forestry, fishing, agriculture and tourism, few women are likely to benefit. However, little information is available on the sex of recipients in most programs but the government has recently released a study of the work sharing scheme which falls under UI/Job Creation. According to this study, "Work Sharing mainly affects prime age workers" and "about two-thirds of the employee-participants have been male."[14] Yet, unlike the other two employment programs discussed above, 70 percent of the Work Sharing agreements were concentrated in the manufacturing sector,[15] where large numbers of women work and where even larger numbers are unemployed. If women cannot acquire a fair share of the jobs created here, they are likely to get very few of those created in agriculture, fishing, forestry and construction.

It could be argued that several of the other job creation programs are directed specifically towards women and other disadvantaged groups. However, when *all* the money set aside for the other job creation programs is added together, it amounts to only *about half* of what is to be spent on NEED *alone*. Moreover, given that these funds have to be shared with older men, with youth, with the handicapped, with Native Canadians and with corporations, it seems unlikely that women will reap the majority of the benefits in terms of jobs.

In late 1983, the government announced a restirring of the alphabet soup of government job creation programs, "representing a consolidation and reinforcement of a number of earlier initiatives." The new strategy, "focussing on two priorities: the creation of jobs for those in immediate need, and the development of a work force trained and ready to meet the challenges of a new age of technology," outlines four major programs and contends that they will have special emphasis "on helping the nation's youth, disabled persons, Native Canadians and women entering or reentering the labour force.[16] In spite of the expressed commitment to finding jobs for the minorities who make up the majority of Canadians, it is far from clear that these new programs will succeed in meeting this objective.

The examples given for projects which fall under the largest program, Canada Works, (with a 1983-84 budget of $865.2 million) include a construction project for improving McNab's Island in Halifax harbour as a tourist attraction, a salvage operation in Quebec involving the restoration and rehabilitation of land damaged by a budworm epidemic, and a salmon enhancement project on a river in New Brunswick. None of these projects is likely to involve a high proportion of women and there is little indication that steps have been taken to ensure them equal access. The second largest program has approximately a quarter of the funding going to Canada Works. This Local Employment Assistance and Development program (LEAD) provides support to hard-hit communities through established community groups or organizations. Examples of eligible groups include Boards of Trade, Chambers of Commerce, Indian Band Councils and economic development associations. Eligible projects include the expansion of a body shop and mobile tire repair service, a fishing tackle manufacturing operation, a pet shop, a furniture manufacturing company, and an aluminum repair shop. While not explicitly excluded, women are unlikely to benefit proportionately from these types of projects. They certainly do not feature prominently in the eligible groups. Moreover, their unemployment is less concentrated than that of men in specific communities. The other two programs have less than $3 million in funding and are designed to provide skills and motivation for the employment disadvantaged. The Job Corps program appears to be primarily directed towards those with physical and mental handicaps, although those with inadequate training or other disadvantages are also to be included. The larger of the two programs, Career-Access, seems to be mainly planned for youth and the elderly. People who are returning to the labour force after a long absence, however, are also included. While women fare better under these two schemes it is difficult to see how any of these programs will go very far in increasing women's employment opportunities. Although women represent nearly half of the labour force, they are still lumped with the handicapped, the Native Canadians, the youth and the elderly. Only a small minority of the labour force remains, but it is effectively the target for most of the job creation programs.

The government has been responding to the crisis by establishing research projects and job creation schemes. Most of these have focused on the problems of the 'prime age males.' Not overtly discriminatory—indeed the new scheme selects women as a target group—they nevertheless seem to be concentrating on the areas of large and growing male unemployment. The effect may well be that women are further disadvantaged, especially as the crisis deepens.

Restraint Programs

On the one hand, the state is responding to the crisis by creating employment, primarily for men. On the other hand, it is introducing restraint programs which mainly affect women. Given the sexual division of labour, wage freeze policies, as well as cutbacks in government jobs and services, hurt women more than men. Since these policies are only now beginning to take effect, they have not begun to show up in the published data but there is strong evidence to suggest that they will do so in the near future.

Although there has been some controversy surrounding the size of the pay gap between women and men and the reasons for the differences in their employment income, there has been little debate about the existence of significantly different male and female wages. In 1981, half of the women with paid jobs earned less than $6 an hour. This was the case for fewer than a third of paid male workers.[17] At the other end of the scale, women accounted for less than 30 percent of those earning more than $18 an hour. Since women, on the average, continue to earn less than men, government wage restraint programs which limit increases to 6 and 5 percent ensure that the unequal pay (and fringe benefits) are reinforced, not challenged.[18] Moreover, almost twice as high a proportion of women compared to men, work in jobs covered by this federal government wage policy. In Quebec, the figures are even more startling. Two-thirds of the workers in the public sector are female and most of these workers saw their salaries cut temporarily by 20 percent and then frozen until 1984.

Women face not only falling real wages but also loss of jobs. Between 1980 and 1982, over three-quarters of the net gain in jobs for women was in education, health and public administration, in government-funded work. If provincial and federal government restraint programs are effective, jobs in these sectors will be reduced. In fact, this has already started, at least in the provincial and municipal levels and among school boards and hospitals. Since women are the majority of the workers here, especially of the new workers, most of those losing their jobs will be women. In Quebec for example, it is estimated that approximately 10,000 teaching posts at the elementary, secondary and CEGEP (Community College) levels will be eliminated in 1983 as a direct result of the government-imposed decrees. There were only 21,000 more teaching jobs throughout Canada in 1983 than in 1980. Thus, the Quebec reduction alone will wipe out almost half of that gain and it is clear that most of this loss will be borne by women. If and when the 20 percent decrease in civil service jobs in British Columbia is added to this total, female unemployment will soar.

What has mainly prevented women's employment situation from deteriorating as rapidly and obviously as that of men has been direct or indirect employment by governments. As governments cut wages and jobs in these sectors, women will suffer more. In addition, women have found their best jobs, their best pay and their most rapid promotions in these sectors. Moreover, women's unionization is highest in the public administration sector. Losses here mean more than rising unemployment. They also mean that women's position relative to that of men may deteriorate and that their union membership may drop sharply.

Finally, cutbacks in public expenditures also mean more unpaid work for women in the home. According to the Canadian Council on Social Development, there has been a 15 percent decrease in publicly-funded daycare spaces since 1980.[19] Although employment in health and medicine has been growing, there has been a reduction in pediatric and rehabilitation beds.[20] If children and those requiring rehabilitation care are not looked after in daycare centres and hospitals, they are cared for at home by women. As services in the hospitals decline, women are expected to be available to provide bedpans to the children in the orthopaedic ward and sick pans for those recovering from tonsil operations. Outpatient clinics are growing for a wide range of operations, sending children, and adults, home while they still require a good deal of surveillance and even nursing care. The loss of special programs for the gifted, the disabled and the retarded also increase women's unpaid workload at home, as does the loss of after-school and lunch-hour supervision. In other areas too, the state is attempting to shift responsibilities away from itself and back to the women. The Nova Scotia government, for example, has announced that single teenage mothers will no longer be eligible for social assistance. Federal and provincial governments have been reducing social assistance benefits and it is women who suffer most from these cutbacks.

At the same time, hospitals, social service centers and schools are using increasing numbers of volunteer workers. Many women are doing this volunteer work because they recognize the inadequacy of the services, because they cannot find paid work, and because they want to keep up their skills and their sanity while unemployed. That the government recognizes this and has no desire to interrupt the trend is evident in the regulations for the NEED program, which state explicitly that the funds cannot be used for work currently done by a volunteer.

Men will also feel the impact of government restraint policies. And it is difficult to tell just how many women will lose their jobs as a result of the programs. However, there is every indication that women will be hurt more. It would also be noted that most women who are union members belong to public sector unions. The imposition of wages and working conditions in many areas by government fiat has already considerably weakened these unions, reducing the protection they can provide. Furthermore, the loss of jobs here means the loss of female union members, reducing the proportion of women covered by any collective agreement at all. Again, government restraint programs mean women will lose.

Micro-Electronic Technology

Government restraint programs will eliminate many women's jobs but the new technology poses an even greater threat to women's employment. The technological revolution is an integral part of this crisis. While the crisis camouflages the unemployment and underemployment created by the introduction of micro-electronics, it also provides a justification of an incentive for technological change.

Employers, as well as the state and its agencies, claim the new technology will provide the solution to current economic problems. The Economic Council of Canada for example, claims that technological change is central "both in explaining the recent slowdown in total factory productivity and in discovering remedies for that slowdown."[21] Like Labour Canada's Task Force on Micro-electronics and employment, which "sees micro-electronics as a tool with the potential to create jobs, to increase productivity, to improve growth, and to enrich personal development,[22] federal Economic Development Minister Donald Johnston is convinced that micro-electronics will improve industrial efficiency and thus increase Canada's wealth. This conviction was translated into policy when the April 1983 federal budget allocated $700 million for technological improvements and development. While the employers' groups submitting briefs to Labour Canada's Task Force admitted that "there are undoubtedly some short-term side-effects of the revolution," they also argue that "it must be realized that some short-term ill effects are more than offset by long-term benefits."[23]

Primarily designed to increase productivity, efficiency, and control over the labour process, there can be little doubt that the implementation of micro-electronic technology can increase profits by reducing labour costs while increasing output. Although the technology does not represent an independent force, although it is, as the Labour Canada Task Force points out, "an inanimate tool,"[24] it nonetheless has been structured, developed and used to decrease employers' dependency on workers and their skills. The ill-effects referred to by the employers' associations will thus be felt primarily by the workers, the long-term benefits primarily by the employers. The anticipated increase in Canada's wealth is unlikely to be equally shared. As the Economic Council of Canada points out,

> Any increase in productivity means, by definition, that less work is needed to produce the same output. If total output does not rise, some people are thrown out of work.[25]

Most research studies indicate that the demand for services will not increase at a rate sufficient to offset the increase in productivity (Zeman, 1979). Employment will fall. *Maclean's* magazine cites a secret government analysis which

> predicts that a quarter to a half of existing jobs in manufacturing and up to 25 percent of business and financial jobs could disappear by 1991—and many of these positions will not be replaced by new ones (McQuaig, 1983:32)

While dire predictions are made about future employment opportunities, defenders of the micro-technology staunchly maintain that the anticipated technological unemployment has not happened, in spite of the widespread use of the new machines. It is difficult to challenge these arguments with the available data because a number of factors combine to obscure the consequences of the new technology. Since Statistics Canada does not collect the necessary information on the changing composition and characteristics of the labour force, it is impossible to tell whether unemployment and underemployment are products of the decaying economic conditions or of technological innovations. The rising unemployment rates of female clerical workers, the lack of job opportunities for young people, the increase in part-time work, the decreasing hours in that work and the falling labour force participation rates may all result directly or indirectly from the introduction of micro-technology but it is impossible to tell from the available data.

Furthermore, the nature of technological change itself delays and obscures unemployment and underemployment. While the new equipment is being put in place, the existing staff is still required to operate the old equipment and additional workers are necessary to introduce the new machines. Once this process is complete, smaller numbers of workers from both groups will be required. Moreover, most companies have only begun to use some new pieces of equipment: the offices and stores essentially function as they have for many years but with a few new machines. However, micro-technology makes fully automated workstations possible, ones where the work and the workers are transformed, eliminating the need for much of the labour force in the process. It is this second phase of technological change which will create the largest disruptions in employment and few, if any, companies have reached this stage yet. Customers and clients also have to be educated. As was the case in gas stations, people are being trained to serve themselves in banks and stores. Once training is complete, many of the paid employees can be fired. All these factors combine to camouflage the impact of the technology, especially during the crisis.

In spite of the major debates surrounding the future impact of the technology and in spite of the difficulty in making precise estimates about employment futures, there is general agreement that the chip will create at least short-term employment and that those who will be hit first and most are women. According to Labour Canada's Task Force, women workers are "Concentrated in those positions which are currently prime targets for efficiency and productivity improvements via the introduction of micro-electrotechnology."[26] More than one out of every three employed women, compared to 6 percent of employed men, held clerical jobs in 1982. With automatic tellers to do the banking, with word processors to type, file and retrieve and sort information, with voice sensitive processors to take dictation promised in the near future, with new systems to handle collect, person-to-person, charge account and international telephone calls, many fewer female tellers, secretaries and telephone operators will be needed. Based on her case studies of various companies introducing the new technology, Heather Menzies calculated that in the best possible scenario, 200,000 female clerical workers will be unemployed by 1990; in the direst circumstances, 750,000 will be looking for work.[27] Even her gloomiest prediction may underestimate the problem however. The supply of female clerical workers was already higher than the highest estimate she used for 1990. Thus there are many more women in a position to be put out of work by the new machines than she anticipated. Whatever the precise impact, it is clear that full-time clerical work has already begun to decline and that this is only the beginning of a dramatic drop in clerical jobs for women.

But not only clerical jobs will disappear. The bar codes and the accompanying technology are designed to replace cashiers and sales clerks with self-service shopping. And more than one in ten employed women now does this kind of work.

Of course, manufacturing jobs are also threatened by a technology that takes robots out of science fiction and puts them into the factory. Since many more men than women hold fabricating and processing jobs, the robots will have a greater impact on male employment, replacing welders, assemblers, spray painters and mechanics in many areas of male work. However, women will not emerge unscathed here either. Many women work in factories, processing food and making cloth or clothes. In part because cheap female labour was readily available, the textile and garment industries have been amongst the most backward in technological terms. The federal budget allocations for technological development and the improvement of facilities are likely to encourage the modernization of these industries and thus to eliminate many female jobs. The food and beverage industry also offers fertile ground for robotic labour. While men will no doubt be replaced by machines, male sectors are already highly productive and therefore the impact of the machines may be less extensive than in female dominated low productive sectors.

Low-level supervisory and managerial jobs are also likely to disappear. Much of the new equipment not only does the work but also supervises the worker. Word processors for example can record the output and the mistakes of each operator. Furthermore, as the secretarial pool and the number of bank tellers are reduced, so is the need for people to provide direction and surveillance. Many of these low-level supervisors and managers are women. Moreover, these jobs sometimes provide the intermediary step in promotions for women, bridging the gap between clerical and administrative work. Many of these bridging jobs will be eliminated and with them, promotions and jobs for women.

In addition, the built-in supervision aspect of this technology makes homework more possible in clerical occupations. At a Labour Canada conference on equality in the workplace, a senior telephone company manager claimed that half their clerical jobs could now be done at home. It is women who do both homework and clerical work. Their numbers are likely to increase at the same time as their outside employment diminishes. While this work does allow women to earn money and still look after children, husbands and houses, it not only threatens the quality of that care but also reduces their ability to resist, since they will be isolated in their homes.

Of the jobs that remain, some will be highly skilled, requiring people who are familiar with the intricacies of the new technology. Men have a head start in the field and women may find it difficult to catch up and compete. Many more jobs will likely be simplified, and consequently made more dull, monotonous and boring. And it is these jobs that will be available to women. As one wag has put it, computer literacy is an idea whose time has past. Much of this new equipment is 'user-friendly', requiring few skills and little training or knowledge of the technology. Workers are thus easily replaceable and can be employed on a part-time basis. The effect is already evident in clerical work, as full-time jobs disappear and part-time ones grow. The robots cannot yet clean house and pick up after children, so women are likely to retain their unpaid domestic labour for a good many years, especially since there is little interest in increasing domestic productivity. Many of the service jobs in the labour market are also less amenable to technological transformation, and it is here that jobs for both men and women are growing. They are also the least attractive and lowest paid jobs, those that are least likely to be unionized.

Although it may be true, as the Labour Canada Task Force claims, that "the diffusion rates of the new technologies have slowed down"[28] during the economic crisis, there can be little doubt that they will pick up quickly in response to the massive infusion of public funds. Clerical, sales and factory jobs for women will disappear, sometimes to be replaced by high-tech, probably male jobs, and often by low-skilled factory-like work that will mainly go to women. Low-level service jobs may continue to expand for both sexes. Women have been partially protected from the full impact of the crisis by their employment in clerical and sales work but this is unlikely to continue to be the case in the future as the micro-electronic technology is put in place.

Domestic Labour

The consequences of the economic crisis for women's domestic labour are even more difficult to monitor through available statistics than are those of technological change. The impact of the economic crisis remains in many ways hidden in the household. However, the research that has been done on the division of labour, combined with some statistical indices, do permit educated guesses about the effects of changing economic conditions on women's domestic work.

Falling wages and rising unemployment change expenditure patterns in the household. The most flexible items in domestic budgets are children's extra-curricular activities such as drama and art lessons, leisure activities, child-care, food, clothes, and paid domestic workers. Women shop and cook more carefully, spending more time bargain-hunting and coupon-clipping as well as planning and preparing meals. Lunches get made to take to work and the food advertisements in the Wednesday newspaper are more systematically surveyed. Clothes get hand-washed in

Zero rather than taken to the dry cleaner. Some are repaired rather than replaced. If there was a cleaning woman, she may be let go, especially since the Consumer Price Index indicates that the price of cleaning services increased more than the overall price index.[29] Babysitters are hired only when absolutely necessary. The expendible after-school lessons are cancelled. As a result, children are home more often, creating more childcare and housecare work for women. Reductions in expenditures on outside leisure activities also mean people are in the house more and are producing more mess for women to clean. In addition, tension may increase as the outlets that leisure activities provide are eliminated. Women's work as tension managers grows accordingly.

While women's work in the home increases during the crisis, women cannot save much money by baking and making clothes. The Consumer Price Index[30] indicates that between 1980 and 1982, the index for flour rose by 107.5, for bakery goods by 44.4. During the same period, the index for potatoes rose by 197.6, for french fries by 23. In other words, the women who bake their own bread and cookies and who peel and cook their own potatoes are having to spend relatively more than those who buy baked goods and frozen french fries. Similar patterns appear when the price of material and finished clothing are compared. The largest increases were recorded in mortgage costs, fuel oil and in private and public transportation, in those areas where women could not compensate for rising costs by intensifying their domestic labour. As a result, the pressure increases for women to stretch the food dollar and to get paying jobs.

Rising male unemployment not only means that there is less household income but also that men are home more, often creating more domestic work. While unemployed men undoubtedly suffer a great deal of psychological stress, particularly in a society which still defines men as primary breadwinners and unemployment as a mark of the failure of the individual rather than the system, women are not spared the pressures. Indeed, one recent American study concluded that "The low-income homemakers, financially dependent on the efforts of other people, showed the highest distress" (MacKay, 1983:33). Moreover, women are more likely to bear the brunt of physical pain. A Toronto study found that "Eighty percent of wife-beaters reported to Metro Toronto Police were unemployed" (MacKay, 1983:33). Children too are more likely to be abused in times of rising unemployment, and it is women who must look after the beaten children. According to the Children's Aid Society of Metropolitan Toronto, the number of child abuse cases was 16 percent higher in the first 6 months of 1983 than it was in the comparable 1982 period. The executive director of the Society maintains that the economic crisis is the major cause of this increase.[31] Furthermore, even when pressure does not break out in physical violence, the stress level rises significantly, increasing women's tension management work.

Not only does rising unemployment keep husbands at home, it also forces many older children to remain in or to return to their parents' household. Enrolment in post-secondary programs is rising[32] while summer employment for students is falling, making it unlikely that many of these students can support themselves. The growth in enrolments is itself related to the extremely high youth unemployment rates. The many unemployed young people are finding it increasingly difficult to collect unemployment insurance or welfare, and those few who are eligible often find the money too low to live on. As a result they are likely to be forced to look to their parents for support. With more older children at home, especially if they are not home by choice, the tension management and housecare work of women rises. So does the pressure for women to get or keep their paid jobs.

While increases in domestic labour are difficult to monitor, given Statistics Canada's neglect of this area and the nature of the problem, it is clear from the data that are available that pressures on the household are increasing. And since the research that has been done clearly indicates that much of the labour there is women's work, it seems more than likely that women's domestic labour is increasing. Moreover, as technology makes "home-work" more possible, and as women's unemployment rates rise, women are likely to be further locked into this domestic work.

Conclusion

Although women's labour force participation rate has been steadily climbing since the 1950s, it did not increase at all between 1981 and 1982. Now that women constitute more than 40 percent of the employed, there are more women in all occupations but the labour force remains highly segregated. This segregation has provided some protection for women from the most obvious and immediate consequences of the crisis, as male jobs disappeared suddenly and in large numbers in primary industries, in manufacturing and in construction. However, there are indications that the continuing high levels of male unemployment will encourage men to compete more directly with women for traditionally female work. The government-funded jobs that have maintained women's employment levels and provided women with most of their best jobs are likely to disappear as restraint policies take hold. Micro-electronics provide an even greater threat to women's employment futures, since the new machines can replace many female clerical, sales and factory workers.

It should not be assumed, however, that women have to date been entirely protected from the crisis. Women's unemployment rates have been readily rising and are higher than those of men in all occupations where there are enough women to make the statistics reliable. More than one in ten women were unemployed in 1982 and most of these women were unemployed because their jobs disappeared. A quarter of those with paid employment found only part-time jobs and many of these workers had their hours reduced. At home, women's domestic labour increased along with the pressure to find paid work. Although the impact on women has been less visible and obvious, women have not escaped the crisis and are likely to suffer increasingly as the crisis continues.

Afterword

Written in 1984, this paper was based on 1983 data. In subsequent years has come a recovery of sorts, and with it has come some improvement in the employment position of both women and men. Between 1983 and 1985, the percentage of Canadian adults with labour force jobs rose, for both sexes, and their unemployment rates declined. Fortunately for women, the cuts we predicted in health care did not materialize in employment terms. Indeed, jobs for women increased significantly in this occupational field, accounting for one in ten of the additional jobs for women and reinforcing our argument that state sector employment is crucial for women.

As we also predicted, however, unemployment rates have fallen more for men than for women, and the female unemployment rate is now once again higher than the male rate. In absolute terms, total unemployment declined during these two years by 120,000 persons, of whom 109,000 were male. Except for the small artistic and recreational occupation, the female unemployment rate remained higher, and often appreciably higher, than the male rate in every occupation with enough unemployed workers of each sex to make comparisons valid. By 1985, even more of those women who found paid jobs had only part-time work, while the proportion of employed men with part-time work actually declined slightly.

Thus, although since this paper was written most of the numbers have changed and women have made some real gains, the experience of the most recent years has reconfirmed our arguments that women suffer as much as men during economic downturns while men gain more from economic upswings, and that state sector jobs are central to the employment position of women.

Notes

1. Before 1975, women's official unemployment rates were consistently lower than those of men. However, when the relevant question asked in the Labour Force Survey was changed to ask respondents directly whether they held or sought work for pay or profit during the reference period, the female rate shot ahead of the male rate.
2. See Armstrong and Armstrong, 1983: 255.
3. Calculated from Statistics Canada, *Labour Force Annual Averages 1975-1978* (Ottawa, 1981), and *Statistics Canada, The Labour Force, December 1982* (Ottawa, 1982).
4. Calculated from unpublished Labour Force Survey data.
5. Calculated from unpublished Labour Force Survey data for January and February 1983.
6. Calculated from *The Labour Force, December 1980* and *The Labour Force, December 1982.*
7. Economic Council of Canada, *In Short Supply: Jobs and Skills in the 1980s,* (Ottawa, 1982).
8. Employment and Immigration Canada, *Job Creation Policy and Programs* (pamphlet, Ottawa, 1983), 1.
9. Armstrong and Armstrong, 1983: 103-108.
10. *Job Creation Policy and Programs,* 1.
11. Unpublished Employment and Immigration Canada data.
12. *Job Creation Policy and Programs,* 2.
13. Unpublished Employment and Immigration Canada data.
14. Employment and Immigration Canada, *Work Sharing: A Perspective* (pamphlet, Ottawa, 1983),4.
15. *Work Sharing,* 3.
16. Employment and Immigration Canada, *Government of Canada Job Creation Programs: An Overview* (booklet, Ottawa, 1983) 5, 7.
17. Calculated from unpublished Statistics Canada data.
18. Most of the restraint legislation does include provision for special treatment for high and low earners. In Ontario, for instance, the Explanatory Note to Bill 179 (2nd Session, 32nd Legislature, Toronto, 1981) says that:

    > Merit increases or other increments are restricted to the extent that they would put a person's salary over $35,000 a year, but low-income workers may benefit from a provision which allows full-time employees to receive an increase of up to $1,000 (if the normal increase provided in the Bill would be smaller). Part-time workers may receive a similar increase on a pro-rated basis.

    Such provisions are possible but not required, and will do little for those earning slightly more than what is defined as low-income. More light is shed on these provisions by recent developments. The Ontario Inflation Restraint Board is reported (Montreal *Gazette,* 4 November 1983) to have ordered 72 Ontario's lowest-paid hospital workers, who make less than $18,000 a year, to pay back up to $1,000 each. In arbitration, they had been awarded an 11 percent increase which exceeded the general provincial limit, in order to bring them up to the lowest rates paid on other hospitals.

Labelled "explicit discrimination against women" by a union official, the rollback affects orderlies, dietary aids, nurses' aids and housekeepers.

19. Canada Council for Social Development, *Social Development Overview* (Ottawa, 1983).
20. Statistics Canada, Hospital Annual Statistics (Ottawa, 1981), Table 18.
21. Economic Council of Canada, The Bottom Line: Technology, Trade and Income Growth (Ottawa, 1983), 35.
22. Labour Canada, *In the Chips: Opportunities, People, Partnerships* (Ottawa, 1982), 4.
23. *In the Chips*, 36.
24. *In the Chips*, 5.
25. *The Bottom Line*, 5.
26. *In the Chips*, 15.
27. *Women and the Chip*.
28. *In the Chips*, 37.
29. Statistics Canada, *Consumer Prices and Price Indexes* (Ottawa, April-June 1982), Table 8.
30. *Consumer Prices and Price Indexes*
31. Cited in Montreal *Gazette* (15 October 1983), G6.
32. According to Statistics Canada preliminary estimates, enrolment in post-secondary institutions will increase to 562,950 in 1982-83 from 536,710 in 1980-81.

Organizing Eaton's*

Carol Currie and Geri Sheedy

"So Much Fun for a Dollar"

The story of organizing Eaton's is a very exciting, stimulating, and interesting one from the perspective of an organizer and someone who is really concerned about people and their rights as workers. Around Christmas of 1983 one of our co-workers was shopping in an Eaton's store in Brampton. The commissioned salesperson explained to him that they have a very small commission, that it had been cut, and that they had difficulties making a decent livelihood for themselves. The rep continued the conversation with him and they discovered that the employees should have a Union. We later made contact with brother Paul, and he indicated to us that the company was supposed to be coming out with wage increases in January of 1984; that the employees had gone through a three-year wage freeze; and that they expected substantial increases when the raises were announced. We received a telephone call from Paul at the end of January indicating that the company had come forward with the raises, and that it amounted to an insult for many of the workers because the increases were minimal: one cent an hour, two cents an hour, three cents an hour. The maximum raise was 4 percent. Many of the full-time sales clerks, who are predominantly women, received increases that were considered to be a gift rather than a wage increase because they were at the top of their payment scale. These people became very upset and angry over this. They had waited three years and they felt that they had helped their company through a very difficult time.

They contacted us and we set up a meeting for February 2, 1984, where we explained the Ontario Labour Relations Act to them. The act requires support from 55 percent of the full-time work force, and 55 percent of the part-time work force for union certification, separated into a retail bargaining unit, and then separated again into an office and clerical bargaining unit. This was one of the first department stores that we organized, and we were not exactly sure how the Labour Board would break down the bargaining units. We made sure that we had 55 percent of every conceivable bargaining unit in that place: the restaurant, the commissioned salespeople, the sales clerks on the floors, the full-time sales clerks, the security people.

*This article is based on an interview conducted with the authors by Charlene Gannagé on September 27, 1985, at the women's conference of the Canadian Labour Congress held in Ottawa.

The employees left that meeting and signed up their co-workers. On February 10, we held another meeting and this meeting was well attended. There were between seventy and eighty people all of whom signed union cards. We submitted an application to the Labour Relations Board. The notification of the application was posted in their store on Valentine's Day, February 14. It moved so quickly that it caught us by surprise. We promised the employees that we would not publicize the fact that they had applied for certification until it had become public to the company, because they wanted to make sure that nothing could possibly go wrong. We indicated to them that nothing could go wrong if the numbers were correct. Unfortunately, the Labour Relations Act allows for delays, and one of the co-workers filed a complaint saying that she was brainwashed, browbeaten, and I can't even recall all the different terms she used in her charges and allegations. Unfortunately, it delayed certification until March 28. The certification of the Brampton Eaton's store caused a snowball in all of the other Eaton's stores. Campaigns started up everywhere. Between February and May 1984 we were successful in achieving six certifications.

The company utilized many tactics to try and prevent us from becoming successful. The Brampton store used the charges routine, which causes delays. People revoke their membership because the company has time to play on them. The companies go through the "I love you" syndrome with their employees—"you're such a terrific employee" and "if it were up to me I would be giving you all the money in the world", "one big happy family" and "how could you do this to me? We have taken such good care of you"; all as if you were personally injuring the employer. They play upon women in particular with a whole guilt syndrome that you are part of a family and that you are disloyal. Loyalty only goes so far; if you don't have money to buy your own kids clothes, food and shelter then it becomes a problem because you can't take promises to the bank manager to get a mortgage for your house or money for food. These people became active with us, and assisted us tremendously in our efforts to organize the other stores. If it weren't for their efforts we probably would never have been as successful as we were. Night after night and weekend after weekend, they went with us to meetings, they talked to their co-workers about all the problems and issues, and they in turn encouraged their co-workers to become unionized.

I think of Leddy, Kathy, and Paul, and that close relationship that we developed because we worked together on a day-to-day basis. I mean you're just about living together because of the whole organizing campaign. Kathy, at 51 years of age, said to me "I thought I would never develop a social conscience like this at 51 years old. I've lived more than half of my life and I see the need for change. I see the need for a union within the Eaton company as well as all other places". And Leddy: "I've never had so much fun for a dollar".

There was so much that motivates you, that makes you feel a part of things. You feel a real self-worth, that here is this grandmother and homemaker, who up until this point was an Eaton's clerk with no real gratification. Now all of a sudden she is affecting social change and she is doing something that is known all over the country and is going to affect the lives of her grandchildren, and the lives of everyone in Canada. It really is a wonderful metamorphosis.

They certainly have achieved and accomplished one hell of a lot since that initial meeting. They brought that message to other workers. It meant so much actually seeing them talking to each other, and saying "I have been an Eaton worker for twenty years and I know what the company is. I know how we have been misused and abused by this company. I am now going to stand up for my rights and I want you to stand up with me, because until we do it nobody is going to give it to us." They were the ones who brought the enthusiasm, the courage and the guts to do it because for so long they had been subjected to totally arbitrary management decisions.

Common Issues

As we went along into each and every meeting, we became more expert at what the problems were, and how to convey the message to the Eaton's workers and then to the Simpsons workers. It became a very tiring, consuming campaign—I mean personal lives were put on hold for the entire duration and our own organization realized that this was not going to just end with the one store. It was becoming a full-fledged organizing campaign of retail workers in Southern Ontario and across the country. What we needed to do was bring in people to assist the two full-time organizers that we had at that time and to provide training for these people to go out into the stores—the number of stores alone was virtually impossible for two people to cope with.

When we were getting calls from the Simpsons stores or the Eaton's stores that wanted to be organized we could not say "Well, you'll have to wait—we haven't got the time, or we haven't got the people—we're concentrating on Eaton's". We had to be out there while the interest was there. We were going to bed at 2:00 a.m. and getting up at 5:00 a.m. to meet people before they went to work. It was just incredible. We found at our meetings with the Simpsons people that their problems were the same; they faced the exact same wage freezes, favouritism and lack of dignity. You could walk into a room whether it was Simpsons, Sears or Eaton's and say "Are you having this problem?" and it was a problem all over. One of the interesting jokes that we used to make was that if you went into a meeting for Eaton's employees one night, and the next evening one for Simpsons, it was just a matter of changing the name plate on the door, for the problems didn't change. They were all very similar.

Customer Profile

One of the issues that was particularly hard to comprehend in the year 1984 was the fact that Eaton's still wanted and persisted in securing the right to promote, demote, lay-off, hire, and re-hire its staff on the basis of appearance and customer profile. As an employee, once your looks start to fade—you develop a few wrinkles or a few pounds—you will be discriminated against and your chances for promotion and even for keeping the job are lessened.

You may be working in ladies' wear and be put into hardware because they want someone in ladies wear who is young and pretty and could wear the clothes. A cosmetician on a partial commission can be a good salesperson and can make a reasonable wage. But she can be taken out of that department and be moved to another department at a straight salary, even though older women also buy makeup and may prefer to buy makeup from an older woman and not from an eighteen-year old beauty. I am not eighteen, and I don't look eighteen; I am never going to look eighteen, and I don't plan to wear makeup like an eighteen-year old. But Eaton's didn't see it that way. They wanted that right: Customer Profile.

An example of the abuse of their rights as an employer is Susan who is from the Yonge-Eglington store. Susan is just an incredible young woman. She is very articulate, very intelligent, and she knows the business of cosmetics. One day there was a posting that came out for a promotion. Originally she had asked to transfer from the Eaton's Centre, where she was working, to the Yonge-Eglington store because it needed an increase in sales and a reorganizing of the cosmetic department. This she went and did. She had more than tripled their sales in one year, so when the promotion was posted, she applied for it. In the job interview with her employer they said to her "You know the job, you're an excellent candidate, you have all of the qualifications you have all of the abilities, but you're overweight, and fat people don't get ahead in this company."

I went in to visit Susan last week in Toronto to ask her how things were going. She is in an organized store, and she is the union steward. Well, now that the union is in, and that she's active in the union, they called her in for a review, and told her she was a wonderful employee, and that they would like to transfer her back down to the Eaton's Centre. They even had the nerve to tell her that she would work in a department with three other women who are a part of the anti-union crew. One of the advantages they mentioned to her was that it would save her having to pay union dues. They are still using the tactic that when the workers go back to work, they don't go back into the department that they came out of.

Wage Freeze

They put them through a three-year wage freeze, and if that's not a concession, then I find it difficult to figure out what is a concession. While other people were enjoying 5 and 10 percent increases, these people were dropping further and further behind. Their bread and milk still cost the same as ours did, everything that they had to buy still cost the same. But add to that the costs of the dress requirements that Eaton's imposes on their employees—you have to be professionally dressed; your wearing apparel has to be acceptable to them. Males are not allowed to just wear a shirt and tie, they have to have on a jacket. That becomes very costly because it is difficult to find a man's sports jacket that you can buy for under eight dollars. Women have to be dressed in co-ordinated suits or dresses, and have to wear panty hose matching the shoes, underwear, and slips. This is stipulated in their brochures for their employees.

The average wage was between $5.50 and $6.00 per hour, and the top rate was approximately $7.20 per hour. Commissioned salespeople, which are predominantly male positions, are higher-paying positions because these people get a percentage of what they sell, so the more you sell, the higher your wages. Even the cosmetic salespersons got a basic salary plus a commission. Eaton's paid a weekly base rate of $218.00; the cosmetic company paid an additional commission rate of 3 percent on sales over $36.00. We all know what kind of markup there is in makeup and what kind of money there is to be made in makeup. And these women had to buy this makeup—they had to wear it.

When you started out part-time at minimum wage, and you progressed up to six or seven dollars, your hours came down accordingly. When you were making the minimum, you might be getting twenty-four or thirty-five hours a week; but, as your rate went up, your hours went down, so that when you were up to making seven dollars, you might only be getting four hours a week. The new person who was getting four dollars an hour was getting twenty-four hours a week. And that was common in both Simpsons and Eaton's. It was a really big problem for the more senior part-time people. They'd come into the company and think that this is great: "I'm getting twenty-five to thirty hours in and four dollars an hour, so I'm bringing home eighty to one hundred dollars a week." What they didn't realize until they progressed through the system was that the eighty to one hundred dollars a week would never increase.

They had no benefits whatsoever. They were totally at the whim of management. If management didn't need them today they were sent home, and they were called back in at a moment's notice. Some part-time workers were single parents or elderly ladies supporting themselves, waiting until they reached the age of sixty-five so they could at least get Canada Pension. When students were available, Eaton's could pay them even less, so you might work part-time, but when Christmas or summer came along, you would find yourself replaced by a student.

The majority of part-timers are women who become conditioned to believe that they are not capable of doing anything else. Employers make sure that they believe that. They give them a little title. They give them a little pat on the back every now and again. The workers say "Isn't this wonderful, I am appreciated, I am worth something." But when it comes to the money and the benefits, there is nothing there. You end up with a very large number of middle-aged women who have come back into the workforce, who are caught in these retail jobs with no place to go. They don't even have enough money to make it worth their while. But they still hope that, someday, there will be a full-time job for them.

We all know what's happening with full-time work, it's being rapidly eroded. Part-time work gives the employers more flexibility and they don't have to pay any benefits. All you end up with is a whole lot of people living below the poverty level, everyone starving to death. This was a big problem to overcome in the organizing, because there is a high turnover rate. And some of the part-time workers hold down two and three jobs to make a living and when they are only in three and four hours a week, it's difficult to reach them.

The employer had said that there was no money available for providing raises or better pension plans. In the meantime, the company was publicizing in its own internal newsletter the building of several large stores in new malls. There were two around the Toronto area, one near the Woodbine racetrack and the other in Pickering. I've yet to see where you can put a price tag in dollars and cents on dignity and respect. Dignity and respect cost nothing monetarily. The elimination of arbitrary management decisions does not cost money. The elimination of favouritism does not cost money. All of these things would provide a better work environment for the people and at least promote harmony and goodwill between the employee and the employer. That was part of what these people were looking for.

Favouritism

I can think of one beautiful case of favouritism. This is the case of Heather Di'Domizio the young lady who filed the complaint against the union, charging that we were harassing, intimidating, browbeating, and brainwashing the workers. Within a few months, Heather was transferred down to the Toronto Eaton Centre. If you have ever been up onto the fifth floor of the Eaton Centre, you will see a little house that's right on the floor, and has been decorated by one of their designers. Heather was given the job of looking after this house. That is one example of favouritism.

One lady who had been with the company for seventeen years was not in the best of health; they pensioned her off at seventeen dollars a month. Another gentleman had been with the company twenty-three years and they transferred him to another store where they put him in the kitchen. This totally devastated the man, who had gone from a job he'd done all of his life into an area where he knew nothing. The man was forced to withdraw his services. Eaton's doesn't fire people: they make their life so unbearable, by putting them into areas where they really can't cope, that they quit. Or, if you are a part-timer, you just don't get called back in, and after a month or two you begin to realize that you are not going to be called back at all.

How many stores does Eaton's have across the country? One hundred and ten. And how many women managers? One. Even if women were going to get promoted above a certain level, they weren't put into the management training programs. Eaton's didn't have to give a reason, they just didn't offer it to women. If you were a woman, you just didn't apply for management positions.

That reminds me of another story. Brenda had applied to become a commissioned salesperson, and she was told that she couldn't sell fridges and stoves because women knew absolutely nothing about fridges and stoves. And her comment back to the personnel manager at the time was "Who the hell do you think cooks on the stoves and who do you think fills the fridges up with food and works with them? The men don't know any more about the mechanics than I do. All they say is that these are the features of these particular appliances, do you want to buy it or not?" And she fought it. She was successful in becoming a commissioned salesperson and she was very effective. She managed to break the ice for other women to come in behind her. Especially since she wasn't just a woman, she was also black.

We weren't successful in achieving all our goals in Eaton's, but we do have a collective agreement, and I think that, in itself, is a positive accomplishment. We do have some language that we didn't have before, we do have a grievance procedure, we do have in writing that the benefits and the plans will be maintained—that in itself is positive. This was also a major battle. Eaton's was not willing to put in writing the benefits the employees already enjoyed. They wanted to reserve the right to take away any of these benefits at any time, and yet, when you talk to some of the people in the unorganized stores, they would say, well there is no way they're going to take that away from us. It's not as if the company wouldn't. There were sixteen hundred and thirty-one Simpsons workers who used to be full-time employees who had their jobs wiped out. So, if Simpsons can take away that many jobs from that many employees, then Eaton's is certainly in a position to remove any of the benefits that the employees had enjoyed prior to the introduction of the union.

Union Bashing

One of the biggest difficulties that we had was the fact that the employer, like all employers no matter who they are, had a captive audience. They are able to put out their propaganda to their employees at their place of work.

In our case they gave the employees letters about the union and they had some excellent legal advice because those letters were right on the line of the law—there was nothing that we could challenge through the Labour Board because there was nothing illegal in them. The letters made people wonder and question and worry, especially people who didn't know anything about the labour movement, what unions involve, and what the whole collective bargaining process involves. They took sections out of the by-laws, like if you join this union you have to be a member of the New Democratic Party (NDP). Well that in itself is not true. We have in our by-laws that we pay a per capita to the NDP on behalf of union members, except for those members who choose not to pay. This union, or any other union, can not dictate to its membership which political party they affiliate to. All we can do is educate our members and hope like hell that they become members of the NDP. So we had all these things to overcome, because the company was able to get to these people; and for every fifty that the company got to, we were only able to get back to one of them.

The Right of Access

Our problems were insurmountable in certain situations, because we were not allowed on company premises. We can't reach the employees—they can't discuss the union at work and can't distribute any material at work. There was nowhere on the street that you could get to them. They came in by subway. They came in by bus. There was one employee entrance. We had no names and addresses. We had a committee—quite a large committee—in there, and its major responsibility was trying to get names. You have to know how many people work there, you have to know who they are, you have to have your 55 percent and you have to be really sure of that. The only way you can be sure is to have good records.

There were in excess of three thousand retail workers in the downtown Toronto store. Eighty percent were part-time people, and 80 percent were women. Even if you were successful in getting some of the names, without the addresses or telephone numbers there was no way of tracking them down. I don't know if you've ever tried to find a woman out of the Toronto telephone book, but believe me it is a monstrous task. If we went into the store, we were followed by security and by personnel. There was no way the employees were going to come and approach us or come and sit down and sign a card there, because they knew we were being watched which means they were being watched; and when security is watching you, you must be doing something wrong.

The Labour Relations Act says that employees have the right to solicit and participate in the union and its lawful activities on their own time—i.e. on their lunches, breaks, before work, and after work, but this was on the employers' premises. Eaton's was able to curtail our activities to such a point that the employer violated the law in our estimation. They kicked us out of the Eaton's store in downtown Toronto; they harassed us; they disciplined their employees; they arrested us. Our only remedy to prevent the company from doing this was to charge them at the Labour Relations Board, which we did do in June of 1984. That case only concluded thirteen months later. In the meantime the company was utilizing illegal tactics, which can't be prevented without a decree from the Labour Board to say that Eaton's was conducting illegal activities and that they had to cease and desist. Well, that doesn't do us a lot of good thirteen months later, when the employer has the union looking like a house of ill repute. By having us evicted from those premises they put us on the same level as the drunks, the derelicts, the shoplifters, the undesirables whom they feel they have the god-given right to remove.

In the meantime they were holding captive-audience meetings on company time, bringing their different sales personnel into meetings, and going through their whole propaganda. The anti-union groups including Stop the Union Now (STUN, very appropriately spelled NUTS backwards), were still allowed to hand out material.

The decision of the Labour Relations Board finally came down. "The union had the right to provide reasonable access to the employees of the Eaton's store in the area in which they stood and we had the right for the Eaton's employees to have reasonable access to us". In the court, where Alderman Layton's case for trespassing[1] was heard, the judge said that we didn't have the right to be there and that we were guilty as charged. We are now appealing that charge. However, the question should have been answered in June and July of 1984, not in 1985, thirteen months after the fact. You win the battle but you lose the war. If we had had the ruling when we were organizing the Eaton's workers in the Eaton's Centre, we would have organized that place, but because the company used delay tactics and the Labour Board allowed the delay, we lost. We lost a year of time for these workers, thereby giving the company and the anti-union people an opportunity to work on them. The year of delay also gave the other employees in other stores an opportunity to become intimidated, frightened, and terrified of unions because they saw their co-workers out on strike for six months.

Eaton's concentrated their efforts in stopping us at the Eaton Centre, because they knew, as we did, that had the Eaton Centre been organized when negotiations were going on, the threat of the strike would have been much more powerful.

We believed that under the terms of the Labour Relations Act in this province we had the right to be there, to distribute material, to organize and to solicit for the union. Our whole purpose for being there was to add legitimacy and respectability to the organization, and to provide material to the employees so that they could make an intelligent decision as to whether they wanted to become a union member or not. With the tactics that the company employed, our image was destroyed, because the employees saw us evicted by police. This doesn't create a very respectable image in the eyes of an employee whom you are trying to convince that what you are doing is right. We tried wherever possible to use the media to bring the message home to people, without actually taking out advertisements ourselves. There is nothing in the Labour Act that says that you have to be a wealthy union in order to organize in this province, but advertising in the Toronto Star, the Globe and Mail or the Toronto Sun is a very costly affair. The other possibilities were taking out advertisements in the subway system, on television or on the radio. Again, for the same reasons, we couldn't afford to do that.

Management Co-optation

In the meantime, Eaton's announced a genuine increase and an improved pension plan; they eliminated their three hour shifts and made them four hour shifts; and they started to pay overtime. They were aware of what the employees' complaints were, and they turned around and said "We are addressing them, you don't need the union." That works. People are impressed. Just the mention of the union has already got them a wage increase, an improved pension plan, and improved working conditions.

We explained to the employees that in 1948, when the first organizing campaign happened, the Eaton company promised its employees a pension plan second-to-none in North America. Well, they did have a pension plan 'second-to-none', because I don't think that there was another quite as bad as that one. The employees were bought off back then, and they were bought off again this time. We haven't really progressed very far in forty years.

The other drawback in the 1948 campaign was that if people who were eligible to vote did not do so, their failure to vote was counted against the union. There were nine thousand votes considered and at that time the union only lost by just over eight hundred ballots. To think that if they had been successful then, the huge difference there would be in the retail department store industry of today. We try to convey this to the people. We were successful with the six Eaton's stores, and with the eleven Simpson's stores, and hopefully we're going to be successful with all of the other department stores as the organizing progresses into places like Sears and Zellers. Eaton's unfortunately, I think is going to be a difficult one to crack, because the employer has had too much leeway.

Between a Rock and a Hard Place

We had six months from the day we went out on strike until we had to have those people back to work, and Eaton's knew that. They knew that if we didn't have those people back to work in six months, legally, they could fire every damn one of those strikers. The scabs who worked for Eaton's filed a complaint that we didn't represent them fairly—by not allowing them the opportunity to have a vote on the contract. We did have a vote, a democratic vote, for the employees who were out on strike. Did they want to go back to work? They chose to go back to work. Our international president, who has the legal right under the terms of our constitution, signed the agreement. If he had not signed that agreement, those scabs who were in a majority would have voted that contract down. The strikers would have had to stay out on strike, and they wouldn't have any jobs or a contract.

If we had had a vote on the contract, we would have had to permit all employees in the bargaining unit to vote on it, which is what the anti-union people and the company both wanted. They knew that if all the anti-union people had their opportunity to vote, they would have voted that contract down. All of those strikers would have been fired. We wouldn't have had a contract. And, we would have had a de-certification. So, in order to protect people who went out on strike for six months, we had no alternative. Legally we had the right to do it, even though it has never been invoked in our union before, and I am sure it's never been invoked in most unions. But thank God we did have the right, because without it hundreds of people would have been fired and no contract would exist.

Broken Dreams

There were approximately nine hundred people in fourteen bargaining units. We had approximately 50 percent of them out on strike. We had another 10 to 20 percent who weren't out on strike with us, but who were staying at home—they just were not going to work. The company was able to run their stores with supervisory staff that they parachuted in from the non-union stores. As the strike dragged on, we did lose a lot of the soldiers for personal, economic reasons, and again that whole lack of a support system with the spouse and the family. You have to remember that most of them were women. Their husbands were on to them to go back to work. They were having family problems. They were single parents running into financial difficulties. We tried to help wherever we could, as finances provided and as the contributions from other unions came in. Wherever possible, we tried to provide the financial assistance as well as the networking, but you do lose people along the way. When we finished up we had about a third of the people still out. So we were looking at probably about three hundred people who would have lost their jobs.

What really saddens me is that two of the people who ended up going back to work were two of the people that I had grown very attached to and really fell in love with, respected, and admired: Kathy and Leddy. Both felt they were justified in going back. Rather ironically, shortly after they went back the contract was signed and the strike was over. But knowing the pressure that those two women went through, it is incredible that they were able to sustain their effort for as long as they did. They were getting it from home, from co-workers, and from the strikers. They handled everyone else's problems. Anytime anyone else wanted to go back into work they turned to them. It came to the point where they were burned out. They just couldn't handle it any more. We weren't successful in getting to them in time to take some of that pressure off. We lost them. But I think the experience is still with them. I can't see them going through so much in their lives, what with the organizing, and the strike, not to have some of it instilled in them.

I think that it's going to take a lot of encouragement on our part to bring them back into the fold. They need that mental rest. I know that a lot of people in the labour movement have difficulty condoning or contending with people that they consider to be scabs. I do too, I have problems with scabs. I have problems with people going in to do the work while their co-workers are out on strike trying to achieve something better for them. But I think what happened to these two ladies in particular is that they thought that they were going to lose anyway, and they couldn't see the light at the end of the tunnel. I forgive them. I don't hold any animosity towards these two ladies because they went back to work.

I think they are fine, strong, courageous women and I love them just as much now. You are talking a year and four or five months that these women had been as involved as we were, without our background, and without our labour history. They were working full-time jobs at the worksite, they were working full-time jobs as organizers, and they were working on the picket lines six days a week. We tried to talk to them early on in the strike when they were working every shift—they were there morning, afternoon and evening, and they were putting in twelve-hour days on the picket line. We tried to tell them that they couldn't do it; but they were so afraid that someone might need their assistance or encouragement that they couldn't say "I'll be there in the morning." They had to be there all the time in case they were needed. They reached out, but they also burnt out.

The Struggle Continues[2]

What do we do? We need tougher legislation. We need first contract legislation. We need tougher labour laws. We need labour laws that prohibit those types of delays that cause such undue anguish and pain.

Through the organizing campaign and then through the whole strike situation, the labour movement itself caught fire. People from one end of this country to the other were phoning, and sending letters of congratulation. They all wanted to be a part of it. When the strike was on we were getting support before it was even requested. We were getting calls:

"Would you send a striker out to Vancouver? We would like to have them talk to our membership, to get them on-board, to get some strike support." When the Congress got involved with the nationwide boycott and everyone else got on-board, it was a total mobilization of the labour movement. And that is something that we haven't seen in the labour movement in Canada in a long time. We have not had another issue that everyone could grasp, that everyone related to. People came up to us on the picket line. Either they worked for Eaton's, or their mother had worked for Eaton's, or their sister had worked for Eaton's. They were related to Eaton's, either when going through school or through someone in their family. They all knew. It was such a common issue.

Notes

1. Jack Layton was passing out leaflets outside the employees' entrance to Eaton's before the store was open to the public. The leaflets explained the employees' rights under the labour Relations Act. He was charged with trespassing. The judge ruled against Layton. When the decision was appealed, he won on the grounds that the Charter of Rights protects employees' rights to organize. The Crown has appealed this decision.
2. Since the writing of this article workers at five Eaton's stores have voted to decertify the Retail, Wholesale and Department Store Union.

Organizing for Daycare

Ronnie Leah

Introduction

The issue of daycare emerged as a focal point for union women's organizing in the Ontario Federation of Labour (OFL) from 1975 to 1980. We have studied the political process of daycare organizing from the perspective of activist union women, as a means of understanding the recent development of a trade-union women's movement in Ontario. The daycare issue has been a significant part of the ongoing struggle for women's rights in the unions. Not only did the daycare organizing reflect union women's growing militancy, but it was also strategically important for women's mobilization and their future organizing efforts for equality in the labour movement.

The OFL Women's Committee (WC) was the primary union formation through which women mobilized support for daycare. The OFL's adoption of the "Statement on Daycare" at its 1980 annual convention helped to establish the committee as a legitimate part of the labour movement. Confirmation of OFL support for free, universal, publicly-funded, quality childcare in November, 1980, indicated a significant development in the growth of labour support for women's concerns, as well as a new commitment by the traditionally male-dominated labour movement to women's equality. In the "Statement on Daycare"—which concluded that "there can be no real equality for women until daycare becomes a social right—women's equality was directly linked to daycare.

Women's trade union organizing developed in response to the changing material conditions of working class women in Canadian capitalist society. Women's work in the family and in the paid labour force was changing rapidly, as growing numbers of women entered the paid labour force.[1] By 1981, more than half the mothers of pre-school children in Ontario were working outside the home,[2] yet most of them did not have access to quality, affordable childcare.[3] Daycare became an urgent demand of working women.

Growing numbers of working women turned to unionization as the best means of improving their low pay and poor working conditions.[4] Women in Ontario more than doubled their representation in unions between 1965 and 1975; by 1981 close to one-third of all union members in Ontario were women.[5] With daycare becoming so crucial for the growing numbers of working mothers, union women began to organize support for this demand within the labour movement.

Changing gender relations in society were reflected in the growth of the modern women's movement in the 1960s and 1970s; this established a foundation for the struggles of working class women in the unions. By 1975, union women had recognized the need to organize collectively in special formations of women, in order to effectively challenge male domination of the labour movement,[7] as they mobilized support for daycare and other special concerns of working women.

This study provides evidence of changing trade-union gender relations in the last decade, as the struggles of working women entered into the dynamic of trade-union politics. While union women continued to face male resistance in some quarters, they reported increasing instances of labour support for their demands. Based on the experiences of women actively engaged in the daycare organizing, as well as analysis of union documents, we have reconstructed this process of struggle. The daycare issue played a strategic role in these struggles, as union activists organized a women's movement within the trade union structure.

The research was undertaken through in-depth interviews with activist union women, including members of the OFL Women's Committee and women active in both public sector and industrial unions.[8] Their personal accounts—based on direct involvement in union organizing—have formed the basis of our assessment of working-class gender relations in the Ontario labour movement.[9] The project was initiated with a strong commitment to both the union movement and the women's movement. The interviews were conducted with the full cooperation of the women involved, who expressed considerable interest in the outcome of the research. It is hoped that the study will contribute to labour action on daycare and other issues important to women, thereby furthering the process of building a progressive labour movement committed to women's equality.

Emergence of the Daycare Issue in the Unions

Daycare had emerged as a basic issue for women active in the unions in the late 1970s. It was identified by members of the OFL Women's Committee as the issue "most problematic for ... women" (Chris).[10] Without daycare, women were unable to "either get a job in the first place, keep their jobs or become active in the labour movement" (Chris).

A number of union women have commented on how their personal experiences as working mothers led them to become active around daycare. Jean, active for many years in the International Union of Electrical, Radio, and Machine Workers (IUE), explained: "Nothing is more inspiring than your own situation. It really is a drive for you." Ann, a Canadian Union of Public Employees (CUPE) member, became active around daycare as she was faced with the need for childcare for her two young children. She commented that her "own personal experience made the link between seeing the problem and suddenly being stuck in it". She added: "Then it becomes something that you don't think about from time to time as one of the issues to consider; it's something you live with every day." Donna, active in the Steelworkers union, explained that she got "drawn into" the daycare issue, having experienced the problems caused by lack of childcare with her own son. She explained that she didn't "want to see other women go through the struggles" that she went through.

A number of the members of the OFL Women's Committee had personally experienced difficulties as working mothers. And even those committee members without young kids "saw it as an issue for their membership" (Chris).

The lack of daycare has also had a negative affect on the representation of working women in the labour movement. In the assessment of the women who initiated the daycare campaign in the OFL, "to get women involved in unions means that you really have to have good daycare" (Chris). Daycare would be necessary in order to increase women's participation in their unions in large numbers "so that it wasn't just still token." Women saw that as "critical" in their "push to be equal members of their unions" (Chris).[11]

Not only was the issue of daycare a priority for union women, but it was also strategically important for women organizing in the labour movement. Although women's concerns had often been seen as divisive by the male union leadership, daycare was one issue that could "bring people together " (Diane).

The daycare issue was raised at the time that women were beginning to organize themselves in the trade unions—when they were "pushing hard for the establishment of women's committees and the Federation Women's Committee" (Diane). Within the Ontario Public Service Employees Union (OPSEU), the effort to establish an equal opportunities program for women had encountered "a lot of very negative backlash", which created a difficult situation for union women. Diane explained that it was "a hard time in terms of fighting around these issues. Everything was presented as very divisive." Daycare was one issue which men did not seem to find as threatening as other women's issues, because men as parents could understand the need for daycare.

> Men and women could recognize the importance of the issue... it didn't seem to generate the same kind of male paranoia that sexual harassment or affirmative action did. (Diane)

Men were also being sensitized to the need for daycare by the provision of childcare at union functions. According to Nancy, this encouraged union men to see daycare as a "concern of the whole union and as a legitimate union demand which required their support".

Daycare was presented to the OFL as an extension of universal education, which was already a union priority. With the "labour movement behind universal education," daycare "wasn't a major thing," Chris explained. "It was a question of extending that care for younger children ... We felt that labour men could easily understand that."

Women activities in the trade-union movement felt that it was crucial to win labour's support for daycare, since it was a basic necessity in order to enable women "to combine work and family responsibilities... and also become active in the union" (Chris). Daycare also proved to be a gender issue which men could relate to in a positive manner.

Building a Base for Women in the OFL

The daycare organizing grew out of union women's efforts in the 1970s to establish an organizational base in the Ontario labour movement. Union women organized in special formations such as Organized Working Women,[12] as well as within a number of unions. A resolution for an OFL Women's Committee was brought forward at the 1977 annual convention through organized pressure by women who "felt that work should be done within the trade union themselves" (Nancy). This made it "really critical that a women's committee exist at the Federation level" (Chris).[13]

However, there was quite a struggle over this issue at convention. Chris recalled that women "fought on the convention floor to establish the committee"; supporters used every opportunity to raise the issue of women's committees in order to win delegates' support for this demand. Chris described how there was a major debate over the formation of the women's committee, which erupted into a "real shouting match." The debate was couched in procedural questions, since Resolution No. 135 to establish a women's committee failed to come to the floor of convention for debate, even though it was initially included in the list of convention resolutions presented by the Resolutions Committee.[14]

Points of order were raised by delegates about "why the issue is being dropped," and the priorities of the Resolutions Committee were called into question by some delegates. The struggle grew more heated as the convention drew to a close without considering the women's committee resolution. The question of a quorum was called by the chair, just as Resolution 135 was brought forward and, for "the first time in years," the annual OFL convention was adjourned for lack of a quorum.[15]

The OFL leadership had argued that only executive officers had the authority to establish OFL committees. Chris feels this was one factor in the leadership's reluctance to have Resolution 135 debated by convention delegates. Resistance of the union leadership to women's demands was thus expressed in terms of constitutional questions. When Resolution 135 was discussed at the next Executive Board meeting,[16] Chris reports that there was still strong opposition to the establishment of a women's committee; however, the resolution for an OFL women's committee was finally approved. Chris suggests that it was less contentious for the executive to approve the women's committee at this level, rather than having to "say it on the convention floor" (given the sharp confrontation over the issue).

Formation of an official women's committee served to legitimate women's organizing within the OFL. Through the Women's Committee (WC), activist union women were able to put pressure on the labour leadership to take action on women's issues, while at the same time they mobilized women in the affiliated unions around their demands. As this study shows, these factors contributed to the successful daycare organizing by women in the OFL.

While gender issues had previously been raised in the OFL, the lack of an organized body of trade-union women had made it difficult to take action on issues important to women. For example, in November 1975, delegates to the OFL Convention had approved a "major policy paper on women's issues" (Chris). However, this resolution, Chris explained, did not lead directly to a program of action since union women did not yet have "a body to implement it actively". As a result, "after that policy paper was passed...there was a push for the Women's Committee to be formed."

The Women's Committee would be able to "keep the pressure on" to implement policies on women; it would ensure that policy paper "didn't just stay as static pieces of paper" (Chris). This would prove important for the daycare issue, as the Women's Committee strategized and developed a plan of action to mobilize support for daycare in the OFL, which in turn led to a major trade-union campaign for universal child care.[17]

The OFL Women's Committee "started off slowly" at its first meeting in April 1978 (Chris), proceeding carefully in light of opposition to the committee manifested at the 1977 Convention. While many of the Women's Committee members were appointed by unions,[18] a number of activist women were attracted to the committee, often as a result of their involvement in particular issues (Chris).

The OFL WC drafted a policy paper on women—"A Woman's Place is in her Union"—and mobilized support for it at the 1978 Convention. Following debate, this resolution was adopted by OFL delegates. The statement presented a strong argument in favour of a women's movement within the trade unions, responding to the opposition which had been manifested earlier in the OFL. The resolution argued against trade unionists who characterized women's organizing as "a diversion from the common interests of all working people." On the contrary, it stated that:

> The interests of all our members will be served if our ranks are opened at all levels to the full participation of women.

Union women argued that raising women's concerns would strengthen the labour movement as a whole.

The OFL Women's Committee was mandated by this 1978 resolution to call the OFL's "First Women's Conference: Bargaining for Equality," held in April 1979 and attended by 295 delegates. This conference served as a catalyst for organizing women in the union movement and encouraged the development of local women's committees. A CUPE member recalls: "As a result of my going to that conference, I came back to my local and said, "let's organize a women's committee and it was an extra impetus" (Ann).

As an official OFL committee, the Women's Committee was able to take advantage of the Federation's organizational and financial resources in calling such a conference, thereby reaching a great number of trade-union women.

Following the "First Women's Conference", members of the Women's Committee realized that "women had reached a point" where they had "been to enough conferences." They said, "let's strategize around an issue and get somewhere" (Chris). After a good deal of discussion, they decided to focus on daycare, as the best issue to take up in the OFL to win support for women's issues in general. Diane explained that combined with "the ongoing fight and struggle" they were having "to gain credibility around all of the issues," daycare seemed to be an issue that they could move forward on. Chris agreed that daycare was "probably a very good issue to pick as the first issue" for the committee to "launch itself on."

Strategy and Tactics of Daycare Organizing

Once the daycare issue had been chosen as a major focus for their work, members of the Women's Committee mobilized support for daycare resolution which would provide official labour endorsement for further daycare organizing. Nine different resolutions on childcare had been submitted by a number of unions in response to the WC's call. The resolution which was finally adopted was "action oriented" and called on the OFL to hold a conference on childcare.[19] This gave the WC an "opening" in making daycare organizing their "major work in the next year" (Diane). The resolution also gave the WC their "mandate to call the Conference on Daycare: 'Sharing the Caring', held in October 1980" (Chris).

It had been the intention of women activists in the OFL to have the labour movement endorse daycare as a priority issue; they had been successful in their goal. It had been only a "short duration from the Women's Committee being formed" to having one of their issues "taken up with the OFL as a main topic" (Jean).

Following through on the 1979 OFL resolution, the Women's Committee developed a plan of action on daycare. Their goals were to "develop a comprehensive policy, publicize the issue, educate unionists, and plan strategies for change." The Conference on Daycare would be "one part of this programme" (Women's Committee Correspondence, June 27, 1980).

The OFL daycare conference was an important step in building trade-union support for universally accessible quality child care. The Women's Committee played the key role in planning and organizing this conference, which was an integral part of their strategy for building support for the daycare issue. Nancy explained:

> The logical thing is to hold a conference and invite people who, by their attendance at the convention, have already shown they'll support the issue. And that will bring people together.

The Women's Committee hoped to have a major recommendation come forward from the conference which would strengthen the OFL's commitment to a daycare campaign; this was accomplished. The "Discussion Paper on Daycare", formulated by the Women's Committee "after several lengthy meetings and consultations with (daycare) activists in the field" (OFL, Daycare Conference Report, 1980, p. 4), had served as the basis for discussion at the conference strategy sessions. This discussion paper, plus the recommendations for a comprehensive child care plan which came from the conference, formed the basis of the official OFL policy paper on daycare. By the time of the daycare conference, the OFL executive had agreed to present a policy paper on daycare to the November 1980 OFL Convention.

The daycare conference was advertised through official trade union channels of communication. Local unions all across the province were urged by the Secretary-Treasurer of the OFL to "send delegates to this important conference" (OFL Correspondence, June 3 and August 26, 1980).

Publicity during the conference served to increase public awareness about labour support for daycare. At a press conference held during the conference, OFL President Pilkey pledged that "the OFL has committed itself to making universal, publicly-funded daycare a major labour issue" (*Ontario Labour*, Nov.-Dec. 1980). Media coverage of the conference was widespread, with reports carried in many local newspapers. The publicity around the daycare issue, and the ability of the Women's Committee to reach large numbers of people on this issue, illustrated some of the benefits of the committee being able to use official trade-union channels to build support for daycare.

Within the labour movement, many trade unionists were educated about the issue of childcare through their participation in debates and discussions at the conference. There were 145 union delegates who attended the conference, most of them from unions with representation on the Women's Committee (OFL Conference Report, 1980, p. 1). By their attendance at the conference, these union delegates had shown an interest in and commitment to the issue of daycare. Many of them were from unions where the issue had been recognized as a priority for their members.

The conference reflected the state of gender relations which existed in the labour movement at that point. There was significant support by trade-union men—including the leadership—for the daycare issue. However, there were still indications of conflict around the priority to be accorded to women's issues in the labour movement.

While the delegates to the daycare conference were "primarily women," according to Chris, there was participation from men "both in the community and the labour movement itself." In her estimation, about 10 percent of the conference delegates were men. Women's Committee members felt it was significant that the "male leadership (of the OFL) attended and spoke" at the conference (Chris).

Despite the close working relationship between the Women's Committee and the male trade-union leadership, there were indications of some conflict around women's issues. While the OFL was publicly committing itself to make daycare a priority for labour, its scheduling of a major OFL demonstration for the same weekend as the daycare conference was perceived by members of the Women's Committee as indicating a lack of concern for the daycare issue.

A rally against plant closures had been scheduled for the final day of the conference. This necessitated last minute changes in the conference agenda in order to "accommodate the OFL cutbacks demonstration" in the afternoon (Women's Committee Minutes). As a result, "the agenda had to be compacted into a shorter period of time, leaving a less than satisfactory time allotment in the plenary session," according to the OFL Conference Report (1980, p. 4).

While this conflict did not disrupt relations between the trade-union women's movement and the OFL leadership, members of the Women's Committee "were furious" about the scheduling conflict (Nancy). At this point, leaders of the OFL WC had felt it was necessary to make an accommodation to powereful interests in the labour movement, by publicly endorsing the OFL rally against layoffs and incorporating it into their conference on daycare. Despite the conflict in scheduling, the WC judged the conference to be a success in terms of building support for a major trade union campaign on daycare.

There was strong support for an OFL daycare resolution at the November 1980 Convention. The Women's Committee won most of its demands around the daycare issue, as Convention delegates endorsed the OFL's "Statement on Daycare." However, there were some minor setbacks. Although a number of workshops at the October daycare conference had proposed that a daycare coordinator be hired by the OFL, this demand was lost even though the Women's Committee members "strategized at Convention and fought" for it (Chris).[20] Despite this, "because of the pressure" around the daycare issue, the Women's Committee found that the OFL leadership demonstrated its "willingness to put on any staff needed to carry it out effectively" (Chris).[21]

OFL endorsement of the November 1980 "Statement on Daycare" represented months of organizing, educational work and lobbying by the Women's Committee. Nancy recalled how the WC had strategized around the daycare issue:

> The whole process, between calling a conference and writing a paper, the paper being amended by the delegates, becoming a policy paper, going to Convention was part of the strategy.

The committee had worked to build support for daycare, "rather than just coming cold to Convention" (Nancy). Members of the WC felt they had gained valuable experience in organizing within the trade-union structure.

Impact of Daycare Organizing

The daycare organizing has been an important part of the process of change in trade-union gender relations. When the daycare resolution was adopted by the 1980 OFL convention, it had both an immediate impact on the trade-union work and long term effects on the building of a women's movement in the unions.

The OFL's policy paper on daycare proposed an "active campaign" in order to achieve a "system of universal, comprehensive childcare"; it outlined a "plan of action" including proposals for internal union action and a political action campaign for legislative change. Internal union action focused on the provision of childcare services at union functions, union education programs on daycare, and collective bargaining for daycare subsidies and workplace daycare.

There is evidence that concrete steps were taken by the OFL—as well as some of its affiliated unions—towards implementing internal provisions for childcare at union meetings, conferences and conventions. Daycare has been provided at OFL conferences and conventions since 1979.[22] Other unions such as OPSEU and the United Auto Workers (UAW) have also adopted internal policies for childcare at union meetings.[23]

Collective bargaining for workplace daycare and daycare subsidies has been a part of negotiations in public sector unions as well as in some industrial unions.[24] Collective bargaining for daycare was linked to negotiations for other parental rights and benefits in the OFL Women's Committee's bargaining guide for unions, *Parental Rights and Daycare* (Acheson and Macleod, April 1982).

At the same time, the OFL initiated a political campaign for publicly-funded, universal daycare. This plan of action was implemented through the organization of a series of regional community forums on daycare, as well as by the formation of a province-wide daycare coalition, the Ontario Coalition for Better Daycare (OCBD). Initiated by the OFL, this coalition of labour and community groups has continued the political struggle for changes in public daycare policy.[25]

The daycare campaign was also of strategic importance for the development of a women's movement within the OFL and its affiliated unions. It facilitated the efforts of women to establish an organized base in the labour movement, and mobilized women around their special concerns as trade unionists. Daycare was the first identifiable issue taken up by the Women's Committee in the OFL, and focussing on daycare enabled women to work as an organized group within the structure of the Federation. Support for the 1980 daycare resolution helped to establish the legitimacy of union women's organizing. In Diane's estimation, the OFL resolution was "politically important in terms of establishing credibility of the Women's Committee" itself, as well as the "women's trade union movement" which is embodied through local "women's committees and the OFL Women's Committee."

In the assessment of its members, the WC "came of age" through this political process of building trade-union support for the daycare campaign. As an organized body of union women, the committee had gained valuable experience "in terms of fighting for an issue and seeing it through" (Chris), a process which would prove to be applicable to organizing for other women's concerns.[26] The WC had demonstrated its ability to mobilize union women and build support for women's issues.

Trade-union women found that women's issues were being taken more seriously than before, given the labour leadership's support for the daycare issue. Jean explained that when "delegates see their executive body endorsing" an issue, "then they think...we've got to follow suit and take it seriously." Official endorsement of the daycare issue provided legitimacy for activity around this issue at the local level. Ann related her experiences in CUPE:

> From my own union local, there was never any resistance from the executive to this kind of involvement...Because they understood that it was a trade union effort, they understood that the initiative was from the OFL. That gave it the legitimacy they needed.

There are indications that many women got involved in trade-union work around the daycare issue, which gave "a focus to the work". Union women found they were "able to work with men" on the daycare issue because they could "speak about the needs of working parents". Ann saw daycare as the specific issue which had mobilized women: "It was the right place and the right time, because daycare was in itself a problem."

As women were organizing around daycare, they also got involved around many other issues which affected them. Donna pointed to "the women's committees that were formed in and around that time, because the drive was on". There have been long term effects on the role of women in the unions, as Ann explained: "There's a stronger network of women who I met in 1979 and '80 and many of them I still know and work with."

Development of a Trade-Union Women's Movement

The daycare issue entered into the process of building a movement representative of women as well as men, as women organized together and raised their demands for equality in the unions. The OFL's support for daycare reflected the growing strength of women in a union movement which was becoming more responsive to women's demands. Women were becoming more aware of their power and demanding "recognition as trade unionists" on an equal footing with men. Chris felt this "showed the strength of women who felt that now they could push this" because they had reached a "point where there was a much greater increase of women's participation within unions".

At the same time, the success of the Women's Committee in organizing for daycare also reflects the positive impact of the women's movement "on the trade union movement and on women within the trade union movement". Chris feels this has led to "the increasing consciousness of trade-union members around women's issues." This growing consciousness was, in turn, the basis of the achievements of the WC in organizing and winning support for the daycare resolution, as women were "becoming active in the trade union movement" and insisting "the OFL take up these issues" (Chris). Thus, positive developments for union women can be traced to the activities of the Women's Committee, the daycare organizing and "just the general way it's moving in the labour movement" (Donna).

Activist union women have provided examples of the growing support for women's issues and the increasing respect accorded to women in the Ontario labour movement. Their experiences confirm that there have been significant changes in trade-union gender relations in the last decade.

Chris described how women's concerns were now being "recognized as serious issues." She explained, "they're not laughed at or snickered at, people don't leave the hall, (although) that kind of thing...used to be the case." Such changes were visible at OFL conventions. Activist union women reported that their concerns were now being taken more seriously, in contrast to their previous experiences, where women generally were not treated with respect as delegates and speakers.

Chris observed that increasing numbers of women were attending conventions. Donna added that not only were women attending conventions, but "more women are even getting up and speaking at the mike, and being accepted by males — where before they weren't." In the assessment of a number of women who have been organizing within the labour movement, there have been significant gains made by women; they are now speaking up on a broad spectrum of trade-union issues and "the men are respecting and listening to what they have to say" (Donna).

In Donna's estimation, union women are "getting the support of men, as they gain experience as trade unionists." However, this "process has taken years to develop." It developed in response to women's growing participation and militancy in the unions. Chris feels that there have been some improvements, with women's militancy "not seen as quite such a threatening thing (to men) as it once was."

The changing responses of union men reflect women's growing confidence in themselves, as they have decided "this is enough of being put down — I'm a person" (Donna). Donna contrasted her earlier experience in a Steelworker local where "women were intimidated. . .and wouldn't talk back" to management, to the present situation where women are becoming stewards and "fighting for their rights along with their brothers' rights".

In Donna's estimation, women themselves have changed as they demanded equal recognition from men, "because women were not going to sit back and take it, like they had for so many years." She thinks "men are realizing that they're dealing with a whole different type of woman." As a result of these changes, a growing "interchange" has developed between women and men in the labour movement which was "never there before" (Donna).

As they have continued raising their demands for daycare and other concerns of working women, union activists like Diane have identified the unions as "vehicles of change" for women's equality. They are hopeful that "male domination is changing" (Donna) and giving way to a labour movement based on equality.

In this study we have documented how women organized around their specific demands for daycare within the unions. This has provided us with a basis for assessing gender relations in the contemproary Ontario labour movement. In the assessment of activist union women themselves, there are grounds for optimism that the labour movement is becoming more effective in representing and defending the interests of all workers, women as well as men. The development of a women's movement within the unions contributes to this process of building a more progressive labour movement.

Notes

1. In the last two decades, there have been profound changes in the labour force participation rates for married women and women in the 25-44 year age group (see Armstrong and Armstrong, 1978; Ontario Ministry of Labour, 1982; Yanz and Smith, 1983). While only a minority of married women in Ontario (31.6 percent) worked outside the home in 1966, by 1983 substantially more than half (56 percent) of all married women were working or seeking work (*Ontario Statistics*, 1984: Tables 5.11, 6.5, 6.7). The increase in labour force activity has been most pronounced for women in the 25-44 year age group (the traditional childbearing years), rising from less than a third (30.5 percent) in 1956 to more than two thirds (73 percent) in 1983 (*Ontario Statistics*, 1984: Tables 5.11, 6.5, 6.7).
2. According to the 1981 data, the participation rate for women in Ontario with at least one child under six was 52.9 percent (Ontario Ministry of Labour, 1982).
3. See Leah, 1981. An expansion in daycare facilities in the 1960s and early 1970s was halted in 1975, as a result of cutbacks in government funding for daycare. Combined with the growing labour force activity of mothers with young children, this precipitated a serious crisis in daycare. The daycare crisis was documented by a number of studies; for example, a Social Planning Council report concluded that "the levels of access to daycare in Metro (Toronto) are frighteningly inadequate" (Sept. 1980:193).
4. See Armstrong and Armstrong, 1983; Briskin, 1983a; Ontario (Ministry of Labour), 1981; White, 1980. In the last two decades, "women have dominated union membership growth...almost doubling their share of organized workers" (Armstrong and Armstrong, 1983:108).
5. While women comprised only 15.3 percent of total union membership in Ontario in 1965, their proportion had risen to 22.9 percent in 1975. In 1981, 29.5 percent of all union members in Ontario were women. See Ontario Ministry of Labour, 1981. However, at the same time women comprised 42.2 percent of the Ontario workforce; thus they continued to be underrepresented in unions. See *Ontario Statistics*, 1984, Tables 5.11, 5.26.
6. See Briskin, 1983b; Colley, 1981, 1983; Egan and Yanz, 1983; and Smith, 1981 (British and American Unions).
7. A number of studies have documented the history of discrimination against working women in the Canadian labour movement. See Frager, 1983; Sangster, 1981; White, 1980.
8. In-depth interviews were undertaken in May and June 1983. Union women interviewed included members and staff of the Canadian Union of Public Employees (CUPE), Ontario Public Service Employees Union (OPSEU), Steelworkers (USWA), Autoworkers (UAW), and Electrical Workers (IUE). The women have been identified by the following pseudonyms: Ann, Chris, Diane, Donna, Jean, Nancy. Interviews were also conducted with four other persons who are not referred to in this part of the study.
9. Other studies employing a similar methodology include Armstrong and Armstrong, 1983; Oakley, 1981; Luxton, 1980.
10. Quotes in the text have been identified by the pseudonyms of the persons interviewed (see Note 8).
11. The OFL "Statement on Daycare" addresses these concerns; it called for the provision of childcare services "at union meetings, conferences and conventions".
12. Organized Working Women (OWW) was formed in March 1976, "to bring more women trade unionists into union activity" (*Union Woman*, Nov. 19, 1980).
13. A precedent had been set by the Canadian Labour Congress which established a Women's Bureau in December, 1977.

14. The Resolutions Committee brings forward resolutions for debate at convention (on the basis of resolutions submitted by union locals), recommending concurrence or non-concurrence to delegates; as a result, the Resolutions Committee weilds considerable political power—regarding what will be debated and when it will be debated.
15. See *Proceedings* of the OFL Convention (1980: 48, 58, 90-91) for details of the debate about Resolution No. 135.
16. According to OFL procedures, resolutions not debated at convention are brought forward at the next Executive Board meeting following convention.
17. The daycare campaign is outlined in the OFL's 1980 "Statement on Daycare."
18. The usual procedure for OFL committees is to have members appointed by the affiliated unions.
19. See Resolution No. 183, "concurrence as amended", (OFL, "Resolutions of 23rd Convention", Nov. 1979).
20. The OFL leadership maintained that the Executive Board—not delegates to annual conventions—reserves the constitutional right to hire staff (see OFL *Proceedings*, 1980: 10, 45-6).
21. For example, Andre Foucault, OFL Programs Director, was assigned to work on the daycare campaign. He coordinated activities in early 1981, including the organization of regional community forums on daycare and the formation of a provincial daycare coalition.
22. A 1978 OFL resolution called for "an examination of the feasibility of providing childcare services at future functions" (Resolution No. 52, see OFL *Proceedings*, 1978:34). Following a pilot project at the first OFL Women's Conference in April 1979—which accommodated 16 children of conference participants—the 1979 OFL Convention approved the provision of daycare at all future OFl conventions and conferences (Resolution No. 202, see OFL *Proceedings*, 1979:40).
23. OPSEU voted to "provide childcare facilities at conventions and educational conferences" at its 1978 convention. In 1980, a more comprehensive policy was adopted, providing for an expense claim for childcare costs, as well as the continuing childcare services (Diane). The UAW provides for childcare at union meetings, including the Canadian Council, its highest decision-making body (Nancy).
24. For example, the Women's Committee of CUPE, Local 1000 played an active role in the four-year process of setting up workplace daycare at Ontario Hydro; this centre opened in September 1985. Workplace daycare was raised as a final demand by OPSEU in the 1981-82 negotiations with the Ontario government. While they did not win the daycare issue during negotiations, since that time the government has set up four pilot projects with on-site daycare (Diane). In its December 1983 contract, UAW Local 1325 successfully negotiated for employer contributions to an employee daycare fund (*Solidarity*, Winter 1983: 11). This contract for Canadian Fab workers in Stratford, Ontario was seen as a milestone in collective bargaining for childcare.
25. While we have made only a brief mention of the implementation of the OFL's 1980 policy paper on daycare, these measures indicate that there was an actual commitment may by labour to implementing daycare policies.
26. Both Nancy and Diane have recalled how their political strategy for the daycare organizing was repeated with the campaign for Affirmative Action. Delegates to the 1982 OFL Convention endorsed the "Statement on Women and Affirmative Action". This policy paper set forth a plan of action for mandatory affirmative action for women in the labour force, as well as a comprehensive program of internal union action to provide for women's equal representation within the labour movement.

Reproductive Rights

Carolyn Egan

There has been a developing relationship between the trade union movement and the women's movement in the past years. The tentative but growing links between the two have the potential of significantly strengthening both and fostering greatly needed changes in the lives of women. In this presentation I want to examine a concrete example of this process: the work of the Ontario Coalition of Abortion Clinics (OCAC), and the support for abortion rights that has developed within the labour movement.

The struggle for reproductive rights has been a cornerstone of the women's movement since its inception, and unfortunately is still a long way from being won. When we speak of reproductive rights we are referring to a whole range of feminist issues: the right to decide when and if to have children, the right to safe and effective birth control, the right to support services such as childcare and paid parental leave, the right to determine our own sexuality as women, control over our birthing process, an end to forced or coerced sterilization, and of course the right to full access to free abortion in our communities. We understand that if we are truly to have choice, then all of these are required. This particular campaign is part of a long-term struggle for full reproductive rights for all women.

Access to abortion for poor, immigrant, working-class women, and women of colour has become more and more difficult. Hospital cutbacks, the committee and quota system necessitated by the Criminal Code, and the increasing number of doctors opting out of the Ontario Health Insurance Plan (OHIP) have all contributed to this. In Ontario in the fall of 1982, a campaign was initiated by activists from the women's health movement to begin to change this situation. The Ontario Coalition for Abortion Clinics was established, and it put forward the demand to legalize free standing clinics providing medically insured abortions, as well as the longstanding call for the repeal of the federal abortion law. The goal was to provide free and more equitable access to abortion for all women and to ensure that we are treated in a respectful and humane manner. A strategy towards this was accepted and won great success in Quebec where CLSC's (Community Health Centres) and Centres de Sante des Femmes (Women's Health Centres) are offering abortion services to women who seek them. It was a combination of a doctor willing to challenge the law by doing abortions in defiance of the Criminal Code, and a broad-based alliance led by the women's movement willing to defend the clinic, and fight for the necessary change.

The OCAC knew that a political campaign of this sort was necessary if we were to succeed. The clinics in Toronto and Winnipeg were our test cases, but the long term goal is to challenge the law so that it would become unenforceable and finally overturned. We want to change the Criminal Code so that community and women's clinics throughout Canada and Quebec can offer real choices to women, at no cost, in a supportive environment. This will not provide full reproductive rights for all women, because we know this requires a more fundamental change in the priority that our society assigns to women's needs. But, it will mean a significant breakthrough in the options that are available, and a real step toward the long-term goal of women's emancipation.

A challenge of the Criminal Code or a political campaign without mass support cannot win the desired changes. That is why the OCAC reached out to involve the trade union movement, the immigrant community, lesbian and gay organizations, neighbourhood groups, and many others who have not been traditionally active in this area. We know through the polls, through our endorsing organizations, and through the tremendous encouragement our campaign has received, that it is we who represent the needs of the majority. The consciousness is there, but our task is to organize that consciousness into a political force that can achieve our goals.

The women's movement, through coalitions such as OCAC, has initiated a major offensive with the possiblity of making the first real gains in the area of reproductive rights that we have seen in a decade. We know that we cannot win this offensive alone.

A victory requires a broad-based movement willing to be vocal in its support. This means a movement that is able to defend the abortion clinics when they are under attack from the right and from the state; a state which, as we have seen by the police raids and criminal charges, is not playing a neutral role. OCAC believes that one of our strongest allies is the trade union movement, both because it is the organized representation of the working class and because it has the potential to be a powerful agent of social change. We have made a particular priority of linking with the labour movement. Outside of the women's community, it has provided the most consistent support for the issue.

This, of course, has not happened by chance. The ground work had been laid by the ongoing work of feminists within the unions over the past years. In Ontario, there has been a string of militant strikes such as Fleck, Radio Shack, Fotomat, Irwin Toy, hospital workers, Bell Canada, and Puretex which have brought forward the particular concerns of women trade unionists... Organized Working Women (OWW) has held conferences and skill-training sessions for the rank-and-file activists. The Ontario Federation of Labour (OFL) Women's Committee has taken a high-profile role in promoting women's issues within the federation and in individual locals. Not enough can be said in recognition of the determination and courage of these women, who have fought for women's caucuses, committees, and conferences, and support for women's issues. The OFL initiated campaigns in daycare and affirmative action with meetings across the province. Issues such as the right to childcare at meetings, contract clauses for paid parental leave, and against sexual harassment and against discrimination on the basis of sexual orientation were bargained for. The demands of women within the unions have had an impact on the consciousness and the structure of the labour movement. There is still a tremendous amount of work to be done, but the work to date has led to a much greater openness towards the women's movement and its objectives, and a greater willingness to work together and to support each others' issues.

This very much set the stage for organizing support for the pro-choice movement. Feminists within the union movement have, by the very nature of their demands, been working towards the defeat of business unionism. They have tried to build an appreciation of the importance of fighting for social as well as economic issues. In so doing they are bringing home the point that workers, particularly women workers, have needs that go beyond an increased pay packet. There is no sharp dividing line between fighting for workplace concerns and taking up broader social and ideological issues such as racism, violence against women, etc. that have a profound impact on working peoples' lives. Reproductive rights and full access to abortion is clearly such an issue.

I would like to deal more specifically with how the issue has been addressed within the labour movement: with the successes and some of the failures that have been encountered. First, we have succeeded in winning solid support from labour councils, locals, and federations as well as from women's caucuses and committees. This has enabled major labour figures such as Cliff Pilkey, Bob White, Dave Patterson and Grace Hartman to participate in our rallies and meetings and to speak strongly on behalf of the labour movement in support of the campaign. They have never hesitated to do so.

When we first began our approach to the unions we were cautioned by a number of otherwise sympathetic staff that we might not win support, because very little work had been done on this particular issue. The strides that had been made on matters like women's caucuses had been mainly work-related, and abortion was viewed as a potentially 'divisive' issue. It was felt by some that there could be a backlash which might harm the campaign, or that we might jeopardize other women's issues, such as the affirmative action which was being discussed at an upcoming OFL conference. We were also cautioned that the waters hadn't really been tested at labour meetings and therefore the question had not been thought through. But others within the trade union movement disagreed, and OCAC chose to go ahead, working through existing women's caucuses and committees as a first step. A subcommittee was established within OCAC to coordinate our work within the trade union movement. It prepared a specific information packet which included a sample resolution, basic information on the issue, and a motivating leaflet entitled "Why Should Trade Unions Support the Legalization of Medically Insured Freestanding Abortion Clinics?" It dealt with the worsening situation, and why we were appealing to the unions, and spoke of the need for unity between the two movements.

Our first test was the Ontario Federation of Labour Convention in November 1982, which we chose because we felt that if a resolution was passed at this level it would set policy for the federation and make our work with individual unions and locals much easier. We were aware that a pro-choice position had been taken at a previous Canadian Labour Congress (CLC) convention, and that gave us confidence that it would be won after debate. Organized Working Women had submitted a resolution through a union local, and OCAC organized a major drive for support. One of our leading members was a delegate, and we were working with others which gave us direct access to the floor. We prepared 500 information packets and were able to use the OFL Women's Committee table to distribute them to interested delegates. We sold hundreds of CHOICE buttons and many of the delegates signed our petitions in support for the resolution, strategizing, planning the lobbying of delegates, and developing a floor strategy for debate. Women delegates raised it in their local caucuses, and put a tremendous amount of energy into discussions with fellow delegates. There was a lot of activity and debate outside the hall, and by the time it came to the floor, everyone was aware of the strong support for the resolution. CHOICE buttons were everywhere, including on the lapels of a number of executive officers.

It was significant that an important vote on an affirmative action policy paper had already been won. This helped to set the stage for further debate on issues of concern to women. Abortion rights could not be dismissed as easily because of the dialogue and debate on the need for trade unions to take seriously woman-defined issues. A strong women's presence was clear, and there was a heightened sensitivity to the need to take women's issues seriously. When the resolution came to the floor woman after woman was in place at the pro-mikes, as well as men such as Wally Majesky, President of the Labour Council of Metro Toronto. An executive member of Organized Working Women spoke movingly of her personal experiences of being forced to seek an illegal abortion after her doctor refused her, even though an earlier child was born with hemophilia. Delegates from Northern Ontario spoke of the lack of access in their area, and how women are forced to travel to Toronto or the U.S.

Women also spoke of the two-tiered health system, where women of privilege have the right to abortion but working class, poor, immigrant, native women, and women of colour were denied this right. The point was made that if the trade union movement was sincerely concerned with women's equality, then it must work in conjunction with the women's movement to support this campaign. Those intervening put forward eloquent arguments for why delegates should support a woman's right to choose, even if they were personally opposed to abortion, stressing that each individual should have the right to make her own decisions without race, class, or geographic barriers.

The issue was placed clearly within the context of choice and women's rights. This perspective convinced many who had expressed personal reservations to support the resolution. When the question was called, the vote was overwhelmingly in favour; for those involved it was a very moving and gratifying moment.

Since that very significant vote, we have consistently won the issue, and in most situations have always opted for the debate because of the educational value, even when there was a risk that the vote could be lost. This has won us the support of the Labour Council of Metro Toronto, the National Council for the United Auto Workers (UAW), the Canadian Labour Council Convention, the Ontario Public Service Employees Union (OPSEU) Convention, the Equal Opportunity Committee of the Canadian Air Line Flight Attendants, and many individual locals. We try wherever possible to set up information tables at labour events, and would like to be able to do more of this type of work. We ask locals: to pass resolutions modelled on the OFL's, to send endorsements of our demand, and to organize with the women's movement to build a pro-choice campaign in their area. This campaign can be undertaken in many ways, including conducting educationals in the local, sponsoring public meetings, establishing local pro-choice groups or locals, circulating petitions in the community, and urging members to send letters of support to the government.

Major labour leaders have regularly spoken at our events and we feel that we clearly have strong rank-and-file support based on the consistent pro-votes we have received. But this, to date, has not translated itself into a mass mobilization by the trade unionists, in contrast to Britain or Italy when the abortion struggle was won there. It is always duly noted by the media when labour representatives speak at our rallies, but the unionists are rarely able to draw out there membership. There has only been one pro-choice labour rally; it took place at the 1983 OFL Convention after an almost unanimous reaffirmation of its pro-choice position. Hundreds of delegates marched to the courthouse where the doctors were on trial and held a vocal rally supporting them. This had a tremendous impact on the media, gave a major boost to the campaign, and was highlighted in OFL publications. But we have been unable to repeat it. The problem of mobilization is not a phenomenon related only to this issue. We know that the trade union movement of today has difficulty mobilizing the rank and file. Since OCAC is committed to the building of a mass movement, we have been disappointed that we have not as yet been able to translate the strong union policy and membership support into mass political action.

We are trying to develop strategies to improve our work in the unions and build on what has already been accomplished. We would particularly like to involve rank-and-file members in our day to day workings, mobilizing in concrete ways the support that is there. We would like to see local pro-choice committees built within unions, more women's caucuses taking this up as a priority, pro-choice literature always available on women's committee tables at conventions, support petitions initiated by the labour activists, etc. We would also like the Ontario New Democratic Party (NDP) to take as strong a stand in support of abortion rights as the labour movement, and we have worked with labour movement supporters to prepare for this within the party and the riding associations. NDP party policy is pro-choice, but the leadership has not spoken out as strongly as it should.

There has been a disturbing decision by the Labour Relations Board relating to union financial support of non-workplace related issues. A complaint was launched by an OPSEU member after one convention took a strong position in support of the abortion campaign and the OPSEU news published a very supportive article. The complainant felt that he should be exempt from paying union dues if monies were used to support abortion rights, which are contrary to his religion. The board ruled in his favour. There has not been any reduction in union support since this ruling, however, and we have continued to receive financial donations. This case is clearly an attempt to intimidate unions from taking progressive positions on such issues and giving them financial support. Anti-choice publications have instructed their members to take similar actions within their unions, and anti-choice resolutions are now being submitted to some conventions. We in the OCAC believe in the centrality of the working class to any movement for social change, and the anti-choice forces have also recognized the impact that labour's support has made on our struggle.

On the ideological level the work being done in the unions on this issue is very important. Women are doing more than asking support for our specific demand for the legalization of clinics. We in OCAC and other women activists as well want to broaden the understanding of the roots of women's oppression, and bring out the ideological as well as the economic aspects of this oppression in our political approach to the issue. We want not only to legalize the clinics, which is important as a specific demand on the state and is vital in economic terms for most women, but also to broaden the consciousness of those with whom we work to appreciate that control of our bodies—our reproductive freedom—is fundamental to our liberation. Even winning this particular demand, as important as it is, will not in itself bring full reproductive choices for all women.

It's important to raise questions of control and social responsibility in our political organizing. We want to make clear that when we use the word "CHOICE" we are addressing something beyond freedom under the law. We mean real alternatives or possibilities for all women. Working class, native, immigrant women, and women of colour need full access to free abortion in their own communities, and not just the legal right to choose. We also need economic independence, paid parental leave, free universal childcare, and lesbian custody rights, if the choice to have a child is to be a real one. We know that only a partial victory is achieved by the demand for freedom of choice, and that democratic rights of this sort can be very limited in winning changes that will concretely impact on all women, and not just those with economic resources. Control or choice is not only a question of legality or illegality, as Mary MacIntosh and Michele Barret have pointed out in The Anti-Social Family. It is not as simple as that, and we must speak to what constitutes real freedom of choice for working class women, immigrant women, and women of colour. I referred earlier to what must be in place to make that possible, and that includes well-paying jobs, paid parental leave, free universal childcare, safe and effective birth control, control of our sexuality, and services in our own communities and in our own languages, etc. Yet until we have all of these, which would necessitate dramatic changes in our economic and social system, we must continue to demand legal rights and choices because we cannot leave the very real questions of control to the church, or to the state, or to any other power.

We also want to make it crystal clear that we are not asking for greater access to abortions only because the economic crisis makes it more difficult to raise children. We are questioning the conventional roles related to motherhood and gender. The right to control our reproduction, the right to decide whether or not to have children is fundamental. We try to make this point in our literature when we speak of a world where women are sexually and economically exploited, where we make up the largest percentage of the poor, where we are denied paid parental leave and childcare, and the right to determine our own sexuality, and where we are raped and beaten and still bear the major responsibility for domestic work and child raising.

The goals in our work with the trade union movement are much broader than winning support for our major demand; they include a recognition of the fundamental oppression of women and the role that the denial of reproductive freedom plays in maintaining it. Our tasks are now to redouble our efforts to maintain the gains that we have made and to develop strategies to mobilize the support that we know is there.

We hope that this campaign will provide important lessons on the necessity and political effectiveness of the trade union and women's movements working together to win advances for all women.

"Famiglia e Lavoro": The Experience of Southern Italian Immigrant Women in Post-War Toronto, 1949-60

Franca Iacovetta

Women played an important role in the immigration of Southern Italian peasant families to post-World War Two Toronto. Within the patriarchal organization of the family, Italian women performed demanding roles as immigrants, workers, wives and mothers. Their active commitment to the family helped to bridge the move from the old world to the new as women's labour, both paid and unpaid, continued to help ensure the survival and material well-being of their families. The transition from *contadina* (peasant women) to worker did not require a fundamental transformation in world view for these peasant women, who were long accustomed to contributing their labour power to the family economy. Those who became workers, however, now had to endure new forms of economic exploitation and new rhythms of life and work. Women who remained at home similarly performed economic and social tasks for their immigrant working-class families and endured the alienating and racist aspects of urban industrial life.

Based on preliminary research and oral interviews, this brief discussion on womens' roles in immigration focusses on family and work roles in Italy and Toronto. It is divided into three sections: old world conditions, migration, and early living and working conditions in Toronto. I concentrate on women's activities and perceptions, but also discuss the economic and social contexts in which those experiences took place.

After World War Two, Italian immigration to Europe and overseas took off. Between 1951 and 1961 overseas emigrants numbered over one million. A quarter of these arrived in Canada, over 81,000 of whom were women. More than 25,000 women, many with children, came to Toronto - a city that attracted some 90,000 (or 40 percent) of the Italian immigrants to Canada in this period. Young, married peasant women, sponsored by husbands and families, predominated; after 1952 they accounted for between 40 and 50 percent of annual waves of Italians to Canada. Most were from the Mezogiorono—the southern agricultural regions of Abruzzi—Molise, Basilicata, Campagnia, Puglia and Calabria (Sidlofsky, 1969; Sturino, 1978: 288-311).

Anticipating their arrival, the Anglican Church in 1941 depicted Southern Europeans as "amenable to the fallacies of dictatorship" and better suited to Latin America's climate and politics.[1] The British Dominions Emigration Society dismissed Northern Italians as Communists and Southerners as poor settlers. Provincial officials, worried about Jews and Catholics entering Protestant Ontario, cooperated with manufacturers to recruit only British skilled workers.[2] Even federal officials—who in cooperation with Canadian employers did recruit Italian men to fill serious labour shortages in agriculture, mining and construction—portrayed Southerners as backward and slovenly, and worried that they outnumbered 'superior' immigrants from the North.[3]

Women received little consideration. Concerned about the drying up of traditional sources of female domestics, immigration officials did welcome some 16,000 single women for domestic service as well as hairdressing and seamstressing. Once again, however, the preference was for women from urban centres in the North. Following several frustrated attempts in 1951 and 1952 to recruit southern single women, immigration and labour agents dismissed these women as "rather primitive and uneducated," lacking the appropriate standards of cleanliness and training, and straightjacketted by their obsessive commitment to their families. Moreover, they were considered mere farm girls who could not be expected to adjust well to "Canadian housekeeping methods." And many Italian immigrant women either rotated their jobs in domestic service, or violated the one year employment contracts and fled service in favour of employment in the garment and textile factories of Toronto and Montreal. Not surprisingly, married peasant women from the South were seen as the least desirable of all, especially because officials did not expect such women—considered homely and untrained—to engage in any form of paid work. A 1950 agreement to permit bridal trousseaus duty-free at least recognized married women's role in setting up a new home. But it also reflected a view of married Southern Italian women as merely dependent wives and mothers who could make no financial contribution to their families or, more importantly, to Canadian society.[4]

Far from being simply a part of the male newcomer's cultural baggage—a view some male scholars have also adopted—Southern Italian women were indispensable to their family. That indispensability was rooted in the peasant mode of production in the old world.[5]

Southern peasants did not come from isolated, closed villages; nor were they completely self-sufficient farmers isolated from the market economy. Rather they resided in hill towns which were characterized by complex social structures and class divisions (evident in the presence of professionals, bureaucrats, artisans, and agricultural labourers). Peasants, who might simultaneously own, rent and sharecrop numerous plots of land, daily walked long distances from the town to the fields below. Their farm lands consisted of highly fragmented, scattered, and underproductive plots located on steep slopes. These factors prevented extensive mechanization and reinforced under-capitalized and labour-intensive methods of farming. While the household was the primary site of production and commitment, peasants also engaged in the cash economy on a local, national and international scale. Women I interviewed had regularly sold surplus wheat and eggs to co-villagers, and these people also frequently visited nearby urban centres to purchase goods and services. Poverty compelled families to supplement their meagre farm incomes by sending out members—usually men—to earn extra wages. These people worked temporarily as agricultural labourers or woodworkers in Italy, or went to Europe and North and South America to labour in agriculture, railway construction and the building trades. These activities, and the cash sent home, brought peasant families into contact with more highly industrialized economies.[6]

Patriarchal structures and cultural mores imposed heavy restrictions on peasant women's behaviour and freedom.[7] Family *onore* (honour) rested upon women's sexual purity and on men's success in guarding their women's virtues and winning the family bread. Central to women's oppression in Southern Italy were basic notions linked to male esteem and dominance: an almost obsessive fear of pre and extra-marital sex and of the shame a 'loose' woman could bring to her family. Males exercised their privileges in the public sphere by leading ceremonial rituals and acting as the family's representative with the outside world. Assunta C.'s father, for example, played a typically high profile role by consulting for two weeks with the local cleric, doctor, and others before granting approval to her choice of husband.[8]

Nevertheless, a pure model of male dominance and female submission is too simplistic here, because it ignores the complexity of gender relations in the South and underestimates the importance of female labour to agricultural production. Though the 'natural' link between women and domestic work persisted, the family economy also regularly drew women outside the home to toil in the fields. Domestic tasks included cooking, cleaning, and childcare, as well as sewing clothes and producing linens and tablecloths for bridal trousseaus. Such tasks could be very time-consuming. Doing laundry, for example, might involve fetching water from the town well, soaking the items, and then carrying them to a stream to be rinsed and laid out on rocks to dry. Women and girls also farmed—clearing plots, sowing and planting, hoeing, and sharing in the work of the summer grain harvest. During fall ploughing, they brought manure stored at home to the fields and, aided by an ox or cow and some basic tools, some even performed the actual task of breaking the ground. All season long, women made lengthy trips to the fields carrying food and supplies stored in baskets carried on their heads.

Women also grew vegetables, fed animals and supervised their grazing, made goat and sheep cheese and preserves, collected wood for fuel, and sold surplus goods locally. In southern regions, they picked olives, nuts and fruits located on either their own lands or on landowners' estates. Young women were also trained in town as seamstresses and hairdressers; and though there were few non-agricultural job opportunities, some families sent their daughters away to work in domestic service or in the garment, textile and silk factories of the region. There, they lived in chaperoned boarding houses and sent their wages home. After the war more and more *contadine* (peasant women) worked part-time as agricultural labourers or cleaned house for local *prominenti* (middle class).[9]

Distinctions between women's and men's work roles were often blurred—a vital point scholars have often missed. When men were conscripted during the war, women ran the family farm. And wives, sisters and daughters compensated whenever men worked in the paid labour force. How much time women devoted to their various duties also depended on the size and character of the household. When there were several women in one household, for example, younger women were released from domestic chores to enable them to spend more time farming or to take up an apprenticeship in town. Maria R. often worked in the fields with her parents, grandfather and brother, because her grandmother laboured at home. Assunta C. noted how life after her marriage actually became easier, because she no longer had to shift between the home and the fields, but instead took charge of household tasks while her in-laws and husband farmed.[10]

Nor were women passive victims with no influence over their husbands and children. Scholars have stressed men's public roles, and have made much of women's tendency to act modestly in mixed company and to claim to outsiders that they acted in their father's or husband's names. This can be very misleading. It was within the private sphere that women could wield considerable power over their family; and indeed they effectively argued, nagged, manipulated, and disrupted normal routines in order to achieve certain demands. In *Women of the Shadows*, a grim look at postwar Southern Italy, Ann Cornelison captured this public/private dynamic well in her description of a married woman who was supporting her elderly parents. This Italian woman told co-villagers that she consulted with her parents on everything, but she admitted to Cornelison this was not true. "The Commandments say Honour thy father and thy mother, don't they?," she explained. "No reason to let anyone know what happens inside the family." Another woman portrayed in the same book endured months of verbal and physical abuse from her husband before convincing him to go to work in Germany in order to raise funds for their son's medical operations, and she even secured the necessary work permit (Cornelisen, 1976). Mothers were also mediators for their children. Julia's mother, for example, instructed her husband who was in Argentina in 1955 to grant formal approval to their daughter's marriage, because *she* favoured it.[11]

Though attached to their families, women also made close female friends. During joint labour projects women from different households worked together and chatted. Many chores, such as laundry and shelling beans, were done outside, in the company of other women. In-laws collectivized home and field duties. Not all women were natural allies; some were suspicious of and cruel to each other. But many were very close. Women interviewed remembered confiding in other women, and having chosen long-time friends as their childrens' godmothers. As social convenors arranging visits and meals between relatives, women also placed themselves at the centre of widespread kin networks. Furthermore, men were subjected to community sanctions if they proved to be poor providers, and in private husbands often conceded to their wives' demands. All these factors came into play in the decision to emigrate.

No longer compelled by fascism to stay, many Italians after the war escaped from worsening conditions in the South—the further pulverization of landholdings, rising unemployment, inadequate housing and sanitation, and malnutrition and disease. A large number of these, attracted to a boom economy and pulled by chain migration, came to Toronto. The poorest—agricultural labourers and urban unemployed—did not immigrate. Rather, it was the peasants, especially young families unable to improve landholdings, who predominated in emigration. Women interviewed typically noted that though they were poor, they have been better off than the landless poor; Assunta C. described malnourished women who used to beg for the water in which she had boiled beans to feed to their own babies. Such people were left behind, though some would later end up in labouring jobs elsewhere on the continent.[12]

Though men's work opportunities abroad largely determined the decision to emigrate, women also tried to influence the process. Desparate to leave war-torn Fossocesia, Molise in 1948, Maria S. persuaded an initially very hostile fiancee that, after marriage, they should join her married sister in Toronto. Against her parents' wishes, Iolanda—a trained seamstress from Miamo, Molise—travelled in 1956 to join her brothers in Toronto. By contrast, the parents of a large Southern Calabrian family in Rocella, Ionica sent away Josephine, two sisters and a brother to Toronto, to raise funds for their butcher shop and for the father's medical bills. Many married women, however, shared with their husbands the dream of the good life in America and eagerly agreed to join family abroad. Impressed by pre-war sojourners who had returned home wealthier men, many Southern Italians also believed that a few years of hard work abroad would guarantee them a comfortable life.[13]

Chain migration occurred in a ragged fashion. It involved the temporary break-up of family members, but secured the long-term survival of the family.[14] Many women were left behind while husbands sought work. Though accustomed to the absence of fathers, brothers and husbands who in the past had immigrated temporarily or had gone to war, women found these years lonely and hard, especially those who separated soon after marriage. Seventeen-year old Vincenza was left behind in Mountaurro, Calabria, while her new husband worked for three years at agricultural and construction jobs in Switzerland and Toronto, though he respected his obligations by sending money home. With only occasional help from her father and brother, Dalinda ran the farm in Vasto-Giardi, Molise for two years while raising two sons, including one born just two days before her husband's departure in 1951 for a Quebec farm. Initially opposed to joining her husband permanently in Toronto, Julia eventually gave in because she felt responsible for her daughter's unhappiness: "My little girl she call 'daddy, daddy, daddy' everyday... she say 'mommy why we don't go see daddy...she's a devil she not let me see my daddy.' Oh she make me cry everyday."[15]

Travelling alone, or with husbands or female kin, women benefited from chain migration which acted as a buffer against the alienating features of immigration. Some were unhappy about leaving home, while others looked forward to it. While some enjoyed the food and dancing aboard ship, others feared their children might fall overboard or disturb other passengers by crying in the cabin at night. On arrival at Halifax, women feared being separated from their children. On a cold November day in 1953, Dalinda was embarrassed by her lightly-clad sons, and feared she might be called a bad mother. The train ride through eastern Canada evoked concern, and the view of scattered wood frame houses resembled more the poverty back home than the expected wealth of the New World. But Toronto brought familiar faces and relief. Women and children settled with their men in the city's east and west ends and within College Street's Little Italy.

In Toronto, women lived in two types of households: an extended familial arrangement, in which one or two kin owned the house and others paid rent, or a flat rented from non-kin or non-Italians who resided on the main floor. Given their clannishness, newcomers felt uneasy about the latter arrangement. Women resented daily infringements on their privacy and were highly protective of their children. Vincenza detested her three years spent in a tiny flat: "I was think was gonna be different but I was living worse than over there (Italy). I was live in a third floor... two kids after six months. I was feel so desparate. I cry lots. I wanna go back home, but money was gone, furniture was sold, nothing was left...." Julia, however, was so fed up with the landlord's complaints about utility bills and her child that she made her husband move to better quarters within a month of her arrival.

Women much preferred the *familiari* (extended family) arrangement because temporary boarding among family, kin and *paesani* (co-villagers) reduced costs; it also permitted kinfolk to pass on household and baby items, take on wine-making and other joint labour tasks, and engage in "fellow-feelingness". Ada is a Molisana woman who lived for five years in a crowded household on Dupont St. She considered these times when *parenti* (relatives) united against the hardships of immigration as special; "We cared for each other more then than now," she added.[16]

Women in their household roles performed crucial economic tasks, stretching limited resources and finding ways to cut costs and earn extra cash. To capitalism's benefit, they daily replenished male breadwinners, and fed, clothed and raised their children. Maria S. spent her days doing her housework, which included caring for children, sewing, making meals, and helping a sick married sister who lived nearby. In extended households, women serviced male relatives who were single or not yet joined by wives, as well as their elders and in-laws. Where families shared eating facilities, women prepared meals for their own family; at supper-time, for example, each woman awaited her husband's return before heating her pot for spaghetti. Since numerous houses lacked fridges until the late 1950s and early 1960s, women had to purchase perishables on a daily basis. With no washing machines and with only hotplates for cooking in otherwise unfinished basements, household chores were arduous and time-consuming.[17]

Women cut costs by growing vegetable gardens and grape vines and by preserving fruits, vegetables and some meats. Many earned money by taking in washing, keeping boarders, and doing babysitting—which only increased their domestic burden. And they frequently acted as the family's financial manager, allocating funds for groceries and other necessities, and depositing savings or putting them towards mortgage payments. Several women described how their husband turned over his weekly pay cheque, and they stressed the importance of their responsibility to 'watch' the money. Men later usurped women's managerial role when finances became complex, but as long as families were merely surviving, women were expected to, and did, play a highly active role in making ends meet.[18]

Extended households also let women collectivize labours, such as cleaning and laundry, and exchanging confidences. Women who stayed at home—one nursing, another sewing and another unemployed—frequently shared housekeeping. For over a year Vincenza and her sister-in-law shared quarters while their husbands worked out of town. She babysat while her in-law worked as a chambermaid, and they shared cooking and cleaning duties. Three working sisters rotated housekeeping, laundry and shopping each weekend. Some, like Maria S., befriended non-Italians in their neighborhood, including Jewish and Ukranian women.[19]

Urban industrial life evoked anxiety in women who no longer enjoyed the protection of the *paese* (village). Maria S. recalled being laughed out of a department store in 1949 because she could not make herself understood, though the experience did spur her to learn English. A misunderstanding at the border resulted in Pina and her sister being jailed in Buffalo for ten days, until an Italian lawyer hired by an American aunt cleared up the confusion. Maria L., who gave birth to a premature son the day after she arrived in Toronto, was afraid to ever leave him. As she noted, the comfort provided by the village midwife had been abruptly cut off. Women also feared going out alone at night, disliked being stared at, and resented being robbed in their own homes. They worried about children at schools where outbursts were common and the boys fought, and they feared being called bad mothers by doctors, school nurses and teachers. When school authorities sent home one girl suspected of having lice, her family was totally distraught. Women also feared policemen harassing their menfolk, who gathered outside after Church and at clubs. Such anxieties were not unfounded, for racism permeated post-war Toronto. In a 1954 letter to Premier Leslie Frost, a local Orangeman provided an extreme but not atypical expression. "The place around here", he wrote, "is literally crawling with... ignorant almost black (Italians)... many with TB disease." Saving his worst criticism for men - "chaps armed with knives... continually holding up people... especially ladies near parks and dark alleys", he expressed total distaste for men and women from what he called "a Vatican-controlled and disease-infested Italy".[20]

Part of the dramatic post-war increase of women, especially married women, in the Canadian work force was the entry of many Southern Italian women into the paid labour force. Italian-born working women, most of whom were post-war immigrants, comprised between 30 and 38 percent of Italian female adults in Canada and Ontario in 1961, and nearly 40 percent in Toronto, where some 17,000 Italian women workers comprised 7 percent of the female labour force (32,000 Italian-born were working in Canada; over 20,000 of these were working in Ontario). While Canadian women flooded into white collar jobs, Italian women took the low-skill, low paying jobs available to immigrant women lacking English and other marketable skills beyond domestic training. These women did garment homework, operated steampresses, sewing, and novelty-making machines, did bottling and labelling, and performed domestic service. Manufacturing, especially semi-and-unskilled work in the garment industry, and domestic service were the two major employers of European women after the war. In Ontario, Italians working in manufacturing included 38 percent leather cutters and sewers, 22 percent tailoresses, 14 percent food processing workers, and 10 percent unskilled factory workers. Over 61 percent of those in the service categories were housekeepers, waitresses or cooks, while 38 percent were laundresses.[21]

Whether travelling alone or with male or female kinfolk, women seeking work headed for the light manufacturing and garment making sections of Toronto. Many benefitted from kin networking as earlier-arriving women arranged jobs for incoming relatives. Though scholars stress how these occupational enclaves helped ease men's fears about women working outside the home by providing traditional checks on them, women themselves preferred to emphasize the camaraderie of a workplace filled with family and friends. But some also said they would have worked wherever they found jobs, and others did indeed work for a time in ethnically-mixed factories, where they learned English and made new friends.

Women's paid labours were part of a well articulated, working class, family strategy of survival—one measured primarily by the goal of home-ownership. Female wages helped support families when men were unemployed, and they also paid for daily living expenses—groceries, clothing and household needs—so men's pay cheques could go into savings deposits and towards houses and other investments. Like other working class women, Italians worked long hours at monotonous or heavy jobs for little pay. Those in drapery and clothing shops endured poor ventilation, high humidity, speedups, and close supervision. Others put up with dust and foul-smelling fumes in leather and plastics factories. Laundry work for others still involved sorting and carrying, and the heat of steampresses in the summertime making the work almost unbearable. Women employed in factories were being subjected to industrial discipline and to impersonal employer-worker relations, while those employed as domestics worked in total isolation from their ethnic and other working sisters.

In the early years of employment in Canada, Italian women workers did not articulate a political response to their exploited position. This was due to many factors: their low status as cheap, unskilled workers; ethnic and language barriers between co-workers; the isolation of domestic workers; household duties that kept women away from meetings; uncertainty about union organizers; employer resistance; a lack of workerist traditions; and a fear of losing their jobs and hence compromising their primary obligation to the family.

Italian women worked in industries characterized by large numbers of unskilled female workers and by high labour turnover rates. Familial priorities, especially for young women wishing to have children, helped shape the timing and rhythm of Italian women's participation in the work force. Some women who entered the work force as single women and continued as married women, never went back once they started raising a family. Others with young kids delayed work until children reached school age. But many others also regularly moved in and out of the workforce. In between having children, tending a family crisis, or helping a family resettle in a new home, these women moved from factory job to factory job, or into service jobs, or on to fruit and vegetable picking. Many left one job as a protest against poor conditions and pay and soon found work elsewhere. Just two weeks after Ada quit work as a shirt packager, for example, she found a better paying job as bow-machine operator in a factory producing wrapping and party accessories. Husbands sometimes urged their wives to quit certain jobs. In 1963 Maria L. quit her hotel chambermaid job because her husband disliked her cleaning up after strangers and working on Sundays, even though his father and sister also worked at the hotel. Several years earlier, though, Maria had quit her Woolworth's cafeteria job when management abruptly shifted her into a more stressful job in inventory. This time her husband approved of her decision, even though he had found her the job. A further source of stress for these women was finding appropriate babysitters. Those who hired landladies or neighbours worried about leaving their children with women unconnected by ties of kin or village. Many quit or delayed working until incoming relatives or women newly returned to their home could provide the service. Vincenza and Julia, however, worked as domestics, bringing their children with them to their clients' homes.[22]

Of course, working for wages did not reduce the burden of housework. Though husbands stoked coal furnaces and shovelled snow, women did all the housekeeping, even when the men were at home unemployed. Indeed, other women often watched the children while working mothers shopped and cleaned. For over a year Maria L. combined full-time steampressing work with caring for a son, a husband, and the husband's father and two brothers: "Full-time work, wash, clean, cook, I did all that. I was just a girl, 19, and thin like a stick. I was with no washing machine. I use the laundry tub, then I had to cook and I had to work. Only 19, and it was not only me." And Julia voiced the frustration of many working women when she said: "Of course he should help in the house. My back I hurt it at work, it hurts to wash the floor, pick up the clothes. Can't have a fight about it every day so I do it, but no, it's not right."[23]

Notwithstanding the real obstacles to unionization, Italian women probably were not as docile, or hostile to unions, as some would suggest. At a time when female militancy was not pronounced, it is not surprising that immigrant women did not become politicized. Nor is there any reason why Italians should have shared any sense of solidarity with Canadian women, especially with white collar workers. In stark contrast to the women radicalized by the Italian Resistance—women who became communists and socialists, and who in the early 1960s spearheaded Italy's modern feminist movement—Southern peasant women lacked prior experience with the traditions of workers' protest. But as peasants long resentful of the exploitation they had suffered at the hand of landowners and middle men, they perhaps instinctively understood exploitative relations between bosses and workers, and they were truly angered by the injustices they experienced as immigrant working women.[24] Even Julia, an anti-unionist, despised what she considered to be ruling class rhetoric extolling Canada as a land of great opportunity: "Why feel grateful, we really suffered for what we got and don't live like Kings and Queens. I have four back operations, have to leave my kids alone and work." Furthermore, many Italian women eventually supported unionization, for higher wages helped their families, and they linked better working conditions and health benefits won in the 1960s and 1970s with a recognition of their labours and with self-respect. Some, such as Ada, lost their jobs over their decision to support local organizing drives. In Dalinda's words, "sure we should get more money, we work hard for it, leave our kids, come home tired, do the dirty jobs."[25]

Southern Italian women's entry into Toronto's post-war work force reflected a pattern of continuity, for women had been important contributors to the family economy in the Mezzogiorno. Traditional values stressing family obligation, and the success with which Italians preserved old world cultural practices and beliefs, eased the transition from *contadina* to worker. But the transition did not occur without considerable strain and difficulty in adjustment, especially for married women. Women at home had also to cope with new conditions of scarcity and restriction under which their working class families struggled. These strains reflected the dialectical process by which Southern Italians became transformed into working class families. Their collectivist and familialist behaviour was both an expression of peasant values and a reflection of their new economic position under industrial capitalism.[26] Scholars who have described Italian women exclusively in terms of family and home have ignored how family and work experiences provided contradictory as well as complimentary demands on women. Motivated by family commitment, housewives and working women linked their self-identification as good family members and mothers to the paid and unpaid labours they performed for the family's benefit. In this process they developed a view of respectability that was rooted in their peasant and ethnic working class backgrounds. It expressed the pride of immigrant women who saw themselves as indispensable to the family. Stripped of notions of reserved femininity and delicate demeanor, it also contrasted sharply with post-war middle class models of womanhood.

Acknowledgements and Notes

I would like to thank my friends in the Socialist-Feminist Study Group for their comments on earlier drafts of this paper.

1. Public Archives of Ontario (hereafter PAO), Ontario Department of Planning and Development, Immigration Branch Files (hereafter IBF), "The Bulletin Council for Social Service", No. 104, Church of England of Canada, 15 October 1941: 15-19.

2. PAO, IBF, E. H. Gurton, Canadian Manager, British Dominions Emigration Society, to Immigration Branch, 1 June 1951.
3. Public Archives of Canada (hereafter PAC), Immigration Branch Records, Vol. 131, Laval Fortier to Acting Commissioner of Immigration Overseas, 4 October 1949; Vol. 651, File B29300, "A Report—Immigration—A Vital Problem Facing Canadians", 22 February 1947.
4. PAC, Department of Labour Records, Vol. 290, File 1-26-52-5, Dr. A. MacNamara to Deputy Minister of Immigration, 15 January 1952; W. W. Dawson to R. Hamilton, 8 April 1952; E. R. Cornell to Regional Employment Office, Montreal, 30 April 1952.
5. See, for example, Cornlisen (1976).
6. On South Italian peasant communities see, for example: Vecolie (1944); Banfield (1958); Brogger (1971); Davis (1973); Cronin (1970); Bell (1979); Lopreato (1967).
7. On women in South Italy see: Yans-McLaughlin (1971); Cohen (1977); Furio(1980); Bravo (1982); Gabaccia (1984).
8. Interview with Assunta Capozzi.
9. See also Mountjoy (1973), Levi (1947), and Tarrow (1967).
10. Interview with Maria Rotolo and with Assunta Capozzi.
11. Interview with Julia Toscano.
12. Interview with Assunta Capozzi.
13. With Maria Sangenesi, Iolanda D'Accunto (with Tina D'Accunto), Josephine D'Agostino, Maria Lombardi, Maria Rotolo, Ada Carmosino, and DaLinda Lombardi-Iacovetta.
14. On chain migration see, for example, MacDonald and MacDonald (1964) and Choldin (1973).
15. Interview with Vincenza Cerullo, DaLinda Lombardi- Iacovetta, Julia Toscano.
16. Interview with Maria Sangenesi, Marie Carmosino; DaLinda Lombardi-Iacovetta; Maria Rotolo; Vincenza Cerullo; Julia Toscano; Ada Carmosino.
17. Interview with Maria Sangenesi, Maria Lombardi and Marie Rotolo.
18. Interview with Vencenza Cerullo and Josephine D'Agostino.
19. Interview with Maria Sangenesi, Josephine D'Agostino and Maria Lombardi.
20. PAO, IBF, James Love to Premier Leslie Frost, 1 September 1954. See also H. K. Warrander to Love, 2 September 1954.
21. On women and the post-World War Two labour force see, for example, Armstrong and Armstrong (1984); White (1980); McLeod Arnopoulous (1979); Johnson (1982).
    On Italian women's labour force participation, calculations are mine based on statistics in Statistics Canada, *Census*, 1951 and 1961; and Department of Citizenship and Immigration, *Annual Report*, 1950 to 1962.
    For a useful theoretical discussion of immigrant and migrant women see Phizacklea (1983).
22. Interviews with Angella D'Accunto (with Tina D'Accunto), Ada Carmosino, Maria Lombardi, Assunta Capozzi, Vincenza Cerullo and Julia Toscana.
23. Interview with Maria Lombardi and Julia Toscana.
24. For example: Hellman (1985); Slaughter (1984); Alaia (1984).
25. Interview with Julia Toscano, Ada Carmosino and DaLinda Lombardi-Iacovetta.
26. On an earlier period see, for example, Tilly and Scott (1978), and Bodnar (1976).

Organizing the Unorganized Farmworkers in Ontario

Erma Stultz

To understand the problems in organizing farm labourers in Ontario, it is necessary to first look at the laws which affect these workers. Farmworkers are excluded from labour legislation protecting the rights of most workers in Ontario. They are excluded from:

1. the Labour Relations Act, which recognized the right of all workers to a measure of job security and the right to collective bargaining.
2. the Employment Standards Act: farmworkers are excluded from the parts of this Act dealing with minimum wage, overtime pay, vacations and vacation pay, public holiday pay and hours of work.
3. the Occupational Health and Safety Act which recognizes the right of all workers to work in safe conditions, to form safety committees at places of work, and to refuse unsafe work. This exclusion means that farm workers can claim benefits if they are injured on the job (through Workers' Compensation), but they cannot refuse work which they reasonably consider to be dangerous without breaching their contract of employment and thereby exposing themselves to the possibility of being dismissed.

Because of these exclusions, farmworkers at present can be and are required to work 12 hours a day, seven days a week, at less than the minimum wage, with no overtime pay, no vacation pay or vacations, and no public holiday pay.

The reasons given for these exclusions are that farming is a family business and family members cannot be covered under the same legislation as other workers, and that wages for farm labour have to be low due to particularly difficult economic times for farmers.

In fact, the trend has been toward a decrease in the number of small farms, with a corresponding increase in the number of large operations. Data from the Ontario Ministry of Agriculture shows that 90 percent of the paid year-round agricultural workers in the province were employed on farms having a total capital value in excess of $150,000.

Although the number of paid labourers in agriculture has increased over the years, total wages as a percentage of total operating expenses have dropped from 16.5 percent in 1951 to 10.5 percent in 1983.

We estimate there are about 150,000 farmworkers in Ontario; of these about 90,000 are seasonal workers. Each year 5,000 workers are brought into Ontario under the government "offshore program", from the Caribbean and Mexico.

In the research we have carried out, we have found many small farmers to be willing to pay higher wages, give benefits and treat their workers fairly in order to have a reliable and skilled workforce. This appears to be much less likely with large farming operations whose prime motive is profit.

Attempts have been made in the past by various groups, including unions, to organize farmworkers. However, without the right to represent farmworkers, those who signed up members and applied to the Labour Relations Board were turned down.

There are many problems inherent in organizing farmworkers:

1. Farmwork is not seen as a skilled occupation. Workers who enjoy their employment feel they are not respected as legitimate contributors to Ontario's workforce.
2. Unwilling to improve conditions for Canadian workers, the federal and provincial governments have consistently depended on new immigrants or have brought in foreigners specifically for farmwork. In the 1950s and 1960s workers who were brought in didn't speak English and were unlikely to be able to gain employment in another area. This was seen as a way to provide a dependent and reliable workforce. As these immigrants were eligible for Canadian citizenship and gradually moved away from farmwork, this program was stopped and the present offshore program introduced. Under this system workers often stay six to eight months, bring no family, have no legal status in Canada, pay unemployment insurance and Canadian Pension deductions but can never collect, can be sent back to their home country if they displease their contracted employer, and are totally dependent on their employer.
3. Farmworkers mostly live in rural areas and have little, if any, contact with other farm labourers outside of their place of employment.
4. Long-term workers are small in numbers in most workplaces, although mushroom workers are a notable exception to this; here there are as many as 400 farmworkers in one workplace.
5. The relationship of employment tends to remain feudal in

nature, with a long tradition of dependency in a conservative environment.

6. Farmworkers often work 70 - 90 hours per week, which means they have little time or energy for other activities including using community social services (even if they do have transportation).

7. Farmworkers often live on the employer's property, or are bussed in from miles away, so that it is very difficult to gain access to them.

8. Farmworkers in Ontario are from many ethnic and language backgrounds. In B.C., where the Canadian Farmworkers Union was founded in 1980, the majority of workers who were organizing were from the same region of India, working together in the Fraser Valley, and living in the same area.

Women face a double day: as farmworkers, and as wives and mothers. As one said: "When there's a lot to pick, we have to stay until 8:00 or 9:00 at night, until all the work is done. It's hard when it's 9:00 p.m. and you have to go home, cook supper and start all the work in the house." Women migrating seasonally to Ontario with their children face the lack of daycare. Children who are old enough work in the fields, but the younger ones, the infants, are left unattended in the fields while the parents work. Women are often paid piece rate and experience wage discrimination.

As agriculture is considered the third most dangerous industry in Canada, women face unusual danger both to themselves and to their children. One example reported: "There was a pregnant woman in Cambridge who was laid off for going to the washroom too often. She was laid off just before her entitlement to maternity leave. I think they didn't want to give her the benefits." The effects of chemicals, pesticides and tobacco poisoning on the unborn fetus are potentially very dangerous. Pregnant women also face other work-related hazards. They must stoop, climb, and haul heavy loads.

When the Canadian Farmworkers Union closed its office in Ontario in May, 1983, a new organization began, now incorporated at Tolpuddle Farm Labour Information Centre. Our aims are to pursue research, information gathering and dissemination, and educational work about Ontario's farmworkers, sharing information among farmworkers themselves, with groups working with farmworkers and with other concerned groups or individuals.

Acknowledgements and Notes
Much of the above information was taken from leaflets developed by the Participatory Research Group, entitled:
1. Farmworkers: the invisible minority in Ontario: an introduction for the public
2. Farmworkers Speak Out: our rights/our health and safety
3. Migrant workers and their families
4. Family life, women, and child labour

Also available is the Canadian Farmworkers Union's film, A *Time to Rise,* and a recently-completed video produced by the Tolpuddle Farm Labour Information Centre, *To Pick is Not to Choose* (these can be rented for $50 per showing). For more information contact:

Erma Stultz
Tolpuddle Farm Labour Information Centre
505 Parkside Drive
Toronto, Ontario M6R 2Z9
Telephone: (416) 767-3277

Organizing Domestic Workers

Carmencita R. Hernandez

Each year, approximately 10,000 women come to Canada on temporary work permits to work as live-in domestic workers in private homes.

Ninety-nine point nine percent of domestics are women and the majority of them come from Third World countries; most of them are visible minority women.

The majority of domestic workers are exploited and are not fully protected by law.

For some of these women, it is an adventure to travel to Canada and perhaps to learn English; to see places to see the world. For the majority, however, it is an opportunity to escape the worsening economic conditions back home. For women from Third World countries especially, it is a means to earn a regular wage that is essential for the families' survival.

Like many others, Filipino domestic workers are becoming aware of the need to fight for their basic rights. But Filipino domestic workers not only have to deal with the lack of justice in Canadian law in relation to their situation, but they also have to deal with representatives of the Philippine government, under Ferdinand E. Marcos,[1] who are trying to prevent them from speaking out about the unfair working conditions in their home country.

The Filipino domestic worker represents the latest wave of Filipino workers in Canada. They are noticeably present at the Eaton's Centre; they go to church services in groups; they are in certain pockets of the community at specific times. There was a case of a domestic worker who died in Montreal. Her permit to stay expired. Out of fear of being sent back to the Philippines, she was always in hiding; she was always on the run. There were reports of women being harassed, there were a number of complaints. The plight of these women workers came into focus in the 1980s. They are victims of a serious political-economic crisis in Philippine society: a crisis that is due mainly to large-scale domination and control of industry by foreign big business in collaboration with their local counterparts, centralization of political power in the hands of the ruling elite, and landlord domination of the peasant majority of the Philippine population.

These factors result in large-scale violation of democratic rights, low wages and inhuman working conditions, landlessness for the vast number of the peasantry, unemployment and underemployment, persistent price increases, acute shortages of decent shelter and poverty-caused diseases.

The political-economic crisis has pushed the marginalized sectors of the Philippine population to seek employment in foreign countries to better their conditions.

The Philippine government officially promotes the export of skilled Filipino labourers and professionals to avert the breakdown of the existing social order. The instabilities are caused by huge loans, trade and payment deficits, inflation, unemployment and poverty.

The Philippine government, through the educational system and other cultural institutions, promotes colonially- oriented culture to maintain the existing social order in general and to promote manpower export in particular.

The current orientation and structure of the Philippine educational system has its roots in the 1969 landmark report of the Presidential Commission to Survey Philippine Education (PCSPE). Funded by a U.S. grant of $200,000[2] by the Ford Foundation, the PCSPE conducted a survey to define how Philippine education could best serve the goals of "national development". Their report constituted "exploratory initiatives" on the part of the Department of Education to interest the World Bank in financing Philippine educational improvement.

In the period 1973-1982, the World Bank invested a total of $212.7 million to fund six major education projects. In 1973, $12.7 million was extended to finance the creation of 10 regional manpower training centres, strategically located near the country's export processing zones and industrial estates. The goal was to train the cheap manpower exploited in factory and agricultural enterprises owned by foreign monopoly capitalists in the Philippines.

In 1974, the World Bank put up $25 million for the production of thousands of textbooks for the country's public elementary and high schools. These materials have blatantly sought to ingrain in the minds of the youth the 'overwhelming benefits' of foreign control of the economy.

The World Bank's export-oriented "industrialization" strategy for national development received a big boost when the Bank poured in $25 million to increase production of surplus crops for export. In 1977, agricultural programs in selected state colleges and universities received generous endowments from this loan.

The single biggest and most ambitious project of the World Bank is the Program for Decentralized Education, a 10-year "development" program for elementary education. Robert McNamara, then World Bank president, explained the agency's interest in funding elementary education in the Philippines: "Effective elementary education...helps make the labour force more easily trainable and mobile. It facilitates skill development during subsequent formal and on-the-job training as well as through agricultural and industrial extension programs."

This state of affairs subjects the Filippino migrant workers to further exploitation and oppression at the hands of the Philippine government, foreign employers, unscrupulous construction firms and private placement agencies engaged in overseas contracts.

The manpower export policy of the Philippine government worsens the existing crisis in Philippine society.

The Filipino domestic workers here in Canada, scarred by the economic policies over which they have no control, fearful of losing their chance to work abroad, and part of an immigrant and intimidated community, were able to organize themselves into an ad-hoc committee to obtain landed status for foreign domestic workers. With the International Association of Filipino Patriots taking the initiative in the Filipino community, and by working with groups like INTERCEDE, Labour Rights for Domestic Servants (LRDS), and the Committee for the Advancement of the Rights of Domestic Workers (CARDWO) in Vancouver, as well as lawyers and other groups and individuals, they were able to have educational forums on why they are in a foreign country like Canada, what their rights are, and what they can do collectively.

The Filipino domestic workers also have to contend with the Philippine Consulate and its particular kind of harassment and intimidation. There was the subtle impression given by consulate people that domestic workers who were participating in various activities with community activists might find it difficult to renew their visas. In addition, there were other groups and individuals which the domestic workers had to contend with. Red-baiting tactics and labels of subversives were applied to individuals who sought petitions and those who joined protest actions. There was the constant fear that militant actions would irritate immigration officers who would retaliate by turning down their application for landed status.

But the work of continuously pressuring government officials to allow domestic workers to apply for landed status had to go on. There were demonstrations in front of the immigration office on University Avenue; the protest action in front of the Sai Woo restaurant (during a dinner where the previous immigration minister Lloyd Axworthy was present); the role of petitions containing thousands of signatures; the letters; the opinions of news writers. These were all part of the motion that forced the government to introduce a policy which allows domestic workers on temporary employment authorizations to apply for landed immigrant status within Canada.

This policy also allows domestic workers who have been in Canada for at least two years to apply if they can demonstrate that they are "self-sufficient" or have the "potential to achieve self-sufficiency". Immigration officers carry out an initial "assessment" to determine eligibility for permanent residence. Here lies another problem. The domestic workers are able to enter Canada on temporary work permits and on the basis of a valid passport from their country of origin, but the very nature of their legal status in Canada exposes them to blatant exploitation in this country.

Domestics don't have the same protection under the laws as other workers. The domestic minimum wage increased to only $3.50 in October 1984 (from $3.25) while the standard minimum goes to $4.00. Unlike offices and factories where the employers are required to keep a record of the hours worked by the employees, this is not the case with the employers of domestic workers. There are cases where a domestic worker's day starts at 6:00 in the morning and ends at 10:00 in the evening. When her employers decide to go out in the evening, her working hours are inevitably extended. More often than not, no overtime pay is given to her. It only follows that domestics find it difficult to upgrade themselves in order to be "self-sufficient". Also, domestics are not covered under the Workers' Compensation Act—thus they are not insured for injuries suffered at work.[3]

At the initial and mid-stages of the struggle, there were very few organizations that gave their support. Except for the YWCA, women's groups were noticeably absent. The labour unions were not even heard from.

There are still many problems being faced by domestic workers. . . INTERCEDE has been the organization that is doing the lobbying work to make possible changes in legislation. In addition, they have a service unit that assists domestic workers with their immigration problems. Our women's movements should interact with groups working with migrant workers, as should our unions.

Whatever the objective of our work may be, any effort to create awareness and to organize people, any gains that are made set a very powerful and meaningful example that gives encouragement to others.

Let us not take the position that the domestic workers should come to us and we will assist. Rather, we should as conscious forces take the initiative to know them and work with them and for them.

Notes

1. This article was written prior to the overthrow of the Marcos regime in 1986.
2. This figure and all subsequent ones are quoted in U.S. dollars.
3. There have been some revisions to this legislation since the time this article was written.

The Garment Workers Action Centre

Winnie Ng

The need for organizing immigrant garment workers stems from my experience in working with immigrant women, in particular, Asian women who are the newest arrivals in the industry's labour force. This need applies to both unionized and non-unionized.

South Asian women experience male domination at home and exploitation at work

In reviewing the scenario of unionized women workers it was found that women comprise over 85 percent of the workforce and over 90 percent of them are immigrants, yet union leadership has failed to reflect this ethnic and gender composition. Certainly, immigrant women workers have more than their share of constraints militating against their coming out to union meetings or running for executive positions in the union. But is it not the responsibility of unions to facilitate their participation by reducing some of the constraints, rather than using those constraints as their excuse to do nothing?

One example to illustrate this point is the lack of interpreters at union meetings. What is the point of sitting through a meeting if one doesn't understand what's going on? Eventually, the original enthusiasm felt by the women when they first sign their union cards fizzles out. The union becomes invisible and the past becomes history. The union continues to struggle in the name of the workers but not with the workers.

Another example is the issue of piece-work versus time rates. It is unfair for union management to say that the workers love the piece-work system and thereby absolve itself of the need to negotiate for time rates, when, in fact, the women have never been offered any alternative—or when the time rate is kept so low that one has to "become one's own boss" to make a decent living. The voice of immigrant women workers needs to be heard. The workers need to be heard. They have to speak for themselves.

With non-unionized women workers, isolation and working conditions are even worse. Yet with the high unemployment rate in the manufacturing industries, a lot of husbands have been laid off. Thus many women are on the verge of breakdowns because they have to take on a triple-day role. A woman will work as a sewing machine operator from 8:30 a.m. to 4:30 p.m., then rush to a hotel to be a chambermaid or to an office building to do cleaning. She returns home at ten or eleven at night to do house work. For those women whose families rely on them to put food on the table, it will take a lot of consciousness-raising and education to get them to organize and break the isolation. At the same time, they also have to realize that, with the unavoidable high tech changes within the next ten years, a lot of their work could become obsolete. What will happen then?

The labour movement in the garment industry must become organized to ensure that technological innovations and international relocation of industries are not carried out at the expense of workers. The workers have got to realize that they are the unon. Building a strong immigrant workers' movement doesn't imply that it will be separate and segregated from the mainstream workers' movement. On the contrary, they will enhance each other's strength. The Garment Workers' Action Centre which I have proposed is meant to serve as a workers' education and resource centre - a stepping stone to organize the unorganize—to develop and empower immigrant women workers towards becoming involved in the larger workers' movement.

When we talk about the future of the garment industry, we are considering not only strategies for its survival, but also the improvement of working conditions and benefits. In order for the garment industry to be publicly recognized as a viable and permanent manufacturing enterprise, it must divest itself of the old image of a fly-by-night or sweatshop operation. This change in image will be realized when there is a strong organized sector in the industry—when justice is done to improve the working conditions of these producers.

When we talk about an industry that provides jobs and livelihood for 15,000 workers and their families, it is not a token industry, and it should not be wiped out in exchange for high tech imports. Furthermore, with the gradual development of technological changes, government, labour and manufacturers have a responsibility to ensure that this process is not implemented at the expense of workers. There is a concommitant need for a better trained and more stable workforce.

The need for a strong organized workers' movement and a better trained workforce are the main essence and rationale for proposing a Garment Workers' Action Centre. This proposal envisions a building, right in the heart of Toronto's downtown garment industry, that will house all the services necessary to the workers, both employed and unemployed, in order to build a common front. The Centre will focus primarily on workers' education, the key to stronger worker participation.

Ninety percent of the garment workers are immigrant women: the union leadership does not reflect this composition

Since the overwhelming majority of garment workers are immigrants from different cultural backgrounds, English as a Second Language (ESL) is essential for breaking down the communication barriers between workers. From our experience in teaching ESL in the workplace, we feel that locating classes in the workplace has its limitations. It only reaches a small sector of the workforce and attendance fluctuates because of seasonal layoffs, overtime and the constant watchful eye of management. Thus an ESL for the Workplace Program at the Action Centre would ideally reach out to more workers, both organized and unorganized.

To better prepare workers to cope with the new tech changes, skills retraining and upgrading, as well as academic upgrading, will be offered to those who wish to attain the equivalent of a high school education. Courses in the academic program would be geared to the needs of working people as well as the unemployed and would deal with such subjects as Canadian labour history, geography, nutrition, literature drawn from novels about working class lives, mathematics and science courses. The labour education aspect of the program would be based on practical concerns of working people with an emphasis on how to organize the unorganized, the problems of racism and sexism, union counselling on legal rights of workers, and courses on the nature and operation of a union.

The Centre will also operate as some form of commercial co-operative, offering rental space for community agencies. Several agencies, each retaining its own autonomy under one roof, would provide: employment counselling, preventive health care, legal clinics, interpretive and information services, general counselling and other public services. Such an integrated services approach will greatly enhance the accessibility and delivery of services to workers.

The Centre will house a library and recreational facilities for workers. The publication of a newsletter in different languages would be a major contribution to workers' development. Further, workers would be involved in setting up clothing and food co-operatives as viable fund-raising ventures for the Centre.

Last, but not least, emergency day care services and regular day programs will be set up. They will offer the convenience and opportunities that promote women workers' participation in all programs of the Centre.

In essence, the main thrust of the Garment Workers' Action Centre is education—the key to empowering immigrant women workers. It is a vision that will truly create a workers' culture and sense of belonging to the labour movement. It is my dream that the Centre will serve as a model for other industries with high concentrations of immigrant workers, for example, hotel, food and assembly-line industries, to adapt and follow in the years to come. That'll be the day...

Acknowledgements
We are grateful to *The Asianadian* for allowing us to reprint this article which appeared in Volume 6, number 2.

SECTION V

Strategy and Tactics for Social Change

Introduction

Among the recurrent themes of this volume is the vulnerability of current forms of labour and left organizations and the necessity of strategies and tactics to repond to the economic assaults of a reorganizing capital and a resurgent right in populist guise. The twin pillars of the welfare state and collective bargaining are under steady assault, and labour and the left have proven ill-prepared to defend previous gains in democratic rights, let alone expand them. Each paper in this section deals with the historic question: "What is to be done?" As the papers demonstrate, there is no single answer. The adequacy of responses will be determined by specific contexts and historical circumstance. Thus, the authors in this section should be read as providing suggestive analyses which may stimulate strategic debate rather than definitive strategies which might be immediately put into practice.

John Calvert states that it is clear that the post-war concessions granted to labour by capital gradually separated union leadership from the rank and file due to the increasingly technical nature of the bargaining system. Unions, once seen as social movements and concerned with the broad structure of society became instead technical organizations, narrowly confined to the provision of services to the membership. As a result, previously existing links to the broader community were seriously weakened. Calvert argues in light of this for a restructuring of union work, in order to reverse the trend where unions become institutions marginal to workers' daily lives.

The next paper by an active trade unionist, directly addresses some of the concerns raised by Calvert. Sean Usher in particular, after describing the impass of government cutbacks on the Ontario Public Service Employees Union's membership and on the general community, discusses the ways in which his union is attempting to build a "Coalition of Dissent" at the level of local communities. It is clear from his paper that the fight against the new right will necessitate numerous tactics, including broad coalition organizations, research/education activities, and legal challenges to cutbacks. In short, Usher argues for a revival of social unionism if the labour movement is to survive the crisis. While his paper refers to the previous Conservative regime in Ontario, little has changed in the overall situation since its defeat.

The next three papers discuss a question which has been extensively debated: What is the role of the professionals in social change? Stan Marshall, in contrasting the Canadian Union of Postal Workers' (CUPW) strategy of confrontation (or class struggle) with the Professional Institute of the Public Service's strategy of consultation (or class collaboration), raises the important question of why unions in apparently similar circumstances would adopt quite different tactics and ideology. He finds the fundamental difference to be rooted in variations in the labour process. Marshall raises the possibility that as control is tightened over the professionals, their tactics may well be transformed in the same direction as those of CUPW.

Jim Ward identifies a further contradiction with respect to social service professionals—the potential conflict between approaches based on community development (or empowering clients) and professionalism (or increasing the dependency of clients). He suggests that this ideological contradiction is now at the heart of a struggle within the social work profession. If professionalism becomes dominant, he argues, then local agencies will be agents of social control. If community development wins out, however, then the social work "professionals" will have a valuable role to play in social change.

Barry Weisleder's paper provides a practical discussion of the difficulties and prospects of organizing part-time teaching staff, a group of workers not previously known for organization or militancy. Given the accelerated growth of part-time work throughout the labour force, his paper is particularly timely and has implications reaching far beyond the current state of a single profession. Clearly, the response of the labour movement to part-timing is going to be crucial to its continued health.

Deirdre Gallagher presents a practical analysis of the development of an alliance between the trade-union and women's movements around the issue of affirmative action. That this change of policy direction took place in the midst of economic crisis is of particular significance, since crisis is as likely to evoke retrenchment as advance. Gallagher argues that the women's movement is forcing a refocusing of the trade-union movement towards social action, linking members' private and public lives in ways that have not been seen for decades. Her discussion suggests that some of the changes proposed by the previous authors are already happening, and that the labour movement will be the stronger for it.

Uncharted Waters: The Labour Movement's Dilemma in Developing a New Role Beyond the Bargaining System

John Calvert

The present crisis of capitalism has given rise to a concerted effort by employers and governments to roll back the gains achieved by labour since the Second World War. Workers are not only suffering reductions in their real standard of living: their bargaining rights are being systematically curtailed and, in some cases, literally extinguished. What is disturbing about this onslaught is the difficulty many unions are facing in attempting to mobilize effective opposition from their rank-and-file members.

To understand why unions have not been more successful in their fight, it is necessary to examine their structure and functions in a critical way. Historically, unions have been reactive organizations. They were formed as a reaction to the abuses by capitalist employers. Their objectives and activities were powerfully shaped by the broader social and political environment within which they functioned. With certain notable exceptions, the Industrial Workers of the World (IWW) for example, they did not seek to supplant the employer but rather to establish appropriate limitations on the exercise of managerial authority. They wanted to humanize, rather than overthrow, capitalism.

In the period following World War Two, governments and employers were forced to concede to certain union demands, such as legal recognition and the dues check-off. However, in granting these concessions to the labour movement, governments also attempted to channel and institutionalize the organizations which represented workers. They began to ensnare unions in a web of increasingly complex labour law. Contracts became longer and more complicated.

The grievance and arbitration procedure, which governments had initially promised would be quick and inexpensive, turned into a legal maze which required the expertise of full-time staff or legal counsel. Unions were forced to adjust their internal structures and style of operating to accommodate the ever more technical nature of the bargaining system. In the process, workers were gradually separated from the activities through which unions represented their interests. The bargaining system deterred rank-and-file participation while simultaneously encouraging the professionalization of union staff.

While the impact of governments and employers in shaping the collective bargaining system in the private sector has been significant, it has been even more profound in the public sector. Workers at the level of local government tended to organize in parallel with those in the private sector, frequently under similar provincial legislation. However, those at the provincial and federal levels achieved bargaining rights during the 1965 to 1975 period normally as a direct consequence of new labour legislation. Frequently this legislation determined who could be unionized, how bargaining units would be structured, what issues unions could and could not bargain over, and even the structure of the unions themselves.

Perhaps most importantly, the very conception of union work was powerfully shaped by these developments. Unions became institutions absorbed with negotiations, arbitrations and labour board hearings. The idea of a labour movement involving social, cultural and community dimensions was supplanted to a large extent by the concept of unions as organizations which provided bargaining and arbitration services.

The shift towards a legalistic, bargaining-oriented conception of union work had other consequences. Although it was not deliberate or intentional, it resulted in a decline in unions' social and community activities where they had previously existed. Working with local community groups, supporting other progressive organizations and encouraging union members to become local activists became less of a priority. Real union work was increasingly seen as bargaining and servicing contracts. Building alliances in local communities, engaging in political action (beyond attempting to elect New Democratic Party MLAs and MPs) and in a broader context, trying to maintain and develop working class culture were concerns which received less and less attention and resources.

Relations with union members were also deeply affected by the tendency of the industrial relations system to focus the energies of unions exclusively on bargaining. Instead of being a movement which attempted to satisfy a broad range of workers' needs and interests, unions came to be viewed merely as one among literally hundreds of organizations competing for their numbers' attention in a pluralist and consumerist society. Unions sold a service—negotiating and enforcing contracts—as did many other organizations and business firms. Moreover, the bargaining system could function quite well without widespread rank-and-file participation.

Of course not all unions followed this pattern. Many trade unionists worked energetically to maintain a role for class politics and working-class culture within the labour movement. But the process of the institutionalization of the organizations representing workers made major inroads nonetheless.

These problems were further exacerbated by the way in which unions came to conceptualize the practice of internal democracy. Union meetings came to be structured in a manner which deterred participation by members. Roberts' Rules of Order, formal parliamentary procedures: a classroom-style division between local officers and members; and an excessive concern with 'business matters' such as reading endless piles of correspondence, minutes and the like all combined to make union meetings uninvolving for the members. Often, although not invariably, the roles of elected union officers also became excessively formal and bureaucratic. The formal procedures of union democracy—which were designed to guarantee democratic control—gave rise to practices which tended to deter democratic participation because they did not take account of the need for a process which fostered participation.

The emphasis that the bargaining system placed on contract negotiations also created a situation in which it was difficult for other problems union members faced, both on and off the job, to be raised. And, when such problems were raised, it was often in such a manner that the feelings and emotions of members could not be expressed. Problems at work were channelled into impersonal grievance procedures. Alternately, union officers were forced to explain that the union could do nothing about them because the contract did not provide a remedy. As a consequence, many union members decided that they would prefer to watch Dallas on T.V., cultivate their gardens, or go fishing rather than attend union meetings.

Of course some of the concerns raised in the preceding pages also reflect the fact that unions did not have sufficient resources to engage in many other activities in a serious way. In some cases membership apathy was a response to the weakness of the unions. Because unions did not have the power to make the kinds of changes their members may have desired, their value was downgraded in the eyes of those members. At the same time, the tendency on the part of many unions to adopt some of the practices of 'business unionism' was also a contributing factor to this weakness.

The impact of employers and governments in shaping the development of unions can be seen in other areas. The excessive concern with bargaining and servicing contracts left unions with little time or energy to contribute to the development of an alternate culture for their members. Unions did not see the importance of providing a vision of a better and more humanely satisfying way to live, a vision which could be contrasted to the mass consumerism being promoted everywhere by capitalist enterprises. The narrow focus on bargaining led to unions being seen as one-dimensional institutions and this increased the tendency for unions to become marginalized in the lives of their members. Low attendance at membership meetings and a general sense of apathy—except during bargaining crises—reflected the fact that unions appeared concerned only with a single aspect of the economic lives of workers.

Consequently, when governments began their attacks on union rights and began enacting anti-labour legislation in the late 1970s, the response from most union members was one of lack of concern. Campaigns to inform members of the adverse effects of the loss of their bargaining rights had little success precisely because workers had been largely unaffected by union activity when they had had these rights. Workers were not prepared to make major sacrifices for the interests of institutions from which they felt largely alienated.

Honest recognition of the marginal status of unions in the lives of most unionized workers is essential if the labour movement is to begin to overcome its current malaise. The question which needs to be asked is this: if workers are not prepared to fight for the kind of unions they now belong to, what kind of unions would they be prepared to fight for? What should unions be doing to overcome their marginalization? While the answer to this question is not easy, a few suggestions seem in order.

First, with regard to the internal practice of union democracy, there needs to be a fundamentally different approach which facilitates open discussion about the problems of working people and dispenses with many of the formal procedures which often restrict the participation of members. Perhaps unions need—symbolically at least—to burn their Roberts' Rules of Order. Many locals could fruitfully experiment with new ways of conducting their internal meetings in order to foster greater participation and give members more opportunities to discuss what is important to them, not only as employees but also as working people who confront a wide range of economic, social and personal problems.

The approach taken by the women's movement—that we must begin with the personal before moving to the political—provides important lessons. Unions must create a forum in which people can talk about what is important in their lives, rather than simply discuss abstract goals and objectives, most of which are unattainable in any event. Unions can also learn a great deal about organizing meetings and other activities from the women's movement. In locals with smaller numbers of members, there is no reason why people should not sit in a circle and face each other. Nor is there any reason why the chairperson should not be rotated so that everyone has a chance to learn about and participate in running meetings.

Second, the conception of what unions are supposed to be doing must be broadened to include a wide range of activities which are currently at the periphery of union activities. This can occur in two ways. At the bargaining table unions can begin to make a wide range of new demands which go beyond the traditional concerns of business unionism. In the public sector, for example, they can demand: improvements in the quality and extent of services; a more open and democratic approach for the administration of services; and, greater access by the public to information about how services are being carried out. In this way the unions can use the bargaining table as a way to build alliances in the community.

Yet, what needs to be done must be still more ambitious. Unions, both individually and collectively, must begin to think about how to mould the bargaining system and the broader activities of unions in a way which places labour's long-term objectives on the economic and social agenda.

Unions must also expand the focus of their activities to involve community organizing in the localities where unionized workers live. At a time when many unions in the public sector no longer have the right to bargain, unions need to devote much more resources and staff time to this process.

Unfortunately, because such activities are not associated with bargaining, many unions—especially those in the public sector—are devoting their time to what can only be described as make-work projects within the bargaining system. In the absence of any strategy, these unions have allowed themselves to become totally absorbed into grievances, arbitrations and appeals, vainly waiting for a restoration of bargaining rights (which, even if it comes, will be in a form almost unrecognizable from that of the 1960s and 1970s).

What, then, is meant by the suggestion that unions should become more involved in community organizing? In part, it means building links with the wide range of groups which are now attempting to represent the interests of working people on other issues. Local women's organizations, tenants' groups, ethnic clubs, peace groups, native rights' organizations, and many more need to become part of labour's network. Links should also be built with progressive factions within organizations like the churches.

However, there is no point in simply talking about 'networking': concrete activities which will involve people working together must be devised. And, it must be a two-way street, with labour giving help, as well as expecting support on union issues.

In addition, there is a real need to work at the project of developing an alternate working-class culture. To the extent that unions provide any culture for their members, it is focussed around the traditional activities of strike support benefits, union local dinners and dances, and annual picnics and similar events. These are important activities. But they are not enough.

Much greater effort needs to be made to link workers with progressive contemporary artists, playrights and singers. Thus while the women's movement, in obvious contrast, has a growing and supportive network of cultural activities, unions have nothing comparable to offer their members. If the conception of union activity is broadened to include building a labour movement, with all the multi-faceted activities involved in such an approach, then the need to enrich working-class culture and provide an alternative to Dallas becomes clear.

There are many other aspects to developing a working-class culture which need to be explored. Unions should be working with other groups to assist in the provision of a wide range of services to their members, such as daycare, housing, community centres and the like. Some of the preceding suggestions are already being implemented by union locals. It is thus a matter of putting greater emphasis on these issues.

Governments and private employers have shown themselves increasingly willing to extinguish the rights of workers and unions. Under such conditions, to remain marginal institutions whose appeal is restricted to a narrow conception of bargaining is to risk being gradually pushed out of existence. Unions will have to change into different kinds of organizations if they are going to survive at all.

Unions and Social Issues

Sean Usher

What we have for ourselves we want for all. That is the tradition of the trade union movement.

Unions have a long and proud history of involvement in social issues. In fact, it is no exaggeration to say that many times workers have initiated reform movements for social change.

We believe the crucial developments in Canada since 1900 to be the growth of immigration, industrialism and urbanization, and as a corollary to these, the advent of social democracy, national minimum standards of welfare, and the organization of workers in mechanized industry.

So say labour historians Irving Abella and David Millar. This set of circumstances helps us to understand why unions have been at the centre of reform movements. Both unions and progressive causes grew from the same soil of social injustice and political inequality.

That is why unions supported the extension of voting rights. For the same reason organized labour was active in winning unemployment insurance.

Unions also mobilized for medicare. And labour was an early supporter of parental leave and daycare rights.

In order to secure the advantages of high quality health and social services, unions have fostered public sector growth. By and large, publicly-owned corporations and fees for services aside, the public sector supplies goods and services intended either for the benefit of society as a whole or for individuals and families who cannot afford to pay for them.

Government revenues to finance these services are not deductions from the national wealth. In fact, collective financing of these services is a payment by society for the economic infrastructure necessary to achieve prosperity.

Today, there are powerful conservative forces challenging this traditional view of social services. There is a growing belief by senior governments and big business that people should be left to their own devices and not rely on public services for social well-being.

In Ontario, we are all too familiar with this 'new right' program to divest government of any responsibility for community well-being. Using the rhetoric of 'de-institutionalization' and restraint, the Ontario government has tried to entrench a regime of public sector cut-backs since late 1975.

Instead of providing a social service safety net, so that citizens are protected from swings in the economic cycle, we see a provincial administration making municipal governments pick up the tab for provincial programs.

"Approximately 75 percent of our expenditures are transfer payments," the 1984 Throne Speech warns. "The autonomy enjoyed by these agencies carries with it the responsibility for effective financial and administrative stewardship."

So the government decides to cut support for social programs, leaving service clubs, churches and others under a greater strain. No longer able to look at simply supplementing government efforts to provide a decent life for all citizens, they are instead forced into the front line of social service delivery.

At the same time the policy of divestment compromises these same charities and social agencies. They scramble to gather scarce public funds by reducing their expectations, so as not to be bypassed in favour of some other group being played against them by senior governments or big business.

With the loss of the traditional 'free' voices in social agencies due to cynical government manipulation of their budgets, it becomes appropriate to ask who else will voice the concerns of the poor and disadvantaged together with the union movement? The experience of the Ontario Public Service Employees Union (OPSEU) suggests that we will find our allies in municipal government and local constituencies.

The Davis government has presided over the divestment of provincial public services. Many program responsibilities are being shifted back to municipalities. These include special education, psychiatric care services, and residences and programs for the developmentally handicapped, as well as family benefit allowances and welfare responsibilities.

All in all, the government's restraint policy has meant the loss of key community services and a reduction in the Ontario Public Service Employees Union membership equal to 1300 employees during 1983 alone.

Inadequate financing has crippled Children's Aid Societies in Ontario. The Metropolitan Toronto Society is seeing its budget cut by $600,000 each year over the next three years. In the Ottawa area, the society is facing an $800,000 deficit. Children's Aid Society staff are reporting increased case loads and as a result, the closing of group homes used by clients.

Privately operated for-profit correctional care is also producing disaster. In one case, the operators of a for-profit farm home for young people in trouble with the law were left saddled with debts of $400,000 when cutbacks in aid to the Sarnia-Lambton Children's Aid Society were implemented by the Ontario government.

When the Northeastern Regional Mental Health Centre in Timmins was closed by the government in December, 1975, many professionals who had provided mental health services left the area. There is now a shortage of psychiatrists, relative to the rest of the province. One qualified psychiatrist, resident in Timmins, serves a population of over 100,000.

The closing of four directly administered government laboratories in the spring of 1976 has also been an experiment in failure. The private for-profit laboratories which have moved in to fill the gap have proven to be more expensive to operate.

The decision to close Lakeshore Psychiatric Hospital resulted in catastrophe for the Toronto area, and went against the government's own $116,500 independent study recommendations.

In an attempt to reduce beds, many patients at Lakeshore were pushed out of the hospital and now live in the community. There are some 2,000 former in-patients who live in Homes for Special Care and boarding houses in greater Toronto. These people, the above-mentioned study showed, are seriously impaired and have not been cured by the shift in 'treatment.'

Government cuts in care of the developmentally handicapped have meant that residents shifted to the community are faced with waiting lists for group homes which number in the hundreds. The government is turning to the private sector for help in implementing its displacement of the developmentally handicapped to the community. Some of the developmentally handicapped are being placed in nursing homes and psychiatric hospitals. We even know of one case where an individual was sent to a facility for the criminally insane.

In another area of government activity—income maintenance—a recent independent report on poverty highlights the fact that Ontario is abandoning its social responsibilities. Expenditures on social assistance schemes represented a smaller proportion of the Ontario budget in 1979-80 than they did in the 1971-72 fiscal year.

Another regressive effect of government restraint policy has been steep health care premiums in Ontario. The premiums, which amount to $680 a year for a family, are the highest in Canada.

However, it is clear that Tory style restraint does not apply with equal force to friends of the government. In one example untendered contracts worth more than $81,000 were awarded to consultants, in violation of the government's own policy guidelines for government contracts.

When it comes to money for public sector workers the province claims it can only pay public employees a maximum 5 percent wage increase. However, at the same time it is increasing advertising expenditures for government cronies by 17 percent.

The poor, the disadvantaged and the handicapped are being pitted against each other to fight for crumbs from the province's table while the wealthy pick and choose. At the same time as the government calls for cut-backs, they offer no accounting for large-scale expenditures on government advertising, Ontario Hydro, and the $237 million that the government transfers to private for-profit nursing homes every year.

The Ontario Public Service Employee Union is responding to the province's right-wing social and economic policies by building a locally-based Coalition of Dissent. Together with the clients affected by cut-backs and shift-backs to municipalities, our union is mounting a real challenge to the 'new right.'

By building alliances with churches, service clubs, municipal politicians, local agencies and other unions, we have substantially slowed the government's attempt to divest itself of responsibility for social services, health care and education.

As part of our union's work to defeat Ontario's cut-back crusade, we conducted a very successful inquiry into the provincial mental health system during late 1981. We produced the book called *Madness* to publicize the findings.

We have conducted stress studies designed to clarify the pressures on union staff in centres for the developmentally handicapped, psychiatric hospitals and correction facilities.

We are also currently engaged in a court battle to stop the government from closing residential centres for the developmentally handicapped. We have evidence to prove that adequate standards for care of the developmentally handicapped have not been provided in the community by the government.

In the course of another legal dispute, we have engaged the government on the issue of public sector wage controls. Though this action we have contributed to a better understanding of our position on restraint among members of the legal profession.

By use of the union's new Pa*ssword* newsletter we have improved our locals' ability to act at a grassroots level with the community and strengthen our stewards' network.

The design of 'hands on', action-based courses for union members has increased our ability to respond quickly to regressive government policies. The course program includes sessions on politics in the community, lobbying, and dealing with politicians.

An educational movie about care for the developmentally handicapped was developed for cable television distribution, and was seen in 50 different locations across the province.

Another movie, "Where have all the Jobs Gone?", about the book by Professors Barry Bluestone and Ben Harrison titled *The Deindustrialization of America,* has also been used as part of our membership education program.

The Ontario Public Service Employees Union has sponsored a public inquiry, chaired by former Ontario New Democratic Party leader Stephen Lewis, into the delivery of ambulance and emergency health services in the city of Windsor. There are Ontario-wide implications for this inquiry.

I am convinced that Ontario's experience with restraint demonstrates that the way to take on regressive social and economic forces is to strengthen this Coalition of Dissent. Unless the government can fracture its opposition, it cannot implement a divestment program.

The message that I want to communicate here is that the way to defeat unfair restraint measures is the development of a strong social-issue profile for the union movement. Unless we win this battle for democracy—and that is what is really at stake—senior government will succeed not only in divestment of community programs and support systems, but also divestment of the humanity and compassion without which no society can survive.

Bishop Remi De Roo of Victoria, B.C., who is Chairman of the Canadian Conference of Catholic Bishops' Social Services Committee, released a 19-page booklet which outlined the "ethical choices" and "political challenges" facing Canada on International Workers' Day. It argues that massive unemployment, cuts in social spending and the devaluation of human labour reveals a deepening 'moral disorder' within the country's economy. The challenge to combat this is left to us.

We in the trade-union movement have no stomach for hiding our lamp under the bushel of social, political and moral compromise. Let's be honest advocates of the system of life we desire as Canadians. Let's include dignity, honour and honesty in that reform and deny the duplicity and degradation of to-day's governments, and let's identify and dialogue with our natural allies to develop the kind of Canada we can be proud of.

Confrontation and Consultation: The Organizational Objectives and Strategies of Two Public Sector Unions

Stan Marshall

The organizational objectives of the Canadian Union of Postal Workers (CUPW) and the Professional Institute of the Public Service of Canada (PIPS), as codified in their respective constitutions and by-laws, could not be more strikingly different. The language of CUPW's constitution is that of confrontation - confrontation with an employer and a government with whom they perceive no common interest. CUPW's objectives reflect an acute awareness that their existing rights have been won through collective bargaining and need to be defended against the attacks of an increasingly hostile employer. The language of PIPS' objectives, on the other hand, is that of consultation—consultation with an employer and a government who is less of an enemy than a partner. PIPS was a leading force in the establishment of the National Joint Council (NJC)—a public service-wide consultative mechanism—and has an explicitly stated position of common interest with the employer.

Needless to say, these very different orientations have been manifest in very different strategies and tactics. If we are to contemplate possible strategies and tactics for social change in the future, we must attempt a more systematic understanding of the historical processes and forces associated with both the general orientations and strategies of unions in the public sector. What follows is not intended to be an exhaustive cataloguing of strategies and tactics but a selective examination of some of the specificities of cases especially as they relate to mangement intervention into the labour process. Toward that end this paper will have four major sections. Firstly, the two dominant orientations as reflected in the organizational objectives will be outlined. Secondly, a distinction between technical proletarianization and ideological proletarianization will be re-cast as types of management appropriation of the labour process. It is argued that this framework provides insights into the nature of the strategies and tactics employed by unions, and provides, more importantly, a basis for understanding the differences in orientations. Thirdly, strategies and tactics will be examined within the contexts of organizational objectives and types of appropriation. Finally, implications for current and future strategies are considered.

Organizational Objectives: Two Dominant Orientations

The organizational objectives of both CUPW and PIPS are formalized in their respective constitutions and by-laws. These objectives can best be characterized as representing an ideology of confrontation in the case of CUPW and an ideology of consultation in the case of PIPS. Table 1 is a summary of these objectives based on selected features. CUPW's objectives are quite comprehensive and narrowly delineated. This has led some to comment that "the size of a collective agreement is inversely related to the trust between the parties" (Finkelman and Goldenberg, 1983: 219) implying that those groups with a consultative orientation do not feel the need to build protections into their agreement and, indeed, "would actually feel constrained by a detailed collective agreement" (Finkelman and Goldenberg, 1983: 304, fn. 82). Aside from this, several features of this comparison are notable. While there is agreement on the role of the union as an economic bargaining unit, it is here that the similarities end. CUPW's objective with regard to affiliation denotes a strong identification with other workers within the Canadian postal system as well as with a national and international working class. This identification is accompanied by a specific recommendation to support all workers. PIPS, on the other hand, makes no specific mention of any form of solidarity either as professionals or as unionists.

The political objectives provide an interesting contrast in that CUPW is very specific about its relationship to the employer. They perceive a hostile employer who is waging an attack on CUPW members through operational changes in the Post Office and through restrictive legislation. PIPS' political objective does not single out the employer as an antagonist. Although it does recognize an obligation to secure rights and to seek redress for infringements on those rights, the tenor of the language is less direct than CUPW's. The educational objectives reveal two fundamentally different conceptions. The professional influence in PIPS is evident in its objective to provide an education which contributes to professional advancement and maintains high professional standards. In CUPW the confrontation orientation is reflected in its desire to educate its membership to the importance of power and trade union strength among postal workers in particular and among the working class in general.

These objectives merely scratch the surface of the orientations of these two unions. Suffice it to say that the orientations are qualitatively different and are manifest in qualitatively different actions and policies.

Table 1: Organizational Objectives, CUPW and PIPS

Canadian Union of Postal Workers

Objectives	
1. Affiliation	• unite all workers in Canada's postal system • cooperate with other postal unions • explicit desire to merge with other unions in the postal system • cooperation with similar workers both nationally and internationally • active participation in the Canadian labour movement
2. Economic	• wages, hours of work, and working conditions • old age security and pension provisions
3. Political	• removal of repressive and restrictive legislation • active program of defense against attacks by employer
4. Education	• make membership aware of relationship between power and collective strength • encourage trade union principles among Canadian Workers
5. Rights	• defend rights acquired by the union
6. Ideology	CONFRONTATION

Professional Instutite of the Public Service of Canada

Objectives	
1. Affiliation	• no specific mention of affiliation with other professionals or the labour movement conditions of employment
2. Economic	• salaries, terms and conditions of employment
3. Political	• seek redress and secure rights founded in contract, common law, and statute
4. Education	• the right to further professional education • maintain high standards of professionalism
5. Rights	• bargain for rights to exercise professional responsibility and professional education
6. Ideology	CONSULTATION

CUPW and Confrontation: Consultation Rejected

The current position of CUPW on consultation can only be considered in terms of its historical antecedents. In the years before the passing of the Public Service Staff Relations Act (PSSRA) collective bargaining for the public sector came under considerable debate. The postal workers were a lone voice in favour of full collective bargaining rights. Other organizations in the public sector were still heavily influenced by the mechanisms of the NJC established in 1944. The NJC was fashioned after the Whitley Councils in Britain and was designed to provide

> ...a greater measure of cooperation between the state in its capacity of employer and the general body of civil servants in matters affecting the Civil Service with a view to increased efficiency in the Public Service combined with the well being of those employed ... (Barnes, 1974: 29).

Postal employees began almost immediately to make demands outside of the stated objectives of the NJC. The first meeting of the NJC was in June 1944 and by July the postal employees began to make wage demands - demands which incidently were resolved in a satisfactory increase for postal employees (Barnes, 1974: 30-31). The result was an on-going debate about the proper role of the NJC, and the NJC was never to become involved in such negotiations again (Barnes, 1974: 32, 72). It was to remain a mechanism devoted to consultation in the most narrow sense of this term. As Joe Davidson notes, "the staff side was free to voice its opinions on ... matters—consultation—and then the management side did whatever it pleased—divine right" (Davidson and Deverell, 1978: 98).

The Canadian Postal Employees' Association (CPEA), very dissatisfied with the lack of real negotiation under the NJC, first began to demand full collective bargaining rights in 1950 under the Industrial Relations Disputes Investigations Act (Davidson and Deverell, 1978: 97). This pressure from postal employees stimulated more open debate about the role of collective bargaining in the public sector. Arnold Heeney's (1959) report contained recommendations which would have led the Civil Service Commission to employ compulsory arbitration as a dispute resolution mechanism but the Diefenbaker Conservative government rejected these recommendations still holding firm to a non-negotiation model by freezing wages in 1959 (Frankel, 1962: 154-155). But it was clear that better mechanisms for bargaining were essential and in 1961 finance minister Donald Fleming introduced legislation to make consultation compulsory. Such a move drew support from the Civil Service Federation (CSF) but not from the CPEA. The CPEA's vision of a suitable bargaining mechanism was beginning to supercede anything the government was willing to provide at that time. Indeed, the CPEA was beginning to reject the Whitley consultation approach and they stood largely alone among public employees in this orientation. Joe Davidson contends the attempt to make consultation compulsory was a "transparent stalling gambit—" and "was the litmus test which served to define the orientations and philosophy of public service unions, and continues to do so right to the present day" (Davidson and Deverell, 1978: 99).

The philosophy of postal employees was now diametrically opposed to that of other civil servants and affiliation with these groups was no longer advantageous to postal employees. "[T]he only answer for postal workers was to put as much legal distance between us and them as possible" (Davidson and Deverell, 1978: 103). Postal employees disaffiliated from the CSF in 1962 and served notice to the NJC in 1966 that they were "debating the advisability of participating further in the Staff Side Conference of the NJC". An uneasy relationship between CUPW and other public sector unions continued until January 8, 1971 when the Council of Postal Unions withdrew (Barnes, 1974: 167).

The success of the 1965 CUPW strike had helped to put in place a hard-line militant philosophy which was to reject consultation as a viable mechanism for resolving negotiations over wages and conditions of work, and to accept instead the necessity of negotiating through the conciliation/strike route. The general distrust of postal workers toward management with regard to the effectiveness of consultation is illustrated in the following account:

> The shortage of lockers and proper washup facilities was another matter close to our hearts. There was a notion in the minds of management that sorting was clean work, so postal clerks, with the exception of a few favourites, had to leave their street clothes, hats, overshoes, work jackets, aprons, lunchboxes, et cetera on open racks. The borrowing and filching, especially when the armies of Christmas casuals came in, drove people to distraction. The CPEA raised the demand for private lockers repeatedly until supervisor George Morley finally said "o.k., you tell me where we're going to put them." This was what we were waiting for, so we showed him a forgotten space that was perfect for the purpose. Two days later it was filled with letter sorting cases. This was the kind of thing that made postal workers laugh bitterly whenever management talked about the advantages of good faith and consultation (Davidson and Deverell, 1978: 50-51).

The philosophy of militancy in the postal unions was formed in reaction to events at both the local and the national level, and the rejection of consultation is now firmly institutionalized into the CUPW national constitution and policies. The duties of the 1st National Vice-President of CUPW includes "mobilizing the membership in struggles against the employer" and "organizing preparatory steps and strike structures". The 2nd National Vice-President's responsibilities for education include "campaigns to be conducted by the Union against the employer and the opponents of the labour movement", and courses on "regressive and anti-labour legislation" and "the dangers of industrial democracy". At the local level the local president shall "impose, as a policy of the union, the rule according to which no Local Officer may meet alone with a representative of the employer to discuss Union matters". CUPW national policies prohibit cooperation with management in employer surveys, courses, or publicity ads. Most specifically the national policies reject consultation which is not binding. "No articles pertaining to Consultation Committees which do not commit the employer to actual negotiations with representatives of the Union shall be included in the C.U.P.W. Collective Agreement". Similarly, the "C.U.P.W. opposes any form of tri-partism" even if it is supported by the Canadian Labour Congress (CLC). "The C.U.P.W. opposes the principle of industrial democracy" perceiving it to contain inherent dangers to the membership, and CUPW policy statements to the membership outline the reasons for rejecting consultation with management at all levels (*CUPW*, 1982: 5). It is evident that the relationship between employer and employee here is well-defined and is one of confrontation. PIPS, on the other hand, seems to embrace consultation as part of their professional ethos.

PIPS and Professionalism: Consultation Accepted

It is well-accepted that professionals have resisted the traditional union form and action because of a professional ideology which "is on the whole favourable to management, and even where they have accepted the instrumental value of a union it is usually only with reluctance" (Prandy, 1965: 142). Cooperation with management and a firm belief in individualism and meritocracy are central tenets of this ideology.

> I don't want a collective agreement that says how many professional conferences I can attend in a year. I'm better off leaving it open then I can go more or less as necessary. The department managers know we have to keep up to date. And I'm glad we don't get overtime. I'd be insulted. I'm not a '9-to-5' guy (Finkelman and Goldenberg, 1983: 305, fn. 82).

The professionals employed in the public service shares the desire of all professionals, namely to derive satisfaction from the work being done. To have a recognizable degree of control over the planning of that work, and within limits to share in basic decisions on operational requirements, deployment of resources, both financial and manpower, to maximize efficiency and obtain the greatest response. It is inconceivable that a person trained to think independently and trained to weigh the alternatives and make decisions in his own area of expertise will accept as compensation for a frustrating life at work sufficient funds to pay for a good life off the job ...(PIPS, 1974: 2-3).

Professionals value independence and wish to have control over their work environment, education and specialized knowledge, and career development (PIPS, 1981: 7). PIPS has been no exception to these generalizations and actively resisted industrial-style unionism for the public sector. By the time the NJC was formed it enjoyed the full support of PIPS in spite of some reservations that Institute members did not share the interests of manual and clerical workers (Barnes, 1974: 20).

The consultative philosophy of PIPS was not lost on the government nor on Arnold Heeney's (1965) Preparatory Committee on Collective Bargaining for the civil service. This committee recommended that public employees not have the right to strike and PIPS did not object. PIPS was found to be a responsible organization who would not be a disruptive force in any collective bargaining process. "The Committee took into account the long and responsible history of the organization of professional employees in the public service and the significant role they played in developing the process of consultation over rates of pay and conditions of employment, and saw no good reason why this group should be denied access to collective bargaining" (Finkkelman and Goldenberg, 1983: 27).

The ideology of professionalism in PIPS is complemented by a 'service ethic' which is a commitment to serve the state and the Canadian public. "We Serve the State" has been PIPS's motto since its founding in 1920. In briefs to the Canadian parliament PIPS has presented itself as partners with parliamentarians in "the need to provide the people of this country with a highly skilled public service" (PIPS, 1981: 3). This service ethic has contributed to a non-confrontational type of unionism among professionals (Thompson, 1977) where most issues, outside of money matters, are decided upon before formal negotiations begin (Finkelman and Goldenberg, 1983: 291). Consultation therefore requires considerable trust and confidence between employer and employee such that negotiations proceed smoothly and detailed collective agreements are unnecessary. Moreover, professionals fully *expect to participate.* "[I]t is often essential that the professional be provided with a participatory role in management, and not be limited to the provision of expertise in a manner unconnected with the decision-making process" (PIPS, 1981: 7). This desired participatory role is consistent with the actual position of many of PIPS' members as 'quasi-management' supervising others and acting as policy advisors.

The history of consultation in the NJC, the ideology of professionalism and an adherence to a service ethic have all contributed to a situation where consultation is institutionally codified in PIPS' constitution and contracts. The explicit aims of PIPS as an organization incorporate many references to consultation and common interests with employers. Indeed, some contracts include clauses such as the following:

> The parties acknowledge the mutual benefits to be derived from joint consultation and will consult on matters of common interests.
>
> The subjects that may be determined as appropriate for joint consultation will be by mutual agreement by the parties and shall include consultation regarding career development and the provision of information to employers and the Institute. Consultation may be at the local, regional or headquarters levels as determined by the parties (Finkelman and Goldenberg, 1983: 313).

Lest one get the impression that there are no disputes between employer and employee, it is important to note that a consultation philosophy has its limitations. PIPS, with decentralized bargaining, requires many individual contracts and does not have the available resources to "play the game". Consultation requires time and money to play effectively. Moreover, bargaining over salary has led to more specificity in contract language—specificity which ideally should not be required in a consultation model. A case in point is overtime compensation. Historically, it has not been an issue but it is currently being incorporated into more contracts because it allows PIPS to overcome some erosion of their relative economic position and to keep pace with other public sector unions.

Nevertheless, consultation continues to be the predominant philosophy of PIPS. Before turning to the implications of the confrontation and consultation philosophies for the formation of actual strategy and action, it is necessary to engage in a short theoretical divergence in order to gain some further insights into the forces of change affecting each of these unions.

Ideological and Technical Appropriation

Since Harry Braverman's (1974) pioneering work the labour process in capitalist society has come under ever increasing scrutiny. While Braverman regrettably did not examine the political responses of workers and their organizations to changes in the labour process, there is a great temptation to attribute any such responses as being directly related to a process of proletarianization. I wish to resist this temptation, as the study of proletarianization has proven to be a veritable minefield for scholars in both its theoretical formulation and its empirical analysis. My major concern here is with the strategies, tactics and orientations of public employees' organizations and not with the process of proletarianization *per se* nor with any analyses of the class locations of these employees. Nevertheless, there are aspects of the proletarianization argument which cannot be dismissed out of hand, and may be particularly instructive in any attempt to draw implications from the confrontational style of CUPW and the consultative style of PIPS. Charles Derber's (1982) theoretical discourse on the proletarianization of professionals serves as a case in point. Derber argues that there is a distinction between technical and ideological proletarianization such that technical proletarianization is

> the loss of control over the process of work itself (the means), incurred whenever management subjects its workers to a technical plan of production and/or a rhythm or pace of work which they have no voice in creating... .

Ideological proletarianization then, is

> ... a loss of control over the goals and social purpose to which one's work is put ... [including] powerlessness to choose or define the final product of one's work, its disposition in the market, its uses in the larger society, and the values or social policy of the organization which purchases one's labour (Derber, 1982: 169).

It is not my intention to quibble over Derber's use of the concept 'proletarianization', but it is my intention to recast the ideas germane to his argument such that they address the specificities of the forces affecting both CUPW and PIPS members. Derber is addressing two fundamental features of management intervention into the labour process. Firstly, changes in the labour process such as changes in the degree of specialization, fragmentation, routinization and degradation are features of management's appropriation of the technical labour process and of the skill and knowledge of workers. I shall refer to this intervention as *technical appropriation*. Secondly, management intervention into the ideological component of the labour process changes the degree to which the worker can "shape or control broad organizational policy and the specific goals and purposes of his own work" (Derber, 1982: 169). This intervention is *ideological appropriation* and is a management attempt to appropriate the ideological commitment and allegiance of employees (cf. Panitch and Swartz, 1984; Rinehart, 1984).

The responses of professionals to this type of appropriation can take two specific forms (Derber, 1982: 180). Firstly, ideological desensitization can occur where professionals no longer identify with the professional aims *or* with the institutional aims of the work. Secondly, ideological cooptation can occur in that the professional no longer differentiates between professional aims and employer (institutional) aims. It is this latter form of accommodation and consultation in the public service. Charles Derber sums up well the major points for consideration.

> ... ideological proletarianization may be the foundation of a new system of labour process control in post-industrial capitalism that does not require technical proletarianization in order to subordinate workers effectively to capitalist production. Technical knowledge and skill controlled by workers is fundamentally inimical to capitalist production only if workers perceive their interests as different from management's and are organized in a manner allowing them to enforce their own objectives. Where workers are characterized by a strong internal discipline and identity with the objectives of their organization, their continuing possession of technical knowledge and skill may serve management's interests more than it threatens them. To the extent that effective systems exist for the integration and motivations of workers, imperatives of technical proletarianization diminish (1982: 189).

Derber's distinction has implications for the analysis of the organizational behaviour of public employees in that type of appropriation influences both the organizational philosophy and action. It is now necessary to examine the differences in strategies and tactics in more detail.

Strategies and Tactics: Reactive and Proactive

Labour strategies and tactics fall into two broad categories. (1) Reactive tactics are generally defensive responses to protect and preserve existing rights which are being threatened by managerial policy. (2) Proactive tactics are actions which place the union on the offensive in terms of gaining new rights or pressuring for alternative arrangements in the workplace. Trade unions have been primarily defensive organizations acting as defenders of working peoples' rights both inside and outside of the workplace, although as Rinehart (1975: 153) observes "unions are paradoxical institutions" serving to integrate workers into the capitalist system and coincidentally serving to attack the capitalist system. In this sense union strategies are neither wholly reactive nor proactive. Nevertheless, the distinction is a useful one providing insights into the relationship between union orientations and the nature of management appropriation of the labour process in the public sector.

Postal workers have been subject to the forces of technical appropriation through the reorganization of the labour process and the massive introduction of technology. Any ideological appropriation of the labour process of postal employees seems to have been rejected by postal workers by the time of their withdrawal from the NJC in 1971. This marked the final rejection by CUPW of any common interests with their employer. Professionals, on the other hand, have not been subject to the same forces of technical appropriation. They have retained at least relative autonomy of the technical part of their labour process. However, ideological appropriation may be a feature of the relations between PIPS' members and management. While they have retained an ideology of common interest with their employer, the autonomy of professionals may be under attack as professional interests become increasingly subordinated to the interests of the employer.

At first glance it would be easy to interpret the confrontational strategies of CUPW as reactive strategies taken to fight back against management's increasing technical appropriation of the labour process. Similarly, it would be easy to interpret PIPS' consultative orientations as indicative of a proactive strategy to establish autonomy for the membership. In point of fact, the strategies of each group cannot be easily categorized. CUPW, with its confrontational orientation stretching the limits of its capacity to act, often incorporates very proactive strategies into its program. PIPS, with its consultative orientation limiting its capacity to seek alternatives, is beginning to react defensively. The initially reactive and defensive unionism of CUPW may be developing in a somewhat dialectical fashion into a proactive and offensive-minded unionism with a more well-developed plan for alternative industrial arrangements (cf. Mann, 1973). PIPS now appears to be at the point of reacting to a process of ideological appropriation and may be entering a form of dialectical struggle with their employer. If this is the case, CUPW and PIPS may not be as diametrically opposed in the future as they have been in the past.

A brief examination and interpretation of some of the strategies and tactics of each of these unions should provide support for the above argument and should enable us to make some conclusions about the potential (and necessary) direction of strategies in the public sector.

The issue of consultation provides a particularly good illustration of proactive strategy within the context of an orientation of confrontation. CUPW's early scepticism about the NJC as a suitable vehicle for negotiation was not solely a negative reaction. It was accompanied by a positive alternative still within the framework of the NJC. Postal employees wished to set up their own separate Staff Side within the NJC because they correctly perceived that other members of the Staff Side (CSF, CSAC, and PIPS) were not in agreement with postal workers' policies or demands

(Barnes, 1974: 138). Postal employees realized that the Staff Side was likely to be dominated by its more moderate counterparts. With this particular avenue closed the Council of Postal Unions (CPU) began to circumvent the NJC by negotiating benefits, previously handled by the NJC, directly with Treasury Board. This strategy is partly reactive but is the forerunner of a later proactive strategy to negotiate items deemed to be illegal under the PSSRA. This will be discussed more explicitly below. This initial circumvention of the NJC is successful in that the employer agrees to pay 50 percent of the direct Medicare premiums for workers. Under the NJC only approximately one-third of the premium was paid by the employer (Barnes, 1974: 146). Indeed, this strategy spurred the NJC to improve its Medicare benefits for other employees.

Many of CUPW's demands were precedent setting demands in the public sector and CUPW's now explicit refusal to consult has often been interpreted as evidence of the intransigence of CUPW's unnecessarily confrontational position. Yet, the very fact that CUPW's demands were precedent setting led to proactive strategies, and consultation was not to be a part of this type of strategy. In the words of Jean-Claude Parrot:

> To say to people that we are not going to consult anymore during the life of the agreement seems to be abnormal, while it is normal in the private sector not to meet. So we are put in a situation where our people would like permanent negotiations. That is what we are seeing more and more, that we should fight during the life of the collective agreement for things we couldn't resolve during negotiations (Parrot, 1983: 56).

That negotiation should be continuous represents a proactive approach in a time when legal strikes can be predicted and planned for by the employer becasue of the structure of the conciliation/strike procedure. Continuous negotiation represents for the employer an unwanted degree of uncertainty.

CUPW has employed the negotiation process itself as a vehicle for change in a very direct way. The PSSRA is very restrictive in what may be negotiated in collective bargaining. Clauses relating to technological change, for example, are non-negotiable under the act. Nevertheless, CUPW proceeded to negotiate technological change under a strategy of 'get it in the contract first, and fight for change in the legislation later'. This strategy has proven to be quite effective generally (but not specifically in the case of technology). "Of what we got in our collective agreement today, probably half of it was considered illegal in 1968 when the law [PSSRA] was passed" (Parrot, 1983: 55). This strategy was accompanied by a strategy which used the grievance procedure as a battleground. Grievances generally are reactive in nature but CUPW used them in a very proactive fashion. The tactic was to grieve on an individual basis the effects of the introduction of technology and the use of casual labour. This resulted in some 60,000 grievances over two years. Indeed, the tactic was to *solicit* grievances in order that sections of the collective agreement could be clarified (Davidson and Deverell, 1978: 131). This clarification had the added advantage of providing an educational tool for stewards. Successes could be explained in terms of what was in the agreement and failures could be explained in terms of what was *not* in the agreement. The battleground of the grievance procedure laid the groundwork for mobilizing support in future negotiations.

Not all strategies by CUPW have been as explicitly proactive. The system of rotating strikes, the series of illegal strikes, the boycott of the postal code, the T-shirt campaign, and others have been largely reactive. This is not to say that these tactics did not have their place or their successes, but rather that this type of tactic places a different kind of pressure on the employer and has a different impact on potential change.

The strategies of PIPS, formed within the context of a consultative orientation, seem to be limited to reactive tactics by the very constraints of that orientation. Consultation should (ideally) have the potential for proactive change. Yet, PIPS' strategy reinforces a status quo in which professionals retain autonomy over their work situation. As such, the Institute's support for the formation of the NJC was a proactive strategy which was tinged with reactivity. Faced with the prospect of formal collective bargaining through unionism, PIPS strove to put in place a formal mechanism of consultation (the NJC) which was a reflection of what professionals were already doing in their relationship with the employer.

In general the strategy of PIPS is a 'strategy of indispensibility'—an attempt to convince the state of the necessity for professionals to maintain their professional freedoms, all in the national interest (PIPS, 1980: 3). This strategy, while not reactive in and of itself, becomes reactive in its application. It is seldom pursued as a goal in itself but is invoked as a defence of professionals in the face of threats from the employer. This is demonstrated particularly well in PIPS' response to expenditure cutbacks. The tenor of the argument against cutbacks is not so much one of promoting the welfare of PIPS' members as it is one of explicating the consequences of Canada of a weakened public service. "To inhibit professional activity by further staff reductions would serve to mortgage to the severest extent the current and future capability of the Public Service to respond to the needs of Canadian society" (PIPS, 1980: 5).

While technical appropriation has not been a significant factor in the professional workplace, ideological appropriation does seem to concern PIPS' members. Control over decision-making and influence into policy-making have been threatened by employer intervention into the uses to which professional labour is put (the subsumation of professional interests into employer interests). PIPS' response has been relatively mild—no real pressure for change by pressure for 'adaptation' with a 'new style of management'. Professionals would be more fully integrated into the decision-making process even to the point of ensuring that line managers are competent scientists. The rationale is that professionals "will be better able to assess scientific performance, make wise staffing decisions, and 'sell' justifiable program proposals to superiors" (PIPS, 1981: 9). Although the language of these demands may imply proactivity, the strategy does not posit a new alternative arrangement as much as it posits a re-integration of professionals into an advisory role in the policy-making machinery of government. In this sense, the strategy is a reaction to the loss of professional freedoms and duties as well as a reaction to a managerial cadre who have institutional goals rather than professional goals.

> If professionals in government are to be adequately utilized in their service to Canadians, it is imperative that they be allowed to stand by their professional opinions, as well as to criticize and advocate changes in accepted theories and existing institutions, and in the policies, programs and administration of the public service insofar as these affect their sphere of expertise. Professional employees today are convinced what is required is a new style of management, one which is more flexible, is characterized by fewer rules and bureaucratic procedures, and which provides for a more open relationship with employees (PIPS, 1981: 7).

The desire for a more open relationship is consistent with their consultative orientation and is, in part, a response to the creation of a Senior Management (SM) category which will place tighter controls, accountability and efficiency on PIPS' members (PIPS, 1981: 10-13). The SM category adds one more level to the government hierarchy and, in PIPS' perception, collegial accountability and peer evaluation are threatened. This threat is real enough for PIPS' members to utilize the grievance procedure as a response. Grievances are not common amongst professionals as they usually try to resolve issues through consultation between the management and the individual involved. Indeed, one of the major roles of the shop steward is to facilitate this consultation (PIPS, *By-Laws* 1977). Still, grievances are lodged over the issue of evaluation of professional performance. The complaint often is not over the accuracy of the evaluation but over the capability and qualifications of the evaluator. The creation of the SM category puts in place a structure where evaluation by peers is less likely to occur. The use of the grievance procedure in this instance is strictly as a defensive mechanism and, more importantly, a defensive mechanism which operates at an individual level.

The individualized tactics of PIPS are consistent with an ideology of professionalism. Individual professionals may, if conditions in the government are not suitable, negotiate a contract elsewhere—often with one of the free enterprise firms to which the government 'contracts out'. On occasion, this may result in the professional working at exactly the same job, on the same project, but with a free enterprise employer. Rather than taking collective action in order to affect change the professional often uses individual action to alter individual working conditions and/or market situation. The emphasis is on resolving grievances individually, one way or another.

From the inception of collective bargaining in the public sector, PIPS has sought to avoid confrontation in bargaining. An aversion to collective action made the conciliation/strike option an almost intolerable choice and they opted for compulsory arbitration in *all* their units. They did make a recommendation to Finkelman in 1973 for Final Offer Selection in order to add some flexibility to dispute resolution (PIPS, 1974: 22-23). Since then however, the successes of other unions using the conciliation/strike route have led several of PIPS' locals to change their method of collective bargaining resolution (Finkelman and Goldenberg, 1983: 716-722). It appears that some aspects of the consultative orientation and the professional ideology are being eroded and this has some interesting implications for any conclusions we may draw.

Conclusions

The strategies of both CUPW and PIPS must be considered in the contexts of their orientations and the nature of the threat posed by management action. Neither the orientations nor the strategies of these organizations should be treated as immutable. However, the confrontational position of CUPW seems to be most firmly established in the face of technical appropriation of the labour process by the employer. The strategies employed by CUPW are defensive in origin but have developed into very proactive collective demands with potential to move *outside of* the existing organizational framework. PIPS' consultative position, while firmly rooted in a non-confrontational past, may be undergoing some change currently in the face of ideological appropriation. PIPS' response has been a defensive one even though it stems from a proactive ideological base and illustrates the limitations of a proactive strategy *within* the existing framework, especially when it is not backed up with the threat of direct action.

The implications for trade unionists and for trade union strategy can be summed up in the following three interrelated points:

1. Direct action in the form of confrontation may be an effective strategy not so much because of its potential for immediate gains but because of its potential for longer term mobilization of the membership toward the formation of alternatives.
2. Confrontation strategies can force the initiating union beyond the limits of its own action and policies and toward strategies which, under certain conditions, become ever increasingly proactive. Managements will almost certainly resist on the grounds that such strategies are disruptive (increasing uncertainty) and that the alternatives arising out of proactive strategy are beyond acceptable limits i.e., the existing power structure in the workplace is threatened. One management strategy at this point is to 'concede' through the consultation process some of its power. In effect, the consultation 'concession' is a form of "premise-setting" or "unobtrusive control" which ensures consistent and predictable resolutions to disputes thereby decreasing uncertainty (Perrow, 1979; March and Simon, 1958).
3. To submit to the current pressures being placed on employees in both the public and the private sectors to adopt consultative mechanisms is to subordinate employee interests to the interests of the employer. For professionals ideological cooptation becomes a predominant form of managerial control *even without* management intervention into the technical labour process. For workers already subject to substantial technical control, ideological cooptation mitigates against any strength the employees have in the form of confrontational strategies, and inhibits unequivocally the formation of proactive strategies designed to further the interests of workers. More importantly, it inhibits the formation of a process of proactive strategizing which stretches the limits of organizational action as outlined in point (1) above. Moreover, any confrontation which does occur under conditions of ideological cooptation are likely to be reactive in nature, defending attacks on the consultative strategy and mechanisms, because the proactive alternatives are inappropriate as outlined in point (2) above.

The Settlement House: Agent of Social Control or Agent of Social Change?

Jim Ward

The Settlement House—A Mini History

Settlement houses were first developed in several of the large urban centres of North America and Britain around the turn of the 20th century. Hull House in Chicago and Toynbee Hall in London are two of the best known examples. Here in Toronto there are six social service agencies that consider themselves to be settlement houses: Central Neighbourhood House, Dixon Hall and Woodgreen in the east end of the city, and St. Christopher House, St. Stephens and University Settlement in the west end.

A basic assumption upon which the settlement-house approach to social problems is built is that such problems can be tackled effectively on a neighbourhood scale. Underlying this assumption is the belief that cities are, to a considerable extent, spatial manifestations of socio-economic structures. To use Timms' (1972) term, there is an "urban mosaic". The city is seen as a patchwork of middle, upper, working class and marginal population residential areas; production areas (industrial parks, etc.); consumer areas (shopping malls, etc.); and financial areas (banks, etc.). Thus, if one is interested in ameliorating the lot of those in the working class or marginal population residential areas, the most effective way to do this is to locate in such areas. And so it was with settlement houses.[1]

In the early years, socially concerned individuals and groups (most often with middle-class backgrounds) actually took up residence in the settlement houses. It was felt that by both living and working in these working-class and marginal neighbourhoods, a more effective understanding of the problems of the poor could be developed. By living amongst them, they could feel the problems in their very bones and thus assist the poor in dealing with them.

The early settlement house members appear to have been genuinely motivated by a deep-seated concern for their materially less fortunate fellows. The early 20th century city, with its glaring inequities, provided fertile ground for the development of such concern. However, many appear to have fallen into what geographers were later to refer to as the ecological fallacy trap—i.e., the notion that social problems are actually caused by the area in which they are found. For example, high crime rates, high mental illness rates, etc. are seen as being a function of a particularly 'bad area'. (The founders of Dixon Hall referred to the 'criminal classes' in the area.) The solution then appears to be to 'clean up' the area. This frequently leads to 'urban renewal' responses, as it did in Toronto with the razing of much of the old Cabbagetown area in the 1940s and 1950s. In this way a narrow spatial focus on social problems leads the search for solutions away from the wider socio-economic system and towards the local geographic area.

A neighbourhood approach can be highly conservative one, analogous to the psychologistic and individual approach to social problems, in which the problem is located within the individual rather than the socio-economic system. With few exceptions, it appears that much of the settlement house philosophy slipped into this narrow framework. A more radical neighbourhood approach is to see the task as one of developing new organization and political strengths within working-class and marginal population areas, and turning the focus of these new strengths towards the wider socio-economic system. In addition the development of a structural understanding of how different urban functions interrelate spatially (see, for example, Pickvance (1976)), in conjunction with the new organizational and political strengths, can provide powerful tools for the explanation of urban inequities.

From the little that is available on the topic, and by looking at the current status of settlement houses, it appears that although many may have begun with a keen understanding of and an urge to ameliorate urban inequities, most of them moved toward a conservative approach to social problems. They either fell into the ecological fallacy trap or, worse still, located the social problems in the individuals themselves.

Settlement house activities became increasingly recreational; pool or basketball could be played, providing the poor with opportunities to mix with middle-class volunteers. The notion is that is the two classes rub shoulders over a game or two, the poorer group will benefit by the absorption of middle-class values—amelioration through value osmosis.

Herbert Gans (1962) critiqued this settlement house tendency harshly in his study of one of Boston's large Italian immigrant reception areas. For Gans, such approaches were little more than a kind of volunteer voyeurism. Out of his study Gans developed the concept of the 'external caretaker'. External caretakers were the middle-class outsiders who would come down to the 'slums' to 'help' those less 'fortunate' than themselves. However, the external caretaker never turns any power over to the 'unfortunates'. Instead he/she simply helps to maintain the status quo, in which the main winner is the external caretaker who leaves with all his/her beliefs intact plus a good feeling that he/she has done something worthwhile.

Settlement houses in general appear to have deteriorated into this kind of approach, at least until the 1960s. Charity tended to win out over the notion of social justice as a driving force. Handouts of food, clothing and goodwill went hand-in-hand with recreational endeavours, so that the settlement house became difficult to distinguish from church-based organizations with their long history of political quiescence and charity to the poor.

Community Development Versus Professionalism

In the 1960s two major developments impinged upon the languishing settlement houses. The first of these was the explosion of concern with urban inequities amongst both left-leaning and environmentalist groups of activists. Most, but not all, of these activists were middle class and college educated. They read Alinsky (1971), Sennett (1971), Marcuse (1964), and Roszak (1973), as well as other authors who expressed an abiding concern for mankind in the latter part of the 20th century. The activist groups were concerned about the ways in which some powerless sectors of the urban population were being trampled on by the powerful. Much of the concern grew out of an environmentalist movement opposed to high-rise living, the wholesale destruction of neighbourhoods, concentrations of noxious industries, etc.

This era spawned a healthy development of urban protest movements. People who had never before thought of organizing went out into the poor neighbourhoods and ghettos. They became the late-20th century Narodniks, working to empower the poor. In a small way the settlement houses became involved in these activities. They began to see that perhaps charity and basketball were not quite enough, and sought out funding to hire community development workers. The task of these workers was to empower the powerless, to redress the imbalance through the development of grass-roots organizations.

However, it was a second development of the 1960s that had the more major impact on settlement house activities. This was the explosion of professionalism within the social welfare sector. Schools of Social Work by one name or another were both growing and proliferating in universities and colleges throughout the Western world. Since it was necessary for graduates to seek out job markets wherever they could, after the large state bureaucracies had been saturated, the smaller-scale social welfare operations provided the next possibilities. Settlement houses became 'professionalized'.[2]

What is a Profession?

Since the notion of 'professionalism' is so important to this paper, it is necessary to take time to discuss it. This section of the paper endeavours to critically analyze the phenomenon.

In recent years there have been several trenchant critiques of professions—see, for example, Illich (1977), Illich *et al.* (1978), and Parry and Parry (1976). For our purposes there are four important characteristics of any occupation that considers itself and is considered by others to be a profession. These are:

a. the claim to exclusive ownership over a certain area of knowledge and practice.
b. The ability to expropriate an outsider's right to know and to practice.
c. The ability to create and further develop a market for the service.
d. The development of a ready avenue to its 'own' for upward social mobility.

Because it is important to understand how professionalism has and will probably continue to influence settlement house philosophies and activities, it is necesary to discuss these characteristics in some detail.

Exclusive ownership over knowledge and practice

Through an internally policed educational system, a profession can convince all outsiders that they have no right to the knowledge within that system. Medical Schools, Law Schools, Social Work Schools, etc. are the only places where one can *legitimately* familiarize oneself with the knowledge, jump through the hoops (manufactured by those schools), and eventually come out at the end of the process with the 'tools of practice' as a doctor, lawyer, social worker, etc.

Access to the school is strictly controlled through various admission criteria. Statewide professional bodies make decisions on how many should be allowed access each year, and set down criteria for access. These are usually measurable academic criteria: certain high school or college courses taken, certain marks achieved, etc. In subtle ways, however, the access criteria are those that will select most heavily from certain parts of the social structure. In the 'more established' professions, such as law and medicine, recruitment is heaviest amongst the upper middle class; whereas in the 'newer' professions, such as social work, recruitment is likely to come from the lower parts of the middle class and even from the working class.

The development of a unique language is important in maintaining exclusive ownership over knowledge and practice. The major function of this unique language is to keep outsiders 'in the dark', but professions are particularly adept at claiming the language is necessary to understand the complexities of knowledge and practice. Hence the difficult nature of legal terminology, the pseudo-Latin of medicine, and the obtuse jargon of social work. Once an individual is fully socialized into the particular profession—i.e. he/she is able to call him/herself a 'professional'—he/she tends to keep the knowledge within the group. A major task for someone who has become a professional is to maintain the myth that the knowledge one has gained in one's professional training is of considerable value to the rest of the world, and that one's social position is justified by the facts that one now knows.[3]

Expropriation of the outsider's right to know and to practice
Professionalism is largely based on the denial of an individual's competence to manage his/her own affairs in particular areas. In medicine it is the denial that one can really get to know one's own body, what conditions are best for one's own health, etc. In law it is the denial that one is capable of selling one's own house or of leaving one's possessions to whom one chooses without an intermediary. In psychiatry it is a denial that one can know one's own mind! In education it's a denial that one can learn for oneself.

An important corollary of this is the fact that particular areas of knowledge and practice have been completely taken over by professions. The lay citizen is stripped of his/her ability to fend for him/herself in some of the most fundamental areas of life without the 'help' of a professional.

Creation and development of a market for the service
For a profession to survive and grow, it must maintain or increase its market size. Medicine, for example, continually develops new reasons why one must use its services; Illich (1977) refers to this as 'the medicalization of society'. Childbirth, until recently, took place outside the medical system. Now it is only the 'cranks' who have their babies at home. As preventive medicine becomes more and more the catchcry, the medical profession will make itself more and more essential to that area. Already it is common practice for medical establishments to offer elaborate (and expensive) preventive checkups and tests.

Psychiatry, through its development of a wide range of 'mental illness' categories, has built up a huge market of users and potential users. Although it is difficult to get more than two psychiatrists to agree what schizophrenia is, there are thousands of afflicted out there clamouring for treatment.[4]

Social work has also done a great deal to help maintain the psychiatric and medical labels. Working hand-in-glove with medicine and psychiatry, it has helped to maintain a large market of 'alcoholics', 'drug addicts', 'inadequate personalities', etc.[5]

An avenue for upward social mobility

One of the most insightful social histories of a profession is Parry and Parry's (1976) *The Rise of the Medical Profession*. The authors demonstrate how medicine has provided upward social mobility for its practitioners in Britain over the past two centuries. Two centuries ago, the recruits for medicine came from the lower end of the social structure. As medicine became more professional, its recruits came from higher up the social structure, until, in recent times, the upper middle class became the almost exclusive area from which came the recruits to British medical schools. Parry and Parry suggest that one of the major functions any profession performs is this collective upward social mobility for its members.

On an individual level also there can be little doubt that membership in a profession is an efficient method of upward social mobility. This appears to be one of the major reasons that certain occupations struggle to become professions.

If social work is to follow in the steps of medicine and recruit from higher levels as it becomes more 'established', then this has important implications for its future role in 'helping the poor and disadvantaged.'

Professionalism and the Settlement House

It is apparent from the foregoing that the move toward professionalism in the settlement house is likely to be a move away from a concern for empowerment of the powerless. Professionalism in the settlement house is more likely to lead to a greater concern for the provision of professional services. A helping model is likely to follow the treatment orientation so prevalent in the private social agency sector. Buchbinder (1981) notes that this orientation "... absorbed and reinforced the development of social work professionalization" in Canada.

This is not quite the same as reverting to the old 'do-gooding' charitable approach. The professional is not simply guided by a fuzzy warm 'wanting to help people' feeling, but by the knowledge of the profession. And that knowledge tells the professional social worker what is best for people.

Counselling is the approach *par excellence* of the professional social worker. It deals primarily with problems on an individual basis and, therefore, has a tendency to locate the problem *in the individual* rather than in the system.[6]

As with any other profession, social work will strive to maintain and increase its market. So it must be constantly labelling the people with whom it deals as 'unable.'

Community Development and the Settlement House

There is a lively tension in the Toronto settlement houses between the community development approach and the professional approach. Several of the six settlement houses do have active community development programs, working at empowerment of local powerless groups. However, it is difficult to know to what extent the tension between the two approaches has been raised to a conscious level.

It may be that through the raising of this tension to the conscious level of debate and action, the community development approach will arrest the move toward professionalism. Debate could be around questions such as: Can the professionalization of occupations, ostensibly aimed at the betterment of the human condition, be other than what it has been in the past? Can the 'helping professions' be truly helpful (to people other than themselves), or are they doomed by their very nature to work as forces for the control of the powerless and as anti-liberatory organizations?

Action could be around the encouragement of self-help initiatives among the powerless; community development workers are familiar with this kind of action. Social work professionals could provide resources and support. The latter would have to deny their claim to exclusive expertise and would have to defer to the expertise of the self-help group. Currently at Dixon Hall there are examples of this kind of joint action.

For the settlement house to become a real agent of social change, it would be necessary for the self-help initiatives to become more than peripheral activities. The settlement house itself would need to become a self-help initiative.

Some obvious ways this might be achieved are:

- Increased proportion of local, low-income people on Boards of Directors.
- An affirmative action local hiring policy, in which local low-income residents are hired for positions at all levels.
- Commitment to community development over professional service provision.
- A concern with social justice demonstrated through direct involvement in distributional issue—incomes, jobs, housing, etc.
- A rejection of charity approaches to problems of inequity.
- A willingness to take a stand on social issues and to publicize the stance.
- An affirmation that the neighbourhood approach can only be useful if it goes hand-in-hand with organizational and political development.
- Unionization of the settlement house staff—particularly the 'professionals'. For such a program to be put into action a great deal of community development work would have to be carried out by all those involved with the settlement house. Community development work can be carried out effectively by anyone willing to follow

a few basic tenets. Si Kahn (1982) points out convincingly that we all have the ability to organize at the local level. This is perhaps why community development is the best antidote to professionalism in the settlement house *milieu*.[7]

Conclusion

In sum, the history of the settlement house approach to social problems began with a mix of radical political approaches and old-style charity models. All believed that 'being there' was important in understanding the problems.

Over the years, the charity models coupled with recreationally based attempts to change values without questioning social structures. In recent years the settlement house approach has been somewhat ambivalent, pulled between professionalism on the one hand and community development approaches on the other. The former implies a move toward greater social control; the latter aims at redistribution of power and social change.

The small-scale, neighbourhood approach to social problems, as taken as the settlement houses, may be equally successful whether the final goal is social control or social change. Neighbourhoods are in a very obvious (if perhaps superficial) sense closest to grass-roots concerns. This closeness may be used to deter the development of social action for change or it may be used to foster it. Settlement houses need to make that choice!

Notes

1. For those who believe social change can be most effectively brought about at the point of production (e.g. through union organization), location in the residential neighbourhoods of workers would be seen as a conservative option, aimed at changing values rather than social structures.
2. Buchbinder (1981) discusses the influence of professionalization in the Canadian social services and its tendency toward social control.
3. McKeown (1976) and Illich (1977) muster considerable evidence to show that medicine has had little to do with the improved levels of health and increased longevity enjoyed by the West in the 20th century. Illich would, in fact, have us believe that medicine is actually inimical to good health. Yet professional medicine has done an outstanding job in convincing us that it is almost exclusively responsible for health improvements.
4. See Thomas Szasz (1961) for a fascinating discussion of the creation of mental illness by professional psychiatry.
5. See Jim Ward (1979), Chapter 4: "Rehabilitation: Helping Who?" for a discussion of labelling and consequent treatment of skid row inhabitants.

6. Corrigan and Leonard (1978) hint at ways in which the individual counselling approach can be used to raise people's awareness regarding structural problems and thus turn the blame toward the system. However, it is difficult to see this as having much effect, unless active community development initiatives follow on from the 'counselling'.
7. A major danger here is the possible professionalization of community development work. There are already college and university courses in community development, and there have recently been province-wide conferences of community development workers in Ontario. The danger is that such 'professionals' will descend on the working class communities with the result of convincing the local working class inhabitants that they know nothing about community development.

Organizing Substitute Teachers

Barry Weisleder

Supply teachers are engaged in one of the largest unionization drives currently underway in Ontario, concentrated in the Metropolitan Toronto area. For the union sponsoring the effort, the Ontario Public Service Employees Union (OPSEU), the current response from supply teachers has not only exceeded all its expectations, but has attracted to OPSEU tremendous interest and support from workers in related fields. Off-shoot organizing campaigns among English-as-a- Second Language teachers, educational assistants, night and summer school teachers, community and youth workers, and substitute teachers at community colleges and at private schools are now under consideration.

How do we explain this phenomenon, arising as it does in the midst of economic depression and social instability? How do we account for this upsurge among education sector workers in a situation characterized by cutbacks due primarily to a systematic underfunding of education by all levels of government? (A situation worsened, it should be noted, by the decision of the Ontario government in 1985 to extend full public funding to the Catholic separate school system.) In fact, those very conditions provide some of the reasons. Cutbacks in education spending, as expressed in teacher layoffs and the elimination of certain programs, have made it extremely difficult for graduates of teacher training institutions to obtain full-time teaching positions in the large metropolitan centres. Since the mid-1970s, there has accumulated a reservoir of qualified, certified and unemployed teachers. Many, like me, have never obtained a full-time position and have survived on the margins of the education system, as well as upon temporary and part-time work in a variety of fields. We are true 'Yuppies'—Young Unemployed Professionals. Educational 'yuppies', their ranks swelled by laid-off teachers, have transformed the social composition of the supply teacher milieu.

Now the majority of supply teachers, like most part-time workers in the labour market, are under 40 years of age, predominantly female, and rely on supply teaching as their sole, or at least their main, source of income. Many families are being raised on a supply teacher's wages. Often these are one-parent families, typically mother-led. As a result, there is a larger, younger supply teacher workforce. The lack of alternative employment, inside or outside education, has somewhat stabilized the pool of supply teachers.

For all these reasons, supply teachers recognize that their present career situation is not temporary; that there is little likelihood of an 'individual solution' or 'personal escape'; and that collectively supply teachers can fight more effectively for gains to make their working lives more tolerable and more rewarding. The emergence of a collective consciousness is perhaps the most significant ideological change in this sector. And a crucial factor it is! A more physically dispersed and fragmented workforce is hard to imagine. In the City of Toronto Board of Education supply teachers are called, mostly by chance, to any of the 142 schools spread across the elementary and secondary panels. Supply teachers work anywhere from zero to 194 days in the school year. In the schools we are the 'loners', socially isolated from the full-time staff, and seldom encountering more than a handful of our supply teacher colleagues even in a busy week. And in the City of Toronto Board there are over 2,000 persons on the supply teaching list.

Naturally, boards of education do not make a habit of providing lists of supply teachers' names, addresses and phone numbers to those who would organize them. The struggle to obtain this vital information is the point where every supply teacher organizing campaign begins. Because of the sporadic nature of our work, leafleting the workplaces would be, in itself, grossly insufficient. And once the information is obtained, by various and sundry creative means, the outreach effort requires an army of volunteers and back-up union staff. Intensive phoning of those on these lists is combined with large and small public meetings, use of the media, in-school contact work, and home visits. All of these measures and still others in a particular combination and tempo for each distinct school board, are required in order to reach, inform and recruit a majority of active supply teachers, and to attain union certification.

Along the road to certification there are obstacles to be circumnavigated. Unfair labour practices by the employer (e.g. restrictions on pro-union activities inside the schools during supply teachers' spare time, or intimidation and discouraging remarks by school administrators who wish to remain 'neutral') have to be dealt with both legally and politically. Interference by other organizations can become a factor. Toothless supply teacher associations, fearful of losing their raison d'etre along with cosy connections to Board bureaucrats, intervene as hostile parties. Or, as in the present situation at a number of school boards where OPSEU has been actively recruiting supply teachers since January, we witness a late and well-financed raiding operation by one of the full-time teachers' federations. With indirect support from management figures in the schools, the federations can effect considerable confusion and intimidation through 'captive audience' approaches to supply teachers—and could play a spoiler role in a unionization drive.

The sudden preoccupation of the federations with supply teachers, after years of neglect and outright refusal to give us organization and representation, is motivated, to put it bluntly, by envy and greed. Envy at the successful organizing OPSEU accomplished at Toronto last year, combined with fear that this example would not be limited to the largest school board in Canada. And greed in the form of federation ambition to control all access to substitute teaching, as well as night and summer school teaching, so as to be able to re-distribute this work to full-time teachers who suffer lay-off or who desire additional income. Naturally, most supply teachers are cool to this approach, and have no great desire to be thrown onto the welfare rolls after serving the school system (in some cases for many years).

Other obstacles to unionization manifest themselves at the Ontario Labour Relations Board—even before the certification hearing. The Toronto school board flooded its supply teaching lists with new recruits from teacher training institutions and other school boards, making it incumbent on the union to sign up as members a larger number of supply teachers in order to demonstrate majority support for unionization. Review of, and disputes over, the 'voters list' occupied weeks of time before a Labour Board examiner.

Finally, a year after OPSEU initiated its organizing campaign in Toronto, a union for supply teachers was certified in June 1983. Automatic certification was granted in the secondary panel. A vote was required in the elementary panel, and it was won handily by the union. This came a little more than two years after the first group of supply teachers in Ontario achieved union recognition—in Brant County, through OPSEU, in 1981.

But union recognition only opens the door to the next stage of struggle with the employer. Since supply teachers enter the fray with nothing but per diem pay, at the lowest step in the teacher pay grid, we have everything to gain.

An examination of the first contract settlement in Toronto, signed in February 1984 following five months of negotiations, indicates both how far we have travelled—and how much farther we must go to obtain a modicum of social and economic justice. Top priority in the first round was union security. Because of the great fluctuation and turnover in the workforce (somewhat reduced though by the rigors of economic crisis), anything negotiated today could be lost in a year or two without some kind of closed shop provision to anchor the union. Despite an ample grandfathering clause attached to it, this was only won after much effort. The newly established Local 595 also obtained customary "no discrimination" provisions, a grievance procedure, and protection against dismisal from the list for supply teachers with a minimum of seniority. In addition, supply teachers won access to their own personnel files, and the union was allocated space on school bulletin boards for posting news about union activities.

A major gain was won in the area of work distribution. Months of negotiation were spent on this point alone. Finally the Board agreed that the supply teacher list, containing over 2,300 names, would be frozen and reduced by attrition down to a figure of 1,900 (950 in each panel). As substitutes leave the field, they will be replaced on the list only up to the ceiling of 1,900—the rest who apply may go onto a waiting list. The union's goal is to further reduce the active list by attrition to afford those on it enough work to make a decent living. We are also interested in providing our students, as well as full-time teachers with whom we work, greater stability and a higher degree of professionalism from supply teacher ranks.

The new Toronto contract also struck a blow against nepotism in the elementary dispatcher system. It now requires that supply teachers must be on the list to be called and that all calls must go through a dispatcher, so that a proper record may be kept of the distribution of work and the load requirements of the system. I should add that we retained a "rotation plus request" calling procedure, so that if a particular school wants a particularly effective and familiar substitute teacher, he or she may be requested out of alphabetical turn. There is also provision for refusal of assignment with valid reason, and a requirement that the supply teacher be given at least 24 hours prior notice before any in-class evaluation of teaching by an administrator, as well as protective language on "late-calls" and reporting pay on a call-out error by a school or dispatcher.

An Employer-Employee Relations Committee was established as a forum for the negotiation of issues and disputes not covered by the collective agreement. This body meets monthly and already has a lengthy agenda.

The Toronto agreement provided for a 5 percent increase in the basic per diem. Although we negotiated a number of paid-leave benefits for Long Term Occasionals (LTOs—those on a 20-days-plus assignment in one teaching position), as well as a continuing commitment to place LTOs on the regular pay grid to reflect experience and qualifications in pay scale, we were unable to reduce the 20-day LTO threshold. As a result, most supply teachers, as daily occasionals, receive no benefits and accumulate no credit for teaching experience garnered on a day-to-day basis.

Like the 2.4 million other part-time workers in this country, the supply teachers' battle for health, pension and other benefits looms ahead. A Letter of Understanding appended to the Toronto contract states a commitment by the employer to study the cost and feasibility of providing benefits to supply teachers comparable to those enjoyed by other school board employees. But the key to success in this area will not be statistics. It will be the degree to which supply teachers are organized and united in their resolve to win benefits. And that means they must be organized at other boards of education across Metro Toronto and across the province.

This brings us back to OPSEU's supply teacher organizing campaign. Prospects are good both for the campaign, and for what it can do to transform the working conditions and rewards for our co-workers. But the massive organizing drive now developing will also act to transform the Canadian labour movement. It will bring more women into membership and leadership of our unions. It will lead unions in the direction of giving organization and representation to the growing part-time workforce. It will strengthen the economic and political self-defence capacity of the working class as a whole.

Organization of the unorganized can rejuvenate labour and help us to forge the kind of militancy and clarity required to meet the challenges of a system in deepening crisis, both at home and abroad. Most of the problems we face as working people cannot be solved in collective bargaining, even were we organized everywhere. Choices are made on regional, national and international levels of unrepresentative elites concerning vital matters of distribution of wealth, production, and social priorities. These are political choices—and working people must develop their own agenda of priorities to counter them, and effect an alternative to them. That requires political action by working people to bring about a government that acts in our interest: a government by, of and for society's majority—a workers' government.

Organization of the unorganized, especially of the exploited, long neglected, and growing part-time workforce, will be crucial to any progress in this direction.

Affirmative Action

Deirdre Gallagher

The Ontario Federation of Labour (OFL) Women's Committee had been working for a number of years around women's rights in the labour movement, particularly daycare, the right to have women's committees, struggles over policy and representation within the labour movement, and support to the struggles of women for first contracts (e.g. the Radio Shack strike and the Fleck Strike). We were an activist group within the labour movement. The struggle over daycare (described by Ronnie Leah in the previous section of this book) had resulted in victory at the OFL convention. After this experience we realized that we had developed a network and credibility within the labour movement, and that we had brought together a whole group of women who had never before worked together. We learned how to work together, and how to think about tactics and strategy. It was a very positive period in which women were coming together in a very strong way.

We were in the midst of feeling incredibly positive about our achievements when we came up against the reality of the recession. Women were getting laid off because they were the last hired/first fired. This happened at Stelco and in all kinds of other areas we saw women losing jobs. The labour movement was beginning to go on the defensive, and we were having fights and battles around concessions. The expectation was that the women's movement within the labour movement would go on the defensive; that we would have to fight just to hang on. Everyone was predicting the imminent demise of this fledgling women's movement. We felt that it wasn't possible to shunt women out of the work force, that there had been major structural changes, that we were in the workforce and the labour movement to stay, and that we weren't just going to fight a holding battle for rights that we had already won. We were going to challenge the government, the employers, and the labour movement for our full rights, regardless of the times. We weren't going to allow women to be the scapegoats of the recession—the recession would not be resolved at our cost.

This was a very heady discussion, and some people thought that our fight for affirmative action in the middle of the recession was some kind of

---

*This article is based on an interview conducted with the author in her home in Toronto by Charlene Gannagé on November 8, 1985.

madness. The program that we developed was comprehensive. We would develop a policy paper, we would debate it at a women's conference, and it would be revised before we took it to the OFL Convention. We addressed three main areas: the economy, politics and legislative change, and the labour movement. I personally had been an opponent of affirmative action and had put forward in earlier times the concept of equal pay for work of equal value as a more effective way of dealing with women's economic oppression. However, we came to understand that there needed to be programs which compensated for the type of historical exclusion and disadvantages that women experienced, so affirmative action made sense at a certain level.

We did not take the very narrow management approach to affirmative action to get only a few token women into management positions. We developed a holistic approach. A strictly economic approach, or even an affirmative action approach in and of itself, won't really address the problems. We not only needed affirmative action programs which had targets and timetables to get women into places from which they had been excluded, like Stelco and Canadian National, we also needed equal pay for work of equal value. Women in the job ghettos where the vast majority of women work would need to be properly valued in their pay. Women are both excluded and under-valued, and both issues needed to be addressed to resolve the economic issue. Systemic discrimination has to be approached in a total or holistic way because many pieces come together to form the pattern of women's oppression. We had to include the fight for childcare facilities, and contract language which included better parental rights; and later on we added the importance of reproductive rights, because that is also a part of the system that puts women at a disadvantage.

In our policy paper we had a section on analysis, looking at the different aspects of women's position in society, and a section on strategy, or how we were to go about doing this. We had a women's conference where we talked about this paper, and we changed and improved it in many ways. People debated the question of joint committees in the workplace, whether to have quotas or targets, and what this or that kind of language meant. We had to decide whether we were really differing with one another, or whether it was a difference of language. It was a very unifying caucus, a very powerful experience. We revised that document.

And then we began to organize—the political lobbying on the one hand, and the organizing within the labour movement on the other, to get women to attend the convention, and to make sure that at the convention we were ready to stand up and fight for this paper. The whole process was very educational. There is a lot of opposition to affirmative action in the labour movement and a lot of fear about seniority. We tackled the question of whether to have preferential seniority. A lot of local union women at the conference were really opposed to preferential seniority, even though the writers of the document had felt that the opposition would come from men. There were a lot of women who had seniority in their jobs, and who really believed in seniority, because they used it to their advantage in keeping jobs. The debate was really quite wonderful. It was hot and very intense. The final resolution said that in those locals or work situations where seniority was the best strategy and where the membership was won to that conception, so be it. We had to be flexible. As a labour movement we couldn't take a unilateral or across-the-board position on that particular question. Some people thought that we had copped out; they wanted to argue more strongly. Others thought that the orientation was wise because it was our first comprehensive discussion on affirmative action in the labour movement, and if seniority became the focus we could polarize men against women in a way that would be destructive to our long-term strategy.

We went on to win the labour movement at the level of policy to this action-oriented proposal. It included proposed actions like organizing regional forums across the province where women would come and make presentations and briefs: a public forum for women to come and talk about the discrimination that they experienced on the job and in their communities. We prepared a brief to organize a legislative lobby. We focussed on certain kinds of employers and organized campaigns for their workplaces. On women's roles within the labour movement there was another whole set of proposals. The one that was the most well-known was to change the OFL representation system to allow for a greater representation of women, on a proportional basis according to their numbers. That was done by a notice of motion, so that we could organize specifically for the following convention. We tested the waters first, around the issues of attacking the employers and the government, and then moved on to the question of women's position within the labour movement.

The process was very good for the women, and very good for the labour movement because we really educated people and really gave power to women. We had never organized this way in the labour movement before. We had everything: notes on how to make the arguments, and caucuses of different unions that met to figure out strategy. We had also lobbied the leadership and we had the support of some of the key leaders which we had worked for a number of years. The United Auto Workers (UAW) was committed at the leadership level to the document, as were other key unions like the Ontario Public Service Employees Union (OPSEU) and the Canadian Union of Public Employees (CUPE).

The convention fight itself was fantastic. We had twenty people lined up at all the different mikes, and women were assigned to different groups on the floor so that we could meet again and see how it was going. The motion for affirmative action passed overwhelmingly. That doesn't mean that the labour movement was overwhelmingly committed to affirmative action, but rather that we were able to exercise enough political power in this situation to win a commitment to this program.

We went on to do the work around the forums and to spread the word. It was important to organize women and for women to be organizing themselves: in the communities, and in all the unions and workplaces. We saw ourselves as having common cause with the women's movement. We wanted to work through the labour councils, and we wanted the labour councils to work with women's groups in their communities. In some places, like Sudbury, the local women's centre was responsible for the success of the event in that community, which is described below.

Women in Sudbury were already well organized. To commemorate the 100th anniversary of Sudbury, the city put out a button/logo with a picture of two male miners. The women were really annoyed because of their exclusion. They put out their own button saying "Every Miner has a Mother". The logo went on T-shirts. They went through all the mothers' and grandmothers' photo collections and got pictures of women working in Kresge's, in grocery stores, in the mines during the war—all the jobs outside the home. There were pictures of women pioneers chopping wood, and of women in the family ironing and taking care of their kids. On Mothers' Day they put up a display in the public library. Women's work and their contribution to their community was valued. The display honoured women who had never been honoured. It demonstrated the sheer imaginative, creative capacity of these women. Their affirmative action conference in October was very successful as part of the ongoing work of women in that community.

The affirmative action brief "Making up the Difference" presented by the Ontario Federation of Labour to the provincial government was an amazing example of women speaking for themselves. Even now when I read it I am moved by the courage that some of the people had to come forward, and the eloquence and anger with which some of the people spoke—their determination to fight in the midst of the recession. It was a very powerful document. It was so powerful, in fact, that it freaked out the government, and they denied everything. Afterwards they got the Human Rights Commission to phone up individual women and ask why they didn't file individual complaints if things were so bad. This was a form of harassment. We think that we live in a free society and that people can come forward and speak their point of view. But, many women risk their jobs to come forward and speak. The Women's Committee organized a counter-attack through the Federation by challenging the government. We went public and got in touch with all the women who had spoken and supported them. We immediately called a news conference and said that the women were being harassed. The government was forced to retreat.

We developed our thinking and our ability to analyze and understand as we went along. The ability to strategize, rather than focusing on issues, was being shared by more and more women at our women's conferences. The most recent women's conference was about all the different struggles that women had been engaged in. We had one panel which really captured the intent of sharing not only the content of the issues, but also how you go about fighting and being successful. Sue Genge from the library workers gave an anatomy of the Metro Toronto Library strike, and really showed how they won that strike, and how they organized: weekly bulletins to inform the membership, open negotiations, and special picket days for different ethnic groups and various support groups like the arts community. She went through the strike systematically, and we could have heard a pin drop because everyone wanted to know how to fight back.

By this time most of us know the shopping list of issues that make up the general movement; we don't have to be convinced. But we have to know how to fight. There are always things to learn, like the effects of technological change or racism, but the common concern is how to organize, how to fight. What are the tactics? How do we plan strategically? How do we build a movement? That is what people are teaching one another. It is manifested in the Eatons' Strike, and, although that has been an extremely difficult experience, anyone who is on a picket line with those women knows that feminism has had its impact on working women, and has felt the solidarity of the women's movement.

We have a social movement perspective on unionism, compared to a narrow focus on collective bargaining in the traditional way. The achievement isn't in better wages for women, even though these are much better than they were—that's not the only issue. We didn't stop women from losing jobs during the recession, but we built the movement during the recession, which is really important. We broke the bonds of the 1950s-type approach to unionism.

The women's movement is teaching, or re-teaching, a lesson to the labour movement. The labour movement couldn't have been organized if it wasn't for a social unionist perspective. The stories of building the UAW, and of the sit-down strikes of the Congress of Industrial Organizations (CIO) organizing drives, these were part of a social movement. Today there is a regaining of that spirit from the 1930s and an understanding of what our movement is all about. We look at the whole person. We look at their private life and their public life. We look at their working life and we look at their existence as an animal on this planet. All of these things belong together. People aren't made up of little compartments. It's not just our organizing of the OFL Women's Committee, but also all the other fights in our communities that have an impact on working women, because women are seen fighting and we identify with them.

A good indication of the impact of the women's movement within the labour movement was the fight for women's reproductive rights (described in Carolyn Egan's article in the previous section of this book). Everyone predicted, including myself, that this was going to be a horrendous battle. The convention was only 20 percent women and we stood there and talked about real life. That was a very moving experience, to see women standing up in front of men, talking about the lack of choices that they faced, and winning overwhelming support. We won 75 percent of the convention the first time, and even stronger majorities the second time.

There's a new mood afoot in the labour movement in Canada. Look at the way the UAW does its negotiations and its ability to speak to the community about social issues beyond the workplace. The UAW has taken a strong public position on peace and disarmament. Their negotiations around Chrysler are in the public eye and they explain why these issues are important. They talk about what's wrong with this so-called 'free-trade arrangement' with the U.S. and where that puts Canadian workers. They really engage the community. The last theme of the Labour Day parade was "We want for everyone what we want for ourselves and we want for all what we want for ourselves." That understanding comes from more of a social movement perspective, reaching out to the community.

OPSEU is engaged in a campaign around the parks. The government is privatizing, cutting back on our parks, and OPSEU is out there in the communities across the province explaining to people the consequences of the privatization of the parks. OPSEU went to agricultural fairs in little towns all over the province to talk to people. This is another example of taking up environmental issues and trying to bridge the barrier between the workplace and the community.

Another good example is solidarity. Here you've got the AFL-CIO in the U.S. supporting a Reagan foreign policy in relation to Nicaragua, while in Canada you have trade-union leaders going on trips to Nicaragua and supporting Nicaragua. As well, a very large segment of the Canadian population is progressive in terms of solidarity issues.

Immigrant workers and people of colour are beginning to organize and to express their rights. They are making us aware and conscious of how we haven't really sufficiently addressed racism. We do have racism within our movement and it has to be addressed. We have to find out why people think that way. It's not enough to just have a nice little policy on it. We have to give power to the people who don't have power. They have to lead their own struggles, with support. It's just like men not being able to lead women's struggles. They can be supportive in every single way, but the real test of whether a man supports women's rights is whether a man can support women who lead. We still have very few people of colour in the labour movement in leadership positions, or on staff.

In the case of people of colour, or immigrant workers, or people from ethnic minorities, it's very hard for them to gain power, because they are outside of the system where power is exercised. We have to make a self-conscious and concerted attempt to bridge certain barriers. There are a great number of immigrant women workers who are not organized, or who, if they are organized, are in unions that are quite weak in terms of their representation of women. These workers generally come from highly exploited sectors of the economy. There are language barriers, and cultural barriers, and just the sheer burden of work—the exploitation. People are so tired, and don't have any energy, or leisure, or money to go downtown to a meeting; all this combined together to exclude people.

We have to develop affirmative action measures to open up the labour movement to people in these situations. We need to work with women's groups, because of their growing strength in the immigrant women's community, and among women of colour, to help organize and to articulate their rights and needs. The OFL Women's Committee is planning a conference to deal with this very question of bringing women of colour and immigrant women together within the labour movement to see how we can work together.

The labour movement became, in spite of tremendous economic gains in the 1950s and 1960s, an institution that has had tremendous boundaries and walls around it. Now, the social movement of women has influenced the labour movement. The latter is more open, more aware of its common cause with different groups in the community. But there are still vestiges, and powerful vestiges, of the old-style unionism. I could give lots of examples of resistance to change: defending the institutional perogatives, not being willing to reach out, not being willing to change, being afraid of changing within our own ranks. Women who are fighting for change within the labour movement will tell you about their very difficult battles for equality. In the back rooms, the men play hard-ball. There is still an unwillingness to let women share power, and a fear—a real fear—of sharing power with women. In some ways, it is a fear of democracy itself, because women's push within the labour movement has represented a demand for a more democratic labour movement. These people who fear democracy, fear women. The CIO was a really progressive movement of workers who had to fight against the old craft-union tradition. Craft unions became privileged and institutionalized bureaucracies: job trusts that protected the privileged few. Workers in industry had to really break with the American Federation of Labour (AFL) tradition and reform the labour movement.

In many ways I see the struggle of women as like the struggle of those industrial workers—a fight to be recognized by the labour movement, and to help the labour movement to become more democratic, and by so doing to regain the kind of vital energy that labour needs. We need to organize and to fight for needed social and political changes, to fight economically with the employers, and to really build the movement. If we don't have that energy, how can we organize? What is the motive to organize? If you are in a bureaucracy and everyone is making $80,000 a year, the few people who are laid off won't bother you very much, and there is no force of energy. But, if there is democracy, then the force of energy and vitality to organize and to build the movement is present.

Abbreviations

AES	Alternative Economic Strategy
AFL	American Federation of Labour
B.C.	British Columbia
BCFL	British Columbia Federation of Labour
BCGEU	British Columbia Government Employees Union
BCTF	British Columbia Teachers Federation
B.N.A.	British North America Act
CACSW	Canadian Advisory Council on the Status of Women
CARDWO	Committee for the Advancement of the Rights of Domestic Workers
CAUT	Canadian Association of University Teachers
CCDP	Canada Community Development Projects
CCF	Cooperative Commonwealth Federation
CCU	Confederation of Canadian Unions
CEPG	Cambridge Economic Policy Group
CIO	Congress of Industrial Organizations
CLC	Canadian Labour Congress
CLRC	Canada Labour Relations Council
CNR	Canadian National Railway (Canadian Northern Railway)
CPR	Canadian Pacific Railway
CPEA	Canadian Postal Employees' Association
CPU	Council of Postal Unions
CSF	Civil Service Federation
CUPW	Canadian Union of Postal Workers
CWC	Communications and Electrical Workers of Canada
DDD	Direct Distance Dialing
D.R.E.E.	Department of Regional Economic Expansion
DS	Dining Services
ESL	English as a Second Language
GNP	Gross National Product
IBF	Immigration Branch Files
ICFTU	International Confederation of Free Trade Unions
IMF	International Metalworkers Federation
IMF	International Monetary Fund
I.D.I.A.	Industrial Disputes Investigation Act
IUE	International Union of Electrical, Radio and MachineWorkers
IWA	International Woodworkers of America
IWW	Industrial Workers of the World
LDC	Less Developed Country
LEAD	Local Employment Assistance and Development

LRDS	Labour Rights for Domestic Servants
LTO	Long-term Occasional
MDAR	Mechanized Directory Assistance Records
MLA	Member of the Legislative Assembly
MP	Member of Parliament
MPP	Member of Provincial Parliament
NDP	New Democratic Party
NEED	New Employment Expansion and Development
NIC	Newly Industrialized Country
NJC	National Joint Council
OCAC	Ontario Coalition of Abortion Clinics
OCBD	Ontario Coalition for Better Daycare
OECD	Organization for Economic Cooperation and Development
OFL	Ontario Federation of Labour
OHIP	Ontario Health Insurance Plan
OPEU	Ontario Public Service Employees Union
OPSOL	Operation Solidarity
OS	Operator Services
OWW	Organized Working Women
PAC	Public Archives of Canada
PAO	Public Archives of Ontario
P.C.	Progressive Conservative
PCSPE	Presidential Committee to Survey Philippine Education
PIPS	Professional Institute of the Public Service of Canada
PMC	Professional-Managerial Class
PSSRA	Public Service Staff Relations Act
RFR	Resources for Feminist Research
RWDSU	Retail, Wholesale and Department Store Union
SM	Senior Management
STUN	Stop the Union Now
TUC	Trades Union Congress (Great Britain)
UAW	United Auto Workers
UI	Unemployment Insurance
UIC	Unemployment Insurance Commission
USWA	United Steelworkers of America
VDT	Video Display Terminal
WC	Women's Committee
W.L.A.C.	Western Labour Arbitration Cases
YWCA	Young Women's Christian Association

Bibliography

Acheson, Shelley and C. Macleod, 1982 (April), *Parental Rights and Daycare: A Bargaining Guide for Unions,* Toronto: Ontario Federation of Labour.

Adams, Roy J., 1982, "The federal government and tripartism", *Relations Industrielles,* 37: 606-16.

Alaia, Marghereta Repetto, 1984, *The Unione Donne Italiane: Women's Liberation and the Italian Workers' Movement,* paper presented to the Sixth Berkshire Conference on the History of Women, Smith College, Northhampton, Massachusetts, June, 1984.

Alford, R., 1963, *Party and Society: The Anglo-American Democracies,* Chicago: Rand McNally.

Alford, R., 1967, "Class voting in the Anglo-American political systems", in S.M. Lipset and S. Rokkan (eds.), *Party Systems and Voter Alignments,* 67-93, New York: Free Press.

Alinsky, Saul D., 1971, *Rules for Radicals,* New York: Vintage Books.

Allen, P., 1984, "The class imagery of 'traditional proletarians'", *British Journal of Sociology,* Vol. XXXV, No. 1 (March).

Anderson, G., 1966, "Voting behaviour and the ethnic-religious variable", *Canadian Journal of Economics and Political Science,* Vol. 32, No. 1: 27-33.

Anderson, Perry, 1980, *Arguments Within English Marxism,* London: Verso Books.

Armstrong, Pat and Hugh Armstrong, 1978, *The Double Ghetto,* Toronto: McClelland and Stewart.

Armstrong, Pat and Hugh Armstrong, 1983 (February), *A Working Majority: What Women Must Do for Pay,* Ottawa: Canadian Advisory Council on the Status of Women (CACSW).

Baggaley, Carman D., 1981, *A Century of Labour Regulation in Canada,* Ottawa: Economic Council of Canada.

Bahro, R., 1982, *Socialism and Survival,* London: Heretic Press.

Banfield, Edward, 1958, *The Moral Order of a Backward Society,* Glencoe, Illinois: Free Press.

Barnes, L.W.C.S., 1974, *Consult and Advise: A History of the National Joint Council of the Public Service of Canada, 1944-1974,* Kingston: Industrial Relations Centre, Queen's University.

Barrett, Michele and Mary McIntosh, 1982. *The Anti-Social Family,* London: Verso.

Baudelot, Christian *et al.,* 1974, *La Petite Bourgeoisie en France,* Paris: Francois Maspero.

BCFL (British Columbia Federation of Labour), 1983, *Federation,* Executive Council Minutes, July 15.

Bell, Rudolph, 1979, *Fate and Honour, Family and Village: Demographic and Cultural Change in Rural Italy since 1800*, Chicago: Chicago University Press.

Blake, D., 1985, *Two Political Worlds*, Vancouver: University of British Columbia Press.

Blauner, R., 1960, 'Work satisfaction and industrial trends in modern society', in W. Galenson and S.M. Lipset (eds.), *Labour and Trade Unionism*, 339-60, New York: Wiley.

Blauner, R., 1964, *Alienation and Freedom: The Factory Worker and His Industry*, Chicago: University of Chicago Press.

Bluestone, Barry and Bennett Harrison, 1980, "Why corporations close profitable plants", *Working Papers for a New Society*, Vol. 7: 15-23.

Bluestone, Barry and Bennett Harrison, 1982, *The Deindustrialization of America*, New York: Basic Books.

Bodnar, John, 1976, "Immigration and modernization: the case of Slavic peasants in industrial America", *Journal of Social History* 10 (Fall).

Bott, E., 1957, *Family and Social Network*, London: Tavistock.

Bowles, S., D. Gordon, and T. Weisskopf, 1983, *Beyond the Waste Land*, New York: Anchor / Doubleday.

Braverman, Harry, 1974, *Labour and Monopoly Capital*, New York: Monthly Review Press.

Bravo, Ann, 1982, "Solidarity and loneliness: Piedmontese peasant women at the turn of the century", *International Journal of Oral History*, Vol. 3, No. 2 (June).

Brint, S., 1985, "The political attitudes of professionals", *Annual Review of Sociology* 11: 389-414.

Briskin, Linda, 1983a, "Women and unions in Canada: a statistical overview", in L. Briskin and L. Yanz (eds.), *Union Sisters*, Toronto: Women's Press.

Briskin, Linda, 1983b, "Women's challenge to organized labour", in L. Briskin and L. Yanz (eds.), *Union Sisters*, Toronto: Women's Press.

Brogger, Jan, 1971, *Montavarese: A Study of Peasant Society and Culture in Southern Italy*, Oslo: Bergen Universitetsforlaget / Scandinavian University Books.

Brown, Douglas and Julia Eastman, with Ian Robinson, 1981, *The Limits of Consultation: A Debate Among Ottawa, the Provinces and the Private Sector on Industrial Strategy*, Ottawa: Science Council of Canada.

Bruce-Biggs, B., 1979, *The New Class?*, New Brunswick, N. J.: Transaction Books.

Bryden, Kenneth, 1974, *Old Age Pensions and Policy Making in Canada*, Montreal: McGill-Queen's University Press.

Buchbinder, Howard, 1981, "Inequality and the social services", in *Inequality: Essays on the Political Economy of Social Welfare*, Toronto: University of Toronto Press.

Calvert, John, 1984, *Government Limited*, Ottawa: Canadian Centre for Policy Alternatives.

Canadian Gallup Poll, 1985, "Canadians losing respect for business, the church, parliament, Gallup says", *Toronto Star*, January 14, p. 2.

Center for Industrial Relations, 1985, *The Current Industrial Relations Scene in Canada,* Kingston: Queen's University.

Centers, R., 1949, *The Psychology of Social Classes,* Princeton: Princeton University Press.

Chamberlain, C., 1983, *Class Consciousness in Australia,* Sydney: Allen and Unwin.

Choldin, Harvey, 1973, "Kinship networks in the migration process", *International Migration Review* 7 (Summer).

Christian, W. and C. Campbell, 1974, *Political Parties and Ideologies in Canada,* Toronto: McGraw-Hill Ryerson.

Clark, Robert M., 1960, *Economic Security for the Aged in the United States and Canada,* Volume II, Ottawa: Minister of National Health and Welfare.

Clarke, H. *et al.*, 1979, *Political Choice in Canada,* Toronto: McGraw-Hill Ryerson.

Clement, Wallace, 1981, *Hardrock Mining,* Toronto: McClelland and Stewart.

Coburn, D. and V. Edwards, 1976, "Objective and subjective socio-economic status: intercorrelations and consequences", *Canadian Review of Sociology and Anthropology* 13: 178-88.

Cohen, Miriam, 1977, "Italian-American women in New York City, 1900-1950", in Milton Cantor and Bruce Laurie (eds.), *Class, Sex, and the Woman Worker,* Westport, Connecticut: Greenwood Press.

Colley, Sue, 1981, "Day Care and the trade union movement in Ontario", *Resources for Feminist Research,* Vol. X, No. 2, Part 2 (July): 29-31.

Colley, Sue, 1983, "Free universal Day Care: the OFL takes a stand", in L. Briskin and L. Yanz, *Union Sisters,* Toronto: Women's Press.

Cornelisen, Ann, 1976, *Women of the Shadows: A Study of the Wives and Mothers of Southern Italy,,* New York: Vintage Books.

Corrigan, Paul and Peter Leonard, 1978, *Social Work Practice Under Capitalism,* London: Macmillan.

Cottrell, W.F., 1951, "Death by dieselization: A case study in the reaction to technological change", *American Sociological Review,* Vol. 16: 358-65.

Cousins, J. and R. Brown, 1975, "Patterns of paradox: Shipbuilding workers' images of society", in M. Bulmer (ed.), *Working-Class Images of Society,* London: Routledge and Kegan Paul.

Craven, Paul, 1980, *'An Impartial Umpire': Industrial Relations and the Canadian State 1900-1911,* Toronto: University of Toronto Press.

Crombie, S., 1986, "Life of the party: the Ontario NDP prepares for its convention", *Our Times,* Vol. 5, No. 4 (June).

Cronin, Constance, 1970, *The Sting of Change: Sicilians in Sicily and Australia,* Chicago: Chicago University Press.

Crozier, Michel, 1964, *The Bureaucratic Phenomenon,* Chicago: University of Chicago Press.

Cuneo, C., 1979, "State, class and reserve labour", *Canadian Review of Sociology and Anthropology,* Vol. 15, No. 3.

Cuneo, C., 1980, "State mediation of class contradictions in Canadian unemployment insurance", *Studies in Political Economy*, No. 3.

CUPE (Canadian Union of Public Employees), 1977 (December), *Brief to the Royal Commission on the Status of Pensions in Ontario*, Brief No. 101, Ontario Archives.

CUPW, *National Policies*, various years.

CUPW, *National Constitution.*

CUPW, "Management Programs. What has Changed?", May-June 1982.

Davidson, Joe and John Deverell, 1978, *Joe Davidson*, Toronto: James Lorimer and Company.

Davis, John, 1973, *Land and Family in Pisticci*, London: University of London Athlone Press.

Derber, Charles, 1982, "Managing professionals: ideological proletarianization and mental labour", in Charles Derber (ed.), *Professionals as Workers: Mental Labour in Advanced Capitalism*, Boston: G.K. Hall and Co.

Dickinson, J., 1985, "From poor law to social insurance", in J. Dickinson and B. Russell (eds.), *Family, Economy and State*, London: Croom-Helm.

Dominion of Canada, 1971, *House of Commons Debates*, Ottawa.

Dominion of Canada, 1976, *House of Commons Debates*, Ottawa.

Economic Council of Canada, 1976, *People and Jobs: A Study of the Canadian Labour Market*, Ottawa: Information Canada.

Economist Intelligence Unit, 1982, "Britain's jobless: No bright road from Wigan Pier", *The Economist*, Vol. 285, No. 7266 (December 4): 29-30.

Edwards, Richard, 1979, *Contested Terrain: The Transformation of the Workplace in the Twentieth Century*, New York: Basic Books.

Egan, Carolyn and L. Yanz, 1983, "Building links: labour and the women's movement", in L. Briskin and L. Yanz (eds.), *Union Sisters*, Toronto: Women's Press.

Ehrenreich, John and Barbara Ehrenreich, 1978, "The professional-managerial class", in Pat Walker (ed.), *Between Labor and Capital*, Montreal: Black Rose Books.

Eleen, John W. and Ashley G. Bernadine, *Shutdown: The Impact of Plant Shutdown, Extensive Employment Terminations and Layoffs on the Workers and the Community*, Ottawa: Ontario Federation of Labour, Canadian Labour Council.

Engelmann, F. and M. Schwartz, 1975, *Canadian Political Parties: Origin, Character, Impact*, Scarborough: Prentice-Hall.

Erickson, B., 1981, "Region, knowledge, and class voting in Canada", *Canadian Journal of Sociology*, Vol. 6, No. 2 (Spring): 121-44.

Finkel, A., 1979, *Business and Social Reform in the Thirties*, Toronto: Lorimer.

Finkelman, Jacob and Shirley B. Goldenberg, 1983, *Collective Bargaining in the Public Service: The Federal Experience in Canada*, 2 volumes, Montreal: The Institute for Research on Public Policy.

Flora, P. and A. Heidenheimer, 1981, *The Development of Welfare States in Europe and America*, New Brunswick, New Jersey: Transaction Books.

Frager, Ruth, 1983, "Women workers and the Canadian labour movement, 1879-1940", in L. Briskin and L. Yanz, *Union Sisters*, Toronto: Women's Press.

Frankel, Saul J., 1962, *Staff Relations in the Civil Service*, Montreal: McGill University Press.

Freeman, Audrey, 1980, "Plant closed — no jobs", *Across the Board*, Vol. 17 (August): 12-18.

Furio, Columba, 1980, "The cultural background of the Italian immigrant woman and its impact on her unionization in the New York City garment industry", in G. Pozzetta (ed.), *Pane and Lavoro, The Italian American Working Class*, Toronto: Multicultural History Society of Toronto.

Gabaccia, Donna, 1984, "Sicilian women and the 'marriage market': 1860-1920", paper presented to the Sixth Berkshire Conference on the History of Women, Smith College, Northhampton, Massachusetts, June, 1984.

Gallie, D., 1983, *Social Inequality and Class Radicalism in France and Britain*, Cambridge: Cambridge University Press.

Gans, H.J., 1962, *Urban Villagers*, New York: Free Press.

Giles, Anthony, 1982, "The Canadian Labour Congress and Tripartism", *Relations Industrielles*, 37.

Glynn, Andrew, 1982, "The Cambridge Economic Policy Group and profits", *Socialist Economic Review*.

Goldthorpe, J., D. Lockwood, F. Bechhofer and J. Platt, 1969, *The Affluent Worker in the Class Structure*, Cambridge: Cambridge University Press.

Gonick, C., 1975, *Inflation or Depression*, Toronto: Lorimer.

Gordon, David, Richard Edwards and Michael Reich, 1982, *Segmented Work, Divided Workers*, New York: Cambridge University Press.

Gorz, Andre, 1982, *Farewell to the Working Class*, London: Pluto Press.

Gough, I., 1972, "Productive and unproductive labor in Marx", *New Left Review*, 76 (November-December).

Gough, I., 1980, *Political Economy of the Welfare State*, London: Macmillan.

Gouldner, Alvin, 1979, *The Future of the Intellectuals and the Rise of the New Class*, New York: The Seabury Press.

Goyder, J. and P. Pineo, 1979, "Social class self-identification", in J. Curtis and W. Scott (eds.), *Social Stratification: Canada*, Scarborough: Prentice-Hall.

Gramsci, A., 1971, *Selections From the Prison Notebooks*, New York: International Publishers.

Gray, Stan, 1982, "The case of Terry Ryan", *Canadian Dimension*, Vol. 16, No. 7 and 8.

Gray, Stan, 1984, "Counting bodies at Mack Truck", *Our Times*, July/August.

Gross, N., 1953, "Social class identification in an urban community", *American Sociological Review* 18 (August): 398-404.

Guest, D., 1980, *The Emergence of Social Security in Canada*, Vancouver: University of British Columbia Press.

Hazelrigg, L., 1973, "Aspects of the measurement of class consciousness", in M. Armes and A. Grimshaw (eds.), *Comparative Social Research*, 219-47, New York: John Wiley.

Heeney, Arnold, 1959, *Report on Personnel Administration in the Public Service*, Ottawa: Civil Service Commission.

Heeney, Arnold, 1965, *Report of the Preparatory Committee on Collective Bargaining in the Public Service*, Ottawa: Queen's Printer.

Hekman, J.S. and J.S. Strong, 1980, "Is there a case for plant closing laws?", *New England Economic Review*, July/August: 34-51.

Hellman, Judith Adler, 1985, "The Italian Communists, the woman's question, and the challenge of feminists", *Studies in Political Economy* 13 (Spring).

Heron, C., 1983, "The ballot box blues: Canadian labour and politics", *Canadian Dimension*, Vol. 17, No. 3 (July): 27-31.

Hiller, P., 1973, "The subjective dimension of social stratification: the case of the self-identification question", *The Australian and New Zealand Journal of Sociology* 9: 14-21.

Hiscott, Robert D., 1982, *Manufacturing Plant Closures and Labour Displacement: A Case-Study of the Beach Appliances Plant Closure*. Paper presented at the Annual Meeting of the Canadian Sociology and Anthropology Association, Ottawa, Ontario, June 6-9, 1982.

Hiscott, Robert D., 1983, *Social Consequences of a Plant Closure — The Experiences of Displaced Beach Appliance Workers*. Paper presented at the Annual Meeting of the Canadian Sociology and Anthropology Association, Vancouver, B.C., June 1-4, 1983.

Horowitz, Gad, 1968, *Canadian Labour in Politics*, Toronto: University of Toronto Press.

Hunter, A., 1981, *Class Tells*, Toronto: Butterworth.

Hunter, A., 1982, "On class, status, and voting in Canada", *Canadian Journal of Sociology*, Vol. 7, No. 1 (Winter): 19-39.

Illich, Ivan, 1977, *Limits to Medicine*, Harmondsworth: Penguin.

Illich, Ivan *et al.*, 1978, *The Disabling Professions*, London: Marion Boyars.

Jackman, M. and R. Jackman, 1983, *Class Awareness in the United States*, Berkeley: University of California Press.

Jamieson, Stuart, 1968, *Times of Trouble: Labour Unrest and Industrial Conflict in Canada, 1900-1966*, Ottawa: Study No. 22 for the Task Force on Labour Relations.

Johnson, Laura C., with Robert Johnson, 1982, *The Seam Allowance: Industrial Home Sewing in Canada*, Toronto: Women's Press.

Johnson, Richard, 1978, "Thompson, Genovese, and Socialist-Humanist History", *History Workshop Journal*, 6 (Autumn): 79-100.

Kahn, Si, 1982, *Organizing: A Guide for Grassroots Leaders*, New York: McGraw Hill

Kealey, Gregory S. (ed.), 1973, *Canada Investigates Industrialism*, Toronto: University of Toronto Press.

Kealey, Gregory S., 1980, *Toronto Workers Respond to Industrial Capitalism, 1867-1892*, Toronto: University of Toronto Press.

Keddie, V., 1980, "Class identification and party preference among manual workers", *Canadian Review of Sociology and Anthropology*, Vol. 17, No. 1.

Kornberg, A. *et al.*, 1982, *Representative Democracy in the Canadian Provinces*, Toronto: Prentice-Hall.

Korpi, W., 1983, *The Democratic Class Struggle*, London: Routledge and Keagan Paul.

Kwavnick, David, 1972, *Organized Labour and Pressure Politics: The Canadian Labour Congress, 1956-68*, Montreal: McGill-Queen's University Press.

Lambert, R. and A. Hunter, 1979, "Social stratification, voting behaviour, and the images of Canadian federal political parties", *Canadian Review of Sociology and Anthropology* 16: 287-304.

Lash, S., 1984, *The Militant Worker: Class and Radicalism in France and America*, London: Heinemann Educational Books.

Latimer, Murray Webb, 1932, *Industrial Pension Systems in the United States and Canada*, Volume I, New York: Industrial Relations Counselors.

Leah, Ronnie, 1981, "Women's labour force participation and Day Care cutbacks in Ontario", *Atlantis*, Vol. 7, No. 1 (Fall): 36-44.

Legendre, Camille and Jacques Dofny (in collaboration with Alain Guenette, Lucie Lapointe and Nancy Thede), 1982, *Catastrophe dans une mine d'or. Etude sur le milieu minier quebecois*, 219 pages, Quebec: Ministere des Communications, Gouvernment du Quebec.

Leggett, J., 1969, *Class, Race and Labor*, New York: Oxford University Press.

Leggett, J., 1979, "The persistence of working class consciousness in Vancouver", in J. Fry (ed.), *Economy, Class and Social Reality*, 241-62, Toronto: Butterworths.

Levi, Carl, 1947, *Christ Stopped at Eboli* (translated by Frances Frenaye), New York: Farrar, Straus and Giroux.

Lilley, Wayne, 1982, "The untimely end of Admiral", *Canadian Business*, Vol. 41 (June): 41-92.

Lipietz, Alain, 1982, "Toward global Fordism?", *New Left Review* 132 (March-April).

Lipset, S. and D. Schneider, 1983, *The Confidence Gap: Business, Labor and Government in the Public Mind*, New York: Free Press.

Livingstone, D.W., 1978, *Public Attitudes Toward Education In Ontario 1978*, Toronto: Ontario Institute for Studies in Education (OISE) Press.

Livingstone, D.W., 1985, *Social Crisis and Schooling*, Toronto: Garamond.

Livingstone, D.W. and D.J. Hart, 1981, *Public Attitudes Toward Education 1980*, Toronto: OISE Press.

Livingstone, D.W., D.J. Hart and L. McLean, 1983, *Public Attitudes Toward Education in Ontario 1982*, Toronto: OISE Press.

Livingstone, D.W., D.J. Hart and L.E. Davie, 1985, *Public Attitudes Toward Education in Ontario 1984*, Toronto: OISE Press.

Livingstone, D.W., (forthcoming), *Class and Class Consciousness in Advanced Capitalism.*

Lockwood, D., 1966, "Sources of variation in working-class images of society", *Sociological Review* 14: 249-56.

Logan, H.A., 1948, *Trade Unions in Canada: Their Development and Functioning*, Toronto: The Macmillan Company of Canada Ltd.

Lopreato, Joseph, 1967, *Peasants No More: Social Class and Social Change in an Underdeveloped Society*, San Francisco: Scranton Chandler Publishing Company.

Low-Beer, J., 1978, *Protest and Participation: The New Working-Class in Italy*, Cambridge: Cambridge University Press.

Luxton, Meg, 1980, *More Than a Labour of Love*, Toronto: Women's Press.

McBride, Stephen, 1983, "Public policy as a determinant of interest group behaviour: The Canadian Labour Congress' Corporatist Initiative, 1976-1978", *Canadian Journal of Political Science*, Vol. XVI, No. 3: 501-17.

MacDonald, L.D. and J.S. MacDonald, 1964, "Chain migration, ethnic neighborhood formation and social network", *Millbank Memorial Fund Quarterly* 13.

MacDowell, Laura Sefton, 1978, "The formation of the Canadian industrial relations system during World War II", *Labour: Journal of Canadian Labour Studies*, 3: 175-96.

MacKay, H., 1983, "Social impact of unemployment", *Perception*, Vol. 6, No. 5: 33.

McKay, Ian, 1983, "Strikes in the Maritimes, 1901-1914", *Acadiensis*, Vol. 13, No. 1.

Mackenzie, G., 1973, *The Aristocracy of Labour*, Cambridge: Cambridge University Press.

Mackenzie, G., 1975, "World images and the world of work", in G. Esland, G. Salaman and M. Speakman (eds.), *People and Work*, 170-85, Open University Press (Great Britain).

McKeown, Thomas, 1976, *The Role of Medicine: Dream, Mirage or Nemesis?*, London: Nuffield Provincial Hospitals Trust.

McKersie, Robert B., 1980, "Plant closed — no jobs", *Across the Board*, Vol. 17 (November): 12-16.

McLeod Arnopolous, Sheila, 1979, *Problems of Immigrant Women in the Canadian Labour Force*, Ottawa: Canadian Government.

McQuaig, Linda, 1983, "The high-tech job threat", *Maclean's*, May 16.

McVittie, James, 1984, *The Canada Labour Relations Council,* unpublished manuscript, University of Western Ontario (January).

Magnusson, W. *et al.,* 1984, *The New Reality,* Vancouver: New Star Books.

Mahon, Rianne, 1983, "Canadian labour in the battle of the eighties", *Studies in Political Economy,* 11: 168-89.

Manga, Pran, Robert Broyles, and Gil Reschenthaler, 1981, *Occupational Health and Safety,* Ottawa: Economic Council of Canada.

Mann, M., 1973, *Consciousness and Action among the Western Working Class,* London: Macmillan.

March, James G. and Herbert A. Simon, 1958, *Organizations,* New York: John Wiley and Sons, Inc.

Marchak, Patricia, 1981, *Ideological Perspectives on Canada* (second edition), Toronto: McGraw-Hill Ryerson.

Marchak, Patricia, 1983, *Green Gold: The Forest Industry in British Columbia,* Vancouver: University of British Columbia Press.

Marcuse, Herbert, 1964, *One-Dimensional Man,* London: Routledge and Kegan Paul.

Martin, Andrew and George Ross, 1980, "European trade unions and the economic crisis: perceptions and strategies", *Western European Politics,* Vol. 3, No. 1 (January): 33-67.

Marx, Karl, 1973, *Capital,* Vol. I, New York: International Publishers.

Marx, Karl, 1975, *Theories of Surplus-Value,* Vol. I, Moscow: Progress Publishers.

Marx, Karl and Frederick Engels, 1964, *The Communist Manifesto,* New York: Monthly Review Press.

Maslove, Allan M. and Gene Swimmer, 1980, *Wage Controls in Canada, 1975-78: A Study of Public Decision Making,* Montreal, Institute for Research on Public Policy.

Matthews, R. and J.C. Davis, 1985, "The comparative influence of region, status, class and ethnicity on Canadian attitudes and values", in R. Brym (ed.), *Regionalism in Canada,* Toronto: Irwin Publishing.

Meiksins, Peter, 1981, "Productive and unproductive labor and Marx's theory of class", *Review of Radical Political Economics,* Vol. 13, No. 3 (Fall): 32-42.

Meisel, J., 1975 (second edition), *Working Papers on Canadian Politics,* Montreal: McGill-Queen's University Press.

Metzgar, Jack, 1980, "Plant Shutdowns and Worker Response: The Case of Johnstown, PA", *Socialist Review,* Vol. 10, No. 53: 9-49.

Michels, R., 1959, *Political Parties,* New York: Dover Books.

Mick, Stephen S., 1975, "Social and personal costs of plant shutdowns", *Industrial Relations,* Vol. 14 (May): 203-08.

Miliband, R., 1969, *The State in Capitalist Society,* London: Weidenfeld and Nicolson.

Miliband, R., 1973, *Parliamentary Socialism,* London: Marlin.

Mills, C. Wright, 1956, *White Collar*, New York: Oxford University Press.

Moorhouse, J., 1976, "Attitudes toward class and class relationships in Britain", *Sociology*, Vol. 10, No. 3: 469-96.

Morton, Desmond, 1977, "Taking on the Grand Trunk: the Locomotive Engineers Strike of 1876-77", *Labour*, Vol. 2.

Mountjoy, Alan B., 1973, *The Mezzogiorno*, London: Oxford University Press.

Myles, J., 1979, "Differences in the Canadian and American class vote: Fact or pseudofact?", *American Journal of Sociology*, Vol. 84, No. 5: 1232-37.

Myles, J. and D. Forcese, 1981, "Voting and class politics in Canada and the United States", in R. Tomasson (ed.), *Comparative Social Research* (Vol. 4), 3-31, New York: JAI Press Inc.

National Council of Welfare, 1982, *Financing the Canada Pension Plan*, Ottawa: Mimeo.

Newman, P., 1986, "A disquieting mood", *Maclean's*, Vol. 90, No. 1 (January): 12-13.

Nightingale, Donald, 1982, *Workplace Democracy*, Toronto: University of Toronto Press.

Nuti, D.M., 1972, "On incomes policy", in E.K. Hunt and J.G. Schwartz, *A Critique of Economic Theory*, Harmondsworth: Penguin.

Oakley, Ann, 1981, "Interviewing women: a contradiction in terms", in Helen Roberts (ed.), *Doing Feminist Research*, London: Routledge and Kegan Paul.

O'Connor, J., 1973, *Fiscal Crisis of the State*, New York: St. Martins Press.

O'Connor, J., 1984, *Accumulation Crisis*, Oxford: Basil Blackwell.

Ogmundson, R., 1975a, "On the measurement of party class positions: The case of Canadian federal political parties", *Canadian Review of Sociology and Anthropology* 12 (November): 565-76.

Ogmundson, R., 1975b, "On the use of party image variables to measure the distinctiveness of a class vote: the Canadian case", *Canadian Journal of Sociology*, Vol. 1, No. 2: 169-78.

Ogmundson, R., 1976, "Mass-elite linkages and class issues in Canada", *Canadian Review of Sociology and Anthropology*, Vol. 13, No 1: 1-12.

Ogmundson, R., 1980, "Liberal ideology and the study of voting behaviour", *Canadian Review of Sociology and Anthropology*, Vol. 17, No. 1: 45-54.

Ogmundson, R. and M. Ng, 1982, "On the inference of voter motivation: A comparison of the subjective class vote in Canada and the United Kingdom", *Canadian Journal of Sociology*, Vol. 7, No. 1 (Winter): 41-59.

Olson, Laura Katz, 1982, *The Political Economy of Aging*, New York: Columbia University Press.

Ontario, 1980, *Royal Commission on the Status of Pensions in Ontario*, Vol. 5, Toronto: Queen's Printer.

Ontario, 1981, *Women in the Labour Force: Labour Unions*, Toronto: Women's Bureau of the Ontario Ministry of Labour.

Ontario, 1982, *Women in the Labour Force: Child Care*, Toronto: Women' Bureau of the Ontario Ministry of Labour.

Ontario Federation of Labour:
Correspondence [Uncatalogued].
____ *Ontario Labour*, Nov.-Dec., 1980.
____ *Report of Proceedings of the 22nd Annual Convention*, Tor: OFL, 1978.
____ *Report of Proceedings of the 23rd Annual Convention*, Tor: OFL, 1979.
____ *Report of Proceedings of the 24th Annual Convention*, Tor: OFL, 1980.
____ "Statement on Women," 19th Annual OFL Convention, Nov. 1975.
____ "A Woman's Place is in her Union," 22nd Annual OFL Convention, Nov. 1978.
____ "Statement on Day Care," 24th Annual OFL Convention, Nov. 1980.
____ "Statement on Women and Affirmative Action," 25th Annual OFL Convention; No.1982.
____ "Report of the First OFL Women's Conference: Bargaining for Equality," April 1979.
____ "Resolutions," 23rd Annual OFL Convention, Nov. 1979.
____ "Report of the OFL Conference on Day Care: Sharing the Caring," Oct. 1980.

Ornstein, M., 1985, "Canadian capital and the Canadian state: Ideology in an era of crisis", in R. Brym (ed.), *The Structure of the Canadian Capitalist Class*, Toronto: Garamond Press.

Ornstein, M. *et al.*, 1980, "Region, class and political culture in Canada", *Canadian Journal of Political Science*, Vol. XIII, No. 2 (June): 227-71.

OWW (Organized Working Women), 1980, *Union Woman*, November 19.

Oulett, Andre, 1983, *Labour and Labour Issues in the 1980's: Presentation to the MacDonald Royal Commission on the Economic Union and Development Prospects for Canada*, Ottawa: Labour Canada.

Palmer, Bryan D., 1983, *Working Class Experience: The Rise and Reconstitution of Canadian Labour, 1800-1980*, Toronto: Butterworth and Co.

Panitch, Leo and Donald Swartz, 1983, "The economic crisis and the transformation of industrial relations in Canada", *CAUT Bulletin*, December: 21-25.

Panitch, Leo and Donald Swartz, 1984, "Towards permanent exceptionalism: coercion and consent in Canadian industrial relations", *Labour/Le Travail*, 13 (Spring): 133-57.

Parkin, F., 1972, *Class Inequality and Political Order*, London: Paladin.

Parrot, Jean-Claude, 1983, "Jean-Claude Parrot: an interview", *Studies in Political Economy*, No. 11 (Summer): 49-70.

Parry, N.C.A. and J. Parry, 1976, *The Rise and Fall of the Medical Profession: A Study in Collective Social Mobility*, London: Croom Helm.

Pentland, H.C., 1950, "The role of capital in Canadian economic development before 1875", *The Canadian Journal of Economics and Political Science*, Vol. 16 (November).

Perrow, Charles, 1979, *Complex Organizations: A Critical Essay*, 2nd edition, Glenview, Illinois: Scott, Foresman and Company.

Phillips, Gerald E., 1977, *The Practice of Labour Relations and Collective Bargaining in Canada*, Toronto: Butterworth.

Phizacklea, Annie (ed.), 1983, *One Way Ticket: Migration and Female Labour*, London: Routledge and Kegan Paul.

Pickvance, C.G. (ed.), 1976, *Urban Sociology: Critical Essays*, London: Tavistock.

PIPS, *By-Laws*, various years.

PIPS, *National Constitution.*

PIPS, *Serving the State II*, brief for presentation to the Parliament of Canada, October 1980.

PIPS, *Serving the State III*, a brief for presentation to the Parliament of Canada, November 1981.

PIPS, Submission to the Special Joint Committee of the Senate and the House of Commons on Employer-Employee Relations in the Public Service of Canada, December 1974.

Piva, Michael J., 1979, *The Condition of the Working Class in Toronto, 1900-1921*, Ottawa: University of Ottawa Press.

Piven, R. and R. Cloward, 1982, *The New Class War*, New York: Pantheon.

Platt, J., 1971, "Variations in answers to different questions on perceptions of class", *Sociological Review* 19.

Popitz, H., H. Bahrdt, E. Juares and G.A. Kestin, 1969, "The workers' image of society", in Tom Burns (ed.), *Industrial Man*, London: Penguin.

Porter, J., 1965, *The Vertical Mosaic*, Toronto: University of Toronto Press.

Poulantzas, Nicos, 1974, *Les Classes Sociales Dans le Capitalisme Aujourd'hui*, Paris: Editions du Seuil.

Prandy, Kenneth, 1965, *Professional Employees*, London: Faber and Faber Ltd.

Reich, Robert, 1983, *The Next American Frontier*, New York: Times Books.

Riebeneck, M., 1905, *Railway Provident Institutions*, Philadelphia: Pennsylvania Railroad Company.

Rimlinger, G., 1973, *Welfare Policy and Industrialization in Europe, America and Russia*, New York: Wiley.

Rinehart, James W., 1975, *The Tyranny of Work*, Don Mills, Ontario: Academic Press Canada.

Rinehart, James W., 1984, "Appropriating workers' knowledge: Quality control circles at a General Motors Plant", *Studies in Political Economy*, No. 13 (Summer): 75-97.

Rinehart, J. and I. Okraku, 1974, "A study of class consciousness", *Canadian Review of Sociology and Anthropology*, Vol. 11, No. 3: 197-213.

Root, Kenneth A., 1979 (October), *Perspectives for Communities and Organizations on Plant Closings — and Job Dislocations*, Ames, Iowa: Iowa State University.

Roszak, Theodore, 1973, *Where the Wasteland Ends: Politics and Transcendence in the Post-Industrial Society*, London: Faber.

Russell, B., 1984a, "The politics of labour force reproduction", *Studies in Political Economy*, No. 14.

Russell, B., 1984b, *State, Household and Economy in the Reproduction of Labour Power*, Ph.D. dissertation, Department of Sociology, State University of New York—Binghamton.

Sabel, Charles, 1982, *Work and Politics: The Division of Labor in Industry*, Cambridge: Cambridge University Press.

Sangster, J. 1981, "Women and unions: a review of historical research", *Resources for Feminist Research*, Vol. X, No. 2 (July): 2-6.

Schlozman, K.L. and S. Verba, 1979, *Injury to Insult: Unemployment, Class and Political Response*, Cambridge: Harvard University Press.

Schreiber, E.M., 1980, "Class awareness and class voting in Canada", *Canadian Review of Sociology and Anthropology*, Vol. 17, No. 1: 37-44.

Schwartz, M., 1974, "Canadian voting behaviour", in R. Rose (ed.), *Electoral Behaviour: A Comparative Handbook*, New York: Free Press.

Sennett, Richard, 1971, *The Uses of Disorder*, New York: Vantage.

Shakeel, G. Sabir, 1980 (August), *Annual Review of Known Permanent and Indefinite Layoffs Involving 25 or More Employees*, Toronto: Ontario Ministry of Labour.

Shultz, George P. and Arnold R. Weber, 1966, *Strategies for the Displaced Worker*, New York: Harper and Row.

Sidlofsky, Samuel, 1969, *Post-War Immigrants in the Changing Metropolis with Special Reference to Toronto's Italian Population*, unpublished PhD dissertation, Department of Sociology, University of Toronto.

Slaughter, M. Jane, 1984, "Women's politics and women's culture: the case of women in the Italian resistance", paper presented to the Sixth Berkshire Conference on the History of Women, Smith College, Northhampton, Massachusetts, June, 1984.

Smith, Dorothy, 1981, "Women and trade unions: the U.S. and British experience", *Resources for Feminist Research*, Vol. X, No. 2 (July): 53-60.

Smucker, Joseph, 1980, *Industrialization in Canada*, Scarborough (Ontario): Prentice-Hall.

Social Planning Council of Metro Toronto, 1980 (September), *Metro's Suburbs in Transition: Part II*, Toronto: Social Planning Council.

Statistics Canada, 1976, *Social Security: National Programs*, Ottawa: Information Canada.

Statistics Canada, 1978, *Social Security: National Programs*, Ottawa: Information Canada.

Steindl, J., 1976, *Maturity and Stagnation in American Capitalism*, New York: Monthly Review Press.

Stern, James L., 1971, "Consequences of a plant closure", *The Journal of Human Resources*, Vol. 7, No. 1: 3-25.

Stern, Robert and Tove Hammer, 1978, "Buying your job: Factors affecting the success or failure of employee acquisition attempts", *Human Relations*, Vol: 31, No. 12: 1101-17.

Stern, Robert, K. Wood and Tove Hammer, 1979, *Employee Ownership in Plant Shutdowns: Prospects for Employment Stability*, Kalamazoo (Michigan): Upjohn Institute.

Stevens, G.R., 1960, *Canadian National Railways, Volume I. Sixty Years of Trial and Error*, Toronto: Clarke, Irwin and Co. Ltd.

Sturino, Franc, 1978, "Family and kin cohesion among South Italian immigrants in Toronto", in B.B. Caroll, R.F. Harney and L.F. Tomasi, *The Italian Woman in North America*, Toronto: Multicultural History Society of Ontario.

Swimmer, Gene, 1981, "Labour Canada: A department 'of' labour or 'for' labour?", in G. Bruce Doern (ed.), *How Ottawa Spends Your Tax Dollars: Federal Priorities 1981*, Toronto: James Lorimer.

Szasz, Thomas S., 1961, *The Myth of Mental Illness*, New York: Harper and Row.

Tanner, J., 1984, "Skill levels of manual workers and beliefs about work, management and industry: a comparison of craft and non-craft workers in Edmonton", *Canadian Journal of Sociology* (July): 303-18.

Tarrow, Sydney, 1967, *Peasant Communism in Southern Italy*, New Haven: Yale University Press.

Therborn, G., 1984, "Classes and states: Welfare state developments, 1881-1981", *Studies in Political Economy*, No. 14.

Thompson, Anthony, 1977, "The large and generous view: the debate on labour affiliation in the Canadian civil service, 1918-1928", *Labour/Le Travailleur*, Vol. 2: 108-36.

Tilly, Louise and Joan Scott, 1978, *Women, Work and Family*, New York: Holt, Rinehart and Winston.

Timms, D.W.G., 1972, *The Urban Mosaic: Toward a Theory of Residential Differentiation*, Cambridge: Cambridge University Press.

UAW (United Auto Workers), 1980, *Auto in Crisis*, Toronto: Canadian Council.

UAW, 1983 (Winter), *Solidarity*.

Vecoli, Rudolph, 1944, "Contadini in Chicago: a critique of the uprooted", *Journal of American History* 51.

Ward, Jim, 1979, *The Street is Their Home: The Hobos' Manifesto*, Melbourne: Quartet.

Warrian, P. and D. Wolfe, 1982, *Trade Unions and Inflation*, Ottawa: Canadian Centre for Policy Alternatives.

Weber, Arnold and David Taylor, 1963, "Procedures for employee displacement: Advance notices of a plant shutdown", *Journal of Business*, July: 302-15.

White, Julie, 1980, *Women and Unions*, Ottawa: Canadian Advisory Council on the Status of Women.

Willener, A. 1957, *Images de la Societe et Classes Sociales*, Imprimerie Staempflt, Bernt.

Willener, A., 1970, *The Action-Image of Society: On Cultural Politicization*, Paris: Editions du Seuil.

Wilson, J., 1968, "Politics and social class in Canada: The case of Waterloo South", *Canadian Journal of Political Science* 1 (September): 288-309.

Wisemann, N. and K.W. Taylor, 1982, "Voting in Winnipeg during the Depression", *Canadian Journal of Sociology*, Vol. 19, No. 2: 215-36.

Wolfe, D., 1983, "The crisis of advanced capitalism: an introduction", *Studies in Political Economy* 11 (Summer): 7-26.

Women's Committee of the Ontario Federation of Labour: Correspondence [Uncatalogued]. Minutes [Uncatalogued].

Wood, Ellen Meiksins, 1982, "The politics of theory and the concept of class: E.P. Thompson and his critics", *Studies in Political Economy*, 9 (Fall): 45-76.

Woods, H.D., 1973, *Labour Policy in Canada*, 2nd edition, Toronto: Macmillan.

Wright, E.O., 1978, *Class, Crisis and the State*, London: New Left Books.

Wright, E.O., 1980a, "Class and occupation", *Theory and Society*, Vol. 9, No. 1: 177-214.

Wright, E.O., 1980b, "Varieties of Marxist conceptions of class structure", *Politics and Society*, Vol. 9, No. 3: 323-69.

Wright, E.O., 1985, *Classes*, London: Verso.

Wright, E.O. *et al.*, 1982, "The American class structure", *American Sociological Review*, Vol. 47, No. 6 (December): 709-26.

Yans-McLaughin, Virginia, 1971, *Family and Community: Italian Immigrants in Buffalo*, Chicago: University of Illinois Press.

Zeman, Z.P., 1979, *The Impacts of Computer/Communications on Employment in Canada: An Overview of Current OECD Debates*, a Report prepared for the Department of Telecommunications, Economics Branch, Montreal: Institute for Research on Public Policy.

Zipp, J.F. and J. Smith, 1982, "A structural analysis of class voting", *Social Forces* 60 (March): 738-58.

Garamond Books:

Books on the leading edge of research and debate in Canadian social science and the humanities, written and priced to be accessible to students and the general reader.

- Robert Argue, Charlene Gannagé, D.W. Livingstone: *Working People and Hard Times*: Canadian Perspectives
- B. Singh Bolaria and Peter Li (eds): *Racial Oppression in Canada*
- Stephen Brickey and Elizabeth Comack (eds): *The Social Basis of Law*
- Robert Brym (ed): *The Structure of the Canadian Capitalist Class*
- James Dickinson and Bob Russell (eds): *Family, Economy and State*
- Murray Knuttila: *State Theories*
- David Livingstone (ed): *Critical Pedagogy & Cultural Power*
- Allan Moscovitch and James Albert (eds): *The Benevolent State: The Growth of the Welfare State*
- Jorge Niosi: *Canadian Multinationals*
- Jon Young (ed): *Breaking the Mosaic: Ethnic Identities in Canadian Schooling*

The Network Basic Series

- T. W. Acheson, David Frank, James Frost: *Industrialization and Underdevelopment in the Maritimes, 1880-1930*
- Pat Armstrong et al: *Feminist Marxism or Marxist Feminism: A Debate*
- Howard Buchbinder et al: *Who's On Top: The Politics of Heterosexuality*
- Varda Burstyn and Dorothy Smith: *Women, Class, Family and the State*; Intro by Roxana Ng
- Marjorie Cohen: *Free Trade and the Future of Women's Work: Manufacturing and Service Industries*
- David Livingstone: *Social Crisis and Schooling*
- Graham Lowe and Herb Northcott: *Under Pressure; a Study of Job Stress*
- Meg Luxton and Harriet Rosenburg: *Through the Kitchen Window: the Politics of Home and Family*
- Leo Panitch and Don Swartz: *From Consent to Coercion: The Assault on the Labour Movement*
- Henry Veltmeyer: *The Canadian Class Structure*
- Henry Veltmeyer: *Canadian Corporate Power*
- Robert White: *Law, Capitalism and the Right to Work*